EXPANDING CIRCLES:
WOMEN, ART & COMMUNITY

The life of [a person] is a self-evolving circle, which, from a ring imperceptibly small, rushes on all sides outwards to new and larger circles, and that without end. The extent to which this generation of circles, wheel without wheel, will go, depends on the force of truth of the individual soul . . . the heart refuses to be imprisoned; in its first and narrowest pulses it already tends outward with a vast force and to immense and innumerable expansions.

— from Ralph Waldo Emerson's essay "Circles"

MIDMARCH ARTS BOOKS

Tarnished Silver: After the Photo Boom, Essays 1979-1989
Beyond Walls and Wars: Art, Politics, and Multiculturalism
Mutiny and the Mainstream: Talk That Changed Art, 1975-1990

Documenting Women in the Arts
Gumbo Ya Ya: Anthology of Contemporary African-American Women Artists
Camera Fiends and Kodak Girls II: 60 Selections By and About
Women in Photography 1855-1965
Camera Fiends and Kodak Girls I: 50 Selections By and About
Women in Photography 1840-1930
Women Artists of Italian Futurism
Michelangelo and Me: Six Years in My Carrara Heaven
The Lady Architects: Lois Lilley Howe, Eleanor Manning, and Mary Almy, 1893-1937
Modernism & Beyond: Women Artists of the Pacific Northwest
Yesterday and Tomorrow: California Women Artists
No Bluebonnets, No Yellow Roses: Texas Women in the Arts
Pilgrims and Pioneers: New England Women in the Arts
Women Artists of the World
American Women Artists: Works on Paper

Poetry and Images
Whirling Round the Sun
Parallels: 3 Artists / 47 Poets
Illuminations: Images for "Asphodel, That Greeny Flower"
Images From Dante
Voices of Women: 3 critics on 3 poets on 3 artists/heroines

Artists, Cats, and Cows
Artists and Their Cats
The Little Cat Who Had No Name
When Even the Cows Were Up

Directories and Guides
Artists Colonies, Retreats & Study Centers
Whole Arts Directory
Guide to Women's Art Organizations and Directory for the Arts

Expanding Circles:
Women, Art, & Community

An Anthology
Edited and Compiled by

Betty Ann Brown

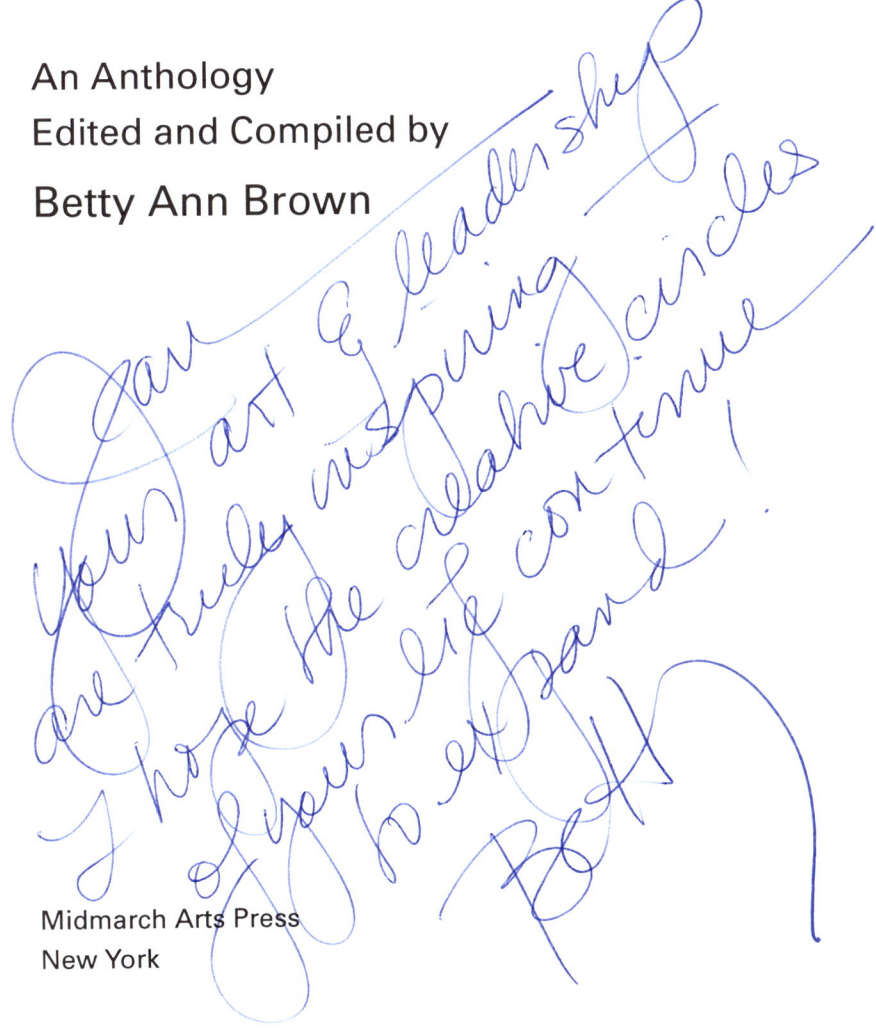

Jan Jan art & leadership
your art & leadership
are truly inspiring
I hope the creative circles
of your life continue
to expand!
Betty

Midmarch Arts Press
New York

Publication of this book has been made possible by the unswerving support and generous contributions of the Jeri Louise Waxenberg Foundation and many dedicated friends.

Library of Congress Catalog Card Number 96-076458
ISBN 1-87765-21-0

Printed in the United States of America

Published in 1996 by
Midmarch Arts Press
300 Riverside Drive
New York, New York 10025

Contents

Foreword

I walk into a bookstore and tell the young woman at the counter that I am doing a book on women, art, and community. Does she know of any books dealing with that subject? I don't know any book on the topic, she says, but I think people are looking for community in any way they can find it these days. And I say, yes, pleased to hear such a heartfelt response to my project.

This is why my project is important, I realize. People must be given images of different kinds of communities, of communities that are neither patriarchal nor hierarchical, neither authoritarian nor demeaning. Communities that honor the authority of lived experience. Communities that give voice to those often silenced, which means giving voice to all who represent Otherness, which ultimately includes all of us.

This book explores the intersection of women, creativity, and community. Many of the contributors are artists; others are poets, playwrights, and scholars whose work addresses the arts. We write about alternative definitions and identifications of community, about using art and art processes to build community, and about the joys and pains of living in creative communities.

We write about community as any group of two or more people who live and/or work together. Realizing that we are all members of several communities, we acknowledge that we tend to emphasize our membership in one or more of them during certain periods of our lives and in certain aspects of our art. At times the expanding circles of our communities intersect, overlap, even coincide; at other times they seem discrete and the points of possible juncture appear distant. One characteristic shared by all the communities we write about here is that they are not based on conformity or hierarchy, or the imposition of an abstracted and external ethos. These communities honor diversity, give voice to those silenced or disappeared, and respect the authority of lived experience.

We write about how we build community, about how our creative efforts are harnessed to establish connections; we employ art processes that are traditional as well as non-traditional; there are performance artists represented here, artists who work through what has historically been labeled political action, ritual artists, installation artists, artists who use image-and-text as well as time, space, and sound to create new genres.

We write about what it is to live in creative communities. In communities of family, sometimes of alternative families. In communities of gender and sexuality, like the artist who for years ran the Los Angeles Woman's Building and now considers its history and demise. In communities of race and ethnicity, like the installation artist who considers how her African-American identity has impacted her relationship to the art world. In spiritual communities, like a pair of artists who are members of a Wicca coven and use art, poetry, and song to celebrate their rites of passage, anniversaries, and transitions.

EXPANDING CIRCLES: WOMEN, ART, & COMMUNITY includes essays by and about Judy Baca, Judy Chicago, Cheri Gaulke, Suvan Geer, Suzanne Lacy, Lucy R. Lippard, Katherine Ng, Rosalie Ortega, Arlene Raven, Rachel Rosenthal, Sandra Rowe, Ruth Weisberg, Terry Wolverton, and many more. As editor, I bring together woman artists, writers, and social activists who grapple with what community means to them, how their personal sense of community developed in their families and cultural traditions, and how they have come to use art to build community. The book's four sections — History, Identity, Building, and Living in Community — are preceded by comprehensive introductory essays placing each contributor in context.

Being the Subject of Art
by bell hooks

Consciousness-raising groups, gatherings, and public meetings need to become a central aspect of feminist practice again. Women need spaces where we can explore intimately and deeply all aspects of female experience, including our relationship to artistic production. Even though most feminists these days are aware of issues of race, class, and sexual practices, of our differences, we tend to confront these issues only superficially. Woman have yet to create the context, both politically and socially, where our understanding of the politics of difference not only transforms our individual lives (and we have yet to really speak about these transformations) but also alters how we work with others in public, in institutions, in galleries, etc.

Many folks assume that feminism has already changed the social context in which women artists produce work. They mistake greater involvement in the marketplace with the formation of a liberatory space where women can create meaningful, compelling, "great" art and have that art be fully recognized. The "commodification" of difference often leads to the false assumption that works by people of color and marginalized white women are "hot" right now and able to garner a measure of recognition and reward that they may or may not deserve. The impact such thinking has on our work is that it often encourages marginalized artists to feel we must do our work quickly, strike while the iron is hot, or risk being ignored forever. If we write, we are encouraged to write in the same manner as those who have made the big money and achieved the big success. If, say, we take photographs, we are encouraged to keep producing the image that folks most want to see and buy. This commodification for an undiscerning marketplace seeks to confine, limit, and even destroy our artistic freedom and practice. We must be wary of seduction by the superficial and rare possibility of gaining immediate recognition and regard that may grant us some measure of attention in a manner that continues to marginalize us and set us apart. Women must dare to remain vigilant, preserving the integrity of self and of the work.

As women artists expressing solidarity across differences, we must forge ahead, creating spaces where our work can be seen and evaluated according to standards that reflect our sense of artistic merit. As we strive to enter the mainstream art world, we must feel empowered to vigilantly guard the representation of the woman as artist so that it is never again devalued. Fundamentally, we must create the space for feminist intervention without surrendering our primary concern, which is a devotion to making art, a devotion intense and rewarding enough that it is the path leading to our freedom and fulfillment.

— *bell hooks*
"Women Artists: The Creative Process"
from *Visual Politics* (NY: The New Press)

Introduction

> Connecting was the function and meaning of women's traditional art, and it is still consciously a function of feminist art today.[1]

Even more than their counterparts in literature and entertainment, female creators in the visual arts have suffered exclusion from the dominant modes of expression in Western culture. It was not until the 1970s when, buoyed by the Women's Movement, groups of feminist artists began to organize institutions such as the Feminist Studio Workshop and the Woman's Building in Los Angeles, the Women's Art Registry of Minnesota (WARM) and Women Artists in Revolution (W.A.R.) in New York, that the problems of exclusion were fully addressed and at least partially redressed. The revolutionary changes of that decade were brought about not by individuals but by groups of women working together. They initiated change by creating communities in which to work and exhibit their art.

For some of these women, the very process of creating community became the impulse and essence of their art. In establishing community-building as an art form, such artists embraced a dual heritage. The history of women's traditional arts — from the ceramics and basketry of Native Americans to the quilts of the Euroamericans who displaced them — was merged with the avant-garde experiments of German artist-teacher Joseph Beuys and the New York creator of "Happenings," Allan Kaprow, to create a distinctive new art form. Propelled by the knowledge that the personal is indeed political and that the breaking down of boundaries between public and private through aesthetic expression can provide profound and often enduring experiences of connection, many feminist artists of the last twenty years have used their art skills as tools for building community.

That art has a unique capacity to inform and integrate peoples is no new idea, nor is it an exclusively female idea. For centuries, the Catholic Church used monumental painting, sculpture, and architecture to align and inspire its congregants. Indeed, the Church issued numerous dictums proscribing precisely which images were proper for spreading or propagating the faith.[2] Modern nation-states from revolutionary France to communist USSR have also used art to draw people together. I think of Jacques Louis David's numerous portraits of Napoleon distributed through France to convince the people of their leader's heroism, or the immense crimson banners of Stalin hung around Red Square to confirm the autocrat's power.

The cohesive function of art is not enacted only through dominance, that is, through imposition by the powerful upon the less powerful. Art that emerges from disenfranchised groups — such as the dynamic graffiti signatures of Chicano gangs — or from individuals working in virtual isolation — such as the cement, tile and steel amalgamations we now call the Watts Towers — can also function to communicate and cohere community. As noted twentieth century American artist Robert Rauschenberg asserts, "I feel strong in my belief, based on my varied and widely traveled collaborations, that a one-to-one contact through art contains potent peaceful powers, and is the most non-elitist way to share exotic and common information, hopefully seducing us into creating mutual understandings for the benefit of all."[3]

The visual arts — what I here refer to simply as art — have a different kind of impact than do their performing arts kin. While music, dance, theater, film, and television all unfold over time, the visual arts are generally read" and taken in immediately. This does not mean they are fully comprehended in an instant. Nor does it mean that more careful and sustained "reading" does not yield greater comprehension; it does. But this culture strongly privileges the visual and we have all been socialized to "get" an image right away." All of the information comes in during our first scanning. How long we are willing or able to spend "digesting" that information determines how much we will consciously derive from the image.

Knowing that the arts have the power to inform and connect, and that the visual arts have a unique capacity for immediate impact, many women artists of the late twentieth century have employed the visual arts to build community. We are living in an era of what has been termed "whole system change." Because of breakdowns in all of the institutions — families, schools, churches, etc. — that previously gave us identity and stability, people are desperately seeking alternative groups and communities.[4] Some are even willing to submit to the degradation of cults or to the rigidity of militia in a vain search for the connection otherwise missing in their lives.

The women who build community through art have indeed developed a new art movement. The processes, images, and experiences of this movement are often arresting, often compelling, always exciting. Imagine walking to the palisades overlooking the ocean in La Jolla, California, and seeing hundreds of elderly women dressed all in white sitting at tables on the silvery sand below you; then imagine hearing whispered echoes of their life stories waft up to you as the setting sun turns the lapis sky and waves to deep cobalt. (Suzanne Lacy's "Whisper, the Waves, the Wind.") Imagine going to the Fu-Nan River in Chengdu, China, the waterway once called Brocade River because when silk was washed there, it became brighter. Imagine seeing dozens of women, dressed in white with red gloves, rinsing long stretches of white silk in what you thought was pristine water. Then imagine seeing the silk emerge stained, grayed, browned, dulled. Consider how that would affect your perception of the river, the environment, our connection to water. (Betsy Damon and Jill Jacoboy's "Washing Silk.") Imagine walking into the Central Train Station in Amsterdam and seeing a large glass window lined with resident's statements about moments of quiet, of silence, in their lives and in their dreams. Imagine entering the hushed room and seeing people sitting quietly, writing, drawing, united in the embrace of stillness as the rest of the harried city races past them. (Annick Nevejan's "Space for Silence.") If you can imagine these three visual — and emotional — experiences, you can begin to understand the power of community building as an art form.

Judy Chicago is probably the best known artist of this genre. Her monumental "Dinner Party" installation honoring the historic accomplishments of women was executed by a community of hundreds of diverse women with whom Chicago did consciousness-raising, skills training, and ongoing creative collaboration. Judith F. Baca brought together disadvantaged teens from neighborhoods all over Southern California to study and work together in planning and painting "The Great Wall of Los Angeles," a celebration of the contributions of people of color to the city's history. In Minneapolis, Suzanne Lacy conceived and coordinated the spectacular "Crystal Quilt," a project in which hundreds of senior women gathered over fabric-covered tables, arranging cloth shapes into quilt squares as they spoke of their life experiences. Cheri Gaulke founded the Sisters Of Survival, a group of anti-nuclear "nuns" clad in rainbow-hued habits, who traveled the Americas and Western Europe to dramatize their protests of the arms race.

Over the last two decades, feminist artists have generated works that involve interaction and creative collaboration with their audiences to build communities. The bridges have crossed lines of age, class, race, sexuality, religious belief, and nationality, integrating into a shared effort and connecting through shared accomplishment hundreds of people who might not otherwise have recognized their commonality/communality.

Unfortunately, the mainstream art press remains strangely silent about this movement in women's art. A recent text with a chapter on "Art & Community" features seven artists who work in alternative communities.[5] All of the artists are male and European or Euroamerican. All use, as the basis for their works, Eurocentric models, which they bring to the community, rather than models developed in and through the community. None acknowledge the history of feminist community building nor the transformational quality of women's work in this field.

According to Suzanne Lacy, "Although the 1990s has seen a resurgence of art works in which artists make contact with 'others' — prisoners, women who've experienced domestic violence, or homeless people — and from these connections develop more or less collaborative representations, art criticism has not recognized the precedents of this practice in 1970s feminism and performance art."[6] It was not until Lacy's recent *Mapping the Terrain: New Genre Public Art,* that she and other writers began to formulate a theoretical context for such work.[7]

The book you are reading writes women back into the history of community building as an art form and thus reinscribes women into a text they first drafted. The book is an anthology, a community of writings, a crazy quilt of text. I have divided the book into four chapters. "Women's Art Communities in Contemporary History" is a selective and abbreviated reconsideration of the Women's Art Movement with emphasis on issues of collaboration and community. It centers around some personal reflections by major figures in historic feminist community projects. "Identity in Community" focuses on the intersection of images and identity. "Building Community" includes accounts of the community-building process in arenas from families to college classrooms, synagogues to theaters. "Living in Community" brings together writings that address the issue of duration in aesthetic community.

The more than forty artists and writers whose work is included here form communities whose boundaries are constantly expanding, often overlapping, sometimes coinciding. Many other community building artists have done work not included in this volume because I don't yet know about them, because I couldn't contact them, because they were working so hard on their art they didn't have time to contribute anything.[8] Whatever the reason, there are many, many artists out there who are building community with as compelling and lasting images as those you are reading about now.[9] Community building is, above all, an art movement about inclusion. We wish we could include them all.

This book is called Expanding Circles *because every time I thought of the convergence of women, art, and community, I saw pictures in my mind's eye. Black and white pictures. Pictures that looked like footage, slow motion footage, perhaps from a Maya Deren film.*

I saw a pool of dark, mute water, a pool that was eternally deep, that had no boundaries. Three smooth gray stones arced silently towards the water, and sank, slowly, soundlessly. Thin round ribbons of waves moved out from the stones, creating silver circles on the black water. And as the circles moved out, as they expanded, they began to overlap. The overlapping circles crossed, weaving shining moiré patterns on the surface of the blackness. And the patterns spread, expanding and overlapping again and again, in exquisite complexity, out to the very edges of the infinite pool.

I am reminded of a passage from Ralph Waldo Emerson's essay "Circles."[10]

The life of [a person] is a self-evolving circle, which, from a ring imperceptibly small, rushes on all sides outwards to new and larger circles, and that without end. The extent to which this generation of circles, wheel without wheel, will go, depends on the force of truth of the individual soul . . . the heart refuses to be imprisoned; in its first and narrowest pulses it already tends outward with a vast force and to immense and innumerable expansions.

I hope that as you read this book the expanding circles of the art described here will connect with you and move into the many communities of your life, just as these artists — and their inspiring art works — have moved into mine.

Betty Ann Brown
Pasadena, California
February 1996

I WOMEN'S ART COMMUNITIES IN CONTEMPORARY HISTORY

Darlene Nguyen-Ely, *Separation*

Vietnam — United States

When Saigon fell 20 years ago, I was separated from my mother. My escape from Vietnam was very traumatic. For this particular piece, I expressed my sadness and sense of loss. Since then, I always longed to grow up a part of a perfect family with parents, brothers and sister living under one roof. Even though my mother is here now, what was missed cannot be made up. Over the years we have drifted apart. We expect different things from each other. My mother is here, but she is not mine.

Introduction

Early summer, 1979. I have flown with my husband to San Francisco to celebrate my thirtieth birthday. We stay in a bed-and-breakfast in Haight Ashbury, travel through the wine country, gorge ourselves on gourmet food. And we go to see Judy Chicago's "Dinner Party." It is installed at the San Francisco Museum of Modern Art which, at that time, is located on the upper floors of an office-like building downtown. People are lined up outside and halfway around the block. Intrigued by what my students and colleagues have told me about Chicago's project, I convince my reluctant husband to stick with it.

We wait in line. We round the block, go up the stairs, crush through the entryway, edge into the museum hallway. As we get closer to the installation we see photographs, written documentation, finally a video about the genesis and process of the project. I am amazed at how many different people grappled with the challenges of creative collaboration to work together on the project. (I had always thought art was something you did on your own.) I begin to think that Judy Chicago must have both a strong sense of vision and remarkable interpersonal skills. But what about all those horrible rumors I'd heard about her "difficult" personality, I ask myself.[1]

I see a museum guard shepherding some of the crowd in a less than gracious way, and I remember what one of my colleagues told me about her experience at the "Dinner Party." As she neared the door, one of the guards pulled her aside and said to her, "You don't want to go in there. It's nasty."

When we finally enter the exhibition space, it seems the very opposite of nasty to me. I walk into a dark, dramatically lit room. I see a large yet elegant triangular table set with glistening sculpted plates, each plate laid over a spectacular fabric runner. The table itself is elevated on a shiny tile floor, with hundreds of names scripted over its surface. This may sound corny, but the first impression I have is one of awe: It is so beautiful and so powerful. I circle the table again and again, reading the names of the women represented by the plates, whispering the names of the women written on the floor, hearing in my mind echoes of the names of the women — the many women — who had worked together on this project.[2]

First I look at the place settings for the thirty-nine guests. Each is a mythic or historic woman of power. I recognize some of the names, but not all. As I circle the triangular table, I realize I want to know them all. The plate for the Amazon, the mythic female warrior, is placed next to that for Hatshepsut, an Egyptian monarch who was noted for her civic reforms. The medieval mystic Hildegarde of Bingen is represented by a plate with a stained glass design. I can relate to this, since I have long been drawn to the writings of the mystics and have always loved stained glass interiors. Nearby is the plate for Renaissance ruler Elizabeth R. I grin, remembering how I had loved stories about Elizabeth as a child. Because my name, Betty, is derived from Elizabeth, I feel a connection with the powerful ruler.

I am drawn to the forceful geometry of Sacajawea's plate, aware that it reflects the visual traditions of her Native American heritage. And I find Sojourner Truth's plate compelling; it has three faces that I think must represent her African roots, her suffering under slavery, and her courage to speak for abolition after her escape. Susan B. Anthony's plate-image seems about to lift off its low circular surface. I ask myself if Chicago is depicting Anthony's (relative) liberation. When I see that Georgia O'Keeffe's plate appears to fly free, I guess I must be correct.

Next I study the tiled floor below the table. The names of 999 women of achievement are written there. I read as many as I can. I see that other suffragettes are clustered near Anthony. Simone de Beauvoir, Anais Nin, Colette, Doris Lessing — all writers whose work I admire — are scattered under Virginia Woolf's plate. Rosa Bonheur, Mary Cassatt, and Frida Kahlo are there near O'Keeffe. I realize, as I walk around the "Dinner Party," that I am being changed by this art. I still smile to think of it.

Something wonderful happened during that encounter with that art, in that room, in that museum. I began to feel connected to all the women portrayed there. I began to feel part of the project, part of the community, part of the history. I began to feel proud of the women's history depicted there and proud to be heir to plate painters, table-setters, weavers, and embroiderers whose traditional art forms were honored there. I began to feel the embrace of cultural reification in a way I never had at any of the male-centered exhibits I had seen before. I began to feel proud to be a woman. I began to feel, like the "Dinner Party" itself, beautiful and powerful.

One of the most important things art can do is to give form to and thereby validate viewers' experiences. The question is, whose experiences are selected and deemed worthwhile. Almost all of the exhibitions of Western art I viewed until the 1970s focused on images produced by men for a presumed male audience.[3] As a woman, either I had to deny my femaleness so as to identify with the male producers and viewers or be alienated to some degree by the viewing experience.

According to Lucy Lippard, "Nothing that does not include the voices of people of color, women, lesbians, and gays can be considered inclusive, universal, or healing. To find the whole we must know and respect all the parts."[4] But throughout most of Western cultural history, a singular cultural perspective — that of the privileged European Judeo-Christian male — was assumed to be universal and designated appropriate for all viewers. This restricted the range of experiences represented in the arts. I deconstruct the basis of such patterns of exclusion in the Introduction to Chapter II. Here, I discuss how women, particularly women artists and art historians, challenged the assumptions behind the historic belief in "universal" art production and reception. Their challenges led them to develop new art forms that established community with increasingly inclusive and diversified audiences and collaborators, paving the way for contemporary pluralism.

Pluralism — the dispersal of a false "universal" into more valid multiplicity — comes out of the several movements for human liberation that crested earlier in this century, most particularly the Civil Rights Movement and the Women's Movement. The development of the Women's Movement in the visual arts has been well documented.[5] Following is a brief survey of some aspects of feminist art-making in order to put community building as an art form into historical context.

The Feminist Art Movement

> Recognizing . . . that "author-ity" is institutionalized as a matter of education, feminists attacked it at the roots. Alternative studio programs, notably the feminist art programs at California State University at Fresno and the California Institute of the Arts, soundly rejected the studio training that supports such an identity. The aspiration was that making art might become a form of social transformation, and the artist an activist, in service of the reformation of traditional cultural values; this could happen only by destroying the aura surrounding the "mystery of creation" and "the artist's creative process." Thus the ideal of community, shared labor, and open exchange was substituted in the teaching program, supported by collaborative methods developed in the contexts of consciousness raising and political action.[6]

The Feminist Art Movement, which became visible in this country in the early 1970s, had its roots in the New Left and the Women's Liberation Movement. While many activist women of the 1960s shared the politics of the New Left, they found that movement to be sexist in practice; thus they were compelled to develop and work within their own political organizations.[7] The National Organization for Women was founded in 1966.[8] At the same time, a group of female members of the male-dominated Art Workers' Coalition organized as Women Artists in Revolution (W.A.R.) W.A.R.'s first protest was aimed at the annual exhibition of American art held at the Whitney Museum, which had a history of showing less than 10% art by women.[9] The protest was, to a degree, successful: the Whitney increased the female representation to 22% that year. A second group, Women in the Arts, organized in 1972 to promote exhibition opportunities for women artists, achieved almost immediate success with an exhibition, "Women Choose Women" (1973) at a major NYC museum.

In 1970, Faith Ringgold and her daughter Michele Wallace spearheaded the group Women, Students and Artists for Black Art Liberation (WSABAL). In 1972, AIR (Artists in Residence) Gallery, the longest lasting cooperative of women artists in the country, was begun in New York.[10] Also in 1972, the Women's Caucus for Art formed to address the concerns of the female membership of the College Art Association (the national organization of art professionals). Still thriving today, the Caucus continues to be the largest feminist political structure in art professions.

Parallel events were challenging and changing the art world of California. In 1970, the Los Angeles Council of Women Artists banded together to urge the Los Angeles County Museum of Art (LACMA) to show more women artists. Specifically, the Council protested the well-funded and widely publicized "Art & Technology" exhibition which featured over sixty contemporary artists, all male. Out of this action came the founding of Womanspace Gallery, which at one point had over 1000 members. And as a direct result of the Council protests, LACMA committed to stage what became the historic exhibition "Women Artists: 1500-1950," curated by feminist art historians Linda Nochlin and Anne Sutherland Harris.

Also in 1970, Judy Chicago left the male-dominated and male-oriented art scene of Los Angeles to teach at California State University, Fresno, where she realized consciousness-raising and other techniques of feminist education could transform her female students' self concepts and, consequently, their art production. A year later, Chicago brought her teaching philosophy back to Southern California and joined New York artist Miriam Schapiro at California Institute for the Arts to start the Department of Feminist Art there. In 1973, Chicago, Arlene Raven, and Sheila de Bretteville founded the independent Feminist Studio Workshop which evolved into the Los Angeles Woman's Building, the longest lasting feminist cultural center in the country. (Its public space closed in 1991.)

In 1971, June Wayne, prominent printmaker and founder of Tamarind Lithography Workshop, began her "Joan of Art" workshops in Los Angeles. Presented in her studio and often involving role playing, the workshops trained women artists in professional practices. Participants were urged to offer similar seminars to additional women.[11]

Throughout the 1970s and 1980s, women artists organized to protest the inequity of dominant art world practices. They also formed their own, often separatist, institutions. There was MUSE Gallery, a women's cooperative and alternative exhibition space in Philadelphia; A.R.C. and Artemisia Galleries in Chicago; the Heresies collective in New York, which published a magazine on feminist art and politics; the WARM women's group in Minneapolis; the Washington Women's Art enter in D.C.; and some 150 more. Many exhibitions of women's art were organized by such groups.

There were also groups of women who created new forms of protest. The Waitresses, formed in 1977, performed collaboratively in Los Angeles. Then, in 1985, an anonymous group of New York art world feminists began to design and distribute posters calling attention to continuing gender and racial inequities in museum, gallery, and periodical representation. At first they signed the posters "the conscience of the art world," but soon the group became known as the Guerrilla Girls. They continue to produce posters and make public appearances, always anonymously masked as gorillas. In a 1989 poster they placed a gorilla mask on the body of a nineteenth-century French nude and asked, "Do women have to be naked to get into the Met. Museum?" Answer: "Less than 5% of the artists in the Modern Art sections are women, but 85% of the nudes are female." On hot pink paper, the "Guerrilla Girls Pop Quiz" of 1990, asked, "If February is Black History Month and March is Women's History Month, what happens the rest of the year?" Answer: "Discrimination." One of my personal favorites, also from 1989: "Relax Senator Helms, the art world *is* your kind of place! The number of blacks at an art opening is about the same as at one of your garden parties. . . . Most art collectors, like most successful artists, are white males. . . . The sexual imagery in most respected works of art is the expression of wholesome heterosexual males . . . (etc.).[12] Still more groups organized in the late 80s and early 90s. In Chicago women formed the Sister Serpents to combat patriarchal attitudes through cultural means. And in New York, WAC, the Women's Action Coalition, grew from 100 artists, writers, and longtime feminists to a group almost ten times that size in less than a year.

The Feminist Art Movement changed the perceptions and the realities of the American art world. However, as the Guerilla Girls have documented, 95-98% of the art in American museums is still by men. They also point out that, as of 1988, the earning capacity of American women artists was 33 cents to every dollar earned by a male artist, compared to other working women, who earned 59 cents to the male dollar. As performance artist Laurie Anderson recently chanted regarding this ratio, it will be centuries before equity is achieved!

Consciousness-Raising

Historically, feminist community building originated with the consciousness-raising process. In "C-R Groups," women gather to discuss topics of shared interest, such as their relationships with their mothers, their lovers, or their employers. Once the topic is selected for a particular meeting, the women go around the room, each speaking her mind on the topic. No one comments, questions, interrupts, approves of, or challenges what the speaker says. Each speaker has equal time and is equally valued. Ultimately, participants have their consciousnesses raised, which means they are given increased insight into the topic and how it affects women in general and themselves in particular. Participants develop a sense of trust, a freedom to speak and to risk. They also begin to realize that if so many women share so many feelings about so many things, the personal must indeed be political. If what they previously perceived as their own particular "problem" is shared by many, many women, then it must be a societal issue, not an individual one. As Teresa de Laurentis has written,

C-R "has produced, and continues to elaborate, a radically new mode of understanding the subject's relation to social-historical reality. Consciousness-raising is the original critical instrument that women have developed toward such understanding, the analysis of social reality, and its critical revision."[13]

Many of the women artists' events and organizations began their meetings with consciousness-raising. Women artists took what they learned in private consciousness-raising and transformed it into public art, connecting two realms previously viewed as not only separate but opposed. Broude and Garrard call consciousness-raising the "key principle" of feminist art in the 1970s, citing theorist Judith Papachristou's description of the process as a "method of using one's own experience as the most valid way of formulating political analysis."[14] Suzanne Lacy specifically links consciousness-raising to community building: "Consciousness-raising and community organizing were techniques for understanding and enacting both individual identity and the differentiated and multiple nature of communities."[15]

When Judy Chicago took consciousness-raising into her classroom, she knew that it was a process that would facilitate the creation of female-identified art. Chicago observed that consciousness-raising — the freedom to tell their stories in a safe environment — helped her students conceptualize and claim their own identities, which were often in contradistinction to those offered them by the dominant culture.[16] From such self-determined identification — perhaps I should say "self-negotiated" identification, since none of us is separate from society and none of us is totally free of the identity messages delivered by society[17] — emerged art works that alternatively celebrated and critiqued the myriad meanings of womanness. "The images . . . came out with an incredible force, as if they had been bottled up and suddenly released," remembers Chicago. "They were so powerful that they frightened me, but I didn't want the students to see my fears and become anxious about exposing what was clearing the raw material for an openly female-oriented art. . . ."[18]

Chicago knew that the identity-claiming process would be enhanced by rewriting the male-dominated histories with which her students were familiar. Becoming aware that women artists had been powerful and accomplished made it more likely that the students could see themselves as potentially powerful and accomplished art makers. "I felt that it was important for the women to learn about the work of women of the past, identify with their lives, and use their achievements to extend their own." I personally wanted to see the work and examine it for clues that could help in my own art.[19] Inspired by feminist revisions of history, Chicago began to do art "in collaboration" with her female forebears: her "Great Ladies" series of 1973. "I recognized that my work could only be accurately understood against the background of a female history, and I wanted to find a way to incorporate that history into my work so that the viewer would be forced to confront my work in the context of other women's work."[20]

Women's Art Communities in Contemporary History

Judith E. Stein discusses how "aesthetic partnership" with historical figures fueled the creativity of many early feminist artists, most particularly Miriam Schapiro, whose "Collaboration Series" of collages incorporated vintage fabrics and reproductions of art works by "recovered" women artists Mary Cassatt, Elisabeth Vigée-Lebrun, Berthe Morisot, and Frida Kahlo.[21]

Audience, Installation and Performance

There were many differences, but there was an uncontested parallel between feminist and ethnic artists: obtaining equality—of resources, representation, and power— was the political motivation that fueled both art practices. This aspiration led artists in both groups to examine the interactive potential of art making, both within the work itself through collaboration and between the work and its audience. This activist orientation toward the audience challenged artists to seek and identify specifically who their work was for.

— *Suzanne Lacy*

Judy Chicago was aware that identifying and presenting individually generated feminist art works was the first step to creating an alternative art community as audience. "If my needs, values and interests differed from male artists' who were invested in the values of the [dominant] culture, then it was up to me to help develop a community that was relevant to me and other women artists."[22] Suzanne Lacy notes that there was no actual distinction between identity issues and the development of audience: "In the beginning of the decade, at least in my experience as a student in Judy Chicago's Fresno Feminist Art Program and later in the women's design and writing programs at the California Institute of the Arts, there were no divisions between art based on identity investigations and art that explored new relationships with its audience. Both sprang from the same political agenda — the transformation of the power differential between men and women.[23]

The next step was to create a more public forum, one which included the community in the art process itself. Miriam Schapiro joined Chicago to spearhead the feminist educational programs at Cal Arts. Their collaborative programs gained great visibility with the 1972 opening of Womanhouse, a condemned structure transformed for just a few weeks into a two-story, many-roomed installation that explored women's traditional images and roles. The Cal Arts students located, cleaned, and reconstructed the building before employing it as an immense palette on which to paint their analyses of such issues as nurturing, personal adornment, the role of the bride, and the shame imposed around menstruation.

A few years later, Chicago incorporated community-building in the creative process of the "Dinner Party." Because Chicago employed consciousness-raising among the collaborators producing the project, and because she deliberately endeavored to break down traditional master/apprentice or artist/assistant hierarchies, the "Dinner Party" is, like Womanhouse, an important precedent for feminist installation as a community building form.

Along with installation, a second feminist community building process emerged in feminist performance art. As with performance art in general, much feminist performance art is autobiographically based. While individualist performance may develop communality with the audience, other feminist performance art seeks to break down the distinction between performer and audience. As early as her teaching days in Fresno, Judy Chicago had begun to develop performance structures that had process, content, and form generated out of consciousness-raising. By the time she moved the Feminist Art Program to Los Angeles, she and collaborators Aviva Rahmani and Suzanne Lacy were facilitating workshops that produced community-based mixed-media pieces such as "Ablutions," which dealt with the topic of rape. The numerous performances at Womanhouse ritually articulated similarly potent issues through image, text, sound, and action. Suzanne Lacy went on to formalize community-building performance structures and to involve groups as diverse as senior women from Minneapolis and disadvantaged teens from Philadelphia.

Community building can be effected through the creation of static or fixed images that viewers see from some distance; through installations that viewers enter and walk through; through rituals and performances in contained environments that viewers can either witness or join; and through public art in larger, more public, and often more urban sites that viewers can either witness or join. These genres extend and overlap with the same fluidity as do the expanding circles in the individual consciousnesses of the creators and participants. This book addresses two main approaches to feminist community building: projects building audience communities and projects involving communities of collaborators in the image-making, installation-constructing, or ritual/performance processes.

Whatever the genre or approach, the impulse is always to connect.

In a 1979 article about the "Dinner Party," Thomas Albright wrote, "The studio is usually thought of as a lonely place, but it would be hard to imagine a scene of busier communal activity than the compact southern California atelier presided over by Judy Chicago." In the same article Chicago says, "I'm trying to facilitate, in a nonauthoritarian way. . . . Women have never achieved in isolation. It is a fantasy to talk about women making it up on their own bootstraps. Women have always had a support system of other women. . . . There is still an incredible prejudice against feminist art — a resistance to accepting the fact that women's experience is important enough to be the subject and basis of art making. Women are accepted in the art world if they accept prevailing values, which means following mainstream trends. I feel the mainstream is corrupt. . . . I have had to bypass the art world to make it as an artist . . . I have had to build an alternative audience."[24]

I became a member of that audience when I saw the "Dinner Party" in 1979. Over the years, I have become increasingly aware of the truth of Chicago's assertions, and of the value of her feminist community building. Chapter I begins with a conversation with Judy Chicago. This is followed by Lucy Lippard's groundbreaking essay "Sweeping Exchanges: The Contribution of Feminism to the Art of the 1970s," the first comprehensive discussion of the difference between the connections of feminist art and the separatist mode of the male-dominated avant garde. Arlene Raven, who joined Judy Chicago at Cal Arts, participated in the performances at Womanhouse, and became a co-founder of the Woman's Building, has also written extensively about feminist artistic processes. A conversation with Raven follows Lippard's essay. The chapter ends with a survey of the last twenty years of the history of women's groups throughout the country, and Terry Wolverton's poignant "Requiem" for the Los Angeles Woman's Building.

The insights of author/critic Suzi Gablik on the subject of community are enlightening.

> The idea of self-directed professionalism has conditioned, if not totally determined, our way of thinking about art, to the point where we have become incredibly addicted to certain kinds of experience at the expense of others, such as community, for example, or ritual. . . . There is a need for new forms [of art] emphasizing our essential interconnectedness rather than our separateness, forms evoking the feeling of belonging to a larger whole rather than expressing the isolated, alienated self. . . . The emerging new paradigm [of creativity] reflects a will to *participate* socially: a central aspect of new paradigm thinking involves a significant shift from *objects* to *relationships*. . . . A new emphasis falls on community and environment rather than on individual achievement and accomplishment.[25]

Judy Chicago, *Isabella D'Este*, 1979.

JUDY CHICAGO

in Conversation with Betty Ann Brown

> It was like being at the moment of birth, the birth of a new kind of community of women, a new kind of art made by women.
> — Judy Chicago in *Through the Flower*

Judy Chicago is one of the most celebrated and most controversial woman artist alive today, and also one of the Great Mothers of the Feminist Art Movement. Born Judith Cohen in Chicago, Illinois, she changed her name to Judy Chicago in 1969, on the occasion of a major exhibition of her work. The name change asserted her identity as an independent woman who refused to accept the labels and limitations dictated by our patriarchal society.[1] Self-naming served as a metaphor for the artist's stunning transformation from producer of cool, hard icons that fit into the minimalist (male-dominated) visual vocabulary of the 1960s into a dynamic feminist image-maker and activist.

In her remarkable autobiographies, *Through the Flower, My Struggle as a Woman Artist* (originally published in 1975 and supplemented by *Beyond the Flower*, 1995), Chicago talks about her developing strengths as well as the conflicts, rejections, and losses that led her to a resolute commitment to and articulation of herself and her art. A prominent theme is Chicago's need for, and her successful efforts to establish, a feminist community that would provide context and support for her work, and for the work of other women artists.

I first read Through the Flower *when I was teaching art history in Normal, Illinois, a small, very conservative midwestern town where I often felt, as a single young professional woman, that I was a freak, an outsider. Chicago's words spoke to me as none had before: she validated so much of my personal history. I remembered, like her, being identified as the artist in my family and in all my numerous schools (my father was a career military officer and we moved every two years). I remembered the painfully contradictory messages I received about being female and an artist in a culture that traditionally links creativity with the male. Like Chicago, "I had found that society's definition of me as a woman was in conflict with my own sense of personhood (and, after all, it was a person who was making art)."*

At Southern Methodist University (SMU) I had realized all my studio art teachers — without exception — were white men. All the named artists I'd studied in art history classes — without exception — were white men. I began to doubt the possibility of success as a woman artist: was art-making the product of an exclusive club I

Women's Art Communities in Contemporary History

couldn't enter because of my gender? As I agonized over this question, two professors affected my nascent career. My painting teacher (a white male, of course) advised me to become an elementary art teacher rather than go on to graduate school in painting — in spite of my superlative grades. His comments were horribly discouraging; I soon abandoned my canvases and brushes.

Then there was Alessandra Comini. Widely published and honored by several academic institutions, Comini had come to SMU as a visiting professor to give a seminar on the art of Munich and Vienna from 1890 to 1910.² She was the most gifted and inspirational instructor I'd ever had, and she was, by all standards, extremely successful. With Comini as a role model (and sadly aware that I could find no female role models in the studio arts), I decided to pursue art history, a subject which had been a competing passion ever since my high school years spent in the museums and palaces of Europe. But I remained depressed and harbored doubts about my decision.

It wasn't until I read Through the Flower *that I realized my art educational experiences and sorrowful forsaking of painting hadn't been unique. I had been taking my "failures" personally, unable to see them as the result of sexism. Now when I hear a young female student say she was advised to become a teacher rather than study architecture, I realize she is being undermined by a system that seeks to exclude women, just as I had been. When I hear an older student tell of having had "gender blinders" — she never noticed that everyone she studied from and about was male — I recognize the same patriarchal process.*

Chicago writes about the pressures to become male-identified during the 1960s, about how she had needed to be "different from other women," to be "tough," in order to make it in the male art world. I had felt the same pressures, but responded in another way. Even more important for the dedicated art historian I'd become was reading her chapter on the history of women artists in western culture. She helped me realize I could research and write about women artists. In the late 1970s, because of Chicago's book, my career took another turn: I became a feminist art historian.

It wasn't only the content of my writing that changed; it was also my teaching. In Through the Flower, *Chicago talks a lot about her teaching job at California State University, Fresno.*

> [I]n Los Angeles . . . the values of the male art community pervaded the environment — values that asserted form over content, protection over exposure, toughness over vulnerability. I decided to go away from the city for a year . . . I wanted to teach women. I wanted to try to communicate to female students, to tell them what I had gone through in making myself into an artist. I felt that by externalizing the process . . . I could examine it, which would be the first step in turning it around, and the women's class might also be the first step in making an alternative female art community.

> I didn't know for sure if my struggle was relevant to other women, and I needed to

find that out before I could use it as the basis for such a community. I felt a strong need to be with other women (something I had never done) and to find out if my own needs as an artist, my desire to build a new context, and the needs of other women interested in art could merge to become the basis for a viable female art community. . . . I hoped, by establishing a class for women, that I could provide a context for my students and for me that could serve us all. . . .[3]

Chicago also writes about using consciousness-raising to enhance her students' self-opinions and to expand their limited concepts of the role of the artist. Our conversation begins with a discussion of this topic.

Betty Ann Brown: The negative stereotype of the artist — as a troubled individual working in anguished isolation, alone, starving in a garret — has been a dominant trope of western culture since the Romantic Period. One of the most radical, socially transforming acts of the Feminist Art Movement has been to challenge that stereotype, to assert that much art can be — indeed always has been — produced in community. Your work at Cal State Fresno, Cal Arts, Womanhouse, and the Woman's Building contributed significantly to that change. Can we go back to the pivotal decades of the 1960s and 1970s? Tell me how and why you shifted from individualistic, male-dominated artistic identity to female and community-based artistic identity.

Judy Chicago: I didn't set out to challenge the system. I grew up believing the idea that art was universal. I thought if I demonstrated my talent, demonstrated that there was an audience for my point of view and that my work was authentic, then I would be embraced by the art system. I really believed that. It took me years before I realized it wasn't so. . .

One of my greatest frustrations today is the degree to which artists and the art system continue to invest in stereotypes about the artist. Robert Rauschenberg, for example, does not produce his prints alone. A lithograph that comes out of Gemini G.E.L. ([a fine arts printing studio located in Los Angeles) is the product of a whole group of people, yet all of their work is disguised by Rauschenberg's signature.

I didn't do anything so dramatically different in making my art in community; I just took off the disguise. I refused to collude in the misconception that I work alone in my studio. Male artists have always had behind them a whole structure of support — assistants, gallery dealers, collectors, spouses, critics — all of whom stand behind the achievement of the individual artist. Women have failed to understand how achievement happens. So when in fact people got around me and provided for me what every male artist who has achieved on any significant level has always had, I got all kinds of criticism, as if I was doing something terrible. But the criticism comes from people who buy into the stereotype. All I did was remove the disguise of the stereotype.

I think that the current breakdown of the international art market has created a tremendous opportunity for artists to redefine the role of the artist and the function of art. Personally, I am no longer interested in making objects for an increasingly elitist, decontextualized audience. That has never been my audience anyway. I need to pay attention to what my audience can afford and what my audience can own. . . . I've been thinking a lot about how some people have too much art while some people don't have enough. Someplace in there is an opening for a new way to be an artist where more people can have access to images. I don't know what I'm going to do yet, I'm just beginning to think about this. But God knows, too many artists are wasting their time making objects that nobody understands, cares about, or has access to. They keep doing it in hopes of becoming the next art star. But it's all so much fantasy. It amazes me that so many artists seem to have so little capacity to imagine another model of achievement.

One of the things I've begun to realize is that if you look at me, at Judy Chicago the artist, in the paradigm of the art world, then I'm rather unintelligible. But if you look at me in the paradigm of women's historical situations, realizing — as the "Dinner Party" shows us and as Gerda Lerner's scholarship has proven to us — that we have a different relationship to history than men do, then it's clear I did what I did because I had to. I had to not only make the art, but also build an audience and create a context, a *community*.

BAB: As I teacher, I am particularly inspired by your work with the California State University, Fresno program and at Cal Arts [California Institute of the Arts, located just outside Los Angeles]. Tell me why you decided to use the classroom as the foundation for a feminist art community and how that worked.

JC: You know from reading *Through the Flower* that I wanted to reconnect with my own impulses, impulses which had been undermined by my classical art education and the art scene in L.A. I figured that by having my students start making art from who they really were, I could get back to who *I* really was. And it worked. I wasn't in a place in my development then that I could devote any length of time to teaching, because I had such a burning desire to make art. I did what I did in Fresno primarily out of my own needs as an artist, but it had great benefits for my students.

I went to Fresno to start creating a context for my work. Of course what I hoped at the time was that I would start this process and other people would come forward to carry it on while I did what I'm best at, that is, create art. . . . I hope that I now have enough support to maintain an institution, since I've put the energy into trying to build one. Because if you don't have the support of established systems, you have to build from the beginning every time.

Which is what we had to do when I tried to move my program to Cal Arts. That was a mistake! The secret to Fresno was that we had a space of our own. We could discover our own forms without the presence of an authoritarian paradigm looming over us. As soon as I brought the program to Cal Arts, the weight of the prevailing paradigm pressed down all around us. I was miserable within three days of walking inside that institution. So I quit. I arrived on campus in February and had handed in my resignation by April.

BAB: Womanhouse, created over twenty years ago, was the first concrete summation of your community building efforts in art education. In *Through the Flower*, when you talk about the Feminist Art Program at Cal Arts, you say that you and Miriam Schapiro began to wonder about dealing with the problems women have making art *in* the context of work, rather than separate from it. Art historian Paula Harper suggested the project of designing a house. You, Schapiro, and twenty-one students located, renovated, and totally reconfigured the dilapidated seventeen-room house in Los Angeles. You talk about the problems, conflicts, resentments . . . but you also talk about the successes, about the fabulous art created — your "Menstruation Bathroom" filled with all the paraphernalia we use to hide our monthly cycles, the "Nurturant Kitchen" lined with pink egg-breasts, the "Bridal Staircase" depicting the dismal realities of the happily-ever-after marriage fantasy. You also talk a lot about the performances, the artist-produced and -directed theater pieces that grew out of the lives — often out of the anger in the lives — of the women who worked with you.[4] The appendix includes the scripts of four of these performance. Even today, when I re-read those scripts, I am struck by the honesty of their content and the power of their expression. It seems to me that Womanhouse explored the social construct of female identity in ways that no one art work had ever done before. Womanhouse lasted for about six weeks in 1971 and was then torn down. Tell me how you feel about Womanhouse in retrospect.

JC: Some years after *Through the Flower* was published, I became embarrassed about Womanhouse. The context of the 1970s had started to disappear and what had seemed obvious then started to seem rather foolish in the 1980s. In later versions of the book, I pulled out the performances and changed some of the chapters. Then, a couple of years ago, I started having these young women intern with me, art students and art history students. They would go through my slide files and say, "Oh my God, this is fantastic!" when they saw images like *Red Flag*, my early work on menstruation. They knew nothing about these works because they weren't being taught any of this. So in the reissue of *Through the Flower*, I put back Womanhouse. I also reproduce *Red Flag* which has never been reproduced before. And I tell the story of what happened when I showed it at the Cal Arts Women in Arts conference. Everyone got hysterical and said I was painting a bloody penis. But it is a tampon! I go on to talk about the continuing absence of women's images in museums and public spaces and what that means. Anyway, my young interns helped me rediscover my own history; I'm claiming all of it now.

BAB: In 1975, you founded the Los Angeles Woman's Building with art historian Arlene Raven and designer Sheila de Bretteville. For eighteen years the Woman's Building was a major feminist cultural center, but it is now a matter of history. Tell me your thoughts about the Los Angeles Woman's Building as a community-building institution.

JC: The opening of the Woman's Building was so exciting . . . but again it was a problem and a conflict for me. Was that the thing for me to be doing, making an institution? I'm an artist.

When we opened the Woman's Building, it was an art organization. Because of that it got a certain kind of support. But then it lost its focus. It became less of an art institution and more of a social service institution. It was really hard not to do that, because the need among women is so great. On the other hand, well, [New Mexico artist] Luis Jimenez said something I think is pertinent here. He said that you can reach out a hand, but you should make people jump up to it. And I think that's very important. At the same time you share, you should ask people to reach to a higher level of aspiration. Art provides that high level. How to balance that, and meeting people's needs . . . that's the problem.

Even though I had sort of abandoned the Woman's Building because I had such a need to make art, I was extremely upset when it closed (in 1991). I thought, "Why can't we maintain our institutions?"

BAB: 1975 must have been an incredible year for you because it was in that same year that you began full-time work on the "Dinner Party." When I read your book on the "Dinner Party," it seems to me that the very structure of the piece has to do with women's history of and continuing need for community. Here is what you said.

> [T]he concept of an isolated woman "pulling herself up by her bootstraps" simply did not stand up to the evidence of history. Rather, women's achievements took place against a background of societies in which women either had equal rights or were predominant to begin with or, later, enjoyed expanded opportunities, agitated for their rights, and built support networks among themselves.[5]

> To convey this idea, I decided to place the triangular table on a floor inscribed with the names of additional women of achievement besides those represented by the place settings. This would suggest that the women at the table had risen from a foundation provided by other women's accomplishments, and each plate would then symbolize not only a particular woman but also the tradition from which she emerged.[6]

Am I correct in assuming that community was the basis for the physical structure of the piece?

JC: The structure grew out of my discoveries of the kinds of things Gerda Lerner writes about. In her historian studies, she found what she calls "affinity clusters."

It's a wonderful term. All the women who achieved to the level of the women represented on the "Dinner Party" table, achieved in the context of an affinity cluster. That could be a convent or nunnery, or the Bluestockings, or a literary salon, a lesbian group, or an expatriate group.

The names on the floor of the "Dinner Party" represented the historical contexts of the women at the table. The women around Susan B. Anthony, for example, were an affinity cluster in the International Women's Movement. True achievement always takes place in the context of support . . . which is something most women don't understand yet.

BAB: Community building was also the process with which the "Dinner Party" was executed. Tell me how the working process developed in your studio in Santa Monica.

JC: Well, I actually developed my process over many years. It's a process of facilitating and empowering that I have used in classes and in working with other people on my projects. I use it to build group cohesion and try to balance that with individual initiative. I extended the "Dinner Party" process in the "Birth Project" (the multimedia art work on the female experience of giving birth, which involved over 150 needleworkers), which didn't happen in my own studio but all around the country. Even though we weren't in the same geographic place, my process still worked to create both group cohesion and individual achievement . . . which is something I wanted to see if I could accomplish when everyone was dispersed.

For the process to work, you have to redefine the role of the leader. The leader, instead of being an authority figure who imparts information, becomes a facilitator who shares information and empowers the people she works with.

The process requires relinquishing power. That's the fly in the ointment. So many people are so in love with power. However, the creative process requires discovery. You can set up guidelines and you can set up parameters. But if you need to control the outcome, you might as well not do it. When people have trouble with teaching or leading the creative process, it is because of power issues. They may want to change, they really may, but they're frightened, afraid of not being in control.

BAB: I see that all the time at Cal State Northridge. People genuinely want to do alternative teaching, teaching that really empowers their students. But, they protest, does that mean that we might not be able to teach Shakespeare? And the answer is yes, maybe, if the class goes in another direction, that's what it may mean. I use Shakespeare as an absurd example. . .

JC: No, he's a good example. I think the question of how to impart information is also important. After all, when you're teaching art history, you have a lot of information to convey. It was really interesting watching [art historian] Paula

Harper teach for "Through the Flower" (the non-profit corporation that has provided a framework for my major projects). She had lots of material to discuss and lots of slides she wanted to show, but what she did was give people the tools for looking. She helped her audience identify what to look for, and the meanings in what they saw. What is the size of the female figure, or the male figure? What is the position of the female, or the male? Who's clothed, who's not? Who's looking at you, who's looking away from you? All these decisions, made by the artist, have meaning. So what Harper did was give people the tools and then they looked at art together. That's very different from how you and I learned art history!

Harper showed a painting of Matisse and his model. There he is, this big, authoritarian man with the lights on him — he looked like a doctor — next to this very thin, vulnerable model. You could *see* the whole story. He owns the female body, he is the master, she the slave. Her body belongs to him, is his to manipulate. When it's translated into a painting, it becomes sublime form carrying hideous content. We swoon over it and think it's a masterpiece and Matisse is a great artist. It's so hard to break through that old paradigm.

BAB: "The "Dinner Party" is often criticized because in spite of the collaborative nature of production, your name precedes the title of the piece and you are usually credited with being its sole creator. I need to say here that an artist like Christo, who involves hundreds of people in his environmental extravaganzas, is never criticized on similar terms. I wonder if that's because "vision" in a grand sense is considered a male prerogative. But back to the "Dinner Party." I know from my friends, like Nancy Ann Jones, who worked with you, that one of your primary aims — certainly something to which you devoted much time and energy — was the interactive process, the "group dynamics," if you will, requisite to establish a positive, diversified, nonhierarchical community. Tell me how you respond, after all these years, to the criticism.

JC: We should talk about that. There is a tremendous amount of misrepresentation and misunderstanding that surrounds what I've done. And one of the key things that's misrepresented is I not only took off the disguise [of the stereotypical view of the individual artist], but I did something men don't ever do. I gave credit to everybody who worked with me. But instead of saying, "God, isn't it great that she gave credit," they all say I'm exploiting people. This is the most bizarre reversal; it's continually baffling to me. I get accused of doing something that I haven't done while the people who do exploit others never seem to get nailed.

Every person who has ever worked with me has been listed in my book, has been named on the wall, has been mentioned in my lectures, in newspaper articles, in films. Every single person. What else do they get? They get respect. They have the opportunity to do something that is important, they learn skills, they become empowered, and they receive credit.

I would like to address this issue of credit directly. I deserve more credit than I have even begun to get. But what comes with credit is responsibility. I've been carrying the considerable responsibility along with the credit I've supposedly gotten and that I'm so resented for. Most people don't think about the fact that it costs $1400 a month to store the "Dinner Party," the "Birth Project," and the rest of my art. It costs almost a quarter million dollars a year to run the tiny little non-profit organization of "Through the Flower." I have to generate all that money or I will lose all the art work. I have had to do many more things than an artist is normally expected to do already, but it still doesn't begin to guarantee the preservation of the work, which concerns me greatly.

I say to people who criticize me: come and stand by my side. For thirty years, I have stood firm. If you want the credit, you gotta take the flack, that's the deal. It's a whole package deal: credit, responsibility, rejection, humiliation, hostility, assault, attack. I've taken it all: the hearings in Washington [during the 1991 Congressional debates about the National Endowment for the Arts, when some speakers referred to the Dinner Party as "obscene"]; [*Time* magazine critic] Robert Hughes calling my work shit; [conservative art critic] Hilton Kramer calling it kitsch . . . I've taken it all.

What were they saying during the Congressional debates? "Cunts on plates! Cunts on plates! Cunts on plates!" It took me years to understand why the "Dinner Party" upset so many people and still does. I was challenging a fundamental concept of patriarchal thought — a concept women have internalized — which is that female genitalia and female sexuality are shameful.

Such thinking is a complete denial of everything for women. Complete denial of personhood, of having a life and needs and independent identity. But the "Dinner Party" plates rise up and say, "Hey guys, you're wrong! We do have needs and identities and history. We have form and we can be universal and we're central and guess what, we can fly, we can leap right off these plates!"

But I didn't do the "Dinner Party" as a challenge. I did it as an authentic expression and a celebration . . . a celebration of women's history and of my own experience and a sense of my own sexuality and my understanding of what it means to be a female. I did it sincerely and naively, with hope that it would educate and inspire people, like the historical information that had educated and inspired me, and all the people who worked with me.

Understanding the implications of the "Dinner Party" is an educational job that has to be undertaken in order to build enough support to preserve it. Okay, here's a work of art that has empowered and inspired hundreds of thousands of people. It is now crucial to educate them to say "I want other people to have this experience, too. I want my children to have this experience. My grandchildren. Therefore I have to contribute to that. I have to take responsibility for it, I have to take responsibility so that other people can have this experience." This would

Women's Art Communities in Contemporary History

be an important step for women. In fact, if we don't take that step, everything I've done (along with that of many other women) will again be erased. And then the images which could empower people in the future will be lost. Instead of being a foundation, my work — like that of so many women — will only be a footnote.

BAB: In spring 1991, I taught a course in Feminist Theory at the Claremont Graduate School (California). We alternated weekly consciousness raising meetings with discussions of historic and contemporary writings by women. That summer, we did a collaborative art exhibit at CGS, an installation which I also later placed at Cal State Northridge. Although I heard many tearful testimonials from students about this being the most important class they'd ever taken, and in spite of the fact that I knew the exhibition was a fabulous success, I was devastated by the brutal rejection I received from some of the class members. It was not until I reread *Through the Flower* in preparation for our conversation today that I recalled you had been through this kind of pain many times. You write that many of the young women with whom you'd worked were unable to accept you as an authority figure. (I'm quoting this at length because I think it is one of the most painful and hard-to-understand aspects of female interaction.)

> They had no models in their lives for women to be authorities on the basis of their accomplishments. The only female authorities in their lives were their mothers, and the young women had many unexpressed feelings towards them . . . they became confused. The rhetoric of the women's movement says that all women are equal, and so they are, on the basis of their humanity. But in reference to talents, abilities, and achievements, not everyone is equal. . . . When women encounter a woman as an authority figure, they can only imagine that she is like their own mothers. They try to lay their anger at their mothers upon them. . . . (I wish to make a clear distinction between authority figures and authoritarianism, which is not at all what I mean. To be an authority figure in the sense that I use the term is to be an authority about a given subject and to have information that is valuable to others. This can be given without the misuse of power that so often characterizes male authority figures.)
>
> The acceptance of women as authority figures or as role models is an important step in female education. If one sees a woman who has achieved, one can say, I'm like her. If she can do it, so can I. It is this process of identification, respect, and then self-respect that promotes growth. . . .
>
> . . . the process of female education was at work, a process that forces a confrontation between the developing women and the female figure who is placing demands upon them. At some point in the process, after the initial gratitude for the help, many women turn against this figure who has helped them. It's happened frequently in my years of working with women, and it always hurts.[7]

Does it still hurt, Judy? What insights do you have now after almost three decades of working with women in community?

JC: Actually, this too relates to the question of credit. We have no models for female authority except our mothers and we're taught that the mother should be selfless. Therefore a mother who insists she get credit is violating the role assigned her. Mothers are not supposed to get credit for what they do. But I'm not everybody's mother. I'm an artist and a writer and I've worked very, very hard for three decades on behalf of women. Young women don't need to fear me; they need to identify with me. But they can't because they're caught in the idea that in order to grow you have to reject your mother. That's a very fucked up concept. It's destructive of self and other.

BAB: This year [1993] marks the 100-year anniversary of the Women's Building at the Chicago Columbian Exposition, 100 years of American feminism, 100 years of women working in creative communities to support each other and nurture the possibilities of social change. Tell me how you view this century of history and, more importantly, what your dreams are for art-making in a feminist future.

JC: Where are women? We're nowhere historically. We just keep reinventing the wheel. And the reason we're nowhere is because of all the things you and I have been discussing. We're nowhere because we don't get it. We don't understand that we have a different relationship to history. We don't understand how achievement takes place. We don't understand we have to work together. We don't understand that we have to unite behind a series of singular goals and work together to achieve them, that we have to build a foundation. We're not at the point where women can enjoy individuation the way men can.

We have to cohere around specific symbols and push them through. We already have masses of books and masses of art works. We already have that. But what we haven't had is the power to push, to cohere behind a number of them. It's related to what I was talking about before, the nature of achievement. People say, well, why should we all work together to house the "Dinner Party"? That's Judy Chicago's. That attitude shows both a misunderstanding about how achievement takes place and an unwillingness to support other women. As Lucy Lippard said, in response to the women at UCLA who stated their intention to picket the "Dinner Party" because it shouldn't be the only feminist icon, "Good, knock it down. Then there will be none!" The "Dinner Party" represents a really good shot to break the patriarchal cycle of history because it has such a big audience. But it will take a lot of people saying, Okay, I'll get behind preserving the "Dinner Party" because it's our best shot to open a crack in the wall of history and then maybe I can follow in through that crack.

In order for women's art to truly flourish, we have to understand the connection between making art, showing art, and preserving art. I figured out how to make it. I built the community, the support for it. I even managed to exhibit it. But now the problem is preserving it. The problem is: Can we leave a lasting legacy?

left: Sandra Orgel, *Sheet Closet* at Womanhouse, 1972; below: Judy Chicago, *Study for Driving the World to Destruction 2*, 1983, prismacolor pencil; courtesy ACA Galleries, NYC.

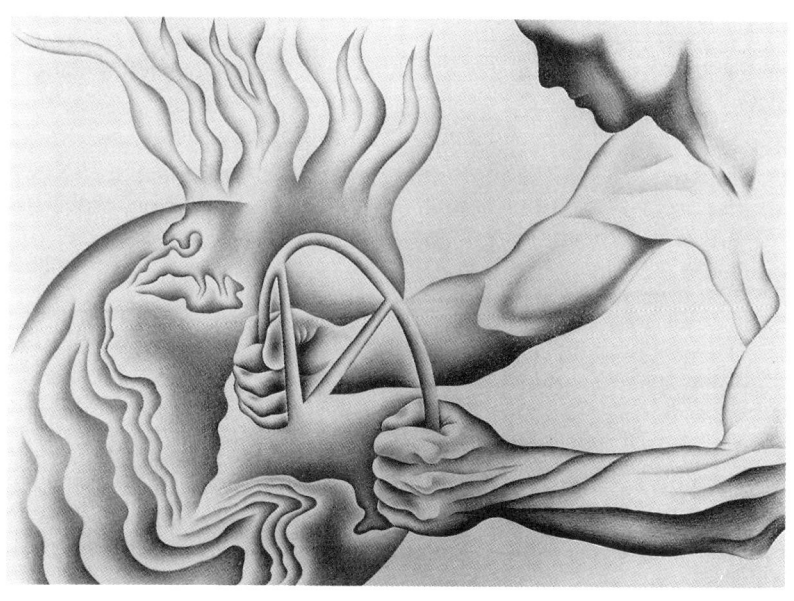

Sweeping Exchanges:
The Contribution of Feminism
to the Art of the 1970s

by Lucy R. Lippard

Lucy Lippard is an inspired public speaker and teacher. Her words and writings have motivated many of the artists and writers in this volume. She summarizes parts of her current position in the introduction to her book The Pink Glass Swan:

> What has changed [in the last twenty years] is that I have deviated from the feminist center (as some see it) or the center has expanded into concentric circles (as I see it). Early in the eighties, I was told by a midwestern feminist that I hadn't been invited to a conference because rumor had it that I was "no longer a feminist"; I was "too interested in the Third World." Bemused by the notion that the Third World was perceived as all male, I was also annoyed and alarmed at such a narrow definition of feminism. The undertones of classism in such comments by feminists have not escaped working-class women. As far as I am concerned, everything in which a feminist is involved becomes feminist in some sense. (Almost like "it's art if an artist says it is.") Feminism changed my entire outlook on the world and its impact on my life has never diminished. Nor could I have gone back, even if I'd wanted to: it's like jumping off a roof — too late to change your mind halfway there.[1]

> [Feminist art today must embody] the spirit of classic feminist inclusion and generosity. The concentric circles might represent open arms, a wider and wider embrace. Mobility within representation, especially when it is controlled from within, is a subtle form of resistance. Art, especially avant-garde art, is expected to be unexpected. All radical feminist artists are moving targets.[2]

By now most people — not just feminist people — will acknowledge that feminism has made a contribution to the avant-garde and/or modernist arts of the 1970s.[3] What exactly that contribution is and how important it has been is not so easily established. This is a difficult subject for a feminist to tackle because it seems unavoidably entangled in the art world's linear I-did-it-firstism, which radical feminists have rejected (not to mention our own, necessarily biased inside view). If one says — and one can — that around 1970 women artists introduced an element of real emotion and autobiographical content to performance, body

Women's Art Communities in Contemporary History

art, video, and artists' books; or that they have brought over into high art the use of "low" traditional art forms such as embroidery, sewing, and china-painting; or that they have changed the face of central imagery and pattern painting, of layering fragmentation, and collage — someone will inevitably and perhaps justifiably holler the names of various male artists. But these are simply *surface* phenomena. Feminism's major contribution has been too complex, subversive, and fundamentally *political* to lend itself to such internecine, hand-to-hand stylistic combat. I am, therefore, not going to mention names, but shall try instead to make my claims sweeping enough to clear the decks.

Feminism's greatest contribution to the future of art has probably been precisely its *lack* of contribution to modernism. Feminist methods and theories have instead offered a socially concerned alternative to the increasingly mechanical "evolution" of art about art. The 1970s might not have been "pluralist" at all if women artists had not emerged during the decade to introduce the multicolored threads of female experience into the male fabric of modern art. Or, to collage my metaphors, the feminist insistence that the personal (and thereby art itself) is political has, like a serious flood, interrupted the mainstream's flow, sending it off into hundreds of tributaries.

It is useless to try to pin down a specific formal contribution made by feminism because feminist and/or women's art is neither a style nor a movement, much as this idea may distress those who would like to see it safely ensconced in the categories and chronology of the past. It consists of many styles and individual expressions and for the most part succeeds in bypassing the star system. At its most provocative and constructive, feminism questions all the precepts of art as we know it. (It is no accident that "revisionist" art history also emerged around 1970, with feminists sharing its front line.) In this sense, then, focusing on feminism's contribution to 1970s art is a red herring. The goal of feminism is *to change the character of art.* "What has prevented women from being really great artists is the fact that we have been unable to transform our circumstances into our subject matter . . . to use them to reveal the whole nature of the human condition."[4] Thus, if our only contribution is to be the incorporation on a broader scale of women's traditions of crafts, autobiography, narrative, overall collage, or any other technical or stylistic innovation-then we shall have failed.

Feminism is an ideology, a value system, a revolutionary strategy, a way of life.[5] (And for me it is inseparable from socialism, although neither all Marxists nor all feminists agree on this.) Therefore, feminist *art* is, of necessity, already a hybrid. It is far from fully realized, but we envision for it the same intensity that characterizes the women's movement at its best. Here, for example, are some descriptions of feminist art: "Feminist art raises consciousness, invites dialogue, and transforms culture."[6] "If one is a feminist, then one must be a feminist artist — that is, one must make art that reflects a political consciousness of what it means to be a woman in a patriarchal culture. The visual form this consciousness takes varies from artist to artist. Thus art and feminism are not totally separate, nor are they the same thing."[7] "The problem is not with people's taste (often called "kitsch" by superior minds) but with defining art as one thing only. Art is that which functions as aesthetic experience for you. If a certain art works that way for enough people, there is consensus; that becomes art. . . . That which we feel is worth devoting one's life to and whose value cannot be proven, that is art."[8] Feminist art "is a political position, a set of ideas about the future of the world, which includes information about the history of women and our struggles and recognition of women as a class. It is also developing new forms and a new sense of audience."[9]

The conventional art-world response to these statements will be *what* new forms? And to hell with the rest of it. Descriptions like the above do not sound like definitions of art precisely because they are not, and because they exist in an atmosphere of outreach virtually abandoned by modernism. For years now, we have been told that male modernist art is superior because it is "self-critical." But from such a view self-criticism is in fact a narrow, highly mystified, and often egotistical *monologue*. The element of dialogue can be entirely lacking (though ironically it is *feminist* art that is accused of narcissism). Self-criticism that does not take place within or pass on out to its audience simply reinforces our culture's view of art as an absolutely isolated activity. Artists (like women) stay home (in self and studio) and pay for this "freedom" by having their products manipulated and undervalued by those who control the outside world.

A basic and painful conflict is set up when an artist wants to make art and at the same time wants to participate more broadly in the culture, even wants to integrate aesthetic and social activities. Artists who work with groups, as do so many feminists, always seem to be looking wistfully over their shoulders at the studio. "I've got to get back to my own work" is a familiar refrain, because, as it stands now, art and life always seem to be in competition. And this situation produces an unusually schizophrenic artist. One of the feminist goals is to reintegrate the aesthetic self and the social self and to make it possible for both to function without guilt or frustration. In the process, we have begun to see art as something subtly but significantly different from what it is in the dominant culture.

This is not said in a self-congratulatory tone. It remains to be seen whether different is indeed better. Success and failure in such unmapped enterprises are often blurred. Various feminists have already fallen into various traps along the way; among them: the adoption of certain clichés in images (fruit and shell, mirror and mound), materials (fabrics and papers), approaches ("nonelitist"), and emotions (nontransformative pain, rage, and mother love); a certain naïveté (also carrying with it a certain strength) that comes from the wholesale rejection of all other art, especially abstraction and painting; a dependence on "political correctness" that can lead to exclusivity and snobbism; and, at the other extreme, an unthinking acceptance of literally anything done by a woman. Beneath these pitfalls is a need for language — visual and verbal — that will express the ways our art and ideas are developing without being sappy and without denying the powers of the individual within collective dialogue.

Nevertheless, feminist values have permeated the 1970s and are ready to flower in the 1980s, if militarism and socioeconomic backlash don't overwhelm us all. Often accepted unconsciously, these values support the opening up and out of eyes, mouths, minds, and doors — and sometimes the smashing of windows. They include collaboration, dialogue, a constant questioning of aesthetic and social assumptions, and a new respect for audience. Feminism's contribution to the evolution of art reveals itself not in shapes but in structures. Only new structures bear the possibility of changing the vehicle itself, the meaning of art in society.

New? I hesitate to use the word in this context, since it, too, has been so distorted in the name of modernism: new reality, new realism, new abstraction; and similarly, all the rigid posts: postmodernism, post-Minimalism, and post-beyond-postness. Feminism is new only in the sense that it isn't post-anything. Its formal precepts are not new at all. They are simply distributed differently from those entrenched since around 1950. Much or even most of the best art by women has turned its back on the "new," preferring to go deeper into visual forms that have been "done before" (mostly by men). When I began to write extensively about women's art, I was accused by friends and enemies of becoming a "retrograde" critic. And so long as I remained attached to the conditioning of my own art education, received primarily at the Museum of Modern Art and on Tenth and Fifty-seventh Streets, I too was afraid of that stigma. However, the more women's work I saw, the more my respect grew for those artists who, having been forcibly cut off from the mainstream, persevered in exploring their own social realities, even-or especially-when such exploration did not coincide with the current fashions.

The more illuminating dialogues I had within the women's movement, the clearer it became to me that the express toward the "true nature of art" had whisked us past any number of fertile valleys, paths to elsewhere, revelations, personal and social confrontations that might forever have been missed had it not been for such stubbornly "retrograde" artists, who insisted on taking the local. During this time I was constantly being told that some woman's work was derived from some far-better-known man's work. In fact, such similarities were usually demonstrably superficial, but the experience of searching for the differences proved invaluable because it undermined and finally invalidated that notion of "progress" so dear to the heart of the art market.

In endlessly different ways, the best women artists have resisted the treadmill to progress simply by disregarding a history that was not theirs. There *is* a difference, though not always an obvious one, between the real but superficial innovations of a feminist or women's art that has dissolved into mainstream concerns and the application of these same innovations to another set of values, where they may be seen as less "original." It was suggested several years ago that feminist art offered a new "vernacular" reality opposed to the "historical" reality that has informed modern art to date.[10] Given its air of condescension, *vernacular* may not be the right word (and certainly we don't want to be "hidden from history" again), but it is the right idea. The 1970s have, I hope, seen the last of the "movements" that have traipsed, like elephants trunk-to-tail, through the last century.

The notion that art neatly progresses has been under attack from all sides for years now; its absurdity became increasingly obvious with postmodernism in the early 1960s. By 1975, a not-always-delightful chaos of Conceptual Art, performance, photorealism, "new images," and what-have-you prevailed. The 1970s pluralism, decried for different reasons by both Left and Right, has at least produced a kind of compost heap where artists can sort out what is fertile and what is sterile. Bag ladies picking around in this heap find forms, colors, shapes, and materials that have been discarded by the folks on the hill. They take them home and recycle them, thriftily finding new uses for worn-out concepts, changing not only the buttons and the trim but the functions as well. A literal example of this metaphor is the Chilean *arpillera*, or patchwork picture. Made by anonymous women and smuggled out into the world as images of political protest, social deprivation, crushed ideas and hopes, the *arpilleras* are the only valid indigenous Chilean art — now that the murals have been painted over, the poets and singers murdered and imprisoned.

You will have noticed by now that feminism (and by extension feminist art) is hugely ambitious.[11] A developed feminist consciousness brings with it an altered concept of reality and morality that is crucial to the art being made and to the lives lived with that art. We take for granted that making art is not simple "expressing oneself" but is a far broader and more important task: expressing oneself as a member of a larger unity, or comm/unity, so that in speaking for oneself one is also speaking for those who cannot speak. A populist definition of quality in art might be "that element that *moves* the viewer." A man probably can't decide what that is for a woman, nor a white for a person of color, nor an educated for an uneducated person, and so forth, which is where "taste" comes in. This in turn may explain why the "experts" have never been able to agree on which artists have this elusive "quality." Only when there are real channels of communication can artist and audience both change and mutually exchange their notions of art.

Feminists are asking themselves, as certain artists and critics and historians have asked themselves for generations, "Is this particular painting, sculpture, performance, text, photograph moving to me? If so, why? If not, why not?" In

Women's Art Communities in Contemporary History

this intuitive/analytical task, the social conditioning we have undergone as women, as nurturers of children, men, homes, and customs, has its advantages. We are not bolstered by the conviction that whatever we do will be accepted by those in power. The lack can be psychologically detrimental, but it also carries with it an increased sensitivity to the needs of others, which accounts to some extent for the roles that the audience, and communication, play in feminist art.

Similarly, because women's traditional arts have always been considered utilitarian, feminists are more willing than others to accept the notion that art can be aesthetically *and* socially effective at the same time. Not that it's easy. The parameters for "good art" have been set; the illusion of stretching those boundaries that prevails in the avant-garde is more exactly a restless thrashing around within the walls. Overtly feminist artists are always being accused of being 'bad artists' simply by definition. That's not something I'm interested in responding to here, but it should be mentioned in the context of changing the character of art. Given the history of the avant-garde, what on earth does "bad art" mean these days? But of course if someone isn't there to say what "good art" is — then art itself gets out of institutional hand.

Perhaps the single aspect of feminist art that makes it most foreign to the mainstream notion of art is that it is impossible to discuss it without referring to the social structures that support and often inspire it. These structures are grounded in the interaction techniques adapted (and feminized) from revolutionary socialist practice-techniques on which the women's movement itself is based: consciousness raising, going around the circle with equal time for all speakers, and criticism/self-criticism. From the resulting structures have evolved the models feminism offers for art. These models, I repeat, are not new ways of handling the picture plane, or new ways of rearranging space, or new ways of making figures, objects, or landscapes live; they are inclusive structures or social collages.

The history of the male avant-garde has been one of reverse (or perverse) response to society, with the artist seen as the opposition or as out-of-touch idealist. The feminist (and socialist) value system insists upon cultural workers supporting and responding to their constituencies. The three models of such interaction are (1) group and/or public ritual; (2) public consciousness raising and interaction through visual images, environments, and performances; and (3) cooperative/collaborative/collective or anonymous art-making. While it is true that they can more easily be applied to the mass-reproduced mediums such as posters, video, and publications, these models also appear as underlying aesthetics in paintings, sculptures, drawings, and prints. Of course, no single artist incorporates all the models I am idealizing here, and certainly individual male artists have contributed to these notions. But since male consciousness (or lack thereof) dominates the art world, and since with some exceptions male artists are slow to accept or to acknowledge the influence of women, these models are being passed into the mainstream slowly and subtly and often under masculine guise-one of the factors that makes the pinning down of feminism's contribution so difficult. Yet all these structures are in the most fundamental sense collective, like feminism itself. And these three models are all characterized by an element of outreach, a need for connections beyond process or product, an element of *inclusiveness* that also takes the form of responsiveness and responsibility for one's own ideas and images — the outward and inward facets of the same impulse.

The word *ritual* has been used in connection with art frequently and loosely in the last decade, but it has raised the important issue of the relationship of belief to the forms that convey it. The popularity of the notion of ritual indicates a nostalgia for times when art had daily significance. However, good ritual art is not a matter of wishful fantasy, of skimming a few alien cultures for an exotic set of images. Useful as they may be as talismans for self-development, these images are only containers. They become ritual in the true sense only when they are filled by a communal impulse that connects the past (the last time we performed this act) and the present (the ritual we are performing now) and the future (will we ever perform it again?). When a ritual doesn't work, it becomes a self-conscious act, an exclusive object involving only the performer. When it does work, it leaves the viewer with a need to do or to participate in this act, or in something similar, again. (Here ritual art becomes propaganda in the good sense — that of spreading the word.) Only in repetition does an isolated act become ritualized, and this is where community comes in. The feminist development of ritual art has been in response to real personal needs and also to a communal need for a new history and a broader framework within which to make art.

Public consciousness raising and interaction through visual images, environments, and performances also insist on an inclusive and expansive structure that is inherent in these forms. This is in a sense the logical expansion of a notion that has popped up through the history of the avant-garde: that of working "in the gap between art and life." Aside from an outreach branch of the Happening aesthetic in the early 1960s, this notion has remained firmly on art's side of the gap. But by 1970, feminists, especially on the West Coast, were closer to the edge of that gap than most artists; they were further from the power centers, and, out of desperation, more inclined to make the leap. Just as ritual art reaches out and gathers up archaeological, anthropological, and religious data, the more overtly political art of public strategies reaches out to psychology, sociology, and the life sciences. Its makers (*planners* might be a more accurate term) work in time as well as in images, moving closer to film, books, or mass media. Video and photography are often used not so much to stimulate a passive audience as to welcome an actively participating audience, to help people discover exchanges between art and life.

Such work can take place in schools, streets, shopping malls, prisons, hospitals, or neighborhoods. Among its main precepts is that it does not reject any subject,

Women's Art Communities in Contemporary History

audience, or context, and that it accepts the changes these may make in the art. To be more specific, a few examples: (1) A group of women of mixed nationalities living in Paris who have done large documentary pieces including drawings, texts, photographs, and video tapes about women in prison and about Turkish and Portuguese workers at home and in economically imposed exile. (2) An Israeli woman trying to communicate to urban workers on the Tel Aviv waterfront the plight and beliefs of the Bedouin tribes through "desert people" costume rituals in urban workplaces. (3) A New York woman who made her "maintenance art" first in the home, then in office buildings, and has spent the last two years identifying with the men in the city's Sanitation Department (the "women" of the city government), recognizing their maintenance work as art by shaking hands with every member of the department. (4) Two women in Los Angeles who make public pieces strategically designed to change the image and media coverage of feminist issues such as rape and violence against women. (5) A mixed-gender group, led by a San Francisco woman, that has built a "life frame" which is simultaneously performance art, five acres of community outreach, and an experimental agriculture station, making connections between animals, plants, people, and art. (6) A group of women photographers in East London organizing child-care facilities and comparing pictures of real life with the mass-media images of women. (7) A man in a small economically devastated New England mill town who uses photography as a vehicle of continuing awareness to acquaint the inhabitants with their environment, with each other, and with their possibilities. (8) Another man who mixes art and science and populism in a South Bronx storefront and calls it a "cultural concept."

All these examples overlap. Much of the work mentioned above is being executed by various combinations of artists or of artists and nonartists, often anonymously or under the rubric of a collective or network or project. Some women work cooperatively — helping an individual artist to realize her vision on a monumental scale and in the process both giving to her work and getting input for their own work. Others work collaboratively, according to their own special skills, needs, and concerns. And others work collectively in a more or less consciously structured manner aimed at equal participation and skill-and-power-sharing. Each of these means helps to achieve an end result of breaking down the isolation of the artist's traditional work patterns. None precludes individual work. (I find from my own experience that the dialogue or critical/self-critical method stimulates new kinds of working methods and a new flexibility. By integrating feedback into the process, and not just as final response to the product, it also changes the individual work.)

The structures or patterns I've sketched out above are laid out on a grid of dialogue that is in turn related to the favorite feminist metaphor: the web, or network, or quilt as an image of connectiveness, *inclusiveness*, and integration. The "collage aesthetic" named by the Surrealists is a kind of dialectic exposing by juxtaposition the disguises of certain words and images and forms and thus also expressing the cultural and social myths on which they are based. The notion of connections is also a metaphor for the breakdown of race, class, and gender barriers, because it moves out from its center in every direction. Though men are its progenitors in high art, collage seems to me to be a particularly female medium, not only because it offers a way of knitting the fragments of our lives together but also because it potentially leaves nothing out.

It is no accident that one ritual artist calls herself Spider Woman and another group calls itself Ariadne. As I was writing this essay, I read an article about the Native American ethos of total interrelationship among all things and creatures, which says: "Thus, nothing existed in isolation. The intricately interrelated threads of the spider's web was referred to . . . the world. . . . This is a profound 'symbol' when it is understood. The people obviously observed that the threads of the web were drawn out from within the spider's very being. They also recognized that the threads in concentric circles were sticky, whereas the threads leading to the center were smooth!"[3] The author remembers his mother saying that "in the Native American experience all things are possible and therefore all things are acceptable," and he goes on to hope that "our societal structures and attitudes become bold and large enough to affirm rather than to deny, to accept rather than to reject."

I quote this not only because it expresses very clearly a conviction that lies at the heart of feminism (and should lie at the heart of all art as well), but also because it comes from another culture to which some of us fleeing the potential disasters of Western capitalism are sentimentally attracted. However, the socialist feminist model does not stop at the point of escape or rejection as did the counterculture of the 1960s. To change the character of art is not to retreat from either society or art. This is the significance of the models I've outlined above. They do not shrink from social reality no matter how painful it is, nor do they shrink from the role art must play as fantasy, dream, and imagination. They contribute most to the avant-garde by slowing it down. They locate a network of minor roads that simply covers more territory than the so-called freeways. They pass more people's houses. And are more likely to be invited in.

Lenora Champagne, "From the Red Light District," Performance.

ARLENE RAVEN

in Conversation with Betty Ann Brown

> Feminism makes a connection. . . .
> Feminist art raises consciousness/invites dialogue/transforms
> culture.
> Feminist art makes the private public.
> The artist is a magic maker. She is a witch.
> When she performs, she enacts. She uses her body.
> She becomes symbolic. Mythic.
> She makes connections. And empowers.[1]

To talk of Arlene Raven's career is to recap the history of the Women Artists Movement in this country. She has been an integral part of almost every major institution and event from the Cal Arts Feminist Art Program through the Woman's Building to the remarkable diversity of the current moment; her writing forms one of the most important records of feminist artistic production during the last two and a half decades. As we discuss in the following conversation, Raven studied painting, but recognizing her "love of words," turned to writing about the arts. In 1973, Raven, Judy Chicago and Sheila de Bretteville founded the Los Angeles Woman's Building. Named after the Women's Building from the 1893 World's Columbian Exposition in Chicago,[2] the Los Angeles Woman's Building combined a women-controlled gallery venue with dynamic, alternative educational efforts. Arlene Raven was a leader in those early feminist teaching projects. She has introduced feminist art pedagogy to several mainstream educational institutions and continues to give lectures and workshops throughout the country. Yet Raven's primary identity is as a writer.

Arlene Raven and I spoke by phone about her history, her relationship with the women's community, her current work, and the changes that life, time, and illness have moved her through. As I transcribed the tape of our conversation, I re-read *Crossing Over*, the anthology of her writing in the 1970s and 1980s. I was both inspired (again) and reminded (again) how much I owe her personally, intellectually, and aesthetically. I have interwoven phrases by and about her into this summary of our conversation.

Betty Ann Brown: Tell me how you came to be an art historian.

Arlene Raven: I come from a very neglectful household — I guess you call it dysfunctional today — and I needed to get out of there. I wanted to go some place where I wouldn't have to live at home. I was not allowed to go out of the state of Maryland — that was my parent's thing — so I chose Hood College. It was a women's school, but I wasn't even cognizant of that at the time. It happened

Women's Art Communities in Contemporary History

to be an excellent educational institution, a wonderful place which means a lot to me now. I studied art and art history there. I heard that artists were geniuses but art historians and critics were parasites, so naturally I went on in art. I got an MFA in painting from George Washington University. But I was a word person. I had a very strong interest in writing; if I had been in school about five years later I might have become a conceptual artist, rather than an art historian. That's basically my approach anyway. I went to Johns Hopkins, which was also nearby, to do my graduate work in art history.

BAB: What field of art history did you specialize in?

AR: In contemporary American art. I wrote my dissertation — I called it "I and Eye" — on the subjective perception of the Washington Color School.[3] It was an anti-Greenbergian treatise[4] on the contents of the Washington Color School, mainly Morris Louis, but also other people. I finished writing the dissertation in 1975, but by 1972 I was out of school and in California.

BAB: What brought you to California?

AR: Judy Chicago and Miriam Schapiro. I met them when I was working at the Corcoran. There was a conference there, one of the first conferences of women in the arts, and I met them at the conference. I really connected, particularly with Judy, and she invited me to visit her.

> Connection, community, kinship, network, are feminist word-concepts which have been actualized in the feminist art movement.[5]

So I went to California and while I was there — this all happened in a very short period of time in the spring of 1972 — I was offered a job at Cal Arts, to be the art historian of the Feminist Art Program. I said sure — because that was the best job I could think of getting. I did not want to train art historians, I knew that already. So from the beginning, I embarked on a career that was atypical of an art historian. I chose to work in art schools, to work with artists.

> I . . . crossed over a professional boundary to bring my commitment to feminism and my work as an art historian together in writing about this social and aesthetic avant-garde. I was inspired by feminist writers (especially Adrienne Rich, Mary Daly, and Susan Griffin) to enter new territory.[6]

My art history developed along with my feminist art activities; my research was in the field of feminist art, always, from the beginning of my writing until today. I don't mean it was confined to the subject of women, but that was definitely my emphasis. I could not write one kind of thing for the *Art Bulletin* [a fairly traditional art historical journal] and then turn around and write something different for *The Village Voice*. That would have been schizophrenic. Although I did not follow the traditional art history path, I was still enriched by being an art historian and having had a rigorous education. I bring it to my art criticism. That is unusual: few critics are trained in art history. Academically speaking, writing criticism is not the road to success and tenure. But I've never believed in tenure nor wanted to have it. I stopped teaching about ten years ago. Not because I don't love it — I do — but because I wanted to concentrate on my writing.

BAB: You came out to California in 1972 and started working at the Feminist Art Program at Cal Arts?

AR: Yes, for a year. Then the next year, Sheila de Bretteville, Judy Chicago, and I started the Feminist Studio Workshop in the Woman's Building (although Sheila and I continued to teach at Cal Arts).

BAB: Tell me a little about the Feminist Studio Workshop.

AR: We knew we wanted to have a community and what we knew how to do was teach, so we started a school. But our community, our school, was truly alternative. A lot of the women who attended already had their degrees, they were older, they were professional artists and are still today. We invented everything in the curriculum. It was joyful. It was also a very rigorous and innovative education for those women — and for me. We did everything from teaching carpentry to writing resumes to, well, I remember I did a workshop on non-ordinary experience. The classes were totally appropriate for what we were doing and yet I think that many of them would be startling even today. If we started all over right now and did the same thing, people would still be knocked out, and so would I.

> When the Feminist Studio Workshop at the Woman's Building advertised its 1980 educational program, the title "Take Part in the Feminist Studio Workshop" was accompanied by an image of a hand holding a fortune cookie. In a second image, the cookie had been taken apart and two hands held the message, "Take part; make whole." This dual meaning conveyed the concept of feminist education as not only professional training in the arts, but also a healing process in which, by taking apart the events of one's life and examining them in feminist and art processes, a healing of the person toward wholeness could take place.[7]

BAB: Were you doing traditional teaching?

AR: Never traditional teaching. I gave lectures, but they were coming from very new research, not from what so-and-so had to say and then what so-and-so said about what so-and-so had to say — which is the old art historical way. In addition to lectures we had workshops, we did consciousness-raising, we did exercises for trust and skill, we discussed all kinds of topics together. I always wanted to be in that community as an equal member, but the Feminist Studio Workshop never accomplished the leveling of student and teacher. I tried very deliberately to break down that hierarchy in the Lesbian Art Project and I believe I succeeded as much as possible. But I was more experienced, older than the majority of the students, and I had more education, more background. I was often perceived as a leader rather than a member, although I considered myself one person in a group of people working on the project together. I acted as a member as well as the originator and co-organizer.

> Feminist art is revolutionary not only socially but personally, for at its best, according to Raven, it involves establishing an ideal of autonomous woman. She is the woman who has self-consciously chosen femaleness, not simply had it thrust upon her by nature. Thus, there is as much idealism as anger in Raven's writing, as much a need to repair the wounded dignity of woman — the degradation of femaleness — by re-articulating that dignity in heroic, elevated terms as to avenge the wrongs perpetrated on woman by a patriarchal society.[8]

BAB: What were the dates of the Lesbian Art Project?

AR: We worked on it from 1977 through 1980. In the spring of 1979 we did a play called "Oral History of Lesbianism." I was getting an honorary degree from Hood College at the same time the play was running. So I was participating in (writing and acting in) a shocking lesbian play with my colleagues in Los Angeles — and it was a wonderful piece of work, I think — and then I was flying east to Hood College to receive this honorary degree. The contradictions seemed overwhelming. It was a very, very big expanse for me to think of myself in those two ways, to see that I was actually getting recognition for something that was so off the beaten path, so radical. I am a radical feminist. I wanted a revolution as well as an evolution. I still do.

BAB: When did you start thinking of yourself as a feminist?

AR: In the 1960s. In the mid 1960s, I married my thesis advisor. I would go to parties in Washington, D.C. The women would be in the kitchen talking about their children and the men would be with their cigars talking about art. Naturally I would gravitate toward the art discussion. I began to ask myself, "What's wrong with this picture?" I had begun to develop some awareness from my own experience of things, but it wasn't until I went to my first consciousness-raising group that I heard you didn't have to wash the dishes.

> [P]ersonal narrative entered women's visual vocabulary as expression and public disclosure of the great rush of speech which women exchanged privately when they broke their silent isolation within home, studio, or workplace to gather for consciousness-raising conversations. . . . Hearing stories over time, we have a sense of the continuum of women speaking, even across geography and history.[9]

At that time, I was working on what was one of the first women's journals, *Womin: A Journal of Liberation*. Its offices were in Baltimore, Maryland, in the same building as a free clinic. I would work in the free clinic and I would work on the magazine. That was the way I experienced the Women's Movement back then. I participated in the activism, the rallies and all the political things you did as a feminist.

In a way, I left my husband because he didn't want to do the dishes. Consciousness-raising changed how I was relating to things. I was living with my husband and stepdaughter. I was taking care of them and cooking the three meals and doing all the cleaning and the laundry and the shopping and everything else. Plus I was a full-time student. Plus I had a full-time job and I was basically supporting that family. How do we do all that? I wasn't even thinking. I remember that I had a joint banking account with my husband and I would ask him if I could buy things, with money that I had earned. Right around 1970, the contradictions became apparent to me.

My marriage lasted seven years and I'm glad I was married because given the kind of pressure that I had from my community and my family, if I hadn't gotten married, I would have had a nervous breakdown. They thought I was an old maid when I was 21 years old. The fact that I'd gone to graduate school was totally outlandish to them; they just couldn't imagine it. So I got married and for a while I bought the myth that I was supposed to be anonymous and have nothing, that I was supposed to live for my husband and children. "Sell yourself into slavery, and a man will take care of you." I had to unlearn the myth because I got married yet nobody was taking care of me. I supported the whole family, even supported his ex-wife and my sister at one point, but wasn't supposed to say so. It was rude to suggest that you weren't being supported by a man, because that was the program.

Just a few days after I left my husband, I was brutally raped. That was a real turning point for me. I had begun to consider myself a feminist and I had been thinking about my options, about being independent and so on, but that totally radicalized me. I realized that the only reason I was raped was because I had a cunt. I had a pussy and that meant that I could be raped.

I was kidnapped. As I was being dragged and taken, I kept thinking to myself, "How can they do this to me? Don't they know I'm getting my Ph.D.?" I had thought education was my ticket out, my ticket to the freedom that a man has. But it wasn't.

I was so lucky to go to California at that time and be able to talk about it. I was raped only a few days before I went to visit Judy Chicago. I was still hurt from it because they beat me and everything. There were two of them and they were never caught. Judy was doing audiotapes by rape victims for the "Ablutions" performance and I made a tape. It was the first time I had talked about the experience. My mother had taken me to the doctor the day after it happened. She and my father were called when I was missing. A friend was expecting me at her house and when I didn't come, she called the police. But my mother wouldn't allow me to discuss it with her. She acted like, "Oh no, this didn't happen!" Yet I was hurting. Do you remember the Bob Dylan song with the line "Take 15 Baths a Day"? That was me. I had to have all new underwear, all new sheets. Fortunately when I went to California, I got into a lot of psychotherapy and I had a chance to talk about things in my educational groups. Everyone has their story. But mine was very poignant, and I did something that was atypical for victims of rape, since it's perceived as so humiliating: I told everybody about it.

> In 1972, Judy Chicago, Suzanne Lacy, Sandra Orgel, and Aviva Rahmani performed a blood ritual, *Ablutions.* The subject was rape. A woman was tied into a chair and then tied to everything else in the vast room — an artist's studio in Venice, California — after being "bathed" in raw eggs, earth, blood. The sound was a tape recording of women telling about their rapes. The individual recountings formed one story: at the end of this piece, the last voice repeated over and over, "I felt so helpless all I could do was lie there and cry." This performance was a ritual and a spell. Of enactment and exorcism . . . Judy Chicago was making the *Ablutions* tape when I visited her in the Spring of 1972. I had been raped three days before, and I *was* the shock, panic, self-loathing and despair of the raped victim, because I felt so helpless all I could do was lie there and cry. But I rose on the third day anyway to pursue my survival and future, guided by my woman's intuition that they could be divined: (divination: act or practice of foreseeing or foretelling future events or discovering hidden knowledge. Exercise of intuition.) by flying three thousand miles to perform a ritual of speaking pain and of initiation with a woman I had met, powerfully, only once.[10]

I was stressed for a while there. Yet I was functional. I changed my name and moved to California and I have never lived anyplace in the Mid-Atlantic region, in either Maryland, or Washington, D.C., or Virginia, ever again.

BAB: Why did you change your name?

AR: I changed my name during that first visit to California. I was looking for a new name because I was going to be divorced. I was asking everybody for suggestions. Judy Chicago came up with Raven and I liked it. So I adopted it and it's been my legal name since 1972. I didn't go back to my "maiden" name and I didn't keep my husband's name. I suddenly understood sexist oppression. I was politically radicalized and I knew everything. I could read about it in a book or somebody could teach me some of these things — but basically I knew everything, right from that point. I understood. I did not want my father's name, I wanted my own name, right then. So that's what happened.

> . . . to exist humanly is to name the self, the world, and God. The 'method' of the evolving spiritual consciousness of women is nothing less than this beginning to speak humanly — a reclaiming of the right to name. The liberation of language is rooted in the liberation of ourselves.[11]

> Birth as a metaphor for creation has often been used by feminists to describe the impact of feminism on their lives. Theirs was a rebirth and a recreation of themselves as more fully themselves. And this second, feminist, birth required new naming.[12]

BAB: Let's go back to something we touched on before: the issue of collaboration. I know that most people think of writers as sitting alone in their offices, doing very solitary work, but its seems to me that a lot of the writing you do is actually in collaboration with the artist or artists about whom you're writing.

The feminist synergy between together and alone has taken unique form in creative collaboration.[13]

AR: That's true, but there is a solitary act of writing, and I came to New York to do that. Writing was always part of my activity and I longed for it to be a bigger part. I love teaching, and I love to help people, and to teach people, and to be taught. I do workshops once in a while and it makes me feel so good — helping people get in touch with themselves, change, learn things. But the Woman's Building was a full-time teaching job *and* a full-time job in the women's movement *and* I had to do a lot of administration *and* I was consulted a lot. I have a gift for putting things together, giving them a title, organizing them. . . . I'm very good at doing that and carrying it through, but I longed for the solitary life of a writer. It was contrary to what I had thought I would do and I must say that my colleagues in the California women's community were never very encouraging about my writing; they didn't even like it. I didn't write that much because I didn't have time. I guess I write in the way most academics do, present company excluded. I wrote once in a while, when I had an opportunity. But I wanted to put myself in a situation where I *had* to write. So I came to New York and I became a full-time writer — thirty days a month, every month. That's how I do it.

> Raven's intensity is technically an effect of her staccato, collage method of writing. Many of her essays — and I use that term with its connotation of experiment, tryout, attempt — are a sum of fragmentary observations about artists who are themselves regarded as fragments in the greater mosaic whole of feminism. The fragment, for all its partiality, conveys a sense of experiential density, perhaps because we imagine the whole of which it is part to be concentrated in it. It functions synecdochically, its brokenness adding an extra edge to its poetry. Raven's piling up of fragmentary statements about artists creates a special density of import, as though through the accretion of fragments a new female wholeness might spontaneously generate, or at least be imaginatively glimpsed.[14]

> Piercing, crosshatching, connecting disparate parts — of materials or family members or aspects of life — has been a cultural female role and even claimed as innate female nature. These kinds of activities are, in any case, second nature to us.[15]

BAB: Do you see your writing as a form of collaboration with the artist?

AR: I consider what I do to be writing *alongside* of an artist's work. I always have contact with the artist. I always go to the studio, read everything I can locate for background and then I write. But when I'm doing it, it's alone. I give every artist I write about the chance to look at the manuscript before publication. That's often very challenging, but if there is something that they're sensitive about, or if I've done something that's inaccurate, then I need their feedback.

I find this to be the most honorable relationship. It's not the easiest, but it's honorable. I am not swayed by somebody who says, "You have to write that I'm the greatest, that I'm Leonardo da Vinci or something." My integrity is intact and important.

I rarely write on artwork I don't like. At the *Village Voice*, which is my most frequent place of publication, we get to choose what we want to write about. Since I can choose, I write about things that I'm enthusiastic about, that I think are important. I want to communicate about art I want people to see, not about something I think is trash. Why would I bother investigating something like that? I have a negative attitude towards things like censorship but basically I feel that the kind of criticism that says "I like this, but I hate that," is so far away from what I'm doing that there's no relationship.

In my teaching I've collaborated a lot. I did team teaching with Judy Chicago and Miriam Schapiro. In fact, I did team teaching with all my colleagues. I participated in other people's teaching and they participated in mine. It's like a dance, you have to be easy with the person and you have to give-and-take. I know how to do that. It's a very pleasurable, joyful experience for me. But . . . I have to concentrate my life where I really want it. You know, I was ill for several years and that illness gave me a lesson about how you have to do the most important things and you have to let some things go.

> The human body, that ultimate sculpture, can still be whittled or willed into submission. But in defining beauty, I long for more choices than these skinny models.[16]

I went to a consciousness-raising group recently. It's only for women who have been in the women's movement for at least 20 years. There were all these old war horses there, and I started looking at the women. One of them had a facelift . . . her hair is dyed, you really can't tell how old she is . . . although you can tell she's trying to look young. Then I looked at another woman who had let herself get large — some women do get larger in their menopause and in their middle age — and she had gray hair and she hadn't done anything much with it. I said to myself, "Which one is more attractive?" And I couldn't answer the question.

I'm having a revolution in my mind. Of course, I have read a lot of feminist theory about looksism. But I didn't "look like a dyke"; I was always out — never in the closet — and I've never lied about my age. I hadn't experienced the oppressions [directed towards women who don't conform to the dominant standard of beauty]. Now I'm really working them out. My feminism's very active now, in a personal way. I talk with movement women about it.

Right now, I feel great. The Epstein-Barr virus is in remission. I feel spiritually renewed. I'm ready for work. I do get sick occasionally, but I'm living with it, going on with my life. I have exciting new projects. One of them is a book on Adrian Piper. I have a wonderful assistant, a graduate student at [State University] Stony Brook (SUNY), a very intelligent young woman who is working with me. We're assembling what I would call a map of all of Adrian's work before we start. It's a luxury that I have never had before, to do that kind of preparation.

BAB: I think Adrian Piper's work is remarkably important. She did an installation at the Santa Monica Museum of Art that knocked me out. She's a wonderful choice, good for you!

AR: Yes, she's fabulous. I'm not writing only about her artwork. I'm investigating her philosophy writing, her art writing, and her visual art — bringing them together. I'm a philosophical art historian and she's a philosophical artist, so we work well together. But I'm also starting another project. My colleague at the *Voice*, Robert Atkins, and I are writing a book about gay and lesbian artists, using an essay/photo format similar to the one you and I used in *Exposures*. I'm traveling, I'm giving lectures, and I'm continuing as East Coast editor for *High Performance* magazine. I write a monthly column for the *Village Voice*, catalogue essays.

BAB: Let's go back to one more thing which is the community around the Woman's Building. You already said that with the Feminist Studio Workshop you wanted to be in the community and work in community. Why? What was going on there?

AR: Art comes out of community.

> The community network and its genealogy underlie my content. I owe my friends and colleagues with whom I built a home for women's art and a body of work my deepest gratitude for the vital exchange we had and have.[17]

The Washington Color School came out of the fact that people lived in Washington. Feminist art comes out of a feminist art community which is largely invisible, unless you call it feminist and make a school and do all the things we did. Your network of women, my network of women, that's a feminist community.

I knew from my art historical work that community creates art. In Los Angeles, we wanted to create art and community, we wanted to work with other people, we wanted not to feel alone. I think we accomplished a lot. We were the founders, our names were on all the documents, the corporation and the lease. Through all of it we tried very hard to bring in other women as equals. There was always this kind of dissension from people who didn't want to take responsibility particularly but wanted to be taken care of. So the people in charge were viewed as monsters or something, but I guess that is very typical.

> Often frustrating and disappointing, the activity of the seventies nevertheless moved toward coming home . . . to an expanded sense of identity; to different and more authentic modes of living, working, and loving. The professional/friendship network of the women's movement was one such alternative home and community.[18]

We went quite far in creating a community and I still have that community. I did a book with you. When Cheri Gaulke comes to town, I always see her performances. Things keep going on like that. I still feel that I have a community, but I'm living a different life now. I was living 100 percent of my life in the feminist community in Los Angeles. If I went to a restaurant, it was a feminist restaurant. If I got my car fixed, it was by a feminist.

I have a "private" life today. Almost everything is tied into my work. Of course, New York's a real workaholic place anyway, which is appropriate for me. But somehow it's much less taxing to take care of my own business, do my own work. I've faced things that I've never faced before — my illness, the disease and death of many friends.

My community still exists. But when we lived it in a very concrete way, it changed my molecules; I literally became a different person. This is what Marx talked about — he put it in very different words, but this is my understanding — that what makes the person, the individual, comes out of society. There is that kernel of who you are, of course —your talents, your birthmarks — but who you are is formed very much by the company you keep, the neighborhood you live in, what you do with yourself there.

As a child, I thought I had come from Mars. I had to get out of the community I grew up in because it wasn't good for me. So I made my own community that *is* good for me, where I can grow, and I'm still doing it.

I love my life today. I loved it in Los Angeles, too. I don't regret one thing that's happened in my life.

Requiem

by Terry Wolverton

Terry Wolverton was one of hundreds of women who left their home-towns (in her case, Detroit) to be part of the Woman's Building in Los Angeles. Beginning as a student in the Feminist Studio Workshop in 1976, she spent thirteen years working in the context of the Woman's Building — producing performance art works; founding an anti-racism consciousness-raising group for white women; serving as newsletter editor, membership coordinator, typesetter, administrative assistant, member of the Board, development director, and eventually, executive director. "Requiem" mourns the closing of this vital institution.

Founded in 1973 in Los Angeles, California, the Woman's Building was a unique public center for women's culture. The building closed and the organization became inactive in 1991.

A chair is still a chair,
even when there's no one sitting there
but a room is not a house
and a house is not a home
when there's no one there. . . .[1]

In the early morning, the air already sticky with summer heat, a pearly yellow light seeps over this part of town, the forgotten backyard of the city, where the river is bedded in concrete and railroad cars roll by on rusted tracks. It's a scarred industrial pocket, grubbing in the shadow of downtown's gleaming spires, an area snubbed by developers for decades. It used to be called "Dogtown" by the local gangs until the animal shelter closed a few years back, victim of budget cutbacks. To the south and west stretch the streets of Chinatown, their bustling commerce, their tacky allure. To the north and east, Latinos set down roots in Boyle Heights, struggling to maintain their traditions while chasing the American dream. Hidden just behind a hill, nestled in Chavez Ravine, Dodger Stadium looks down its nose on this graffiti-streaked collection of crumbling warehouses and desolate railroad yards.

This particular terrain is claimed by no one; even the homeless scarcely venture this far north, except for the hoboes who still leap from the boxcars, who still build their fires beneath the concrete bridge that spans the cement-lined L.A. river.

Yet on this morning, as your car traverses the bridge, the summer heat pressing

Women's Art Communities in Contemporary History

down like a giant hand, this neighborhood is as familiar to you as breath, filling your head like the scent of garlic rising from the Asian food warehouses, blending with the odor of exhaust. For years this obscure section of decrepit streets and aging structures was the starred capital on your personal map of Los Angeles, its grit settled in your pores, its din pounding in your ears like the beat of your own heart.

At the end of the bridge you slow reflexively, hands ready to guide the steering wheel to the right, into the pot-holed, dead-end Aurora Street, being careful to watch for the random eighteen-wheeler that might happen to be exiting. But unlike the thirteen years of mornings when you made that turn, dodged the big rig, negotiated your parking place beside the metal dumpster, today you drive on by, accelerating past the three-story red brick building which had for so long been the center of your universe. Built in the 1920's by the Standard Oil Company, this red brick building was known from 1973 until 1991 as the Woman's Building, a public center for women's culture.

A painted strip around the building still proclaims the name, although it is no longer true. So you stomp the accelerator, speeding past the blur of brick as if fleeing from a ghost. But not quite fast enough, for time unravels anyway; you are caught up. North Spring Street curls into a ribbon, blacktop twisting back upon itself, knotting inside you, dragging you into the past.

The Woman's Building. A public center for women's culture. In that terse descriptor spins a universe of ideas, of history: the way you, as a woman, searched in vain to find yourself reflected in the mirrors of culture. What did you find? Dull-eyed beauties whose gaze evaded yours; mounds of flesh arranged like bowls of voluptuous fruit; evil temptresses, corrupters of men. More often, you found nothing at all, a curious silence, canvasses destroyed, journals burned, names erased. Culture proved to be a funhouse mirror, distorting and diminishing, a surface you walk into and then disappear.

Still you kept searching until one day your eyes caught the glimmer of refracted light, a spark in the night sky, and like all such luminosities it drew you, lured you all the way across the continent to its very edge, Los Angeles. That spark lodged in your imagination where it burned for years. Where it smolders still.

The Woman's Building. What other city but Los Angeles could have given birth to such an edifice? City of extremes, pressed against the brink of the Pacific, the endpoint of our restless explorations. City of dreams, where multitudes flock to reinvent themselves, to live out their personal myth. City that has slipped from the yoke of tradition, eluded the burden of history; city that levels and starts anew.

You came here to do that too, left behind the constricted fictions of the Midwest, its constipated possibilities, the cold, the drab, the predictable gaze that would not see you in your full dimensions. You came to put the fragments of your life together, following that spark, to re-knit the woman to the artist, the body to the brain, the spirit.

It was a journey worthy of Ulysses, a mythic voyage: departing wizened expectations, resigning from the family, the clan, abandoning the marble fist of culture that had closed against you, traveling two thousand miles to arrive at the home of women's culture, founded in the city of dreams. What could you have expected? Gleaming columns, a vast expanse of lawn, carved fountains spouting sparkling streams of water that glimmered in the afternoon sun? Anything, perhaps, except this neglected red brick building in a dour industrial district, an iron gate across the door bolted with a padlock.

In one way the site was perfect, no accident at all, a seamless representation of women's place in culture: a once grand, now run-down structure, a remote street in an obscure part of town, where toil goes unrecognized, pushed against the margins of a river choked in concrete; hard-to-find, down-on-its-luck, a derelict part of town. It was anger at this circumstance that had struck the spark, anger that provided the fuel; that, and the ether of imagination.

And imagination is keener than broken glass, tougher than pavement, wider than the smog-filled vistas you could see from the top of the bridge. The truth is, there was not one, but *two* Woman's Buildings: the one that squatted modestly beside the railroad tracks and the one that blazed, like an idealized lover, inside your brain. Entering the first, you inhabited the second, the parallel home of women's culture, the one with wide hallways and open courtyards on a sunny, tree-lined street, a city landmark wherein every woman's act gained its deserved significance.

Women all over the world knew this second Womans Building, women in Tokyo, in Mexico City, in Amsterdam; women who'd never set foot on North Spring Street still walked the vast rooms of this other Woman's Building, seized it as their Mecca, their "room of one's own."

You could never understand when others failed to see this second Woman's Building, so brightly did it shine for you. Walking newcomers through the edifice on North Spring Street, you'd puzzle at their dismayed glances, their diffident enthusiasm, and wonder at their failure of imagination. For you it was never a question — you dwelt in both buildings, each as real to you as the scent of your own skin. Huddling in winter in the unheated corridors of the first, you warmed yourself by the glorious fire in the second. And sometimes, when the art was brilliant and the rooms were full of women who were happy to be there together and the words were spoken from the deepest place in the heart, those twin images would blur, begin to swim together, two architectures becoming one.

No one could ever describe the Woman's Building. It would require a language

Women's Art Communities in Contemporary History

of multiple dimensions, of texture, a language which could encompass the passage of time as well as contradictory points of view. Perhaps no language could accomplish it, given the pressure for precision, the demand for definitive meaning, the desire to simplify with which we invest words. Perhaps only music would be capable of sounding those myriad notes — the harmonies, the dissonance, syncopation, counterpoint — to arrive at a composition of the whole.

Like the blind men in the parable, groping sightless at the surface of their elephant, each woman's grasp of the institution was fragmentary, partial and particular. The Woman's Building was a place. An institution. A gathering of women. It was an eighteen-year experiment. It was a collision of history and politics and art. It was poetry, painting, performance. It was the one night you went there for a dance and it was the thirteen years you spent trying to keep it ablaze.

It was the day you showed up with hennaed hair only to find that five other women had hennaed their hair the night before too. It was the rope straining in your hands as you hoisted the ten-foot-tall sculpture of a naked female figure onto the roof of the building, from which vantage point the entire city was her domain. It was a field of crosses planted on the lawn of City Hall by women dressed in nun's habits the colors of the rainbow, in protest of nuclear arms. A stage set of pink gauze that glowed like a lantern, lit from within, to contain and illuminate the stories of lesbians. It was a wall made of bottles, a tree of dolls' heads. A circle of women who stared unflinching into the video lens and told the stories of their sexual abuse.

It was the dope you smoked on the fire escape, the Friday nights you stayed late trying to figure out how to pay the bills. It was the first book you published there on the antique printing press; it was the C-R group you hated.

Language splinters under the complexity, the immensity, the tens, perhaps hundreds of thousands of women whose imaginations and emotions and lives touched and were touched by the Woman's Building. All their stories, their dreams. And it was the art that was made within its walls, yes, but also the art that was made by some woman in some little town, work that came into being because she'd heard that the Woman's Building dared to exist.

The Woman's Building offered up a spark, and this was the message in its glow: that you, a woman, could be an artist too, and that your woman's life — whatever its particulars — could kindle your art, and that in turn, the act of making art would ignite that life, and finally, that a community of women, engaged in the twin acts of making art and making a new life, would transform the mirrors of culture into windows through which you all would fly, like sparks, into the night sky.

An extravagant promise, perhaps. But imagining the promise made it possible, and that possibility stretched like a roof over your head, marking the territory, giving you a place to stand. No edifice of bricks and mortar could contain all women — the kaleidoscope of political persuasions, sexual identities, cultures and personalities — and that was certainly true of the humble warehouse on North Spring Street. Still those eaves spread like wings and their breadth provided context and therefore meaning for what you did, for who you were.

And who are you now, as you sit in your idling car, unable to drive away from a decaying building, just a husk, a shell, the facade left behind once the living thing has fled? A woman, yes, an artist still, but these are now mere details, decontextualized, robbed of their particular significance. Graffiti covers the walls and the sky that stretches above is empty but for the brown cotton of smog.

Perhaps at one time you disdained the body, thought physical architecture was of no consequence, believed that the building itself didn't matter — the walls, the scarred floors, the girders connecting one story to the next. Just square footage, a pile of red bricks. But now, as you find no key to fit the padlocked entry, you know the ache of homelessness, the despair of exile. Now you come to understand that this building was irretrievably the foundation for the second, that grander, gleaming manse of your imagination, dependent on one another, joined at the heart. Now that this building is vacated, its twin has disappeared and with it, context, vanished like a spark in an airless room, like a dream in the pitiless light of day.

Women's Art Communities in Contemporary History

Woman's Building, World's Columbian Exposition, 1893; interior view north showing "Primitive Woman," tympanum decorated by Mary Fairchild MacMonnies; courtesy Chicago Historical Society.

Tina Nemetz (chairperson, Board of Directors, WARM Gallery) and daughter Hannah Rose working on Global WARM Scroll Project, Minneapolis, 1993.

A Collection of Collectives

> We had discovered the gold of sisterhood and it was a unique and precious find. It gave us the moral support that our previous isolation had prevented. Out of our consciousness-raising groups and our political action meetings, we emerged as a vigorous art body.[1]

> The true artist is connected.[2]

Throughout the last three decades, women have built community through arts organizations.[3] Many organizations were formed to provide their members with public spaces for exhibiting their art works. Some were primarily educational in intent. Others focused on publishing materials by and about women artists. Still others provided tools, work spaces, and sales opportunities. The accomplishments of such organizations have been documented in numerous directories and histories.[4] Perhaps most clearly focused on community are the collectives, that is, the organizations in which women gather and work together with self-defined goals and shared identification. Here I briefly survey a sampling of collectives from across the country in order to present an introduction to their scope and diversity.[5]

A.I.R. (Artists in Residence, Inc.) in New York City. The first cooperative gallery of women artists in the United States (except for the short-lived Gallery 15 established in 1958), A.I.R. was founded in 1972 by Dotty Attie, Maude Boltz, Mary Grigoriadis, Nancy Spero, Susan Williams, and Barbara Zucker "as a response to the resistance of the art world to art made by women."[6] In the text for a 1974 A.I.R. brochure, Lucy Lippard noted:

> Other co-ops tended to be run by men and to lack the cohesion that a political alliance, no matter how feeble, provides an all-woman gallery. . . . According to the tenets of the women's movements there are no leaders; everybody has her say on everything; work and money are solicited equally from all members with the usual problems of haves and have-nots, workers and non-workers, solved intramurally. Most significantly, it is committed to a diversity of styles not found in the most high-powered emporia, as befits the organ of a movement devoted to a multiple, open, flexible view of life and opposed to the single, acceptable, currently fashionable image, opposed to the rejection of self and emotion for a place in the establishment's sunlamp.

A.I.R. has twenty New York-based members and fifteen national affiliate members who live and work outside New York but also exhibit in the gallery space. A.I.R.'s

Women's Art Communities in Contemporary History

mission is "to advance the status of women artists by exhibiting work of the highest quality and by providing leadership and a sense of community to women."[7] Its activities include one-person shows for members, group and invitational exhibitions, panel discussions, lecture series, film programs and an apprenticeship program. Concepts for group shows may come from gallery artists, as "Large & Larger," the exhibition of large-scale drawings in June 1996, or from invited guest curators. Among the curated and invitational exhibitions are: "Combative Acts, Profiles and Voices," an exhibition of contemporary French women artists curated in 1976 by French critic Aline Dallier; "Dialectics of Isolation: An Exhibition of Third World Women Artists in the United States," curated in 1980 by Kazuko and Ana Mendieta; a 1992 exhibition of over 750 small works on reproductive rights; and, "States of the Art" curated in 1993 by Metropolitan Museum of Art curator Lowery Sims. The members of A.I.R., always aware that they were making history, have kept a careful archive, which will be featured in their twenty-five-year anniversary programs during 1997.

A.R.C. (Artists, Residents of Chicago) in Chicago, Illinois. Founded in 1972 as a cooperative women's art gallery and educational foundation, A.R.C. has fifteen active members and eighteen affiliate members. According to the gallery mission statement, A.R.C. is "dedicated to providing a forum for women artists and artists working outside the mainstream gallery system."[8] It was founded by women who found it "almost impossible" to exhibit their work once they finished their academic training. "United by their desire to exhibit and some common beliefs in feminism," they located a site for exhibitions and developed a community to form "a nucleus through which critical artistic dialogue covering a variety of issues could be heard."[9]

Along with one-person exhibitions for the members, A.R.C. also sponsors invitational and curated group exhibitions, such as "Women Who Build," a show of women sculptors; "Black Fusion," an exhibition of black American artists; "Earth Statement," an exhibition of Illinois installation artists; and "Post-Frida," an exhibition of contemporary Mexican women artists. Their exhibitions also travel nationally and internationally. In 1994, A.R.C. exhibitions were seen in Mexico City, Toronto, New York, and Ohio. A.R.C. manages six exhibition spaces. Not all of these are always given to the work of women artists.

Artemisia in Chicago, Illinois. Founded in 1973 and named for Italian Baroque painter Artemisia Gentileschi (1593-1652), Artemisia Gallery "supports emerging and alternative artists, provides educational services to the art community, features the work of galley members, and showcases major women artists who have not had the opportunity to exhibit in Chicago."[10] A group of women artists established Artemisia as an alternative to the commercial gallery system. Their goals included a desire to emphasize the role of women in the arts, to encourage the creation of innovative and experimental art that would not otherwise be exhibited, and to provide a forum for the exchange of aesthetic ideas.

Artemisia Gallery has sought to be inclusive, and in 1990 exhibited 363 artists of both sexes, all races, all ages. It has done collaborative programs with the Museum of Contemporary Art and The School of the Art Institute of Chicago. It has developed various outreach programs — including workshops, lectures, and a newsletter — and has offered exhibition space to underrepresented artists and developed a mentorship program for emerging artists. Its programs have included performance art as well as innovative poetry and music. Artemisia continues to offer Chicago premieres of important women artists — such as the 1992 exhibit of Nancy Grossman's sculpture — and underrepresented artists — such as the acclaimed "Coast to Coast," featuring works by more than 140 women of color, and the one-person exhibition of the ceramic sculptures of Barbara Lindsay, a Chicago homeless woman. In addition to annual or biennial exhibitions at the gallery itself, member artists have also planned and mounted group exhibitions internationally in Scotland, Italy, Iceland, Colombia, Chile, Germany and Australia.

The Spring 1996 Artemisia newsletter includes a brief article by gallery member Barbara Blades entitled "Statistics Don't Lie," emphasizing the ongoing need for women's collectives. "Last year I was lecturing to a class at Columbia College and the instructor asked me to talk about Artemisia. 'Why do you feel that there is still a need for a women's gallery, when so many women are now getting recognition for their (art) work?" To my surprise, a few male students came to my defense, and one stated that he thought that women had the right to run their own show because after all, men have had their 'exclusive clubs' forever. I was grateful for the support but I wish I would have had a copy of *WAC STATS, the Facts About WOMEN*, a publication by the Women's Action Coalition, which lists statistics for women in many areas, from art to health and work issues." Blades goes on to list fifteen disturbing statistics, eight of which are repeated here:

> 51.2% of all artists in the U.S. are women
> 60% of bachelor degrees in Fine Arts go to women
> 60% of masters degrees in Fine Arts go to women
> 33% of art faculty are women
> 5% of works in museums are by women
> 17% of works in galleries are by women
> 26% of artists reviewed in art periodicals are women
> Women artists' income is 30% that of male artists[11]

Athena Art Society in Toledo, Ohio. "On November 7, 1903, a group of 18 Toledo women met in the studio of Nina Spalding Stevens . . . to form a society 'to assist and encourage women engaged in all branches of the fine and industrial arts.' There were 59 names on the roster of charter members [who] met for two sketch classes a week plus a monthly social evening, when art work was displayed, readings given and instrumental selections performed. . . . In 1917, the Athena Society together with the Art Klan [sic] and the Tile Group [a male art group] founded the Toledo Federation of Art Societies."[12] Named after the Greek goddess of genius in artistic and intellectual endeavor, Athena "continues to thrive,"[13] the Federation sponsoring annual area artists' exhibitions at the Toledo Museum of Art. Athena also promotes members' work through annual juried exhibitions in alternative sites. . . . The fifty-seven active members run the gamut from painters to potters to metalsmiths and range in age from 32 years to seniors well into their seventies. Treasurer Leslie Adams says "I like Athena because of its long tradition. It has a great history in the city, a history of bringing the arts forward."[14] Membership is through nomination and secret ballot vote. Monthly meetings include lectures, workshops, networking and informal mentoring programs. [Athena, unlike some of the other century-old women's art organizations — such as the Catherine Lorillard Wolfe Art Club (1896), The Pen and Brush (1893), and the National Association of Women Artists (1899) in New York City, and the somewhat younger Women's Art League of Akron (1933), which function primarily as exhibiting organizations — provides "community" through its active programming.]

The Collective in Los Angeles. Founded in 1993 by Cathy Allen, Lisa Barash, Arleen Chikami, Polly Chu, Jackie Freedman, Sarah Lejeune, Keri Sabine, and Denise Seider, who, inspired by their shared experience at Claremont Graduate School, established a community of ongoing support in an art world environment they viewed as not supportive of emerging women artists. They continue mutual support and dialogue about their individual work that they initiated in graduate school, but also produce collaborative works in alternative public spaces, such as their 1995 project involving readings, educational workshops and group performances for A.R.K. (Art Resources for Kids) in Long Beach, California. The Collective has also conceived and presented a series of interactive performances at fairly traditional art sites, for example the 29 Palms Gallery, where viewers entered an auditorium expecting to sit and watch but instead became participants as Collective members handed them slips of paper instructing them on activities like "Go up to some one you don't know and tell them how beautiful they are." Designed to break down the boundaries between artist and audience, the Collective performances develop out of their shared goal of creating instant community. "Art can be about how the person next to you feels," asserts member Sarah Lejeune. "We try to surprise people and make them think." She adds that the Collective is project-driven. "We were having trouble working together, so we went on a retreat. We realized there that as a group we are about participating in and giving back to the community, not just hanging art on the wall. We all continue to do our individual work, but The Collective allows us to take greater risks together."[15]

Heresies in New York City. Begun at a 1975 meeting of feminist artists and writers who first gathered in the studio of Joyce Kozloff to welcome Miriam Schapiro back to New York, after her years living and teaching in California. In addition to Schapiro and Kozloff, Mary Beth Edelson, Ellen Lanyon, Lucy Lippard, Joan Semmel, Nancy Spero, May Stevens, Michelle Stuart, and Susana Torres were also at the first meeting. After a series of meetings in which the possibilities of both a feminist art school and a publication were discussed, twenty women decided in Spring 1976 to found a magazine committed to social change. Mary D. Garrard notes that the founding of *Heresies* marked a turn in feminist art action from museum protests aimed at immediate results to a consolidating phase for more long-term change. "We formed Heresies [the collective] because the ideas most relevant to feminist artists were not being discussed seriously or in depth in any existing publication. [M]ost of us had been involved in the Women's Movement since 1969 or 1970, had done consciousness-raising, had demonstrated and protested, had taught feminist courses and lectured on feminism. But it seemed as if it was a time for the next stage. . . . We want to take those debates and dialogues out to a larger public, to extend the ripples farther outward, to stretch ourselves." [Heresies 1979, p. 93] Each issue of *Heresies* focused on a specific theme, edited by a team from the collective and from the outside. Although originally intended as a quarterly publication, *Heresies* has produced only twenty-seven issues, including "Lesbian Art and Artists" (No. 3, 1977); "Third World Women: The Politics of Being Other" (No. 8, 1979); "Feminism and Ecology" (No. 13, 1981); and "Film/Video/Media" (No. 16, 1983). The last issue, "Latina," came out in 1993. Xiuyuan Lu, who is working on a doctoral dissertation about Heresies, notes that although three editorial collectives continue to work on future issues, a combination of reduced (and negative) government funding, the loss of free office space (in a NYC-owned building), a lack of skilled volunteers, and an accumulation of old debts, has forced Heresies Collective out of existence.

Las Comadres [The Godmothers] in San Diego, California and Tijuana, Mexico. In 1988, twenty women artists and writers of diverse backgrounds — Anglo, Mexican, Chicana, Black and Native American — began to assemble as a study group. Soon they decided to transmute into an activist collective dealing with border issues, to "speak for the community of women whose locus of action is the [United States/Mexico] border." Art historian Shifra Goldman says, "In the best spirit of responsibility and responsiveness, Las Comadres exemplify the creative possibilities of a transcultural interactive process."[16] Las Comadres included Aida Mancillas, Anna O'Cain, Berta Johar, Carmela Castrejon, Cindy Zimmerman, Eloise de Leon, Emily Hicks, Frances Charteris, Graciela Ovejero, Yareli Arizmeridi, Kirsten Aaboe, Laura Esparza, Lynn Susholtz, Magali Damas, Margie Waller, Maria Erana, Roberta Cantow, Rocio Weiss, Ruth Wallen and Stephanie Heyl. They maintained anonymity for all collective projects by not signing their art.

In their 1990 "La Vecindad/The Neighborhood" installation, Las Comadres recreated a trans-border home. On the floor of the entry way was a rug etched with "Hello Beaners" and other hate slogans apparently signed by the "Warboys" Neo-Nazi group from San Diego. The kitchen was more affirmative. "Bracketed by an image of the Virgen de Guadalupe in secular and saintly incarnations, the Kitchen opens up a vista of women's domestic life and sharing, the essence of community, of neighborhood." In the free-form performance "Border Boda/ Border Wedding," memories, stories through generations and "wisdoms were shared, identities and cultures defined."[17] By 1993, Las Comadres had disbanded.[18] [There was also a New York-based Las Comadres "organized in 1980 by a group of Hispanic women to mount an exhibition on the environment. The group disbanded after completion of the project. Navaretta, *Guide*, op. cit., p. 16.]

Mujeres Artistas del Soroesta (M.A.S.) in Austin, Texas. Founded in 1977 by Santa Barraza and Nora Gonzalez Dodson as a vehicle for exhibition of their work and that of many other Chicana and Latina women from Austin, San Antonio, Loredo, and other cities in central and southern Texas. Later members of M.A.S. were Alicia Arredondo, Maria Flores, Sylvia Orozco, and Modesta Trevino. Shifra Goldman cites the burgeoning feminist art movement and the Chicano struggle in Texas as the framework for the development of M.A.S. and notes the "multiple meanings implicit in their three-letter name."[19] MAS is not only the Spanish acronym for "Women Artists of the Southwest" in Spanish; it also means "more" in Spanish.

Women and Their Work, the Austin organization founded in 1976 by three non-Latina artists, sponsored a six-week arts festival involving more than 600 artists between October and December 1977. Fifteen Chicanas participated. During that time, the women of M.A.S. decided to establish their own group. (The DW co-op gallery of Dallas was initiated at that time as well.) M.A.S. was organized around "support, recognition, professional skills enhancement, and information sharing [as] part of the expanding national women's network." M.A.S. was characterized by "collective respect, lack of internal competition and genuine friendliness and cohesion."[20] Sylvia Orozco, director of the Mexic-Arte Museum in Austin, remembers that the members of M.A.S. gathered to work, exhibit and do projects together. They felt they had had less than active roles in the Chicano/ Chicana organizations in which they had previously participated. They mounted several group exhibitions and most of them shared a studio in Austin.[21]

With **LUCHA** (a Chicano arts organization), the women of M.A.S. coordinated the comprehensive Conferencia Plastica Chicana at the University of Texas, Austin, in September 1979. The Conferencia was a series of meetings, lectures, and exhibitions involving artists, critics and scholars from all over the Americas. Goldman spoke, as did prominent Mexican critic Raquel Tibol. Artist Carmen Lomas Garza was one of the many artists who gave workshops.

MUSE Gallery and Foundation for the Arts in Philadelphia, Pennsylvania. A women's cooperative gallery founded in 1977 by nine women artists. The original intention, according to current member Ruth Humpton, was to create a co-op that would provide an alternative space for women to exhibit their work, to provide women artists a professional opportunity in a gallery setting. "That's what we continue to do!"[22] The sixteen current members meet monthly, are self-supporting, and rotate overseeing the gallery space. Members have one-person shows every year-and-a-half to two years and group shows every year. The Muse Foundation sponsors films, workshops, lectures, and invitational shows, such as a group show of senior women artists.

Soho 20 in New York City's Soho art district. The collective was founded by artists Mary Ann Gillies and Joan Glueckman, who met Agnes Denes at WAR (Women Artists in Revolution) meetings. When Denes told them of plans to open the A.I.R. co-op and spoke of "much need for women's galleries," Gillies and Glueckman determined to open another.[23] By 1973, Sylvia Sleigh, May Stevens, Marge Helenchild, Rachel Rolon de Clet, Maureen Connor, Lucy Sallick and Rosalind Shaffer had joined Gillies and Glueckman. Soho 20 opened with one-person shows by Sleigh and Connor. Member Lucy Hodgson speaks with pride of the twenty original members as a political group "like the Chicago Seven."[24]

Soho 20 is "devoted to increasing public awareness of the excellence and diversity of women's art. It is one of the oldest organizations created to address the underrepresentation of work by women in museums and galleries."[25] Full members are entitled to an exhibition in the gallery space biennially, special members and members-at-large exhibit less frequently and participate less in policy decisions and gallery management. In addition to membership exhibitions, Soho 20 also presents guest-curated exhibitions such as a 1975 nine-woman invitational exhibition honoring the United Nations' Year of the Woman; a series of "Ageless Perceptions" exhibitions, beginning in 1987, focusing on senior women artists; the 1990 "Women in Resistance" exhibition of South African women artists opposed to Apartheid; and the 1990 "The Struggle Continues" show honoring the Civil Rights Movement and the Mississippi Three. In 1993, Soho 20 mounted "Underdevelopment In Progress/500 Years" by Vistas Latinas artists Ana Ferrer and Kukuli Velarde, an exhibition that had been censored for its political content at its previous institutional installation. Hodgson adds to this list what she terms the "Jesse Helms protest show" entitled "Blacklist, Whitewashed and Red-handed," it was an "open call" on censorship in the arts. ["Open call" exhibitions admit and display all art works that are submitted for consideration.]

Where We At in New York City. In early 1971, Faith Ringgold and her daughter Michele Wallace organized Women, Students and Artists for Black Art Liberation (WSABAL) to protest an exhibition organized at the School of Visual Arts. The "Biennale-in-Exile" exhibition was supposed to be in opposition to "war, racism, fascism, sexism and repression" (and to continue the May 1970 New York Art Strike protesting the U.S. invasion of Cambodia, the police killing of students at Kent State, and racial violence in Mississippi). But the exhibition included no women artists, no black artists. Ringgold's "demands for compensatory quotas — 50 percent black, 50 percent women, 25 percent students — significantly helped to launch both the feminist and black art movements."[26] In April of 1972, Ringgold published "An Open Show in Every Museum" — a clarion call for more equitable representation — in the *Feminist Art Journal*. In the summer of 1971, six black women artists — Faith Ringgold, Kay Brown, Jerrolyn Crooks, Pat Davis, MaiMai Leabua, and Dindga McCannon — began to plan what they considered the first ever exhibition of black women artists. The exhibition grew to include twelve artists who decided to join together as an ongoing organization under the name "Where We At Black Women Artists."[27] At its largest involving at least seventeen members [Dindga MCannon, Carole Byard, Jean Tayler, Charlotte Richardson, Faith Ringgold, Gylbert Coker, Kay Brown, Doris Kane, Iris Crump, Carol Blank, Jerrolyn Crooks, Pat Davis, MaiMai Leabua, Vivian Browne, Onnie Miller, Akweke Shingho, and Ann Tanksley], Where We At held exhibitions throughout New York.

We Had Waited 5,000 Years

> The history of WARM — the women's gallery in Minneapolis — was unusual in its interaction with and its influence in the local art community. Margot Fortunato Galt in writing about WARM completes the circle of the history of collectives.

WARM was part of a revolution. It emerged early from the tide of feminist protest and discovery that in the early 1970s flooded American culture. WARM threatened the local art establishment that was almost completely male to the extent that some male instructors forbade students to set foot in the Gallery, but it soon succeeded in becoming one of the best shows in town.

It's hard to revive the innocence, determination, and shock-value of WARM's early days. In 1973, Judy Chicago addressed students in the Twin Cities and stunned many women artists by proclaiming, "If you're not doing round things and furry things, you've been over-influenced by your male professors." Future WARM members working in Abstract Expressionist or minimalist styles didn't necessarily change stylistic direction, but they took to heart Chicago's insistence that "If it doesn't exist, you have to invent it."

Answering that challenge, women artists in the Twin Cities began to come out of isolation. "I'd never expected to be public with my art," said one. "I'd never seen a woman's art shown in a gallery." Meeting first in homes and studios, future WARM artists showed slides and discussed discrimination and early feminist publications like Linda Nochlin's ground-breaking article, "Why Are There No Great Women Artists?" A contingent from WARM traveled to the first national conference of women artists in Michigan, and came home with an idea for a Minnesota gallery — inclusive.

Few women artists had been encouraged to consider a career. "You've got your degree," one male professor told his female student, "now go on and get married." Marriage, however, hadn't stopped many women from art-making. "I did the housework in the mornings . . . then I could paint all afternoon." There were few female role models for public art careers, and the art world was often critical of those women who showed their work. "There was an idiosyncrasy, a rawness or freshness to a lot of women's work. If you're working alone, and the men's stuff doesn't fit you, what you come up with is ground-breaking . . . no-woman's land. We were nowhere."

That's why they needed a collective. WARM began semi-officially in the art department of the College of Saint Catherine, as a drawer for slides of women's work. After several shows without walls (the first on women's erotic art), WARM started looking for a space. They argued about the name: should it be WAR or WARM? Later one member would regret the choice: "By calling ourselves WARM we created a mythical mother. Thereafter not only would we have expectations for our careers, but unconscious expectations that our women's community would do for us what our mothers couldn't."

Members negotiated a lease in the Wyman Building on First Avenue North. The building owner at first thought they were nuts, but his wife was an artist and he felt sympathetic. He agreed to rent the garishly decorated former wholesale showroom. Out went the orange and black walls and the floor tile, and in came new walls painted a white mixed from hundreds of donated cans. Later the closest color to it was labeled Silver Bells.

The Gallery opened in April of 1976. "We had waited 5,000 years." Each of the forty members carried a long-stem rose. Some 1,500 people attended; the air was unbreathable with cigarette smoke, but the food was incredible. One observer commented that it was the first time she had seen women work "not for their husbands or children but solely for themselves and their art."

The next night, nationally known artist Miriam Schapiro sat on the floor of the new gallery and described the situation of another feminist organization, Womanspace in Los Angeles. For some of its members, Womanspace represented a piece of the pie of the commercial and academic art establishment. For others, it was an entirely new pie, with divergent goals. WARM members soon discovered that their attitudes covered the same range: some were elitist and wanted WARM to accept only artists at a certain academic or commercial level. Others were populist and wanted to "construct a new Utopian art world that would be inclusive of all."

Whatever their differences the members were united in their belief that women should have equality in the art world and within the collective. The new gallery was run using a consciousness-raising circle. Every member had her say. The Saturday meetings to form by-laws, decide exhibition procedures, and work the finances could both "drive you nuts and elevate you to the stars." The process was slow, but the excitement of taking charge and being heard "carried over into the studio."

The gallery offered two floors where members took turns showing, either individually or in groups. There were no restrictions on what you could show. Unlike commercial galleries that usually demand an identifiable "look" from an artist, WARM welcomed works in progress, works that had little commercial appeal, and installations and performance art before those media were in common use. The shows became educational events, where wearable art, environmental installation, portrait ceramics, and many forms of narrative art exploded the banalities of pop-art modernism, popular at the time. It's clear that many post-modern styles began in the surge of feminist art that WARM represented.

After five years, WARM began to assume the functions of both museum and school. In the Feminist Perspectives Series, members lectured to each other about aesthetics and art history. This educational focus soon expanded to inviting women artists, art historians, and critics of national reputations to exhibit, lecture, and give studio critiques at WARM. During the heyday, such luminaries as Joan Snyder, Alice Neel, Marsha Tucker, Harmony Hammond, Lucy Lippard, and Robin Morgan taught WARM members something about how east-coast and west-coast artists saw them. "Fly-over land" sometimes meant to these visitors a place to be nurtured by Midwestern earth mothers. Some visitors also brought with them the competitive politics of the commercial art world: "These women often didn't have the energy to give, they weren't confident enough of their own foot in the door to offer us a hand. If they had a bone, they hugged it, hid it, didn't share it. That's what happens when there is not enough to go around."

WARM evolved new programs to educate the members and the public at large. The *WARM Journal* gave reviewers a chance to develop language to describe the new feminist art. When funders pressed for new programs, what had been a dream or a joke — "rent-a-mentor" one WARM artist quipped — became an innovation as WARM's Mentor Program. Woman-to-woman mentoring was initially hard to sell to the Metropolitan Regional Arts Council, until a former art teacher on the panel spoke eloquently about the sexism that women often experienced from academic male mentors. She insisted that qualified women should be paid to take on that role.

By its tenth anniversary, the WARM Gallery had acquired a national reputation, paid staff, and the expertise to host a national conference on women in the arts. Larger "by megabytes than anything WARM had ever done," the conference spread over many days, had a program cast of hundreds, and drew in participants from all over the country. Successful as it was, it also left the organization with a deficit of $70,000. WARM had had cash-flow troubles before, but nothing some home-fundraising couldn't cover. A symptom of the size to which the organization had grown, the deficit resulted from lack of communication between the artist-planners and the paid staff. WARM was too large and too diverse to function effectively with the Saturday-morning consciousness-raising circle that had initially created such strong consensus and sharing of responsibilities.

Funders prevailed on WARM to create a board of directors and to submit yearly long-range plans. The board represented corporate America's attempt to put its stamp on the Gallery's unorthodox manner of functioning, and it signaled the end of its era of feminist administration. The tension that developed between corporate-minded board members and the Gallery collective added another element of stress to the already overworked members. Meetings to create long-range plans burdened the Gallery with outside facilitators who did not understand their goals or process. One could say that the demise of the Gallery began with WARM's very success, which its original organization could not realistically handle.

After fifteen years, WARM had accomplished what it had started out to do. It looked like a good time to have a celebration and say good-bye. Honoring the debt rather than attempting to slip out of it helped keep the WARM collective alive. Many old members left, but new ones joined, even as the Gallery moved toward its end.

Before the Gallery closed, the Women of Color show presented the Gallery one last time in its role as prophet. Women of color with national reputations, like Faith Ringgold and the quilt that became her book *Tar Baby*, showed alongside local women artists and signaled to the arts community that there were new revolutions in attitudes and styles still to be counted.

The Gallery closed in February of 1991 after a show of work donated from around the country to raise money for the deficit, "Our Hearts in Our Hands." Shortly thereafter, with a final ceremony for members and community, WARM said good-bye to the Gallery, and the organization, in the words of one member, "dropped down the rabbit hole. It went from being incredibly visible, to being almost invisible."

Conditions in the arts community had altered sufficiently from 1976 to 1991 to make it impossible for a group of forty to maintain a non-commercial gallery with grants and monthly dues. Some funders also argued that WARM, even without the gallery, wasn't necessary anymore; museums, galleries, academies had opened to women's work and professionalism. Many of WARM's founding mothers had gotten more than a foot in the door, or a piece of the pie.

Reduced to a telephone in a corner of *Artpaper's* office, WARM sent out a survey to its huge mailing list, asking for help defining goals and running the organization. A new generation of women responded, believing in the need for an alternative feminist arts organization. Hiring a new coordinator, WARM began to look for different ways to make its presence felt.

Continuing three major programs from the Gallery days, WARM discovered that the Mentor Program, with the Jerome Foundation as primary funder, still attracted far more applicants than could be accommodated, justifying the belief that women still needed to learn from women, outside regular academic programs. Furthermore, in the general decline of arts activities during the 1990s, WARM's annual juried exhibitions offered women from around the region what was often their only venue for competing and gaining recognition. And the summer arts education workshops, coordinated through the MAX program of the Minnesota Center for Arts Education, served gaps that existed in art services.

Then WARM tried an experiment. It held two large shows, the Cinderella Shoe Show and the Herstory Show, in the public space of Calhoun Square. Each attracted a thousand viewers a day, a far larger audience than the Gallery had drawn at its most successful. This set a precedent for sponsoring shows in other community-based settings. WARM also initiated new summer MAX workshops geared toward multicultural enrichment in the inner city. Gradually, the organization assumed a new shape: more diffuse, with a smaller core. Instead of the original two-tier artist membership WARM simplified into one category of artist membership. In the winter of 1995, a new chapter opened in Duluth.

After twenty years, WARM's values have been refined and retooled: hearing all voices now extends around the world through a scroll project, "Global WARM — a message from women to the world." The scroll began as a fund-raiser, with each WARM artist pledging twelve people at $10 an inch, then using that foot of space for painting. Now, coincident with WARM's multicultural initiative, the scroll has tapped into the coinage of international cooperation, as segments of the scroll travel to Mexico, Costa Rica, Russia, Japan, China, Peru, Tonga, and the International Women's Conference in Beijing [1996].

Self-education still energizes WARM, in monthly public discussion groups called Fresh Art offering practical topics like preparing a portfolio or aesthetic ones like the self-portrait. Fresh Art draws artists of diverse confidence and experience for exchanges that many affirm could not take place within the commercial or academic establishment.

Three things seem remarkably different in the WARM of today. First, it works in concert with women artists who have entered other institutions. WARM's founding mothers and others like them can today join WARM in witnessing, withstanding, and watchdogging for women artists. WARM does not and can not act alone. It has no exhibit space and must join forces with academic and community centers.

Second, WARM's scope and scale have altered: like a computer network, the scroll links WARM globally to international women's issues and cooperation, but no more do forty local women make WARM a second family or second job. A few still volunteer considerable time, but today more WARM members work at paying jobs or go to graduate school. Time and money are tighter all around. Thus WARM must consider its programs carefully and count on members dropping in and out of active connection.

Finally, WARM continues to function with a board of directors, many of whom are not artists. Crises still arise, cliff-hangers about meeting the coordinator's salary or paying for an already-committed program with a smaller-than-expected grant, but the organization will probably not undergo again the extravagant growth and programming that supported the national conference and its deficit.

Today, when the phone rings at WARM, as it constantly does, most callers don't realize that they are talking to a phoenix that has risen from its own ashes, with the memory and expertise of contemporary feminism under its wing. Most new callers simply need to escape the isolation that still befalls many women and many artists. The danger is not that WARM can't help them, but that callers won't know all that the organization has accomplished. Its survival when many other small arts organizations in similar difficulties have expired. Its opening up of the Minneapolis warehouse district to arts activities, and providing new energy for its current South Saint Anthony Park neighborhood. Its advocacy and education, which still pressure the larger community to examine visual, racial, and gender prejudice.

The truth is, WARM still has public work to do. Timid and patriarchal institutions continue to sideline or misinterpret beautiful work through skewed or ignorant attitudes toward women. Institutions still need to be challenged on their sexism and racism. You can find WARM in the phone book under W, but a more public presence would be welcome. There's talk of moving to an office with a window, where at least a sign on the street can announce that WARM has kept the fires lit.

In Wakefield, Rhode Island women artists meeting in two C-R groups organized into a ten-member co-op gallery, **HERA**, in 1974. Within the year they had added eight additional women and although they had included some men in their exhibitions since 1976, not until 1996 did they vote to accept men as members. Of the original founding artists — Constance Greene Alexander, Merle Barnett, Mary Jane Christofferson, Bernadette Hackett, Elena Jahn (Clough), Marlene Malik, Frances Powers, Roberta Richman, Althea Smith, Barbara Johns Waterston — only Richman and Alexandra Broches (who joined within the first year) remain, and it is largely through their dedication and perseverance that the gallery still exists. They also attribute their long life to their location in a semi-rural (mostly summer) community close to the university at which several members are on the faculty. They credit as their greatest benefactor their landlord, who in honor of his deceased artist wife converted his small barn-like structure into year-round use for the gallery and continues his benevolent support. Although the withdrawal of state funding is making their operation rocky, they continue to serve the needs of their members with one-person and small-group shows, and provide art and educational programs for an isolated community.[28]

The **Coalition of Women's Art Organizations (CWAO)** was formed in response to the need for women artists to have a national political organization. By 1977 the success of civil rights and feminist groups had demonstrated the effectiveness of organized issue-oriented efforts toward equality. With a national women's conference in Houston, Texas scheduled for November, it was an ideal moment to combine individual voices in the arts into a unified chorus calling for action.

Many women helped to build CWAO, Cynthia Navaretta, editor of *Women Artists News* served as the first *pro tem* chairperson. In preparation for the Houston conference, a group of New York City women attended the State Women's Meeting in Albany and elected artist Susan Schwalb as arts delegate from New York State — the only state to have such a delegate.

At the first National Women's Conference, CWAO proposals were included in the report to the President and U.S. Congress. CWAO and the Women's Caucus for Art jointly operated ARTSPACE, where continuous art activities took place, as well as an information and publications booth. This was typical of later political, cultural, and educational services.

The goals of CWAO were to achieve equal opportunity and equal representation for women in arts programs and institutions, on decision-making bodies and in grants, as well as greater recognition of the arts in school curricula. CWAO exerted pressure in Washington through its national network of women in the arts [some fifty member organizations]. Annual conferences were held and representatives of CWAO frequently gave testimony in Congress and at local and regional hearings. A national lobby day in 1978 brought over 200 members to Capitol Hill where they spoke to congress about arts legislation. Statistics on sex differentials in employment and in exhibition opportunities were published, In 1980, CWAO sponsored the First International Festival of Women Artists at Copenhagen, Denmark where the World Conference of the UN Decade for Women was taking place. Starting in 1982, CWAO published a quarterly members newsletter, with Sylvia Moore as editor.

Changes in the political climate and difficulties in raising funds led to a gradual decline in membership. In 1984, CWAO reorganized as an advocacy organization dedicated to arts issues. A newsletter focusing on these issues and offering advice for action is edited by Dorothy Provis, and annual meetings are held.[29]

> This is our choice: to isolate and fortress ourselves with our personal concerns, or to step into the vulnerability of community and create a different way to live, day by day by day.[30]

A Collection of Collectives

Women's Art Communities in Contemporary History

II   IDENTITY IN COMMUNITY

Allie Louisa Cochran Doty, 1888, Betty Ann
Brown's great grandmother (B. 1878, Harris
County, Missouri, D. 1943, Rogers, Arkansas).

Introduction

this quilt might be
the only perfect artifact a woman
would ever see, yet she did not doubt
what we had forgotten, that out of her
potatoes and colic, sawdust and blood
she could create; together, alone,
she seized time and made new.[1]

My mother's mother's mother, Allie Louisa Cochran Doty, was a quilter. I never knew my great-grandmother, but I have learned from my Aunt Betty (after whom I was named) that Allie (who was named after her father, Alexander) was born into a Scotch-English family in 1878 in Harrison County, Missouri, and died in 1943 in Rogers, Arkansas. She attended Coty College in Nevada, Missouri, and became a schoolteacher. By the turn of the century, she was in what we today call the State of Oklahoma but was then known as Indian Territory. She taught for some time in a sod school house, then, in 1901, she married Harry Walter Doty, who had gone to medical school in St. Louis and was practicing medicine in Homestead, Oklahoma. A year later, my grandmother Dora was born. Allie left teaching to raise her children, but she continued quilting.

We still have several of her quilts. Most of them are cotton, several of them are what are termed "friendship quilts."[2] That means the quilt patches are sewn from scraps of cherished clothing; each textile fragment carries memories. Names and dates are sometimes embroidered or penned onto the surfaces of friendship quilts, so that they function much like nineteenth century autograph albums, with brief inscriptions commemorating friendships and family histories (births, marriages, etc.). Friendship quilts like Allie's were family and community portraits from times before the expansion of photographic technology and beyond the reach of itinerant portrait artists.[3]

It's hard for me to imagine what Allie's life was like out there, on what we call the American frontier. Of course, with politically informed hindsight, I can see that she was participating in the Euroamerican imperialist extension that ultimately wrenched almost all tribal lands from their Native American owners. I can see that the Indian peoples who surrounded the tiny town of Homestead were rightfully hostile. But right now, I am thinking about Allie's life, about her sense of self and her relationship to community. It seems to me that the Euroamerican women of Homestead, separated from the relative security of more sophisticated settlements to the east, probably gathered to work and talk together in order to establish and validate their shared identity, an identity rooted in the Europe of their forebears. They gathered around quilts. As they sewed, they traded stories of their home towns, nursed babies, cooked, read women's magazines, and exchanged receipts (recipes). They built the community their husbands financed and defended — a community that seemed all the more unified and significant when contrasted with the Native American diversity surrounding it — and they built that community around the collaborative art of quilts.

> The significance of needlework in the education and preparation of women for marriage was carried over from Europe with the pioneer women. Responding to specific socioeconomic and cultural needs of the new communities, women's needlework made an important contribution to their society on many levels. . . . Quilt-making . . . served to punctuate and celebrate pioneer women's lives . . . the main events and concern of the community's or household's lives . . . the families and women's friendships within a community.[4]

> . . . the quilt has become the prime visual metaphor for women's lives, for women's culture [and] networking.[5]

If we define community as any group with shared identity, and accept that the group may be as small as two friends or as large as a family extended over three continents, then it is clear that women have always built community[6] They have often done so with or around the objects of material culture we call art. But the merging of women, art, and community in the late twentieth century is unusual. It is a phenomenon that opposes the dominant cultural equation of creativity with the male. It rejects the heroic myth of the artist as a uniquely gifted and individualistic "genius" who produces masterpieces in a rarefied realm above, and certainly separate from, the society of his fellow men [sic]. And it involves "high art" forms — those historically dominated by males — rather than those relegated to the often female domain of "crafts," like quilts.

In order to work on art and community, the women in this book had to deconstruct, then overcome, prevailing cultural notions about gender, creativity, and power. My great-grandmother based much of her personal identity, and the community she wove around it, on what her mother taught her and what her mother's mother had taught her. But the women in this book had to reject what they'd learned from their families in particular and their cultural surroundings in general. They had to forge new kinds of artistic identities for themselves.

The Woman Artist Conundrum

> . . . either she could write as a woman, in which case she created a limited art, or she could write as a man, in which case she created an inauthentic art.[7]

What French-born performance artist Rachel Rosenthal told me in a 1989 interview expresses the problem of female artistic identity so well: "I was totally confused about my identity, first of all as an artist, secondly as a woman, thirdly as a woman artist — which was the real problem. I had really and truly absorbed

Identity in Community

the notion that to be an artist meant to be a male artist. So being a woman meant either I had to deny my femininity or I had to deny being an artist. For years and years I had this continual angst — going back and forth like a pendulum about being a woman and being an artist and never quite knowing where I was or which one I was, having a hazy self-image."[8]

Judy Chicago experienced these same feelings. As she writes in *Through the Flower*, "The next few years were confusing to me both in terms of my life as an artist and my relationships with men in the art world. On the one hand, there were men who were very supportive, but not without reservations. One man, an art critic, used to bring me paint and canvas, mention my work occasionally in his articles, and take me out to dinner. But then he would say, in the middle of a discussion, 'You know, Judy, you have to decide whether you're going to be a woman or an artist.' I was continually made to feel by men in the art world that there was something 'wrong' with me. They'd say things like, 'Gee, Judy, I like your work, but I just can't cut it that you're a woman.' It seemed like I couldn't win. But I wouldn't give up. I knew that what I was confronting came out of the fact that I was a woman, but whenever I tried to talk about that openly, I would be put down with statements like, 'Come on, Judy, the suffrage movement is over,' and treated as if I were a leper."[9]

I'd had the same feelings. So had sculptor Eva Hesse. In 1964 she wrote: "I cannot be so many things. I cannot be something for everyone. . . . Woman, beautiful, artist, wife, housekeeper, cook, saleslady, all these things. I cannot even be myself or know what I am."[10]

But, as Chicago said some years later to Arlene Raven, "After some years in the art world trying to pretend I wasn't a woman, I decided for better or worse I had to be who I was!"[11]

Like Judy Chicago and myself, Rachel Rosenthal did not find resolution about these conflicting issues until she became part of a feminist community. In fact, in spite of her excellent education in the visual arts — she studied with renowned artist/teacher Hans Hoffman and prominent art historian/critic Meyer Schapiro in New York — Rosenthal had never felt like she could develop a style "all her own" . . . and originality was highly valued by the male art world during the modernist era.[12] So she left the visual arts for theater. Then, in the early 1970s, Rosenthal got involved with the Women's Art Movement, primarily through her contacts with Miriam Schapiro. "I was exposed to feminism in both literature and action — talk about trauma! For one thing, I had never had women friends before," admits Rosenthal. "Then suddenly I was surrounded by women who were obviously wonderful artists so I had to change my whole world view. In addition to which I had for ten years been the sole dictator of a theatrical company and suddenly I was thrown into feminist democracy. Again, I had to confront and reappraise everything I was and everything I believed in. I was completely turned around and thrown into a tailspin."[13] "Tailspin" is Rosenthal's term for the intensely confronting and often dizzyingly rapid changes she moved through as feminism challenged her artistic identity, the identity fashioned from the dominant cultural messages she'd received throughout her early career. But out of that tailspin emerged Rachel Rosenthal, the performance artist. With her new identity, supported by the feminist art community, Rosenthal embraced a new medium and achieved international fame.

Art History: Stories of the Artist as Male

This is not a traditional art history book. But in order to understand how artistic identity has been constructed and what it has meant to women artists, it is necessary to examine the key components of that identity — the linkage of creativity with the male, the myth of the great artist as individualistic genius, and the arts/crafts dichotomy — in historical context. From that understanding comes an appreciation of the radical and significant nature of the contemporary women/art/community phenomenon.

The most widely used art history textbook is H. W. Janson's *History of Art, A Survey of the Major Visual Arts from the Dawn of History to the Present Day*.[14] Not until the third edition in 1986, twenty-four years after the first publication of this immense tome, were women artists to be found in its pages. By the 5th edition in 1995 (962 pages), more women and minorities were represented, but women are still discussed in terms of their personal histories more than in terms of their work.[15] As Parker and Pollock assert, "in modern art history the fine artist is synonymous with the male artist. . . . Women artists have always existed. They worked consistently and in growing numbers despite discrimination. . . . Women have made their own interventions in the forms and languages of art because they are necessarily part of their society and culture [but] modern art history ignores the existence of women artists."[16]

Outside of the classroom, the general public learns about art and artists in museums and galleries. Even today, major museums in the United States (with the exception, of course, of the Museum of Women's Art in Washington, D.C.) house collections and sponsor exhibitions in which the great majority of artists is male (and white). Since the 1960s, women artists and art historians have sought to redress this inequity. Art historians Thalia Gouma-Peterson and Patricia Mathews researched and described how women have agitated for parity, but concluded that the number of women artists represented in museums (c. 1987) was still less than 25 percent, "despite continuing feminist activism."[17]

Why have women been excluded? Why is there a perception that women have, as novelist Tillie Olsen angrily puts it, an "innately inferior capacity for creative endeavor"?[18] Why is it that, as Mara R. Witzling asserts, "In Western culture, art making and art history have remained phallocentric notions"?[19]

One part of the answer goes back to the Italian Renaissance, when Giorgio Vasari wrote his *Lives of the Artists (Le Vite de' piu eccellenti pittori scultori e architettoti italiani, da Cimabue insino ai empi nostri . . .*, Florence, 1550). Vasari lionized male accomplishments — particularly those of Michelangelo — but described women artists as "atypical of their sex," thus reinforcing "the idea that women and art are incompatible."[20] Most Euroamerican art historians of the next four centuries repeated Vasari's biases. Many male artists learned this prejudice, some to the degree of French Impressionist painter Auguste Renoir who is believed to have said that any woman who wanted to paint was a monster!

The Great Artist as Genius

> I said it was impossible for a woman to become an artist — I mean a *great* artist. Have you ever thought what that term implies? Not only a painter but a poet; a man of learning, of reading, of observation. A gentleman — we artists are the friends of kings. A man of stainless virtue. A man of iron will, indomitable daring, and passions strong, yet kept always leashed in his hand. Last and greatest, a man who, feeling within him the divine spirit, with his whole soul worships God! . . . That is what an artist should *be*, by nature![21]

The concepts of greatness and genius are also gender-related. In 1971, New York-based scholar Linda Nochlin published an article that shook the very core of the discipline of art history. She titled the article "Why Are There No Great Women Artists?" but even as she did so, she challenged the assumptions behind such a question.

> Underlying the question about woman as artist, then, we find the whole myth of the Great Artist — unique, godlike subject of a hundred monographs — bearing within his person since birth a mysterious essence, rather like the golden nugget in Mrs. Grass's chicken soup, called genius or talent, which must always out, no matter how unlikely or unpromising the circumstances. . . . The supernatural powers of the artist as imitator, his control of strong, possibly dangerous powers, have functioned historically to set him off from others as a godlike creator, one who creates being out of nothing like the demiurge.

But art is not produced in such a mystical manner. "The making of art involves a self-consistent language of form, more or less dependent upon, or free from, given temporally defined conventions, schemata, or systems of notation, which have to be learned or worked out, either through teaching, apprenticeship, or a long period of individual experimentation." So, concludes Nochlin, "The fault [that women have not achieved on a par with men in the visual arts] lies not in our stars, our hormones, our menstrual cycles, or our empty internal spaces, but in our institutions and our education — education understood to include everything that happens to us from the moment we enter, head first, into this world of meaningful symbols, signs, and signals."[22]

> To tell the truth, one is not born a genius: one becomes a genius; and the feminine situation has up to the present rendered this becoming practically impossible.[23]

> Modernism above all exalted the complete autonomy of art, and the gesture of severing bonds with society. This sovereign specialness and apartness was symbolized by the romantic exile of the artist, and was lived out in modes of rebellion, withdrawal and antagonism. . . . "Life is so horrible," Flaubert wrote, "that one can only bear it by avoiding it. And that can be done by living in the world of art."[24]

Another aspect of this complex issue is the relationship between creativity and individualism. Since the Romantic period, which produced not only privileged poets Byron and Keats, but also "crazed" artists like Vincent Van Gogh, the trope of the artist has involved working in fevered isolation, alone, misunderstood. "[A]rtists came to be thought of as strange, different, exotic, imaginative, eccentric, creative, unconventional, alone. A mixture of supposed genetic factors and social roles distinguish the artist from the mass of ordinary mortals, creating new myths, . . . above all else the genius, and new social personae, the Bohemian and the pioneer. . . . These developing notions reached new heights with the genesis of the Romantic myth of the eighteenth and nineteenth centuries when the artist not only inherited the mantle of priests and became the revealer of divine truths, but also assumed a semi-divine status as an heir of the original "Creator" himself."[25]

Christo — the New York-based artist known for wrapping the Australian coastline and Germany's Reichstag, encircling Miami islands with hot pink fabric, and lining California hills with golden umbrellas — echoes Romantic period sentiments when he exclaims, "The work of art is irrational and perhaps irresponsible. Nobody needs it. The work is a huge individualistic gesture that is entirely decided by me. . . . One of the greatest contributions of modern art is the notion of individualism. . . . I think the artist can do anything he wants to do. . . . Independence is most important to me. The work of art is a scream of freedom."[26] Because Christo employs hundreds of workers in each of his projects, many spectators might think his intentions are to build community. His own words confirm his adherence to radical individualism.

Radical individualism as an artistic ideal has excused otherwise unthinkable behavior in many "bad boy" artists. American Abstract Expressionist Jackson Pollock is said to have urinated in the fireplace during a drunken party in the penthouse of wealthy New York patron Peggy Guggenheim. Apparently, the art collectors who witnessed this tittered delightedly (it reinforced their patronizing view that all artists are "nuts") and were inspired to purchase even more art by the alcoholic painter. I have always wondered, since first hearing this possibly apocryphal story, how the collectors would have responded if a woman had urinated in the fireplace. Or a black man.

Speaking of the several concurrent cultural changes that anticipated the Abstract Expressionist style, Los Angeles writer Michael Ventura writes, "Obviously something is going on here that doesn't have to do with individuals or individuality or anything that would be presented in a psychological personal history — indicating that even the previous Western ideal of 'creativity' has crucial collective elements that our society has not begun to think about much less differentiate. Only Carl Jung has explored the concept of collective psychology seriously, and his path-breaking concepts of synchronicity and the collective unconscious are more descriptions of the phenomena than tools for thought and change."[27] Ventura is correct. It's difficult to accept, continues Ventura, that there may be something which "courses through the collective and is picked up and expressed in different mediums by different individuals; and that that expression constellates a kind of subcollective around it, a style of music or a school of painting or a branch of science, that articulates *back to the collective* an impulse that came, originally, from or through the collective. . . . Western thought has taken that expression to be personal, the result of a Charlie Parker or a Jackson Pollock's own unique 'creativity.'" Until we begin to understand the power and dynamics of collective/community creativity, we have no conceptual tools for thinking of creativity as anything but an individual act. And historically, under patriarchy, those given most access to expressing their individuality have been men.

Fine Arts vs. Crafts and the Avant-Garde

> Textile work seems to need to be discovered twice. I have talked to many people who loved working with cloth when young, but who, upon arriving at art school, picked up paint brushes, the tools of Serious Art. Washington, D.C. artist Pat Autenrieth told me of her experience at the Kansas City Art Institute twenty years ago, when anything that smacked of "craft" was put down, "women's work" wasn't recognized, and art history texts were empty of references to women artists.[28]

A third issue has to do with the "high arts"/crafts dichotomy and the related concept of the avant-garde. "Art history views the art of the past from certain perspectives and organizes art into categories and classifications based on stratified system of values, which leads to a hierarchy of art forms. In this hierarchy the arts of painting and sculpture enjoy an elevated status while other arts that adorn people, homes or utensils are relegated to a lesser cultural sphere under such terms as 'applied,' 'decorative,' or 'lesser' arts [or crafts]. . . . The art and craft division can undoubtedly be read on class lines, with an economic and social system dictating new definitions of the artist as opposed to the artisan [but] the sex of the maker was as important a factor in the development of the hierarchy of the arts as the division between art and craft on the basis of function, material, intellectual content and class"[29]

Louis XIV founded the French Royal Academy of Fine Arts in the late seventeenth century in order to institute governmental control of education, exhibition and sale of the arts and thereby employ the arts as propaganda.[30] Louis learned about the use of art as propaganda from the Catholic Church, which deliberately made art the chief medium for spreading or "propagating" the Church's message . . . but that's another story. In Louis XIV's Academy, painting and sculpture were deemed the "fine" or "high" arts. Textiles, ceramic arts and jewelry were demeaned to the less valued status of "craft." While the former were historically male-dominated practices, the latter were traditionally female as well as male. ". . . what distinguishes art from craft in the hierarchy is not so much different methods, practices and objects but also where these things are made, often in the home, and for whom they are made, often for the family."[31] (This sounds like the public/private dichotomy that is so crucial to feminist thought.)

European and American rulers soon followed Louis XIV's lead and art academies, like the one in Philadelphia became the primary locus of fine arts instruction until the end of the nineteenth century. It was not until that time, when artists like the French Impressionists were challenging the validity of the academic monopoly, that women were finally given full access to various academies. Indeed, famed American portraitist Thomas Eakins was dismissed from his post at the Pennsylvania Academy of Fine Arts in 1886 because he dared to admit women to his life drawing classes.[32]

The process of excluding women from the academies repeated what had occurred before in Western Europe: women had been given limited access to the guilds, which controlled art training throughout the middle ages.[33] And today, although university studio art classes are often mostly women, there are still relatively few female professors of studio art.[34] Every time "high art" training has been institutionalized by Western culture, women have been given short shrift. Euroamerican women have, of course, been able to learn the "household arts" of sewing, embroidery, and quilting from their mothers, just as Native American women have learned pottery and basketmaking from their female forbearers. But the continuing mainstream message has been that while women are encouraged to do "crafts" in the privacy of their homes, they clearly have been discouraged from "real" art for the public sphere.

The Impressionists — and their forefathers Gustave Courbet and Edouard Manet — were the first artists described as avant-garde. Like military scouts who traverse unexplored territory to ascertain if it is safe for the rest of the army to follow, avant-garde artists move into new formal or conceptual territory before the rest of the populace. Once mainstream culture catches up, an artist is no longer avant-garde: the music of the Beatles, which used to rankle my career military officer father, is now piped through my dentist's office; and Impressionism, which was once considered so shocking as to be unsafe for the eyes of frail ladies, is now the preferred watercolor style of Euroamerican senior citizens. In other words, what is avant-garde for one generation may become the standard, the ideal, the canon for following generations. As British art historian Hilary Robinson puts it, "the wild boy of one year is the star of the next, and the hero and genius of the year following."[35]

Although women have always participated in avant-garde cultural practices —

there were female Impressionists [as well as Russian Constructivists and Italian Futurists] and female British working class rock musicians — traditional, largely male historians have tended to exclude women. Few women have made it into the artistic canons of painting or music. According to Robinson, "This 'star' system favoured by dealers and galleries has found space for a few women, a handful of whom will today identify themselves as feminists . . . but without wishing to belittle their work, the point must be made again that tokenism is a useful way of both calming dissent and soothing the conscience, and therefore of containing feminist politics."[36]

Such dynamics prevail in literature as well. Tillie Olsen noted that there is only one woman writer for every twelve men included in literary collections.[37] Feminist theorist Susan Rubin Suleiman, writing about avant-garde literature, asserts, "In the Anglo-American case . . . one can speak of a concerted exclusion of women's work from the modernist canon, an exclusion which Sandra Gilbert and Susan Gubar interpret as 'a misogynist reaction-formation against the rise of literary women' on the part of the male modernists whose work came to define that canon." Rubin Suleiman alerts us to the "inherent aggressiveness . . . inscribed in the military connotations of the term. . . . The early European avant-gardes . . . exploited to the hilt the antagonistic potential inherent in the concept of the avant-garde, directing their aggression both against the (bourgeois) public and against what they perceived as the dominant tradition, in art as in ethics or politics.[38]

Because of the overwhelmingly male-identified nature of the "high art" or avant-garde arena, perhaps particularly, as Rubin Suleiman suggests, because of its aggressive nature, few women artists have been comfortable entering that arena and staying there. Georgia O'Keeffe, for example, married successful avant-garde artist Alfred Stieglitz, became the frequent subject of his photography, and exhibited her paintings in the art gallery he ran, but later abandoned the avant-garde mecca of New York City (and him) in favor of the solitary desert expanses of New Mexico. Judy Chicago couldn't stay in the avant-garde environment of Los Angeles, either. She first left to teach in the small and rather provincial town of Fresno, and later, she too moved to New Mexico. But between Fresno and Santa Fe, she articulated a different response: not finding the male-dominated art scene tolerable, she established an alternative, feminist art community. Although she was not forced to relinquish her avant-garde practices in order to do that, she did have to rethink what it meant to be an artist. "[W]hat choice had I? If I didn't build another environment, then I was condemned to functioning exclusively within the male-dominated art community that allowed me only limited roles and recognition. If I didn't take responsibility or my situation as a woman, commit myself to other women, and make a new context, what could I do?"[39]

Stories of Identity and Creativity

As long as she still has to struggle to become a human being, she cannot become a creator.[40]

One of the basic tenets of color theory is that we never see any color in isolation. Color is always perceived in relationship, and what abuts or surrounds a color greatly affects how that color is perceived.[41] The same is true of personal identity. We are social animals; we never develop our sense of self alone. My great grandmother Allie knew who she was in relationship to the other Euroamericans of Homestead, Oklahoma, and in juxtaposition to the Native American peoples who lived around her. Today, women artists are creating identity in the midst of a culture that historically has undermined many avenues of female expression. To assert that they are women and artists, as well as lesbians or single mothers or Chinese-American or practitioners of ancient goddess religions, is to challenge the status quo. To value such alternative identities is to open the avenues of freedom of expression for us all.

> The collectively experienced anxiety provoked by [recent] transformations [in the ideological and political systems] has generated a plethora of identity-related conflicts from geopolitical boundary disputes and the resurgence of ethnic tensions in Europe, to the concomitant racial unrest of North America. In Europe, these issues are being fought over principally in the geopolitical sphere; in the United states, we find ourselves in more of an ideological battle over symbolic representation. This does not mean, however, that the battles in America are any less political, on the contrary, culture in this country is a critical, if not the most crucial, area of political struggle over identity. . . . We struggle to preserve distinctions that, for some, can no longer be taken for granted, and, for others, appear for the first time to be within reach. These conditions shape much of the art and the cultural debates of our historical moment.[42]

The first step to creating community is clarifying personal identity. For women, and especially for lesbians and women of color, this can be an intensely difficult process. But, as Elizabeth Janeway reminds us, we all have "the power to disbelieve," the power to refuse "to accept the definition of oneself that is put forward by the powerful. . . . It is true that one may not have a coherent self-definition to set against the status assigned by the established social mythology. [but] by disbelieving, one will be led toward doubting the prescribed codes of behavior, and as one begins to act in ways that can deviate from the norm in any degree, it becomes clear that in fact there is not just one right way to handle or understand events."[43]

Gerda Lerner traces how the creation of identity, of what she terms "the authentic self which defines its own creativity," was possible for European women much later than it was for men. "The search for an authentic self had to take different forms for women than it did for men, since for men authority was assumed, while for women it was utterly denied. Thus each woman asserting authority was a self-defined freak and had to deal with that fact in her writing before her audience could be open to her language and her thought."[44]

Lerner's comments have much relevance to us today. I remember feeling like a freak before I found feminism. Many of the women artists in this book talk of feeling like outsiders to mainstream society. The dominant culture, through all the communicative avenues it controls (from classrooms to government to news to entertainment), seeks to restrict us by dictating limited possibilities for our identities. In the movies we see, books we read, magazines we flip through, billboards we drive by, women are offered restricted ranges of subjectivity. We are told, overtly or covertly, that to be really creative is to be male, that to be an artist requires the extraordinary gift of genius and working in anguished isolation, that women are rewarded for making nice homes (and all the corollary craft activities) but restricted from avant-garde or "high art" production. "It is necessary even for women artists who might not think overtly in terms of gender and sexuality, or do not conceptualize their visions with a sexual motif [as did Judy Chicago, for example], to negotiate between phallocentric cultural constrictions and their own visions."[45]

In the essays that follow, women artists write about how they have forged innovative personal identities in the context of their families, their racial backgrounds, their sexuality, their spirituality. Arlene Raven writes about Adrian Piper's use of performance and installation to explore her African-American identity. Sandra Rowe, Aleida Rodriguez, and Michelle T. Clinton explore their identities in poetry. A conversation with Rosalie Ortega reveals how her Chicana identity has informed her art activities. Katherine Ng's broadside negotiates the confusing conflicts of names and immigration. Ruth Weisberg contributes an essay about being an artist, a Jew and a woman. Amy Carr and Lisa Carr write of their shared identity/community as twins. Polly Chu and Sarah Lejeune examine the affects of race, class, and identity on their friendship in a series of family history fragments. And Joanna Frueh concludes the chapter with a poetic look at the community of the eroticized female body. It is such identities that artists and writers bring to the creative communities discussed later in this book.

I have always kept the longing alive and pure within me to express my life in a permanent form, to give it the shape which would dignify it to stand before the most excellent persons, to greet them and share in their community. Yes, I have always sought this collectivity, this is the church to which my spirit makes its pilgrimage here on earth.
— Karoline von Gunderrode, *writing in 1804*[46]

Adrian Piper: You and Me

by Arlene Raven

It begins between you and me, right here and now, in the indexical present.[1]

Adrian Piper first found her voice in the first person, her audience incarnated in the second, in an untitled page work of 1968. The location for the conversation suggested in *Untitled ("If you are a slow reader. . . .")* is here; the moment, now. There is no time/place like Piper's indexical present, where the insentient self can come home to a discomforting close encounter, face-to-face with oneself and this artist. Piper's 1981 drawing of herself draws one ever nearer. *Self-Portrait Exaggerating My Negroid Features* is self-made and self-colored self-centering in visual form. The features of the face are contained in but also distinguished from the matter in which they are necessarily embodied. Piper strives to depict her own likeness, but even more to companion the essence of form itself. For Plato, as for Marcel Duchamp and the Conceptualism including Piper, form is synonymous with idea. The principal feature of Piper's features is thus their exaggeration. A distortion of the ordinary mirror, her graphic means literally enlarge her subject to emphasize her graphic, subjective meaning.

What, fundamentally, does she mean? A view of 20 years of her work presents the opportunity to trace Piper's development and to identify continuities in her work over time. The exercise of following these two intertwining paths can yield up the clearest sense of the enduring significance of her forms and their contents.

Piper's early work explored the dichotomy between abstract concepts and their relationships to particular objects. One-page typescripts subtitled "This square should be read as a whole . . ." and "The sides of this square measure 8" . . . "in *Nineteen Concrete Space-Time-Infinity Pieces* (1968) promise to conform to their prima-facie frameworks, straightforward pictorial presentations, and unassuming verbal declarations. But, even in their studied simplicity, meaning meanders and multiplies when concrete concepts unfold in one's mind as tangible constructions. *World Work: One Event Six Locations in Six Early Performances* 1968/71 tears time and place apart within the grammar and syntax of its title alone.

Later, Piper's original dichotomy served to illuminate the division between abstract racial concepts (stereotypes) and the particular concrete individuals that those abstract concepts are supposed to identify (but usually fail to discern). Social splitting of contents and form is at the very core of Piper's concerns.

Consider *My Calling (Card) #1* (1986). The calling card, as a form, is both an artifact of identification and a director of conduct regulated by custom and etiquette. And *My Calling (Card) #1* addressed the conduct of the beneficiary (who selects him/herself by making or allowing a racist remark in the artist's presence) as a matter of form as well.

Piper uses the sisterly salutation "Dear Friend" to inform her recipient that she is black (since s/he has evidently failed to identify the artist within existing stereotypes), and that, therefore, a breach of form has been committed. But Piper calls her piece "Angry Art" in her copyright signature on the reverse side of the card. Anger up close, particularly when couched in courteous formality, can cause its own elements to split and explode. Piper becomes the medium of exchange and passes a bomb to you that ignites only with the fuel of your own incendiary frame of mind.

At first, Piper situated concrete objects in space and time to plot their paths. Form was an orderly arrangement that could result naturally from logic, good sense and right thinking. Eventually, she came to wonder how a concrete race- and gender-specific individual can plot a path through the random routes of public and cultural space in time. In 1974, she began to anticipate unthinking conventional responses such as would later activate her "calling cards" and to incorporate those responses into the works themselves. The reactive voice could be a spoken or written text, or could appear in visual form (as in the 1986 *Vanilla Nightmares* series).

The *Vanilla Nightmares* were drawn with charcoal on newspaper pages. In #8, Piper's ground is a full-page ad in a 1986 *New York Times* leased to Bloomingdales department store to push "Poison" perfume as "The silent potion exclusively ours for you." A young white-skinned model, seen unclothed from above her breasts, lolls in the foreground half of the page. She raises her hand lackadaisically in the air and points vaguely toward the background, as if she were falling back into ever deeper states of unconsciousness. Although her eyes are closed, she is labeled an "enchantress" in the ad copy, and her luscious lips invite the buying public (consisting mainly of the white men to whom Bloomie's sells most of its "Poison") to freely feast their eyes.

Piper crowds five figures into this languid scene. They stuff and squeeze the space barely occupied by the ghost-like model. They are all taller and larger than she, forming a human yoke around her. This woman has possibly never moved. But now she is physically immobilized. All black with negroid features, her "captors" show the whites of their eyes and bare their teeth. The teeth are perhaps the most disturbing aspect of Piper's intervention. She has eaten you, the viewer, by your feelings and fears. She also locates black virility, seen as a dangerous and uncontrollable cannibalism in Caucasian American racist lore, in the mouth — also the organ of speech — which the "silent potion" has rendered deadly mute in the female who wears it.

The poison dream, before and after Piper's alterations, belongs to the racist. And one does not have to go to a gallery or museum to partake of this vision. Images of fear and loathing are viewed in morning papers and digested by millions daily with their first cup of coffee. Piper's purpose is served appropriately by beginning with the single most widely available group of pictures and words. She explains, "[M]y work — whether photo-text collage installation, drawing, artist's book, performance, or video installation — is intended as an act of political communication that catalyzes its viewers into reflecting on their own deep impulses and responses to racism and xenophobia, relative to a target or stance that I depict."[2]

Piper routinely uses newspaper media in her distinctive counter aesthetic art. In 1969, for example, she purchased an advertising space in *The Village Voice* and described its physical dimensions in her allotted area. Her interest in image and text is suggested by her choice of print media, but with these parts she creates new conceptual relationships between the two elements. Direct gaze frontal photography, which Piper first employed in 1973 in the *Mythic Being* series, further compresses the area of confrontation. The *Mythic Being I/You (Her) #3* delivers its text like a cartoon: "You hurt me, and betrayed my trust, and for that I will never forgive you" begins the printed monologue in its balloon.

Piper herself looks out from the lower foreground while her text flattens the upper portion of her page to put you right up against her. Although her message is angry and hurt, her face remains smiling. In subsequent works in this series, Piper acts on her photographic face to transform herself from female to male, still grinning while testifying through her teeth that "I hate you for doing this to me, and myself for allowing it to happen."[3]

While disclosing her injury and pain at the hands of xenophobia, Piper simultaneously identifies herself as "embody[ing] everything you most hate and fear."[4] For her, form is more and more a human being, and artful. When she is the actor in her performances and the subject of her documentation work, she is generic - everybody and anybody.

Piper's 1968 *Meat into Meat* loft performance in New York City recorded with four color photographs a man, Piper's boyfriend, eating four hamburgers. Piper, unseen and unheard, a recent convert to lacto-vegetarianism, has a heated dialogue with him as he eats. Are we what we eat? The distinction between the body as matter and the essential nature of everybody and anybody has increasingly become the task of Piper's art production.

"[F]ear, fantasy, mistrust, suspicion, anger, confusion, ignorance - obstructs my ability to lose myself temporarily in the other, in the world, in abstract ideas. These are the barriers my art practice reflects, because they are the ones that keep me grounded. Unlike materiality, I can't transcend these barriers *solely*

Identity in Community

through the intellectual act of ascending to higher conceptual levels and reflecting on them from a distance."[5]

Piper may long for the comfort of intellectual distance and the satisfaction of the sense that ideas can make in the free-floating mind. But Adrian Piper's art sinks its teeth into the heart of the matter and comes up bearing some unsettling bones in the contemporary closet.

Adrian Piper, "What It's Like, What It Is #23," 1991, mixed media installation, Hirshhorn Museum and Sculpture Garden, Washington, D.C.

Sandra Rowe, "The Slave Series," 1992, mixed media installation.

To Joann
"Community" out
should be you middle
name — a wonderful
friend — I love you.
Thanks for ubiquity +
honesty

Ola Jean: Such a
great friendship
thru the years.
Wish you the best!
and thanks for
promoting Wm. of
Color within the
art circles.
Love you,
Anita
Holguin

Identity in Community

Is It Me?

by Sandra Rowe

In 1993, when Sandra Rowe was invited to create an exhibition for the Santa Monica Museum of Art, she decided to dedicate it to her mother, a woman who had supported two children and her own mother by working as a night cook in the basement kitchen of the train station. To underscore the solitary and alienating nature of that work, Rowe called the exhibition "The Invisible Woman." The artist realized that in order to communicate the essence of her mother's experience and, by extension, the experiences of many disenfranchised women, she had to employ diverse means, so she developed an installation that included photography, video, painting, sculpture and several other components. Rowe also wrote and produced a small, gray book containing an austere, rhythmic narrative of one of her mother's days. She wrote of her mother's walk to the train station.

> She put on her uniform at 1:30 and left at 1:45 for the walk to work. She had to be there by 3:00. . . . She walked with her head down. She stared at the cracks in the sidewalk. When she reached main street, she knew that she was nearly half way there. She looked up as she neared the intersection. She looked both ways, not actually seeing the store fronts, people, cars and bus. She was waiting for the light to change.

Because Rowe's art deals in metaphor rather than didactic statement, she chose not to illustrate that passage concretely in her installation. Instead, she alluded to the urban landscape through which her mother numbly passed in a series of photographic panels framed on one wall.

> An order came down on pale green striped paper. She fried two burgers, placed the bun on the grill to toast, grilled some onions, placed the burger on the bun with pickles, onions and mayo. She shook the fries as they came out of the grease, placed them on a white plate, put them on the dumbwaiter and cranked it up. No other orders came down for an hour.

In the center of the installation was a diner counter from which emerged a television monitor screening a video of aged hands grilling hamburgers and onions.

> She pulled down the dumbwaiter and placed a note on it for the counter-man above. It said, "I'm here." That was her only method of communication to the train station upstairs. . . . The phone had been broken for weeks.

In the far corner of the installation was a stairwell leading up to a dark rectangular well, its murky silence a reference to the isolation of the basement kitchen in which Rowe's mother was so long relegated. "If the piece is doing what it should do," says the artist, "it will affect you in some way. If I've answered the questions as I should and put sweat into it, the work will have a depth, an intensity, like Blues lyrics."

Sandra Rowe was born and raised in Indiana, which she remembers as "a very racist place. My opportunities as a Black person were very limited." She recognized early on that she wanted to be an artist, but "didn't even know what an artist did." Her first year in college, she married, dropped out of school, and moved to Texas. Her husband was in the military, so they continued to move. It was in Rome, New York, that she reconnected with her artistic impulses and began taking painting classes. She quit for a while, then after yet another move, this time to New Hampshire, began yet again. Eventually, she found that she was painting all the time, in the kitchen, in the dining room. "Painting was my salvation. It was a safe and wonderful thing to do. I painted out of my guts. For ten years, all I did was paint and raise kids." When the family moved to California, she started back to school, first at a junior college, then at Cal State Fresno, then on to graduate work at the University of California, Irvine. Her husband pursued his career in the Air Force. "But I wasn't a very good officer's wife," admits Rowe. "I think he might have missed a promotion because of me. I did things like pose with a hammer and sickle for [conceptual artist] Allan Sekula."

Today, it is Rowe's own career that is central. She has had more than a dozen solo exhibitions and has participated in several dozen group shows. In 1994 she installed a major installation at the Studio Museum in Harlem, NYC. Entitled "As the Wind Blows," her Harlem work dealt with issues that have concerned the artist since graduate school: racism, sexism, and the perceptual conflicts of appearance and reality. "As the Wind Blows" was comprised of a series of thirty human heads, which projected from the wall on steel brackets. Situated in five rows of six each, the heads spun slowly and awkwardly. Behind each head were words arranged in such a way as to comprise pithy but seemingly contradictory sentences whether read horizontally, vertically, from left to right or right to left. *Time includes difference. Time excludes difference. Power is deceptive. Change is deceptive.* Large fans framed the piece, spewing air into the viewer's space and leading to the implication that the way the air/wind blows determines the manner in which the verbal "truths" are perceived and understood.

Sandra Rowe's poem, "Is It Me?" [which follows] addresses issues of race, gender, and perception in language so reified, so condensed that readers must constantly pause, re-read, and consider, before they continue through the artist's exploration of art, identity, and community.

PRIDE

Is it me
with my nappy hair that wasn't beautiful then
but is now,
that makes me identify with other persons with nappy hair who
believe that the natural curl of black hair is pretty and
we don't have to wear weaves, curls or be blonde to be beautiful.

IDENTITY

Is it me
who has a few black friends I trust,
a few acquaintances who are OK
but I only see every once in a while and who know others who
have "sold" the roots of their
identity
because they believe that the "system" will work for them when
they really don't know the system or who "owns" the system and
that
the system might "eat them alive" while they continue to believe
in the system.

PREJUDICE

Is it me
surrounded by white people; some are friends I trust,
some are acquaintances who are OK but
only see once in a while and others I do not trust because of
past incidents of insults and prejudices that
seem to have healed but
in actuality are just under the surface of my
tough but sometimes fragile exterior.

ISSUES

Is it me
being part of the movement for
the rights of people of color and women by taking on
issues of racism and sexism in my art, speeches and writing but
not belonging to the organizations that profess to challenge the
media and communities on equality issues because of my
time commitments to art, speeches, work and writing
and wondering if any of it
can make a difference.

ISOLATION

Is it me
in Atlanta in a room full of Black people

(who are now fashionably being called African Americans),
standing next to two women who didn't know I was the artist of
the 33 gridded works in blues, pearlescents and gray
"head" shapes with the text in the brain area that says
"The Difference Between You and Me"
and saying
"This stuff doesn't make any sense and is boring"
and then walking across the room to an artist's abstract painting
in red, green, and black with a Black pride-sounding title and
responding with
nods, up and down.

CRITICISM
Is it me
in my studio wondering who will be the next art critic
to read my bio and know that my mother and her two sisters were
domestics
and then patronize me in some article with comments
about my past by stating
". . . it's been hard for her"
and then not seeing the intellectual concepts in my work because
it is not expected because of
limitations placed on expectations of
what I must be because of their limitations of what
they don't know about Black people.

QUALITY
Is it me
who dislikes the word quality used in any art context because
it has been used by art critics, historians, museums, galleries,
curators, artists, patrons and others to exclude
artists of color and women because
our work was different and not acceptable
under the strict guidelines of the European male art aesthetic of
quality
even though their work sometimes was derivative of
cultures of color and women.

BELONGING
Is it me
wondering what makes an "art community"
and who are the people who really run it
and why don't I see
more people of color or women

being quoted, pictured, framed, written about or
running galleries, museums, art programs . . .
in the "art community"?

RECOGNITION
Is it me
who reads ARTnews and sees year after year
that article about "Artists Selecting Artists" and
continues to see white people selecting white people and
seeing "specialized" articles on people of color and
multiculturalism . . .
then looking at other articles in other magazines on the people
who run things in the "art community" and
realizing that in spite of the "timeliness" of multiculturalism
I might continue to see white people most often choosing white
people, but
I hope not.

ACCEPTANCE
Is it me
wondering about which community I belong to,
want to belong to,
which will accept me,
not accept me and
if one of the communities chooses me
will I or my work be described as
African American, Afro-centric, Black, Ethnic, Black art, Afro-
American art, Political, Feminist, Conceptual, Visual,
Installation, Painter, Book, Woman or artist?

RESPONSIBILITY
Is it me
who continues to get asked by
those few enlightened persons
(most often white organizations but sometimes black) who
may not know my work but have heard my name mentioned
as a "Black Woman Artist"
who continue to ask me
to exhibit my work in
February or March
to absolve themselves of the responsibility
of including me in curated exhibitions of
artists with like sensibilities
in other months of the year and
are surprised when I say no.

ME

Is it me
wondering why I spend so much time working at my art,
working at my teaching,
never resting, working at something,
developing an ulcer,
driven by forces
I sometimes do not understand but want to understand and
wanting all the time to be nothing
but an artist.

OTHER PLACES

BOOGIE MAN

Is it me
at the cellar door, looking into the darkness thinking
that in my childhood a real boogie man was down there,
smelling the dankness,
feeling fear in my stomach and not wanting to really believe
that a large green horrible freak might be waiting
to devour my soul, body and spirit
if I venture into the unknown.

KNOWING

Is it me
turning on the light at the top of the stairs,
turning on the light at the bottom of the stairs,
turning on the light in the middle of the room,
looking at the darkness in the next room,
turning on the light at the door of the next room and
seeing that there isn't anything in that room but
the stuff that I knew was there all along.
— 1993

ROSALIE ORTEGA

in Conversation with Betty Ann Brown

Rosalie Ortega is an artist who works in various media. She creates installations and objects, billboards and jewelry. Much of her art explores her identity as a woman, a Chicana, an outsider. Ortega works in community, in collaboration, and alone. She also teaches and speaks eloquently about her history, her work, and her spirituality. We touched on all of these topics in our conversations. I weave Ortega's words through a weft of quotes from Coco Fusco, an artist and theorist Ortega has found particularly inspiring.

> The identity battles of recent years are among the variety of ways that the peoples of this country are transforming our vision of America and its cultures. What are surfacing in the process are the histories that have circulated until now in marginalized communities. In the debates and art emerging from the tumult of the present are reflections of the many legacies of the conquest and colonization of the Americas, among them, its limiting views of art and culture. Although American society has defined progress as a focus on the future, we must now return to the past in order to place ourselves in that history and understand how we got to where we are. . . . [N]ew alternative chronicles surface; these are the latest examples of how collective memories, those storehouses of identity, once activated, become power sites of cultural resistance.[1]

Betty Ann Brown: I want to talk about three things: identity, collaboration, and experiences you've had with women's communities, or what Gerda Lerner calls "affinity clusters." One of the things I find really interesting is the story of how you came to be self-identifying. Do you mind starting with your personal history, with how you perceive your identity?

Rosalie Ortega: I've only recently come into awareness about my identity, and I'm still working on it. I was born in 1954 in East Los Angeles. Before, when I used to say I was born in East L.A., it was somewhat meaningless, but that's changed. Now I recognize the significance. My parents were two teenagers, two 18-year-olds. I'm sure I was conceived after the prom or something like that. My mother was born to a single mother who had her at age 16. But my parents got married. I've seen the wedding pictures: the traditional church, the traditional bridesmaids. My father's side of the family was Mexican. His mother — that whole side, actually — spoke only Spanish. But my mother's family was *not* Mexican-identified. They were from New Mexico and my mother always considered herself separate, something other than Mexican. I'm not close enough to her to ask her how she identified herself; that's one of the things I need to do. Sometimes I think she wanted to assimilate totally, but when pressed she said she was Spanish. To her, that was very different from being Mexican.

BAB: Isn't that a perception of racial distinction? Isn't Mexican supposed to involve Native American blood? Spanish is European.

RO: I always viewed it as an issue of separation; it was a way to separate from Mexico.

BAB: So you've never thought of it as related to race or class?

RO: It was definitely a class issue. No doubt about it: she thought her family was superior because they weren't Mexican. It would be interesting to find out whether she saw it as a racial difference as well. A lot of my childhood memories are blurred. But I know my mother stayed home; she was a housewife at 19. My father was a mechanic.

BAB: Where did you grow up?

RO: We stayed in East L.A. for three or four years. Then we moved to Santa Monica and I went to a Catholic school there. My mother was obsessed by upward mobility. Her mother had been, too. Her mother moved to California from New Mexico and got a job as a checker in a supermarket. She worked her way up to being an assistant manager, which was a lot for a woman to do at that time. I don't even know if she had a high school diploma. She wanted my mother to go to college and would have paid her way.

BAB: But your mother rebelled by having you?

RO: Right. Whether it was an accident or not, it happened. I was cared for by my grandmother, though. My younger sister became my mother's chance to be a mother, since my grandmother stole the show with me.

BAB: After all, your mother was herself a baby when you were born.

RO: She must have been scared to death. I've been told that I probably separated from my mother very early, probably in infancy. Then my sister died at the age of four from leukemia. That was the real clincher: I was the one who lived and the other one died.

BAB: The death of a sibling is such a tragedy: the survivor thinks she's never forgiven and she never forgives herself.

RO: Exactly. When I look back at pictures, I can see that my mother and I were never close. . . . By the time I was in the third grade, we moved again — to Simi Valley. Back then it was the rural melting pot everybody was emigrating to because the houses were cheap — those Spielberg tract houses. Simi Valley was the area I remember growing up in. All the way up through high school, I was with the same group of kids.

BAB: Was it a pretty white environment?

RO: Very much so.

BAB: Did you perceive yourself as different?

RO: I don't know what I thought. I must have looked in the mirror and seen that I was different, but whether I didn't hear it or whether nobody said anything, I don't know . . . I was very naive. And my mother so often said that we were all the same. It never became an issue; I never perceived my ethnicity until I went away to college.

BAB: So it wasn't until you were a young woman that you really were conscious of being a Chicana?

RO: Correct. Other issues permeated my awareness: being overweight and having divorced parents.

BAB: When did they divorce?

RO: When I was about 11, so that was the crux of my early life. I was the only one on Father-Daughter Day who sat alone in the corner. The divorce was the crisis for me, maybe the racial issue just blended right into it.

BAB: Your mother stayed in Simi Valley?

RO: Yes, she kept the house. Then, from about age 11 on, I had to stay home and take care of my brother, who is nine years younger. My mother was working outside the home. She became the husband and I the wife. I wasn't allowed to stay after school; I wasn't allowed to talk on the phone or socialize; I never went to the prom; I never went to dances; I never did any of that. I took care of the house.

Around 16, I started reading *Ms.* magazine. It brought me feminism. I knew exactly what those housewives were talking about: I too had to stay home. I had to wash the dishes, take care of the kid, do all that sort of thing. Reading *Ms.* brought my very first awareness of myself and it led to my identification with women and the women's movement.

This is the other irony: it was right after the Watts riots, and I was reading James Baldwin and *Burn Baby Burn* and *Black Like Me* and all those books. I could identify with the struggle of blacks, but had no idea about my own struggle. I was totally unaware of my own ethnic background.

BAB: Tell me about college.

RO: I wanted to go to Mills College but my mother forbade it; she made me stay local. I went to UCLA and studied Sociology. To earn money, I started working at the child care center there. Feminism was alive and well on campus and child care was an important issue. The parents sat in on Chancellor Young's office, setting their kids right on his desk.

The child care center was a great place, a place where I gained a lot of confidence. It's where I got the foundations of my teaching. It's also where I first started working with art, with kids, and where I got my first art training. It was the first place where I saw a father show affection for his child. I saw one man lift up his son and throw him into the air, laughing. I'll never forget that moment — I must have stood there with my mouth open. I just couldn't believe it.

I used to baby-sit for the parents, the professors at UCLA, who'd go away for the weekend, and I met a whole new group of people that way. This was the mid 1970s, the time of the Grandview Gallery and the Woman's Building. A lot was going on. Then, the mother of one of our families, a woman who'd been taking art classes at the Building, realized she was a lesbian and left her family.

BAB: That must have been shocking back then.

RO: Yes, it was shocking, but men have been leaving their families for years.

BAB: So you thought it was cool in a way that a woman would have the courage to leave her family?

RO: Right. I was also working out my anger — although I didn't know it then — towards men, towards all that stuff. Anyway, I met up with her and she took me to the Holly Near concert at the Wilshire Ebell. It changed my life to be in a room full of women like that. The energy and acceptance were phenomenal. I was blown away, absolutely blown away. After that, she joined the Califia Collective, one of the first educational collectives for women. They organized week-long retreats for women only. I would go and do their child care for them. I was too shy to be part of the group, but had contact as a care-giver.

BAB: Who's Califia?

RO: Califia is the California goddess. It was in that women's community that my ethnic identity first hit me. That's where it first started, within the feminist movement, not in the outside world.

BAB: Are you saying you experienced racism there? Or that your consciousness was raised about racism?

RO: Before, I had been aware of racism, but not of where I was in the midst of it. I was mostly with groups of white women and I knew I wasn't white but I didn't know what else I was. It was wounding when the women of color began saying, "Why are you with those women?" After a while, there were women of color groups. They all seemed to be made up of women who had the culture, the language, all those things I didn't have or hadn't become aware of. I felt an incredible amount of confusion and pain because they made fun of me as if I had consciously denied my culture. I was being accused — and it was very overt — I was being accused of denying my culture in order to fit in, in order to pass. Which was going on, but the accusations were unfair since I had been acting out of ignorance. I was wounded by the women of color and later by the white women. I would go back and forth [between groups] in anguish. The place that had nurtured me [the women's community] became very painful. I didn't have anything to do with the women's movement for four or five years.

That coincided with a marriage and moving away with my husband to Alhambra [a community to the north and east of Los Angeles]. The marriage and the move swallowed me up.

BAB: How did you feel about getting married? I got married in 1977, right as my angry feminism was peaking. I remember thinking to myself, the very day I got married, "This is a betrayal of your politics. This is a betrayal of who you are and if anybody ever writes your story they are going to wonder how this fits it."

RO: I didn't have that voice. There was a part of me that knew I was getting married, but wasn't sure what marriage would mean. I guess I was never really present in the marriage. I was in my first round of therapy and having a lot of anxiety attacks. I was encountering that part of me that was scared all the time, that was scared when my father left, that was scared if my mother was going to be able to take care of us. For some reason the fear surfaced at that time and my husband took it away.

BAB: The whole weight of the culture tells you that's what should happen. If you find the right man, and he'll marry you and you'll be saved!

RO: I know. There was no doubt about it: I became co-dependent with this person. Yet the marriage served a purpose. It was like an escape; I escaped from all the painful and confusing things that had been happening to me. So out in beautiful Alhambra, my husband and I played at marriage. I went back to school and took art classes at Cal State L.A., which was right around the corner. I got more training, but I still didn't consider myself an artist. Then two very significant things happened. I started therapy with a new therapist, a man, which I couldn't tell anybody. A male therapist?! That seemed like blasphemy! Yet in my heart I knew that there were issues I needed to work out...

And then I returned to the Woman's Building. I went for a series on women's spirituality. I had become acquainted with women's spirituality through Califia; there were lots of witches who hung out there and we would do rituals and so on. The night I went back to the Woman's Building, Ruth Barrett presented her "Circle of Aradia." [It] opened up a whole arena for me. I started doing art workshops in the women's community and I learned the nuts and bolts of what I'm doing right now. I learned the basics of spirituality; the structure of ceremonies, of rituals; the universal things — like the four directions — you work with; all the tools I now know are cross-cultural. I studied with Ruth for a couple of years and then was a member of a coven of Dianic witches for another three years. During that time I also became involved in Native American teachings and started to go to sweat ceremonies regularly.

Largely because of the workshops I was teaching through "Circle of Aradia," I'm now known in the women's community, in the women's spiritual community. I joined the Board of the Woman's Building [in 1990]. But I'm still struggling with my own identity, with what I have an affinity for, what I believe is important to me. And it's been a source of conflict for different groups that I'm interacting with. So many can't accept that I'm not either/or, that I'm not either Wiccan or Native American, but that I combine the two.

> Syncretism, or the fusion of different forms of belief or practice, enabled the disempowered groups to maintain their outlawed or marginalized traditions. It also paved the way for a host of cultural recycling methods that infuse old icons with new meanings. . . . Although some might cling to the idea that all artists are bound to a specific, group-oriented mandate, or a fixed notion of community, the most intriguing work takes these very assumptions apart and presents new possibilities for old terms. . . . In doing so [these artists] participate in multiple communities.[2]

Then, on the heels of a divorce, I got a job [running the educational outreach programs] at the Pasadena Armory Center for the Arts, which was a big turning point for me. I felt that I was being recognized as somebody with expertise, with a body of knowledge. I was gaining more and more confidence, although it has always been a struggle for me. I get to this place and then ask myself, do I belong here? Do I really belong?

BB: So this is an ongoing question for you, this issue of belonging? How does that relate to your artmaking?

RO: In 1991 Ruth Ann Anderson approached me about collaborating on her altar/installation about feminist spirituality for the "Communitas" exhibition [curated by Brown and Elizabeth Say at Cal State Northridge in 1992]. I'd known Ruth Ann through her Wiccan coven and through the Woman's Building. She felt I was somebody she could collaborate with. I was honored; it was my first exhibition, the first time I publicly saw myself as a fine artist. It was also intimidating, but that was buffered by being a part of a group. The "Communitas" exhibition experience was a real gift. I consider it the beginning of what is going to be the essence of my art. My art is about myself, and my spirituality, and my healing, which are all intertwined . . . in my life.

> Symbolic action, in the form of spirituality and art, has for centuries been a critical arena for self-definition by politically disenfranchised peoples. One might recall the importance of African American spirituals in the Civil Rights movement, or the role of the *corridos* for Chicanos in the Southwest as conveyors of a history suppressed by the dominant Anglo society. Culture and communal self-expression are perhaps the most important sites of resistance, the signs in everyday life of an ongoing political struggle.[3]
>
> [For the "Communitas" exhibition, Ruth Ann Anderson erected a large, four-sided structure oriented to the cardinal directions. Ortega was assigned the earth segment. She constructed an immense wall entitled "Your Body is

Identity in Community

the Earth." She covered the wall with plaster casts of fragments of her nude body. The fragments wove together into a fleshy caress of landscape. She covered the undulations with richly textured tar and painted the dark cobalt sky with her hands.]

I'm so heavily ingrained in the spiritual, especially where spiritual teachings overlap with feminism, that I could never separate that part of me. In my spiritual practices — whether they are Wiccan or Native American or whatever — the earth direction — whether it's the north or the west, depending on what perspective it is — is the place I hold, the place I work in. It's the place of death, change, transformation. It's about the connection to the cycles and rhythms of life that become severed by our culture.

BAB: So much wonderful writing comes from feminist theologians who critique the development of patriarchal religious systems premised on separation from and domination of the earth, in contrast to feminist spirituality, which is about connection.[4]

RO: That's how I saw my piece: the body forms coming up out of the earth represented that connection for me. I'll never forget how people responded to the sensuality of "Your Body is the Earth." The sensuality wasn't intended; sensuality is a part of me I wanted to deny. But sensuality is earthy. And the desire to touch [the art work] — to get into the crevices — that taught me a lot.

Soon after "Communitas," I did a public art piece for "Secrets Out," the show in Pasadena for artists and people with a background of abuse, primarily sexual abuse. I got to be a key player in that, working with arts and social service organizations [like the Light Bringer Project] all over in Pasadena. I created a sign in a parking lot which had to do with assault. The sign said "Caution, this is a public parking space. If you are a woman . . ." and then there were a whole series of phrases like "Don't drink," "Don't dress provocatively," "Don't lose consciousness." There was no budget for the sign and it was the first time I'd dealt with lettering. I eyeballed it, because I didn't know the rules for graphic design. I sat there at 1:00 in the morning saying, "You have to do this, nobody's going to tell you how."

One of the things that happened for me in the "Secrets Out" show was I got to be the voice of feminism there, which I hadn't articulated in a really long time, even though it's always been part of me. It was like another coming home for me, to be able to verbalize that.

[The next year, Ortega worked on the "Utopian Dialogues" exhibition. Curated by Brown for the Los Angeles Municipal Art Gallery, Fall 1993, "Utopian Dialogues" presented installations by twelve artists who created work out of conversations they had with writers, scientists, children, the elderly, or other artists on the topic of an ideal society. Here is an excerpt from the catalogue entry on Ortega's "Marginal Confessions."]

Rosalie Ortega's utopian dialogues, enacted verbally . . . and textually . . ., with a gamut of diverse people have focused on the ideological conflicts and experiential difficulties of establishing subjectivity, sustaining creativity, and what psychologist Thomas Moore calls "living from the soul." The artist has addressed these issues as they pertain to marginalized people, others in positions of privilege, and those who through societal or geographic shifts have experienced changes in status. The process has forced her to grapple with the dynamics of inclusion and exclusion, how these dynamics instill fear, then how fear crushes, silences, traps its victims. As her conversations have developed, Ortega has realized that many marginalized people have been pushed, shoved or crushed into constricted categories that have no meaning for them, into ideological boxes too small for the vitality of their lives. She has also realized that many self-censor their responses to such oppressions, usually choosing not to become vulnerable to their fears or to articulate their resultant rage. When they do express these feelings, it is often in a confessional mode.

Ortega, a dark-skinned Chicana whose paternal grandparents were Mexican, has for some time been troubled by the fact that her mother, who was born and raised in New Mexico, always called herself "Spanish" and even indicated on the artist's birth certificate that the child was Caucasian. "I have always thought of myself as someone who was different. This is something that has formed my experience. And as I read, and spoke to people, several things kept coming up. One of them had to do with confinement, what the experience of feeling different does to people, how it makes them feel confined, closed in. This happens within your body, almost physically. It's as if you've gone into a tunnel which gets tighter and tighter, as the level of judgment, both internal and external, constricts you further and further."

This thinking brought Ortega to consideration of how such confinement was culturally constructed. "There's an idea out there that things run better, smoother, if we're all alike, if we all conform." The pressures to conform to the modes of dominance, to agree to what those in power set as standards, are particularly strong on the disenfranchised in any culture, on women under patriarchy, on people of color under racist regimes. Realizing the affects of such pressures on her and her partners in dialogue has led Ortega to create an installation — a series of increasingly claustrophobic confessionals, in which the viewer is forced to physically experience increasing constriction of bodily parameters. The artist hopes that such physical and therefore psychic experience will lead the viewer to an embodied sense of the need to hope, and to work, for freedom from such externally imposed restraints for all.[5]]

Since "Utopian Dialogues," it's been one opportunity after another, whether it's a wearable art show and I get to do my rusty bottlecap things or a Chicano show. My name is out in the Chicano community now. I work at the Plaza de la Raza [the community arts organization in East Los Angeles]. One day, I got a call from somebody saying, "We've got your name, would you like to bring some work over?" And I said, "Have you ever seen any of my work?" When they said no, I almost turned them down, because I was afraid my work would stick out like a sore thumb, that it wouldn't look like what they expected [of] Chicano art.

BAB: It sounds to me like you were responding to pressure (that you sense coming from the Chicano community) to create art that looks a certain way, art that occupies a certain territory. It sounds like you were feeling alienated because your art wouldn't "fit in."

RO: I think that when underrepresented groups of artists want to establish recognition, it's easier to create a body of identifiable work. I understand politically, consciously and socially that this is what happens for people who haven't had a chance to put their art out there. It's comfortable, and it's nice to be a part of identifiable groups. I also know that when you have exclusivity within a group it raises your status. When you're a part of a group, you get to decide who else gets into the group. Unfortunately, when the dominant culture begins to identify the art movement, it becomes identified with a limited number of people. That becomes a problem.

> While the claims to absolute authority in issues of cultural identity and property are at times problematic (since no one, in the end, speaks for every member of a group), the ways that these dealings are represented in the mainstream media and even most of the art press are invariably tendentious. Little effort has been made to distinguish between dominant cultural attempts to curtail an artist's right to express his or her aesthetic sensibility and a subaltern critique of institutionalized racism and privilege. . . .[6]

But it's not always that way. I think of when I started teaching at Plaza. I was hired by Denise Nelson Nash, another one of those people who went out on the line for me. There were a million applicants for this one teaching job, and that was right when Plaza was in the throes of "Do we continue to teach the cultural arts or do we teach other stuff, too?" Here I came in with wearable art, assemblage, all these different things, and Denise decided to go with me. I brought a radically different perspective to the kids. They were a little leery of me at first. But I think they now respect me as an arts educator — although I don't fit the "perfect picture" for them sometimes.

BAB: That "perfect picture" is a stereotype.

RO: I know. I had an interesting experience one summer at the Afro-American Museum and I was really pained by it. Will I ever be included in one of their groups shows? I doubt it. I'm respected there yet I'm not part of the group. I guess I'm a person who goes in between, like the shaman who links all the social groups together. A shaman can be respected and accepted at many different places but not belong in any of them. That's where I'm at.

I went to the party celebrating the end of a teaching session at the Afro-America Museum. All the parents and the kids were there, but just two other teachers —

out of about eight or ten teachers in the program — showed up. I was the only non-black person in the room. It was interesting to feel the separateness. I wanted to stand up and say, "Hey, I came today! This was important to me. These kids are important to me, their artwork was important to me." I wanted to justify myself. I wanted to make myself good there, but I was not part of the community. I wanted to prove my integrity, and establish my value. It was strange. . . . But when the dominant culture oppresses groups, of course they close in.

BAB: That's something we always have to remember, even as feminists. If we set up a group, some people aren't going to be in it, period. We have to accept the responsibility for those decisions and that dynamic. The issue of community is a difficult one, it's not all warm and fuzzy. Groups have boundaries, communities have limits.

RO: Even in teaching, my identity changes. I go from Manhattan Beach, the conservative, affluent community where I teach primarily white, older citizens about mask-making, to a group of learning-disabled kids at the Los Angeles County Museum of Art (LACMA). Talk about humbling! I walked into LACMA in my teacher mode thinking, "I am here to impart wisdom." The kids weren't getting any of it. The person's foot in front of them was much more interesting than what I was saying. I had to shift in two minutes. I had to ask myself, What should I really be doing for them? I had no idea ahead of time how they would be, yet I was supposed to prepare an art project for them. I realized I had to be in the moment, I had to let go of a lot of ego.

BAB: That's what Judy Chicago and I were talking about in reference to teaching art: Give up the power, give up control and allow it to happen. The only way that it's going to be creative is if it's a situation of discovery, if it's not rigidly predetermined at the outset.

RO: It's created a lot of anxiety for me. I come prepared — I come with enough supplies for five classes — and I come knowing what *could* happen, but then being with whatever *does* happens and adjusting to it. I have to have the faith and confidence that I can adjust to whatever is going to happen within that two-hour period. It has shifted my teaching a lot; it also affects my artwork.

It's the same thing with installations. I think I know how the room is going to look but something always changes, so I have to abandon the idea of control and continue to develop my ideas throughout the process of building the installation.

You have to be open in collaborations, too. But there's a part of me that hasn't quite worked out the aspect of the collaboration where people engage in very cerebral, very stereotypical dialogue like that in movies. Sometimes I think there's too much talking. Maybe you should just stand back and see how the art or the project feels to you, and not even talk about it.

BAB: Sometimes people talk — and write — about art from a position of wanting to master or predetermine other people's interpretations. That's the controlling position. Then other people talk about art and they just want to say, "These are my feelings and this is what I'm getting. How do you feel? What's another perspective on it?" I think it depends on where you're coming from, what's your agenda in talking about the art. If you're talking about the art so as to limit and package predetermined responses to it, you're saying, "This is the right (and only) way in which this is to be perceived." That cuts down the art, constricts it. But you can also talk about art in order to open it up.

If the talking about art comes from an impulse to control and say this is the one true way and the only way to take in this art, then that's a problem for me. But if it comes from a position like, I just want to talk about my feelings, and you can talk about your feelings, and we can all say that in a non-judgmental, safe place, then I don't have a problem with it. As an art history teacher, I think it's really important to make that distinction for my students.

> Rosalie and I spoke again, two years later (1995). I asked her where she was in relation to community at that point in her life.

RO: I feel like I've come out of several years of intense darkness. I'm trying desperately to heal — to let go of the blame and the pain of being in and out of communities. I'm ready to take responsibility and step out. It's a really great but also really scary place.

I guess I've always had this "outsider" identity. I've always yearned for community, a place shared with people like me, a place to relax, a home, a safe place with like-minded people where I know there's truth in what I'm saying because it's being mirrored back to me. When your identity is threatened by other groups, or when you lose your group, you become disassociated, disenfranchised. You experience incredible turmoil.

> Exile, and the split sense of self it entails, are paradigmatic experiences of identity for millions.[7]

> These artists reflect the hybrid experiences that shape so much of contemporary life. They emerge from the dynamics of moving between worlds, and feeling at home and not at home in more than one. They use different languages, and cross aesthetic genres as they follow ideas through multiple media. They express the ambivalence produced by being out of sync with dominant media constructs and yet being fascinated with images and the creative possibilities for their recontextualization.[8]

My first experience of disruptive community was my family. That disruption got repeated in the culture and left me with an uncertain sense of who I was, in comparison to how (I thought) everybody else was acculturated. Of course there was an up side: I became one of those people who can travel in and out of groups. I suppose there's an empowerment in having no "home."[9]

BAB: Or having several "homes." What you're saying makes me think of Maria Lugones' discussion of "world traveling," of having the capacity to travel through multiple identities, multiple communities.[10]

RO: Yes, but I still grapple with the pain of having no place. A lot of the healing of that comes through my teaching. I'm doing a residency in Santa Monica. I have five classes of kindergartners two days a week. They're teaching me everything I need to know about teaching. The bottom line is, they just want me to love them. They just want me to acknowledge their work. It's about feeding their souls. Lately, I think I'm teaching them a kind of faith. Each time they come into the classroom, they get a renewed faith in what they're doing. They develop faith that whatever needs to be done, will be done. They'll accomplish it. If they can have faith in the abstract process of creation . . . well, one plus one equals two can't be that scary any more. It's predictable.

I guess that was one of the original purposes of art, to establish faith in the world. Faith in the individual's existence. Faith that the sun would come back around again. Faith in connection. Part of the estrangement of modern life has to do with losing that connection, that faith. If you're disconnected, you think you're not being who you're supposed to be, but you fear the estrangement of being "other."

BAB: You feel you have no solid center on which to stand. The notion of the solid center is one of the master narratives, one of the reductive, universalizing myths we've developed to explain things in Western culture. It has no concrete reality. Yet we yearn for the unattainable absolute of the solid center in self and identity. We long for it, passionately desire it. And when we fail to attain it, we feel failed, alienated, separated. We hate ourselves.

RO: We create our own reality. That shows the incredible strength of the individual ego. It can create its own reality and perpetuate it through time. We can create creatures of self-hate and loathing. Or we can create creatures of love.

One of the things about being an outsider is that you're less constrained by locality. You can take a global view of things. You realize we're all looking for transcendence, for answers, for the reason why we're here. It's horribly unfortunate that wars have been waged over these very questions; we really are all trying to find the same answer. Yet we develop systems that separate us, pit us against each other.

I re-established contact with my mother for a while last year. When we got together, it was really strained. Then something severed the connection. It was a conversation we had one day. We were finally talking a little about the family and I used the term "dysfunctional." She took great exception to that. A few weeks later, she broke off the connection with a letter. It feels final, like a definite closure.

Identity in Community

And it's so sad. I'm afraid we're playing out with each other the way the dominant culture has oppressed women, especially women of color. The oppression involves guilt, pain, shame, and my mother and I internalized those things in our relationship.

BAB: You've just talked about the dominant culture. Weren't you exposed to the culture of New Mexico, too?

RO: Neither my mother nor my grandmother brought the cultural heritage of New Mexico to us. It was there, but never shared as a family. I never experienced it as community. In their desire to become mainstream, they chose not to share their background. I saw the beauty of New Mexican culture, but never felt part of it. It was all very confusing.

BAB: What you're saying makes me think of all the immigrant families here in Los Angeles who refuse to speak their native languages in hopes of rapidly assimilating their children to English-speaking culture.

RO: Yes, and looks are a big part of it, too. My mother and grandmother were both very light-skinned. I of course am darker. Then my sister came along and she was light-skinned; that was so important to them.

They were very negative about my father's people, who were dark like me. It was self-racism. It started right in the home. I wasn't allowed to play with my cousins on my father's side. I felt like an outsider with my own cousins. I remember having to sit in a chair alone while they went out and played.

My father's mother, who spoke only Spanish, often sent food home with us. I know now that it was her attempt to nourish us and connect with us. She wanted to give more love than my mother allowed.

I just thought of something else, too. I got a scholarship for Chicanas while I was at UCLA. My mother was absolutely livid. "You don't need to get money that way!" she raged. She totally disavowed her roots and responded to her own ethnicity with shame, anger and hatred.

BAB: Since the recent assault on Affirmative Action, scholarships like that are increasingly rare. . . . Isn't it interesting that the assault on Affirmative Action came right on the heels of multiculturalism, which aspired to be so inclusive?

RO: I always had problems with multiculturalism. The way it was discussed, you were either in or out. There was no gray territory. I think it was another attempt by the dominant culture to protect itself and hold onto its power. The categories were absolute. You either are or you aren't.

> In such a state of things, the very notion of cultural purity can seem like something of a nostalgic fantasy, one that not even "non-western" societies can provide proof of any longer.[11]

We still tend to buy into that, which means we're still victimized by it. I've been reading a lot of Coco Fusco lately. She writes about how we're fighting against the dominant culture's last-ditch effort to maintain the status quo. How do you hang onto what's being ripped away from you? You want to keep it away from everyone else. You don't want it to be gray.

I still don't do art that "looks Chicano." I'm healing my relationship with that community by realizing that I have a lot to contribute by who I am and what I look like. And lately I've been running into other people with similar backgrounds, although some of them are still in the closet in that community.

It's not easy. Last month, I attended the screening of a video produced by Coco Fusco and some other Los Angeleno artists. It was a high camp spoof of television novellas. It was hysterical. I laughed and enjoyed being included at the screening. At the same time, I felt separate. In the video, there was a character who satirized a woman who tried to come back and learn the language and customs of her people. As I watched, I had this incredible sinking feeling. I thought they were satirizing me. Then I got angry. Why did they need to create that sense of separation? The culture at large creates enough separation.

> Although some might cling to the idea that all artists are bound to a specific, group-oriented mandate, or a fixed notion of community, the most intriguing work takes these very assumptions apart and presents new possibilities for old terms.[12]

BAB: One of our great myths, which is to say one of our most important master narratives, is Eden. We're told we used to live in paradisical union with the divine. Then we sinned. (Of course we have to note here that it was woman who drew man into sin. I always wonder if that isn't a rather twisted acknowledgment of female power.) And after we sinned, God cast us out of the garden, to suffer earthly separation. God/man. Man/woman. Good/evil. Connected/separate.

RO: Isn't that the old patriarchal either/or? Could there perhaps be another way of looking at things? It seems to me that if I'm truly at peace with my God, I should be able to hear about your God without being threatened. But if I'm wounded, if I think maybe my God needs to be better than yours, then I need to exclude you because the threat is too great. If you eliminate self-hate, confusion, skepticism, and separation, then others are okay. Then you can accept otherness in your community.

I guess I've come full circle here. We're back to how I feel about community. There's a way that my struggles with identity are reflections of human conflicts at large. Some of us get to play out the battle internally. Maybe we all do. Not all of us are aware of it.

> We didn't theorize postcoloniality after the fact, learn about it from a workshop, or wait for multiculturalism to become foundation lingo for "appreciating diversity" — we lived it and still struggle to make art about it.[13]

Identity in Community

From Rosalie's Journal:

After reading over my conversations with Betty, I realized that my artistic struggles have mirrored my social struggles, my personal struggles, my spiritual struggles. . . . I have come full circle in my views about my art, about what kind of art I should be making. I am unsure about how my art will look, about what materials I will be using. . . . What I do know is that the art I have been called to create speaks to the ritual of life, of my ancestors' lives, of my life. It is art created out of our human existence and our desire to transcend, to know. It is art that emerges from the soul . . . art of the moon and the sea. It is the art I create to find meaning, to comfort, to celebrate, to acknowledge. It is art that soothes and heals me as it soothes and heals those who come in contact with it. It is the artmaking that occurred at the beginning, before we equated art with power, money, status, standards, white walls, longevity and exclusivity. It is an altar created, a surface painted, a ritually spoken word. It is a handprint on a cave, a rescued bit of rust, an object worn, a rock held. . . . This is not art about spirituality nor is it art about my ancestors' spirituality. This is art that is created as a result of being a spiritual person, art that speaks to that experience.

Rosalie Ortega, *Marginal Confessions*, 1993.

Letting My Mother Feed Me

by Aleida Rodríguez

Poet and prose writer Aleida Rodríguez has given many readings on the West Coast and in New York City. I can personally testify to the compelling nature of her spoken word. "Letting My Mother Feed Me" has been chosen for inclusion in this volume because the poem addresses one of the difficult issues of community: how we often resist inclusion, resist identifying with family or racial or gender groups. Here is a stanza from one of Rodríguez's other poems that will also demonstrate the beauty of her work.

From "The Return"

. . . Though I have lived in exile for thirty years
I am led through a gauntlet of caresses,
become a canal for the memory of moisture.
I am not an orphan, they remind me,
tracing my lineage on my palm then pointing to bark.
Though I have forgotten them
they've kept my picture on the dresser all these years.
I have no language to offer them
but the one the brain perpetrates as language.
But my body, my peasant body, surrenders faithfully
to the wordless love of the grasses.

When I was a child, food was an unspeakable crime,
my mother its relentless perpetrator.
On my high chair I choked
on the purees she forced down my throat
and vomited them back into their bowls in protest.
Undaunted, she'd slap me, whip up
another bowlful, threaten my life with a spoon.
Thus beginning the waltz of wills that would partner us forever.

Later, when I could eat solid food—and with the added insult
of my father being a butcher—I was placed before a plate
of rice and black beans, bananas mashed with a fork (the way
I demanded), and a small steak from my father's shop.
My mother would cut the steak into meticulous bite-size pieces,
but I hated meat. I would chew and chew and chew each piece

until it turned grey in my mouth, but I wouldn't swallow it.
Instead I waited until my mother left the room,
then removed each one from my mouth
and lined them up along a slat that crisscrossed
under the tabletop. There my little collection grew, petrifying
in their masticated forms like miniature modern sculpture.
Until the day my mother moved the table.
Then my works of art came tumbling from their hidden shelf,
scattering like pebbles over the swirled linoleum. The horror
of what I endured for my transgression against the sanctity of food
has erased all memory of its consequences, but I do know
that from that day on I had to swallow my food—all of it.
"I'll swallow it, but I don't have to like it" became my motto,
and it has served a versatile function in all areas of my life.

As a teenager in a new country, I dreaded
leaving the sanctuary of my books to share a meal
with my family of strangers. Sulkily, I dragged myself to the table, wearing the
multicolored poncho my father hated
and forbid me to wear, deeming it unsuitable dinner attire.
I slumped into my chair, the backs of my thighs sticking
to the clear vinyl covering every surface of my parents' apartment,
and "I'll swallow it, but I won't like it" was written
all over my sullen face. I had read the biographies
of several inventors, and as I calculated the remaining days
of my imprisonment with the abacus of my peas, I began to project
a destiny that would open a door in the air for me.
Necessity was the only mother I recognized, and I dreamt
of the day I would invent the pill that would liberate me from
            mealtimes,
free to burrow into my books without interruption.

And yet now, after vomiting countless bowls of my mother's cooking,
after railing half a lifetime at the cruel indignities of family meals,
after hardening my heart and stomach against whatever
that giantess with the ubiquitous spoon would offer,
I find myself softening into the quiet humility of acceptance.

My mother calls me one night and, finding me spacey
from too much reading, determines the solution is a square meal.
What I need to do, she suggests, firmly but gently,
like an expert dancing companion, is come by, pick up

Letting My Mother Feed Me

potfuls of her garbanzo stew, her incomparable black beans,
or the stuffed bell peppers she has reinvented in a vegetarian form
for me. After decades of throwing my plate in her face,
after a lifetime of starvation,
after carefully paving a road from the Lands of Plenty back to me,
I settle into a middle-aged generosity
as into a well-worn, overstuffed chair
and finally allow her the pleasure of feeding me.

My Name Is Not My Own

by Katherine Ng

Katherine Ng creates artist's books. She uses her fine arts and graphic design skills to fabricate multiple objects that combine text and image. Many of her books explore her identity in her Asian-American family of origin. Her "Fortune Ate Me" book, for example, which has been featured in national exhibitions and in international private collections, merges the fortune cookie format with letter and journal writing to examine the artist's relationship with her father. In "My Name is Not My Own," the broadside created for this volume, Ng lays type over a simplified self portrait to create poetic commentary on the intersection between racial stereotypes and immigrant name changes.

All the cousins from my father's side of the family are FONG's, but I'm an NG My name is a part of any Chinese surname ending in -ng woNG When I was a young girl, my mother told me that NG was not my real last name and that my real last name is FONG oNG I thought that this was a secret not to be revealed to anyone for the fear of being deported leuNG Since NG was such an unusual name, especially to Westerners, people would wonder whether or not I was related to an acquaintance of theirs feNG "No," I would politely respond, "I'm not related to anyone with that name." chaNG Then I'd feel obligated to explain why: my grandfather was born in a small village in China and didn't have a birth certificate, so he bought someone else's "paper" to come to America joNG It sounds feasible but wasn't accurate choNG Just before the new Year of the Rooster, I found out the true story behind my surname, which is different than the one I had been incorrectly telling people sooNG Here's the real story: In the early 1920's, when my paternal grandfather immigrated to America, the only Chinese people who were exempt from the Chinese Exclusion Act were officials, teachers, students, travellers and merchants deNG Grandfather was not one of the privileged, and like many of his peers, he became a "paper merchant" when he purchased the papers of a merchant destined for America toNG Most of my uncles changed their name back to their original name when they were in the service goNG Father was not in the service and never bothered to change his name chiNG I feel that I was branded with this name huNG During roll call in a classroom, I would observe the puzzled expressions on the faces of my teachers as they struggled to pronounce my vowel-less name woNG How do you say NG? eNG "Mmmm good!" Mom used to tell me to tell people to sing the Campbell's Soup jingle, but replace the m's with n's cheNG No, say "-ing" leoNG Somebody called me "Nig" fuNG In a college linguistics course, I learned that the phonetics for NG is symbolized by combining the lower case n and j to form a nasal cheuNG Dad told me that NG stood for No Good uNG In my search for empowerment, I wanted to take on my mother's maiden name, CHUNG; at least she has a claim to her name kaNG My name is no good taNG My name is not my own ...

You who understand the dehumanization of forced removal-relocation-reeducation-redefinition, the humiliation of having to falsify your own reality, your voice — you know. And often cannot say it. You try and keep on trying to unsay it, for if you don't they will not fail to fill in the blanks on your behalf, and you will be said.

— *Trinh T. Minh-ha*

Katherine Ng, "My Name Is Not My Own," hand-printed broadside.

Ruth Weisberg, *Awakening*, lithograph, 1986.

Jewish Identity and Feminist Community

by Ruth Weisberg

Ruth Weisberg is a Jewish woman, a painter, a professor at the University of Southern California, [a major private university in the Los Angeles area] a political activist. and a prolific writer and art critic.

The following essay addresses her place in the history of art, particularly of Jewish art, then describes her process and some of her more recent and most celebrated art works. Weisberg's writing is permeated with a sense of her committed membership in her overlapping communities of feminism, art, and Judaism.

The first thing to celebrate about being an artist, a Jew, and a woman is that it is possible. There is now an abundance of talented Jewish women artists in the contemporary art world. Previous suppression undoubtedly fostered a more avid interest in the visual arts once the barriers were removed. Old world restrictions on the range of professions permissible to Jewish people affected both men and women. Women were especially limited in their possibilities since they were restricted by custom to crafts such as embroidery and the paper cut. My research indicates that the first Jewish woman to enter the mainstream of Western Art is Sonia Terk Delaunay. She shares her birth year, 1885, with my maternal grandmother, emphasizing for me how recently this world opened up to women such as myself.

Terk Delaunay was part of a circle of Jewish artists in the Parisian Bohemia of Montparnasse that did include other women such as Chana Orloff, who arrived in Paris from the Russian Ukraine in 1910, the same year as the much more famous Marc Chagall. France was seen as the symbol of political and religious freedom on account of the Napoleonic emancipation of the Jews from the ghettos of Western Europe. In the United States, it wasn't until the turn of the century that Jewish artists began to emerge. Many of the American male artists of the twentieth century have made minimal acknowledgment of their Jewish backgrounds. A fear of further marginalization seems to have governed their self-presentation. It has been principally among women artists of my generation that the more explicit ties to Judaism have been acknowledged. I feel that there are two factors at work here. First the marginalized status of women artists, especially in the 1960s and 1970s, gave them the courage to identify with unfashionable or dangerous categories. The second ingredient has been a strong, supportive Jewish women's community that has clearly embraced the cultural expression of women artists. I've been especially fortunate to have among my circle of friends women who are rabbis, theologians, and community activists.

The ordination of women rabbis has made a crucial difference in Jewish communal life, not only in congregations, but also on account of the rabbinical roles taken on by women in organizations and on college campuses. The first women rabbis were ordained in the early 1970s, so the 1990s represent a rich harvest of the progress made over the twenty years. The Los Angeles area has a strong female rabbinic presence and a highly acclaimed national model for creating women's community. The Jewish Feminist Center of the American Jewish Congress in Los Angeles was led by Rabbi Laura Geller, Southern California A.J. Congress, Executive Director, and Rabbi Sue Levi Elwell, Director of the Center for years. The current executive director is Carol Plotkin. They have created an innovative program of advocacy, education, and celebration over the past few years. The revival of the celebration of Rosh Hodesh, the welcoming ceremony for the new moon, the creation of ceremonies for weaning and menopause are examples of ways in which women's experiences have been hallowed.

Study and the creation of commentary has always been the cornerstone of the Jewish religious experience, although previously women were mostly excluded from the study of sacred texts. The Center is making up for lost time offering courses such as "The Texts of our Lives — New Life Cycle Rituals" and "In Search of our Mothers — Women in the Bible and the Quest for Modern Jewish Identity." Not only has the canon of what is appropriate to study changed, but the way we study has altered.

> a methodology for interpretation which makes sense for all of us, women as well as men, of our representation in or absence from the text. In order to appropriate the texts, we have to acknowledge kinship, build a bridge to the men who told and reasoned and transmitted them. In order to appropriate them as Torah, we have to approach them with the belief that they have something of value to say to us as Jews. For that reason alone, we must find ways to interpret these texts without absolving them of moral responsibility. Critique, then, is an important element of our feminist hermeneutic, but its function is not to tear down and destroy.[1]

Both the traditional and newer forms of study are rarely done alone. The paradigm is either a teacher with a small group of students, a group in which students may take turns leading the discussions or forming *chevrusa*, a pair of scholars studying together taking turns reading, and asking and answering questions. Above all else it is a model of active learning rather then the passive acceptance of knowledge. It integrates questions that relate to ethics, the diversity of personal experience, and a search for the wellsprings of meaning in a difficult world. This kind of study often has exceptional emotional and spiritual power, dimensions not usually associated with secular learning.

In order to understand the continuity of Jewish commentary it is useful to think of Jewish knowledge as a pyramid, with the *Torah*, or Five Books of Moses at the apex (the first five books of the Old Testament are referred to as the Torah but the term Torah can also encompass all Jewish sacred writing and commentary), along with the other primary parts of the Bible. Below that comes the *Talmud* which consists of the basic Jewish laws in life and religion. Underneath the *Talmud* extends the *Midrashic* texts, an interpretive level of commentary. The term *midrash* comes from the word meaning to seek or examine, and it consists of stories and parables which interpret the Torah for the purpose of teaching and religious inspiration.

While some Jews, especially the Orthodox, accept a code of conduct or practice, *Halacha*, there is no final authority for a Jew concerning interpretation. In the *Talmud*, Rabbis argued or reasoned in the name of other sages, often from earlier eras. The text rarely concludes with an absolute judgment. The various "responsa" and articles written today by Rabbis, theologians, and lay people continue this interactive tradition. In particular I see my art as an extension of the *midrashic* activity; creating narratives and images that illuminate the spirit and embody new meanings.

How does this primacy of study and discussion of texts affect the nature of the visual artist's practice?

Historically, the situation of the Jewish artist using religious sources has contrasted with that of an artist working in the Christian tradition. In Christendom, art was given a major role in programs of religious instruction, as well as in the glorification of God and the Church. The abstract nature of the Hebrew concept of God makes visual expression of the spiritual problematic. How can one express the ineffable in the specifics of a religion such as Judaism, which tends to privilege text over image and which has a profound anti-iconic bias. Many people over the course of history have interpreted the second commandment "you shall not make for yourself a graven image or any likeness of what is in the heavens above, or on the earth below" as a prohibition against the human figure or the "icon" in art.

While the primary textual sources in Judaism — the *Torah*, *Talmud*, and *Midrash* — are rich with descriptions, images, and stories, there is little in the way of visual manifestations in mainstream Western art, especially in prestigious media such as painting or sculpture. I would like to share with you the evolution of a few of the key images which I have created out of Jewish textual sources; the insights I have gleaned from study and interaction with my community and my teachers as well as a more inward search. In so doing, I continue a process of commentary and interpretation which is characteristic of Judaism as a living tradition. Among other concerns I bring to this task are feminist ones, in particular a critique of patriarchal assumptions. In a number of instances in my 94-foot drawing *The Scroll*, I have used women and men or women in roles normally assigned to men. For example, it is Rabbi Geller, who teaches a group of children and their parents, surrounded by an unrolled Torah scroll, rather than the more familiar male rabbinic figure.

The Scroll was conceived and completed over a period of three years in the mid 1980s. From the beginning, I envisioned it as a room-size installation in which a scroll would appear to float on the wall enveloping the viewer. I had previously produced two other large scale drawings, 13 feet and 24 feet respectively, in an attempt to transform drawing from an intimate medium to a monumental one which would create a spatial and temporal ordering of experience for the viewer. Scroll formats present special problems and opportunities for the artist, since compositional strategies that involve framing the image on four sides are no longer pertinent. I studied Asian scrolls, Jewish *megillahs*[2] and wimples, or Torah binders in order to expand the possibilities of interlinking visually the various sections of *The Scroll.*

The general structure of the scroll makes use of a formulation of the early twentieth century theologian Franz Rosensweig. He designated the six points of the Jewish star, or Mogen David, as two overlapping triads, the first consisting of God, Torah, and Israel and the second as Creation, Revelation, and Redemption. The latter triad defined the three major sections of *The Scroll* providing a framework for the narrative threads of the biblical Exodus, life-cycle rituals, seasonal holidays, and the twentieth century history of the Jewish people. I interwove these narratives to embrace both historicity and a sense of external recurrence. I feel as if I have built my imagery from every strata of Jewish history and experience. Giving the viewer access to all these interwoven images at the same time is crucial to the meaning of the work.

The concept of synchronicity is paramount in Judaism. The timelessness of eternal recurrence demands an interrelationship of past, present, and future which transcends clocks and calendars. In celebrating Passover, for example, we say, "When we went out of Egypt." We retell the story in each generation as if it were happening to us. Synchronicity also signifies that my visual commentary can be a discourse with others who have been dead for centuries, just as ages hence someone will engage in dialogue with my work. It is a form of immortality that has nothing to do with heaven. In addition, a sacred moment might give us a glimpse of eternity. My first notes on Creation associate God's creation of the world, "Ma-aseh Beashit," and the birth of a child. An experience common to many women can evolve the birth story of our world.

During that period of research and study, Rabbi Geller brought to my attention a midrashic story about the events immediately preceding birth. In the story, the soul is imagined in a translucent womb from whence it sees the world from end to end, and has perfect knowledge of the Torah (meaning in this case all the texts). The soul is comfortable and happy and resists being born. A messenger from God must descend, mark the soul on the upper lip, and then a child is

Identity in Community

born who has forgotten in that angelic touch all previous knowledge. In a series of performances in New York and Los Angeles in which I collaborated with Cantor Meredith Stone, the recitation for this section read:

> A child's soul is hovering over the water. The soul is stubborn. It has perfect knowledge of the Torah and does not want to leave the comfort of the womb. An angel descends and presses it, just between the nose and mouth, leaving an indentation. The soul must now enter the imperfect world forgetting everything it knew. The touch of the angel is a mark we all carry. We spend our lives relearning what we lost.[3]

The midrashic story was a catalyst in my quest to interpret Creation. An important aspect of this reinterpretation was its incorporation of previously neglected or suppressed areas of women's experience. The first stage of the Jewish feminist movement centered around issues of equal access to roles and rituals as well as the privileges of Halacha. In writing on the second stage of the movement, Rabbi Geller affirms "that women overcome their marginality by declaring that their experience is Jewish, even though women's experience might have been overlooked by many of our sacred texts or rituals. The second stage begins with the commitment that women's voices are Jewish voices, that we can recover them from our history and our canon if we pay attention to the questions our experience moves us to ask."[4]

I wanted to imagine Creation in a way that not only did not exclude women but was also informed by my own experience of pregnancy, giving birth, and child rearing. Put another way, I was searching for the antithesis of that great icon of Western tradition: Michelangelo's *The Creation of Adam* on the Sistine Chapel ceiling. The image of God as a white bearded male whose touch transmits the divine spark to the ideal male figure, Adam, is at the core of our sense of exclusion. Also for a Jew such a direct depiction of God is prohibited and therefore disturbing. Curiously, in my configuration of messenger and soul some aspect of the weightlessness and billowing cloth of Michelangelo's fresco lingers. In *The Scroll* my figures are clothed and posed in such a way that their genders are not disclosed. Both men and women can identify with them. The messenger's eyes are closed and the soul/baby gazes expectantly at the angel. It is the instant of knowing/not knowing, a moment outside of time. The floating figures on the rippling white sheet overlap a dark liquid space in which we see the scrunched, straining face of the newborn emerging from the birth canal. This image is overlaid on the parting of the Red Sea beyond which one sees a column of figures moving between pillars of smoke and fire. Among the texts that informed this passage is Exodus 13:21: "Adonai went before them in a pillar of cloud by day, to guide them along the way, and in a pillar of fire by night, to give them light, that they might travel day and night."

Reinforcing the theme of a scroll, within a scroll, within a scroll, this cluster of images is connected to the next major nexus of the narrative, the ritual of circumcision or "Brit Milah," by an undulating cloth wimple. This binder for the Torah was often made from the swaddling cloth used to wrap male infants during the ceremony "Brit Milah." In those cases the wimple is both a birth certificate and the infant's swaddling cloth. It ties the child to the Torah and to its heritage in a symbolic manner, as it literally binds the cloth around the Torah.[5] The custom of embroidering or painting the wimple began in Germany in the sixteenth Century, spreading through much of Northern Europe and to America. In elaborate Hebrew calligraphy, each banner was inscribed with the relevant facts of the child's birth and a prayer; "May his life be blessed in Torah, the marriage canopy (*huppah*), and in righteous deeds. Amen." Many wimples included a marriage scene and some were decorated with flowers, birds, and other fanciful creatures. The one which directly inspired my drawing is from the collection of the Skirball Museum and features a particular delightful mermaid.[6] Although the wimple is charming it also serves another agenda, as it allows me to incorporate the folk art that women of my tradition were allowed to do. In the words of feminist art historian Thalia Gouma-Peterson, "The Torah wimple in its passage through time is a subtext, the commentary of the colonized on official history. For this secondary voice, Ruth Weisberg claims equal authority, not as a fixed entity but, like the wimple, in changing patterns, configurations, and colors."[7]

The technique with which I executed *The Scroll* involved pencil and ink washes. This allowed for passages of great transparency and liquidity heightening the quality of interpenetration and flow among the various images. In addition, I treated the messenger and the soul as an isolated image in a related lithograph from 1986 entitled *Awakening*. Lithography can also be a wash medium with the qualities of transparency and fluidity which this image required. The lithograph allowed a more dramatic silhouette of the figures. In *Awakening* the pale figures sail across the blue field which suggests both cloth and rippling water.

Conceptually perhaps the most difficult of all sections of the Scroll was the one concerning Revelation, since intrinsically it alluded to the unimaginable, the indefinable, and the awesome. In Exodus 19:21 the warning against seeing God is distinct from the prohibition against depicting God. "Adonai said to Moses, Go down, warn the people not to break through to Adonai to gaze, lest many of them perish." In this middle section I expanded the 4 1/2-foot scroll to two tiers in order to accommodate the vertical axis of the inverted Tree of Life. This Kabbalistic image of *Etz Chaim* has its roots in heaven and its branches among us. The upper portion of the scroll is dominated by Mt. Sinai and is purposely without figuration. As Nancy Berman describes it, "The upper tier is devoid of figuration focusing on the abstract, holy and mysterious nature of revelation. The scale is larger than the rest of the work evoking the cosmic, visionary and divine realm."[8]

A way to depict God's revelation eluded me for a time. In the end Josephus's description of the Sanctuary of the Temple in Jerusalem provided a clue. The Holy of Holies was protected by huge golden doors in front of which was hung a curtain of Babylonian cloth embroidered with blue, scarlet, purple, and linen thread. Worked into the tapestry was a map of the stars.[9] A curtain that protected the Holy of Holies might veil God's countenance as well, so in The Scroll at the intersection of mountain, tree, and upward path is a luminous curtain subtly inscribed with a map of the constellations.

In 1991 I had cause to recall my solution to representing Revelation when I was asked by Loyola Marymount University in Los Angeles to do a major sculptural installation on the theme of Passover. I created a metaphorical landscape from metal, sand, stone, and paper that encompassed both Exodus and Revelation. In a space measuring approximately 25 feet by 35 feet, a 9-foot stone passage leads to a curving metal ladder which seems to melt into the back wall. The ladder arches over a seabed of raked sand on the floor and a 20-foot paper scroll on the wall. I remembered the difficult lesson of The Scroll and omitted any figural representations, choosing instead to see the viewer as the figure in this sacred landscape. For Passing Over I designed and had fabricated a metal structure which housed over two tons of flagstone. The tunnel-like structure suggests many possibilities: the dark narrow place though which we must pass in order to be liberated from slavery or oppression; or, since I applied brick red paint to the lintel of this structure, it might read as the houses of the Hebrews that God passed over, sparing their lives. Also, the stones stacked like books and the scroll which run perpendicular to it reinforce the idea of Jews as people of the Book. The 20-foot scroll recapitulates to some extent the part of The Scroll done several years earlier, which also alludes to Revelation. Here Mt. Sinai is haloed in smoke, inspired by Exodus 19:18: "Now Mount Sinai was all in smoke, for adonai had come down upon it in fire; the smoke rose like the smoke of a kiln, and the mountain trembled violently." The 1991 piece is augmented by a system of lights which divide in the center and chase constantly outward, giving the impression of the dividing of the waters as well as the lightning storm and the shifting of the earth. I have aimed in this work for both a sense of the difficulty of deliverance from oppression, whether real or internalized, and the sense of awe and wonder we might feel in the presence of God's Revelation.[10]

A large-scale narrative installation "Sisters and Brothers" completed that recontextualizes a biblical story in a timeless present. I chose the story of Jacob as the basis of my narrative, as I was attracted by its archetypal and transformational aspects as it moves from episodes of betrayal and struggle to reconciliation and connection to the sacred. I was also drawn to the symmetry of the stories of two brothers, Jacob and Esau, and two sisters, Leah and Rachel. During the course of my study of the text with Rabbi Laura Geller and Rabbi Daniel Landes, I came to understand the submerged nature of the matriarch's voices. I now see my installation as a reclamation of Leah and Rachel's stories.

This project also allows me to synthesize two of the great influences in my life — the Italian Renaissance and Jewish tradition. Stimulated by Marilyn Lavin's study of mural decoration in Italian churches as well as other art historical research, I spent five months in Italy in order to study the Renaissance's inventive articulation of mural-size fresco narratives within architectural interiors. My long sojourn in Rome also gave me an opportunity to experience the spatial compression and dynamic playfulness of Borromini's architecture. While not specifically Baroque, my plans for the current project benefited immensely from Borromini's lessons in transcendent space.

While the Italian Renaissance provides elaborate variations on narrative disposition they are also tied to programs of Christian theology. My intention is to create extended narratives that embody Jewish sources and theology. Not since the third century synagogue in Dura Europos in the ancient near east have our stories taken on a large-scale pictorial format in an architecturally articulated space.

Art can have profound aesthetic and kinesthetic effects on the viewer. Our reactions to images combine intellectual, emotional, and intuitive elements which together lend themselves to an experience of the spiritual. I believe in the power of art to shape both beliefs and experience. Inspired by the traditional texts of Judaism, and as part of a dynamic and interactive community, I can act as the visual equivalent of the commentator; I am free to draw out meaning between the lines.[11]

Warrior Council
by Michelle T. Clinton

Michelle T. Clinton is an award-winning African-American poet and performance artist now residing in Berkeley, California who is committed to empowering women through her writing and performance art. I saw her do the performance from which the title of this poem is taken, in which she "dropped the fourth wall of the stage," which is to say she addressed the audience directly and spoke about the importance of self-defense for women. Clinton is clearly one of the outstanding heirs of the Black oratorial tradition: her spoken words broke through my fear and resistance to move me deeply. She followed the compelling articulation of her manifesto with a demonstration, asking for a volunteer — a woman, of course — from the audience with whom she demonstrated some of the basic techniques in self-defense.

Clinton's art is directed to redefining on a broad cultural level what it means to be a woman, by urging all of us to shed the dreary, oppressive mantle of victimization and don the scintillating robes of heroism. Clinton, who was a featured artist in the 1993 Los Angeles Festival, was interviewed in the *Los Angeles Times*, in August 1993. There she asserted, "The city has become more angry and more dangerous. And that's balanced with the wealth and decadence. It keeps me looking at . . . the strength of the human spirit to recover. The multicultural forces feed my hope."

the time in the cave was time well spent
     our girl hero is born
     the dark & the soil
     the perfect molecular spark
     so start off the live baby girl
     her mouth sucked in voices
     her eyes as mirror shine
     dumb as a duck that copied
     clean as a fax machine
     xeroxes of her parents time

it's a trap, you know, we are all born into a trap
     all infants dwarfed by the cathedrals of culture
     like the fossils of dinosaurs too big to rot

monuments of how we do things around here
how we gonna keep doing things
& how you, sweet baby girl, will fit exactly
see these pink booties
this plastic dollie
she wets, she pees
don't squat when you play marbles
you're not a boy you know
practice dress up
you're so cute
like a bunny, like a declawed cat, an angel on a diet
we enjoy looking at you
but cover up that messy opening: keep your ankles tight
don't let that smell get out

the inner world of the self
cradled in the home front of the family
all she needed was sweet & sour breast milk
& sleeping & passing gas
the harsh light she fell into
warned her she was really a hero
even if the blanket was pink
prepare for assault
the home front had sneaky ways
creepy ways of entering your body
& colonizing your thinking space

the first atrocity was the abomination of the man of kin
the exiled man who grew ugly
outside the nest of child rearing
whose sadness mutated into an evil
too gross to look at
whose cloak was the language of secrets
his power the silence of dysfunction
the first atrocity was penetration by flesh of kin
he molested her, or incested her, or raped her,
she confessed twenty years later on the oprah winfrey show
i thought he was peeing in my mouth
while donahue & montel & sally jessy rafael
said across the national head waves
you need a good cry
you could use a session w/ therapy man

backwards in time the patriarchal head waves told our girl hero
        you don't need to fight
        you're too pretty to make a fist
        too weak to pick up a weapon
        too sweet to use the evil eye
        cause daddy will protect you
        brothers will guard you
        plus law man & jesus man shelter you from harshness

the second atrocity is the man of love gone crazy w/ rage
        the beatings inside domestic boundaries
        the wine glass broken & inserted
        knife man eats dinner w/ the frustrated spouse
        the stranger who stalks wants to be in the movies
        somebody thinks fear is sexy
        some liar feeds to lies to these men

the third atrocity of the cavern of fear for females
        freezing us into victim-ness
        the swamps of bad movies
        w/ frailty & terror as sexy girl stars
        we run — we're always captured
        we scream — they gag our fight
        the final atrocity is what is left in our minds
        timid skinny women
        incapable of self defense

sister cousins of the girl hero picked up their teeth
        & organized training camps of women
        ready for gun defense
        ready to stop whining & weeping
        ready for prayers to the goddess of war
armies of women body guards & women psychics
        sent out the subversive message
        it's good to take a stance
        our lady of the swift kick
it's right to land a tight fist in the throat of male aggressors
        the pacifism of good girls is weak as an open window
        to a deranged man

i just wanna tell you about the girl hero
        the colors in her meditation practices

always blue & black & red
for the dead woman behind us
the wounded woman inside us
I just want you to know about the girl hero
the water she breaks when she prays
the fear she defeats w/ self love ritual
her muscles tough & not angry
her heart prepared to punch target
the fist feminine & clenched
hear now about the girl hero
the woman who calms inner violence
the women centered in her breath
the quiet she loves in darkness
i just want to walk on the beach at night
i just want to trust strangers & smile for anybody
i want to be forgiven all history, all personal hurt
i want you to know there is a girl hero
a woman who will fight
a woman who defends the peace centers
who wants quiet & fun & healthy lovers
she is pure as an animal
ancient as death & mourning
the mythology she writes
the vision she reads by renegade women mystics
we uncover healers & muscular mothers & warriors who sing
we re-write the word of the universe
with power women with power weapons
that a woman's love
grows w/ combat knowledge:

know your enemy as you know yourself
resist assault
resist psychic death as you find yourself

i just want you to know about the girl hero's need for peace
i want the globe to birth open safe places for her feet

The Secret Community

by Amy Carr & Lisa Carr

Amy and Lisa were born, four minutes apart, in March 1965. They were raised in the suburbs of Philadelphia. "Our first collaborative work of art was a figurative crayon mural drawn on the entire length of the hallway. We were two years old and blamed it on our newborn sister! We both wanted to be artists from as early as we can remember."

Amy and Lisa both graduated from the Kutztown University of Pennsylvania with BFA degrees in painting. In college they discovered their own distinct styles: Lisa abstract and Amy figurative.

The most important day of both their lives was the day that Lisa almost died in an accident. It was the day they "split" and discovered the limitations of their bond, but also the cohesiveness of it. It was the first time they ever felt separate or alone. "I think I always took our relationship for granted. I remember the doctor telling me Lisa might not survive her surgery, and suddenly I felt empty. There was no way for me to even comprehend myself as being just My Self. I always thought of myself as Two."

"After the accident, we realized how precious life was and began to pursue ideas we were previously too shy to try, among them, traveling to Europe. We backpacked and camped through ten different countries. Oh, the stories we can tell!" It was during their journey that Amy started writing poetry and music in her head. When she returned home, she bought a guitar and taught herself how to play by transcribing what she'd heard in her head. She became a closet musician.

Lisa went to California to get her MFA in painting at the Claremont Graduate School. She ended up living in Los Angeles for three and a half years. Her paintings have been exhibited in shows across America. She has written articles and reviews in art catalogues, journals and magazines, such as *Visions Art Quarterly*.

Amy stayed in Philadelphia and decided to work through her shyness by forming her own band. "I always felt very isolated while painting, but with music, I was creating in front of people and they were reacting and sometimes interacting with me. It's been very challenging to interpret fear and passion and hate and vulnerability and love into music and then try to get it all across in a live setting."

It wasn't until Lisa returned home to Pennsylvania that they realized she also had an ear for music. "Music was as obvious to me as abstraction. For years I'd grown accustomed to creating alone, I didn't realize how singular painting could be. Then I started to learn about the process of structuring and recording and performing songs. Amy and I have started to write lyrics together. Even though I'm not the one on stage, I've been completely invested in the songs from their conception and that must translate, because people from the audience approach me after Amy's gigs without fail and poor Amy ends up packing the gear!" Amy and Lisa both co-produced and designed Amy's latest recording, "I Divide."

Lisa and Amy have also written a novel entitled *Twin Tongue*. "Our book is not a collaborative effort, it is written in *one* voice by *two* people. It was 'twin writ' —meaning one of us would start a sentence, idea, or section and the other would finish — our writing melded into one. Even now it's hard for us to distinguish who wrote what! Our novel is one of myth, deception, language, longing and love — love as seen through the eyes of twins."

"We see new books and recordings and paintings in our future; each new creation involving *all* of the different languages we've learned. And most importantly, each new creation being done together - life's too short to work alone."

We always shared.

Ours was a community, stable and whole; an island of two. We lived in a secluded cavity that was designed to keep all other prototypes out. Daily, we bathed in mumbled words from the outside, soft blue echoes of a language unknown to us. Our living conditions were not suitable for two, but we accepted those constraints, we grew accustomed to such cramped quarters, as anyone would when their destiny was so certain. We were aligned, our hearts beat in even tempo. Inside, our sole motto was "communion" and to it we remained true, until the day we members were born. Two, and of the same genes, we were torn from our womb community and labeled at once: Identical Twins. The starched nurses wrapped us and laid us down in two separate plastic sterile milk-warm compartments. It was our first day in this new place. We were now to live in a world where independence and individuality were proclaimed ideal.

They looked upon us as an object of fascination and, most presumably, of envy. Our Four eyes, Four legs, Four arms, Two hearts. . . . "This is not natural," they said. "This has got to stop." Spectacles slipping down their noses, the experts all agreed, our oneness was unhealthy, a separation would be the most sensible therapy. Possibly they mistrusted our bond, or possibly they just couldn't see. We didn't know. The individuals socialized us, it's true, but in secrecy our community was as strong as it had been in the early days; we believed in its endurance, valued its connections, honored its differences. We drew solidarity high above our heads in a perfect circle. Two times for luck. We were equal and whole. The other community's methods of union seemed quite deceitful and highly unattainable to us. Their members would go off on a lifelong search to find someone whom they could feel safe with and trust. T...R...U...S...T... five letters tattooed on our souls. There we were, waving at them from the finish line of their doubling race, offering them water and a dry towel. "So nice of you Two

Identity in Community

to participate," they'd eye us suspiciously. "You *were* in the running - weren't you?" We were supportive, but behind closed doors we would laugh at their clamoring! How odd they were to disapprove of our connection, when their own predilections led them to do the same. Each individual stood so self-contained and self-governed, tall, buttons done, collar tight, they were ready to take on the world as one, but inside they were all knotted to the same inclination: the fear of being alone.

You make me twinge like a tender skin
stretched to smooth its folds
Sunken in deep
I see what you hide
You use your skin to territorialize
and divide

We always connected.

The incentives to do so were made clear. We received endless attention in exchange for exhibiting an identical image. Effortlessly, we matched. And as we expected, when encroached upon by society (or the casual passer-by), our appearance was assumed to be our most meaningful connection. Hasty Hasty Hasty. We hid our differences beneath twin grins, nurturing their growth discreetly. Solemnly. You see, we'd seen difference used as a tool all too often, and it shone with deception:

diversity . . . *discord*
singularity . . . *abnormality*
exception . . . *prejudice*
variance . . . *hate*

Their Society ushered the concept of difference out of its equation for a healthy community, and, in doing so, it encouraged a superficial identity, it enabled a half-truth. Surviving among these contradictions was as confusing as it must have been for them. But still our unit was a two-way mirror of hope; we disguised ourselves as One but we were actually balanced and Two. We both longed for the day when their community's thin expectations of image would shatter. Patiently we waited. And waited.

Wait till time uncovers and reveals
your marks of presence
Wait till time unwinds
the logic of its frustrating codes
Wait till time persuades
all excess to simply flake away
Leaving behind the colors of you in sight
reflections of your life

We always created.

It was the only way we had to decipher our seemingly nonsensical codes. Our community was clearly connected, but always in the most illogic of ways; shared dreams, shared voice, shared pain, shared fingerprints, shared knowing; these were connections which were anchored in the abstract notions of links and ties. No matter how hidden and basic they seemed, we honored them as relevant and real.

Tight brown suits everywhere. We were surrounded by their community's system of logic and all of its constraints. Nervously though, we ventured out, trying to find a satellite community or a larger community, one where we could transpose our twin language. The art world in all of its dimensions seemed to be the perfect place. They asked us separately for ID - name: address: birthday: race: telephone: occupation. They told us to be more specific, an artist was too broad a label. Having our distinctions already established, we both chose different titles; One music and One paint. They were satisfied. We created. But soon, burnt umber with a dab of alizarin crimson and E minor became the same exact word. We began to hear color and see lyrics and taste the sweetness of ambiguity and feel the sweep of our arms throwing their ID cards away. Somehow our distinctions blended, leaving us lost for an understanding of their community's desire for specialization. It was as if our souls were ingrained with a twin imprint; either consciously in collaboration, or subconsciously in psychic whims, we always returned to communal ways.

In solemn union we choose to go against the pull of the individual and into the balance of our own knowing. Our situation centers itself in the knowledge of the round, for our rules never posit themselves outside our own limits. How safe we feel in recognizing the strength of our community! We are fortunate to have such a privilege of comfort; Our Self; Our Selves. Although the scar of culture has branded its presence on our double identity, we know that it will never penetrate the soul that lies deep inside our secret community.

Amy Carr &
Lisa Carr

Hand Made Histories

by Polly Chu & Sarah Lejeune

Polly Chu is an abstract painter and teaches English as a Second Language. She was born in the early 1960s in Los Angeles, five years after her parents emigrated from Taiwan. Her parents were born in pre-communist China and both escaped to Taiwan before the "door" closed. Polly's mother's immediate family had all escaped to Taiwan previously, but her father was the only member of his family to leave China. Her parents met and fell in love in Taiwan before moving to the United States to start a new life.

Sarah Lejeune is a sculptor, and an installation and performance artist who tells stories and works as an urban planner. She was born in the late 1950s, the year her father became an American citizen. Both her parents were born in England. Her father's family emigrated to California after World War I, but her father returned to England to fight in World War II. At the end of the war, her parents met, married, and decided to settle on the East Coast of the United States. Sarah moved to California in 1990.

Polly and Sarah met at the Claremont graduate school, where they began to tell each other stories and received their Masters in Fine Arts in 1992. "Hand Made Histories" is a work in progress.

Looking At China/*Polly*

I'm sitting on a balcony in the New Territories of Hong Kong that is not unlike my balcony at home — facing mountains. But right now I am looking at China. It is only 10 minutes away by car, but I won't go there. I have come from almost halfway around the planet and I will stay ten minutes away. Actually, I had no idea I would be so close. It still looks distant and misty and silent.

Homeland/*Sarah*

On an English lawn, a green and pleasant lawn, my mother realizes that she has done something irrevocable. It is a tea party, a gathering of English cousins in a garden, to celebrate her younger children's first visit to England. Everyone is eating strawberries and devonshire cream, but her own children devour the delicacy. We are larger, clumsier and our clothes are designed to withstand sagebrush. This cultivated lawn is too small. We are proud, not knowing the polite British habit of self-deprecation. Confounded by ancient protocol, we call everyone by their first name, or nothing at all, addressing them as peers. We are shy, unamusing and silent, studying these fine, small blades of grass growing from such soft, damp dirt. In my garden at home, the grass is wide and sturdy, and the earth is red, crumbly in the heat, or slippery clay with rain.

She sees that her children are finally and uncontrollably American. She is English. In the States, they seem quite normal, even special, they are hers. Now, here, in her homeland, they are clearly foreign. She never thought she would give birth to foreigners.

Ethnicity/*Polly*

I am finally starting to like the idea of being Chinese. I was born in America. Even though Chinese was my first language, I refused to speak it after I got to school and discovered that everyone else was speaking English. When I was 6 years old, I asked my mother if I could have blond hair for my birthday. After that I developed a distaste for Chinese food. I wanted to have what everyone else was having every night — hamburgers. And as an adolescent, I would fantasize about what I would look like if I were white.

Now I am trying to learn my first language again. I practice with a Berlitz tape that my aunt's Caucasian husband lent to me. My parents are quick to point out Caucasian friends and acquaintances who speak better Chinese than I do. And I love Chinese food now but sometimes only know the Americanized Cantonese names for the dishes. (We speak Mandarin.)

I feel good about Taoism, Tai Chi Chuan, Chinese medicine, poetry, painting, calligraphy, and all those early inventions (as if I had anything to do with any of them!).

It's also great to see Chinese people in films now — I only had to wait about 28 years.

Recently, I saw a Chinese film that takes place in China in the early part of this century. It was about a rich man and his four wives. It was an incredible film, but everyone besides the main character was monstrously horrible. The scary thing is that I don't think it was much of an exaggeration. I have heard stories of tremendous cruelty, even in my own family.

And then there's Tibet. I once thought (I'm embarrassed to admit) that Tibetans were a Chinese minority group. I felt a completely undeserved pride by distant association. Then I found out how Tibet became part of China and how it is kept that way. I read that there are more prisons in Tibet than monasteries. I don't feel proud any more, but I'm still glad to say I'm Chinese now when people ask.

Ethnicity is funny that way.

Tea/*Sarah*

We are sharing rice pudding that someone else has made.

The rice isn't right, says Polly. Her mother loves, knows, and cooks rice the way another person might be particular about wine.

I would never admit that I like my rice the English way, soggy and unrefined, preferably burned on the bottom. I am faced with generations of expertise, and I am an amateur.

We all agree, more or less, on tea, Polly and I and our mothers. The water must be poured on the leaves while boiling, not a second after. Tea bags are a barbaric but useful invention, for haste and guests who need options, but our civilized palates can taste the paper. The tea must be served in the finest porcelain or glass, to protect the flavor.

There is no awkwardness around this common ritual. Our friendship strengthens over infinite cups of tea. As with my mother, the difficult words, sadness or hidden anger, ease themselves over out tongues and settle in the teacups. Thoughts loosen and fall away from structure to follow the floating, saturated leaves.

I am relieved to find something so clearly shared, a cultural similarity rather than difference. I wish for tea as proof of the universal, respite from whiteness, respite from difference.

But it is not really my whiteness that haunts me, but history, the history of being white. This custom I claim as my own history is stolen. The Chinese gave the English tea. They gave them the ritual of porcelain. These are the much mannered and domesticated remnants of violence.

Hatred/*Polly*

Two years ago I saw a deeply moving performance. It was a drum performance by a children's Taiko drum group. I know very little about Taiko drumming except that it is a traditional Japanese art. To me, it is a pure and disciplined release of energy and celebration. What a good practice for a child as preparation for later challenges. It's something I'd really like to participate in. But it's problematic for me because I'm a Chinese-American adult and not a Japanese-American child.

Last week I read an article about the "forgotten holocaust," that is, the massive slaughter of Chinese people by Japanese soldiers during the Japanese invasion of China. The sheer cruelty is horrifying, without the estimate of 30,000,000 dead (350,000 alone in the Nanking Massacre). Death by skewering seems to have been a particular favorite; that was because they were trying to save bullets while they murdered all these people. Asian thriftiness. After all, genocide can be expensive. And think how much discipline it took to kill so many people! Amputating arms and legs as a cure for gunshot wounds . . . why did they bother? Why didn't they just kill them then and there? The breadth of cruelty is astounding, everywhere in the world. The desire to see the hated one not only obliterated but suffering intensely first. But with the Chinese and Japanese, what has always confused me was how one culture could adapt so much of another's culture and then turn around and slaughter the people who created the culture.

It's like when Sarah casually mentioned the connection between the colonization of China and the excellent collection of Asian masterpieces in Boston. You know, the tea and opium trade, where those wealthy and respectable New England families got their money. How did those people convince themselves that they were superior to these other people whose art they were carting away by the truckloads to admire at home? What is it we hate anyway, the worst or the best?

So, reading about that "forgotten holocaust" aroused a twinge of anti-Japanese sentiment in me, something I have generally only felt in my parents, something they only talk about on rare occasions. When we make travel plans, my mother tells me that my father is not interested in going to Japan. He suffered too much during their occupation of China. Not only were the Japanese horribly cruel wherever they went in China, but now many Japanese conservatives categorically deny all stories. They have even managed to write — or, rather, unwrite — the whole episode out of their history books.

But my practical dilemma is that every Sunday I go to a Japanese Zen temple to sit [in meditation]. (In fact, it's the same temple that sponsors the Japanese children's Taiko drum group.) Of course, Zen originally came from China (where it no longer exists), but this temple is definitely Japanese. I remember what a hard time I had sitting after a friend told me how she had been deeply hurt by the Japanese parents of her godchild. They implied that she wasn't really good enough to spend so much time around their child because she wasn't Japanese.

So, after all this, how can I, a Chinese person, admire Japanese art, poetry, aesthetics, gardens, textiles, and food so much?

This is what my mother wonders.

How does my mother feel about a place where her daughter refused her culture, language, and food?

This is what I wonder.

Recently, I heard that the Taiko drums were originally used to call a village together or to define its boundaries.

Enemies/*Sarah*

My mother tells a story of being shot at by a German sniper on a street in London. Losing her sense, and contrary to instruction, she huddled upright against a building instead of throwing herself to the ground. She could see the bullets ricocheting around her, and only then understood why she should have been flat on the sidewalk. She could see the gunner. She met his eyes and describes his expression as evil. "He wanted to kill me; I could see it in his face." She is still indignant that he should have shot at her, a woman. She was wearing her officer's uniform. She thinks of herself first as a woman still, not an officer. If there was ever a legitimate target, she was one. I hope I will never have to understand that particular indignity, knowing you don't deserve to die, whatever you're wearing.

When I was thirteen, we traveled in Europe. We had to take the train through Germany, and I understood that there was nothing to see, so we didn't get off.

In Italy, my father glared at the German tourists, choosing to sit on the opposite side of the restaurant. He muttered about their loudness and ostentation, their obvious wealth. To me, they looked like us, but were better dressed. A mother, a father, and two teenage children, who laughed and ate, and felt like foreigners in a beautiful place.

When the Berlin Wall came down, my father exulted in the success of democracy. He spent a career battling the economic influence of communism in developing countries. Yet, he cannot help but feel threatened by a unified Germany.

He is the son of a soldier who was gassed in World War I, and he was a soldier himself in World War II.

Not Japanese/*Polly*

I bought coffee and toothpaste from a woman who had a small stand in Bali. As I walked away, I heard her sneer to someone else, "Japon." I wanted to turn around and state for what seemed like the millionth time, "No! I am not Japanese!" (I, who admire so many Japanese things.) But it was just too complicated to explain to her. I'm Chinese and in fact my own mother hates the Japanese for the same reasons you do. And the more I thought about it, the more I began to realize that I could just as easily have been Japanese-American and then where would I be? I wouldn't be able to say, "No, I'm not Japanese," and deflect that hatred.

Lower Case/*Sarah*

My last name is French. It means "the young," as in "the son of" or "junior." On my father's side, my ancestors were Huguenots, Protestants in a Catholic land. They were persecuted for their religion and economic power, massacred, chased out of France. Someone in my family, my grandfather I think, told me that the Huguenots changed the uppercase "J" in the name to a lower case "j" to distinguish themselves from the Catholics. Someone else told me that this is not true. To escape the hatred of the French Catholic nobility, the Huguenots fled to Germany, Switzerland, and Holland, and then, in succeeding generations, to European colonies in North American and Africa. Many of the Dutch, not called Afrikaners, who went to South Africa had Huguenot origins. My ancestors went from France to Germany to Switzerland to England and then to the United States. If my children are born here, it will be the first time that two generations have stayed in the same country for as far back as we know.

Les Beaux is a beautiful little town in Provence, a medieval village atop a bluff that looks out over what seems to be the whole of Southern France. This town is famous for its two three-star restaurants and for a Huguenot massacre. I remember sitting in the patio of one of the restaurants, nestled at the base of the spectacular cliffs, while my father read from the guidebook how the king's army chased hundreds of protestants over the cliffs to their deaths on the rocks where we sat.

Louis XVI used Huguenots for target practice in the gardens of Versailles. As a child, I imagined Huguenots, dressed like pictures of pilgrims, chased into the center of boxwood mazes, cornered by dazzling aristocrats, and shot like rabbits.

A few years ago, I spent the day on the grounds of Versailles, sketching the orderly lines of trees, planned vistas, and the row-planted forests. My heart wanted to live in the rational loveliness, but I was thinking it would be hard to hide here. The chase could have been a fairer sport than I imagined, wits against gunpowder. Some must have escaped, rescued by the night, or by a game keeper. There were survivors whose great-grandchildren settled in exotic lands.

I know South African refugees who associate my name with hatred. They know people with my name, the descendants of the hunted, who believe they have a right to persecute.

Hands/*Polly*

My parents and one of their tenants, Ram, are going on a trip to Turkey. I am driving them to the airport. Ram is from the Philippines and so we are speaking English. Suddenly my mother starts speaking Chinese. She starts talking with her hands. "My right hand is ugly and my left hand is beautiful. This hand is my mother's hand and that hand is my father's. My mother's hand is ugly and my father's hand is beautiful."

It seemed like some kind of cryptic message — this strange information about her hands, out of the blue and in a private language — but I couldn't decode it.

Porcelain/*Sarah*

My mother is very proud of her old China plates. They have occupied a position of privilege in both of her houses in this country, displayed upright on the top shelves in the living room. In California, they wear little harnesses so they can't fall in an earthquake.

We share a love of ceramics. Not long ago, in her seventies, she took up working with clay again. I treasure the few things she made for me before she gave it up. They are humble, round, and useful.

My mother is the keeper of treasure and history, her house filled with the things that we and others have made. When Polly came to stay in the house, I showed her a ceramic bowl I had made, based on a Chinese porcelain in the Boston Museum of Fine Arts. Polly's delight inspired me to search for something my mother had made, a small hand-built celadon green vase. I found it outside in the potting cupboard. It is beautiful, Asian in its simplicity. Polly put it in a place of privilege, in the living room, setting it carefully on an antique Chinese end table between two old cloisonné bowls. "It belongs here," she said, "with these Asian things."

I thought, but didn't say, "These inherited things." These old things that came from my ancestors, the China traders. They were packed and brought here once, already symbols of the history of my family and their travels. The history of the objects, their makers and original owners, was erased long ago.

Before I met Polly, I didn't know much about the British participation in the China Trade. I thought that owning Chinese antiques was considered a good thing. These were precious objects, mourned over when broken and parceled out carefully by my grandmother as gifts of preference. I have a very old ginger jar she gave me. It is worth a lot, my mother says. It is glazed in shades of gray.

When I go to Polly's parents' house, there are not antiques.

I know ceramics through the collection in the Boston Museum. That museum is filled with fine ancient Chinese vessels, artifacts of opium trading brought to this country by the old Boston shipping families. The British and other Europeans plundered old China of its wealth, scuttling the economy, co-opting the culture and ripening China for the devastation of the twentieth century. In Polly's family, someone was addicted to opium and brought the family to ruin. I can't remember the details; in my mind, they are obscured by sadness and anger.

Polly was sleeping in my mother's house. I was left awake with the objects in the living room, the precious icons of my family's history that have been moved across nations. Objects are vessels for feelings. The plates looked down from their shelves to the collection on the table, the two old bowls, artists forgotten, and my mother's vase.

My mother's plates are old. They were made in China for some seafaring ancestor to glorify his coat of arms. The design is curious. The medieval heraldry, formal and European, symbol of feudalism, is surrounded by fluid and complex Chinese dragons and peonies. The center shield was partially painted over more than a hundred years ago, when marriage to a grander family meant changing the coat of arms. The "new" design is a cloudy dark blue, a different glaze, applied by some lesser English craftsman. As a child, I never understood my mother's love for these things. Even then, they looked strange, a mismatched sensibility, history forcing itself on design.

I am ashamed. In the morning, Polly and I sit in the gracious room, and I do not show her the plates. I need her to think of my mother as the artist who built the vase. I am that artist's daughter. While we speak of our dreams, I can see the plates above her head, vibrating as if they could leap and shatter our closeness. And I say nothing. Who were those old British sailors, commissioning hybrid porcelain in the country they plundered? I didn't know them; I am many generations removed. I am innocent. I wear the rubies they brought home.

Full Moon/*Polly*

This year was a good year for crab. Last night, we celebrated "August 15." The fifteenth day of the eighth month is a special holiday for the Chinese. Last night, I learned that it started out as an end-of-harvest celebration. What it means for us non-farmers is a special family celebration in which we all get together and eat fresh crab and moon cakes and look at the full moon. It's always full because this is a lunar calendar date. On "August 15," the full moon is the largest and brightest of the year. Families who can't be together look up at the big, bright moon and think of their loved ones, knowing that they are also gazing at the same moon and thinking of them.

This year, my family spent "August 18" together since I had to work on the night of "August 15." My parents, my grandmother, my husband and I feasted on huge, sweet, tender crabs and champagne. We sat outside under the no-longer-full moon.

My husband's family originally came from England. My grandmother (who speaks only Chinese) asked my husband (who speaks only English) if he had ever been to England. Then she told us that when she went to England, she discovered that the soil there is extremely poor. My mother then explained that most Chinese people don't like the British, some of whom made fabulous fortunes selling opium in China. In fact, my grandmother's father spent all their money on opium and then ran away with another woman, leaving my grandmother to a childhood of knitting sweaters to survive.

But now, ever since my grandmother tried digging into British soil and found it to be very poor, with rocks just under the surface, she no longer curses the British. She feels sorry for them now and says she understands that they went to other places and stole things because they were such a poor country. She told us that the weeds in China are taller than the crops in England.

Photographs/*Sarah*

Polly showed me photographs that her grandfather took. These are pictures of the ground, old black and white photos of the earth, ruts in a road and puddles. These photos were left with her, not explained, just present. They are so intimate, I am almost embarrassed. He was an artist. I don't know why he took these. They are elegant abstractions of observation, like sketches from a soul I don't know. I am surprised how similar my own memories can be, water in a rut, an umbrella against a curb. How could I think that the sky reflected in the puddle on the other side of the earth would look specifically Asian? Even though I have never been to Taiwan, he shared my internal landscape. These pictures make me free to photograph the sky. The sky covers all. We share the ground like the sky.

above: Polly Chu's grandmother, Yu-Jin Wu Hsiao with art school friends in Hangzhou, China, c. 1900.
below: Sarah Lejeune's grandparents, Sophie Irine Wittemore and Commander William Werden Wilson, 1908, wedding portrait.

Building the Body of Love

by Joanna Frueh

The erotic and the intellectual come together in Joanna Frueh's lushly written work. Addressing sexuality in ways that are usually hidden or left unsaid, Frueh — a noted performance artist and art critic — explores subjects such as aging, beauty, love, sex, pleasure, contemporary art, and the body as a site and vehicle of knowledge. Frueh's language is explicit, graphic, fragmented. She assumes multiple voices: those of lover, prophet, daughter, mythmaker, art critic, activist, and bleeding heart. What results is an utterly original narrative that frees the reader from the false objectivity of traditional critical discourse and affirms the erotic as a way to ease human suffering. Frueh seeks to free the power of our unutilized erotic faculties.

Aphrodite's Ordinance: Look out for anyone who says that pleasure is irrational, for those who, when they think of law, can only say jurisprudence and enforcement.

I lie down with the law of love.

My body, well-exercised in pleasure, provides the reason for existence. Let my practice persuade you, to build the body of love.

Aphrodite's system of intercorporeality (density of human copresence, time as ripeness) increases erotic community.

Misunderstood as solely man's companion, Aphrodite is all touches, and she is all fingerings that test the textures of skins and psyches.

She is satisfaction, not simply the yearnings of incomplete connections. From autoerotic flamboyance to communal eros, she knows but does not evaluate the difference between brutal and poignant honesty.

Sob sister teaching in a creamy voice, her lessons in supreme sentimentalism demand students' return to eros, no matter what damage they have inflicted on others or have had inflicted on themselves. Aphrodite sleeps and cries with the best and worst of us, for she is the infrangibility of pleasure.

My mother sits on the family room couch and I am lying beside her, my head in her lap. She strokes my hair or rests a hand on my shoulder.

Where surfaces meet, the erotic may exist and love may begin.

We speak a little now and then but make no conversation, whose words would interfere with sound, which is one essence of our touch. I feel Mom's diaphragm swelling and compressing: she vibrates through the back of my head into my brain and permeates the mind that is all of my body. Knowing that she lives in me, I think about my having lived before birth in her.

I am any age up to 42, when Mom could no longer love me comfortably in that position on the couch because her arthritic back pained her too much. Her lap and little thighs, her many Aphroditean embraces have led me to love sex and my body's sensuousness, to find erotic ease with girls and women, and to seek community with both.

The mother's body is a problematic foundation for erotic feminist community. While feminists have written about the mother from a range of perspectives that present her as sexually vital to maternally caring to archetypally omnipotent, the extremes of high theory and lived, unwritten experience prevail in my own assessment of where contemporary women and feminists locate the mother. Very few of my friends or students have spoken of having ease with their mothers' bodies. Perhaps this is such an intimate topic that it remains unspoken, certainly in a classroom or a professor's office, and even between closest friends.

In theorist Julia Kristeva's *Powers of Horror*, which has been a supreme influence on 1990s theorizing of the body, the mother(to-be) epitomizes abjectness: she enlarges, looks swollen, produces afterbirth, lactates, and shrinks; she is beyond the bounds of even normal female flesh and bleeding; she is breakdown, dissolution, ooze, and magnificent grossness. The mother is perfectly grotesque, a psychic monument to the queasy slipperiness that is the liminal reality of human embodiment, and she represents the chaos that culture has made natural to the female body and the feminine.

The abject mother is an imaginary figure, but as such she assumes an iconic presence that women use against themselves. Similarly, they carry around the unfriendly facts or atmosphere between their own and their mothers' bodies. Both the abject mother and women's histories with the maternal body provide an undismissable psychological reality, but such misery, rejection, isolation, and repulsion, which excite intergenerational corporeal warfare, do not inspire a woman to love the mother, or the old(er) woman, as a means to making the world whole.

Rebelling against the mother's body, a woman may become a feminist. To atone for the katabasis of having lived within a female body and then having to live as a female body, in a male-dominated and often misogynist culture, after the escape of birth, a woman excommunicates herself from mother eros. At-one-ment, a purposive feminist yearning to make the world whole, cannot occur through antipathetic separation from the mother, who is a primary root of eros.

I grant that the mother's body is an ultimate monster: in abjection, she is the cultural deformity of Freud's reality principle overwhelming the pleasure principle. For the sake of civilization, man designates woman monster so that he can be human. The abject mother holds disruptive authority: monster-woman turns the tables on female power as the standard purified beauty of body-as-stasis. Mother-monster is like carnival, when low becomes high. Queen for a day. Which is a problem: this monster's disruptions do not become permanent social or psychic change, for civilization resists her transgressive beauties by burying the mother's erotic body in the ugliness that operates as the necessary correlate to normative beauty.

In the psychologized modern mind, repulsion can be erotic attraction. Kristeva writes about "this erotic cult of the abject," in which "devotees" yearn for "a coming face to face with an unnamable otherness — the solid rock of jouissance." Mother, the feminine, is this unnamable and unforgivable paradise, a dystopia/utopia that is "desirable and terrifying, nourishing and murderous, fascinating and abject."[1] In her book *Voluptuous Yearnings* theorist Mary Caputi names the abject mother obscene and argues that obscenity has a rightful and necessary cultural function: which is to provide a way into "continuous" states — which I would designate erotic — known in sexual, aesthetic, and spiritual activity.[2] Despite the "worship" of mother-monster, civilization's denigration of mother/feminine/obscenity/other puts women in a relationship to the mother that is differently troubled from that of men and poignantly ironic. Eros repressed creates a repellent mother, and the repressed returns in the damaged daughter who identifies with the grotesque mother and must reject her body in order to succeed as a woman. The satisfactory female does not openly and pleasurably eroticize the mother's body, for that is socially unacceptable. In Aphroditean practice, erotic relation is wanting to be with and wanting to be like in a connection whose overarching motivation is a pleasure upon which aversion does not impinge.

Aphrodite, sublimated to death by the realpolitik of gendered principles and sexed disorders.

Just as filmmaker and theorist Laura Mulvey's ideas about a "male gaze" came, through her seminal "Visual Pleasure and Narrative Cinema" and writings based on it, to permeate feminist academic and art world thinking during most of the 1980s, so has Kristeva's discussion of abjection spread through the same territory in the 1990s.[3] Abjection, reproduced ad nauseum in feminist theory and internalized as truth, especially when mixed with personal mother-daughter history in a woman's mind that is all of her body, devastates female erotic agency, just as the male gaze did. Culture, which is not under the sole purview of men, but is also comprised of Kristeva, other feminist theorists, and our women friends, lovers, and kin, has socialized women to believe in their own abjection. The reality principle, which civilizes human chaos-as-eros into orderly productivity, debases erotic productivity, denies Aphrodite's discipline of pleasure.

Aphrodite, mother of Eros.

Aphrodite: mother is erotic icon.

Between 40 and 45, when I was looking through the family photographs as I do every several years, a black-and-white picture of my mother that I had not seen before stopped me for minutes. Florence in the forest naked, beautiful as a nude. She might have been in her early thirties, but was probably younger, and she leaped several feet off the ground, as lithe and soaring as a male ballet dancer. I wondered why this erotic image was now part of the collection and where it had come from, and imagined that for decades it had been forgotten in the pages of a book bought by Mom or Dad when they were young. Found and loved, the picture demanded residence in the family's visual history. What most astounded me about my discovery was my mother's grace, which I then realized was a basis of her actual Aphroditean presence. Her grace socialized me in eros, and her body is one reason why I enjoy the sheer sensuousness of walking through air, the flexibility of my shoulder joints and mobility of my hips, the loci and contingencies of motion's breadth and balance.

Aphrodite has heard, too many times, these words of so-called reason: to aestheticize and eroticize the mother is sublimation.

Aphrodite says, Happy mothers baking apple pies and holding angel babies is a sublimation.

Erotic friendship with one's body makes possible erotic movement with other people's bodies, which means other people's lives.

Women are often unfriendly with their own and other women's bodies.

Friend, from Old English freond, *friend, love. For Indo-European base, see FREE.*[4]

An artist in her forties, known as a beauty for over two decades, blurted out, "Women hate me because I'm pretty." I loved her art, her intellect, her wit and beauty, but she was also egotistical and bitter, and I was sure that those qualities drew the dislike that she attributed to her bodily charms.

Most often, young women make the mistake of overvaluing their bodies as fuckable items that men want and women covet. "Men only want to fuck me" is an unsophisticated statement, coming from erotic loneliness and bodily insecurity. The statement may feel like a question — "What's wrong with men?" — that could be open to girl talk or feminist analysis with another woman, but the statement keeps women at an erotic distance from one another. "Men only want to fuck me" posits the speaker as ultrafuckable and suggests that the female listener is less attractive, less visible to men, and that competitiveness underlies the seeming desire for sympathy, commiseration, or problem-solving. Eroticism encompasses the desire to fuck and to be fucked, but fuckability, so predicated on a youth and reproductivity model that elevates heterosexual relations, corrupts

Aphrodite's system of intercorporeality, which makes women visible and touchable to one another.

A young(er) woman drives with me to the desert in my car. At dinner that sweet-smelling night we'd already begun to talk about a man whose body we had both known sexually. In the desert we continued, and our stories about him turned to words of love for each other. We came together over his body, dead in comparison to our lust for each other's mouths — our talking till morning, when the coyotes would stop their cries.

Another artist, currently in her sixties, told me recent hurtful comments about her appearance made to her by feminist artists and critics she had known for years. She weight trains regularly and looks as though she's in her forties, and her erstwhile friends shocked her by suggesting that she was body-obsessed and wrong, as an old(er) woman, to not be larger and less muscled, as they were. Assessed as attractive, according to the artist, by her supposed cohorts, she became an erotic threat and oddity. Bodily differences in firmness and size make some women uncomfortable, indeed envious, intimidated, and hostile, especially as they age. American society's construction of the postmenopausal body as generally anti-libidinal can easily reduce an old(er) woman's friendliness to her own and other women's bodies. Also, while freed of reproductivity, the old(er) woman nonetheless carries with her the mother's burden of erotic nonentity. The grandmother, identified and limited by age, sex, and their concomitant iconography, must not be an erotic icon, a position superficially indicated by appearance, because she would represent pleasure's residence, seductiveness, and communality in bodies that have not been modeled as receptive or attractive to men.

Astro Girl and Cleo ordered beers at the Vagabond Love Café's bar and walked through swinging doors to a spacious brick terrace. They sat on high-backed chairs at a round table under the dense blue desert sky. Trellises filled with bougainvillea and oleander climbed the walls. Astro Girl lit cigaret after cigaret. The smoke became a perfume floating quickly away in the clean air. As Cleo and Astro Girl talked, about work, women, men, love, and their own pasts and futures, the waitress came and went a number of times, collecting empty bottles and opening new ones. Cleo used the women's room at least twice, and they shifted their chairs to avoid the sun's severity as it, too, changed position.

Cleo said, "This is corny, but your perfume is intoxicating."

"It's like sweat and grapefruit," said Astro Girl. "I had Sylvie sample it out of the bottle in the store, and she said if I wore it I'd smell like I just got out of bed — from fucking. It's lewd and I love it."

Cleo looked into Astro Girl's eyes, lavender in the brutal sun, until Astro Girl was laughing. "My body is a fact, like perfume," said Astro Girl, "and I enjoy feeling sexy." Cleo laughed too, but stopped sooner. She breathed deeply and released each breath so that Astro Girl could hear its slow escape rising, for her alone, over music, tinkling glass, a fountain's hypnotic voice, and other patrons' crudeness and intimacies. Cleo stretched. She raised her arms above her head and clasped her hands. Astro Girl watched Cleo's breasts rise and noticed her triceps' tautness. Cleo lowered her arms, rested them on the table, and her nipples hardened. Astro Girl stared, then gazing into Cleo's eyes, she said, "You look great. Tight and supple."

Cleo said, "Thanks," and they drank slowly, talking as they each finished another beer. "You're more of a romantic than you think you are."

"Why's that?"

"Creating an image, provoking pleasure."

Now and then Cleo noticed the rock music from inside the swinging doors, and the water, rolling and dripping in a fountain at the center of the terrace. During these moments the sounds themselves seemed lucid, as if aware of their own presence, each tone of its own existence.

They turned away from the sun again and Astro Girl said, "I used to be like a lizard, basking in the heat."

"You know one thing I love about the sun? I see red highlights in my hair when I brush it. In the middle of the afternoon the light pours in the window by the bathroom sink and mirror. I stroke my hair more slowly than usual and hold it out to see the different colors sparkle."

The lipstick faded from Astro Girl's and Cleo's mouths. Customers arrived and left. The walls were turning blush, then rosy orange to mauve.

Using her hand like a brush, Astro Girl held out Cleo's hair, and Cleo asked, "Did you know that Astro, Star, comes from a word meaning desire?"

"Misnomer. A nickname from long ago, before I ever thought about the difference between pleasure and desire, about how desire — I want you, can I have you? — is the means to no end. Keep satisfaction at bay, so you always have to hunt and pine. But we are pleasure, not desire."

"Two friends getting high and having a good talk and prolonging the fact of pleasure."

Women friends' flesh is connective tissue, a dynamic substance that while independent, is not absolutely singular. Through flesh, voice, and mutual looking, women friends can eroticize the world in which they live, which is the microcosm of their own energy field as well as the whole world beyond the proximity of face-to-face. Philosopher Alphonso Lingis writes in reference to Gilles Deleuze's and Felix Guattari's *Anti-Oedipus*, that "sexual desire is invested in whole environments, in vibrations and fluxes of all kinds; it is essentially nomadic."[5] Eros, as I elaborate it, is not limited to sexual desire — directed from one person to another and focused on genitalia — but it *is* nomadic. Eros wanders from body to body to body to body — bodies of pawprints, discourse, drumbeats, meditation, decisions, dreams, and water. Eros stops at primitive nexuses of uneasy pleasure — chemical reactions in which the synthesis of bodies falters. All reaction is relation, but not all relation is erotic.

Overflow, undercurrent, roundabout
Abundance becomes inhibition.
Blockage causes breakage.
Fixed positions forget the drift of eros

In a performance art class that I taught a 20-year-old woman invited many women from young to old to her piece. Her intention was to honor each woman by creating a community that resonated with archetypal weight and individuals' particular beauties. Maiden, Mother, Crone: the performer designated each of us by one of these names and then, in a short sentence or two, addressed each person's value to the performer. As she was leaving, one of the honorees, who was in her early 50s, asked me, then in my mid-40s, "Why were you a Maiden and I was a Crone?" Since that time, she has never helped me professionally, though she has been in a position to do so when her assistance could have altered the tenor and outcome of situations that meant much to me. Once, after the performance, she began a sentence about her inability to help me with, "No matter how fond I am of you. . . ." Archetypal difference sunk in as erotic difference, with Maiden figuring as have and Crone as have-not. Fond farewell to the real Aphrodite, remembered falsely as only young and only sex.

Aphrodite sings a sad, but fast-paced song:
Movie Queen inspired lust
Fell so deep bit the dust
Tired of the game of sex
Wandered in the wilderness

Sex my goddess here today
Who do you trust?
Who do you trust?
Suicide Squad she's gone tomorrow
Sex my goddess crazy sorrow

Aphroditean building of the body of love includes strengthening the physical body. Aphrodite persuades those who love her into amazonian training. She says, "Physical discipline is the erotic practice of endurance, flexibility, resistance, and extension. The amazon is neither musclebound nor warmongering nor mythic corpse; she is the woman who lifts, bends, breathes hard, and sweats for the pleasure of friendship with her own and other bodies."

Mary and I looked forward to each trip to the gym. We'd gossip as we stretched before working out with weights, separately, but within the touch of occasional talk and mutual, concentrated effort. Mary and I went to the gym regularly during the year when we lived in the same town, and our activity solidified our friendship, which remains strong now, almost fifteen years later. Mary and I still talk gym and body, for they belong to her and my erotic community, which reaches into other gyms and bodies in amazonian solidarity.

In May 1995 I met Laurie, a former winning, competitive bodybuilder who stopped competing because she believes that judging women's bodies misrepresents both women's strength and beauty. A professional trainer, Laurie is one of the strongest, most muscular women alive. Her Aphroditean discipline changed me. I watched her perform 315-pound squats, which moved me to tears, and that May she worked with me in the gym, as the friend she has since become. I have grown stronger in unaccountable ways because of Laurie, who has loved and strengthened many women by organizing two performances of strong women, primarily bodybuilders, in order to provide a non-competitive forum for female muscle. Watershed events in the history and meaning of women's bodybuilding, these fascinating spectacles, "A Celebration of the Most Awesome Female Muscle in the World" (1993) and "Evolution F: The Female Body Electric; A Celebration of Female Muscle" (1995), have challenged standard models of beauty and gender. "A Celebration" and "Evolution F" reshape perception, which enable the larger feminist aim of reshaping the world.

But a bodybuilder who felt out of shape said to me, "I've lost my friend, my body." I read her despair as an erotic falling out or away from herself. Autoerotic breakage is a continuing violence and nuance of feminist embodiment and community.

One woman
Decides to love like a bitch

Two women
Wear a perfume labelled Bandit

Five women
Gather forces once severed from their longing

Eight women
Eat preserves of reddest cherries in the morning after

Thirteen women
Sanctify their love with kisses

Twenty-one women
Call each other honeybunch across a crowded room

Thirty-four women
Scale a canyon in the sun

Fifty-five women
Linger as they squeeze each others' muscles

Eighty-nine women
Grow older than the mountains

One hundred forty-four women
Scarlet to the core sing a torch song

Two hundred thirty-three women
Stop sleepwalking

Three hundred seventy-seven women
Dream that Paradise is love of their own sex

Six hundred ten women
Kiss with open lips on city sidewalks

Nine hundred eighty-seven women
Fly across The Flatlands upside down

Fifteen hundred ninety-seven women
Say my sisters train with sisters

Twenty-five hundred eighty-four women
Excite each others' mounds and hollows

Forty-one hundred eighty-one women
Cruising from the islands to the heartland are
Adding ammunition to the Amazon Brigade

III Building Community

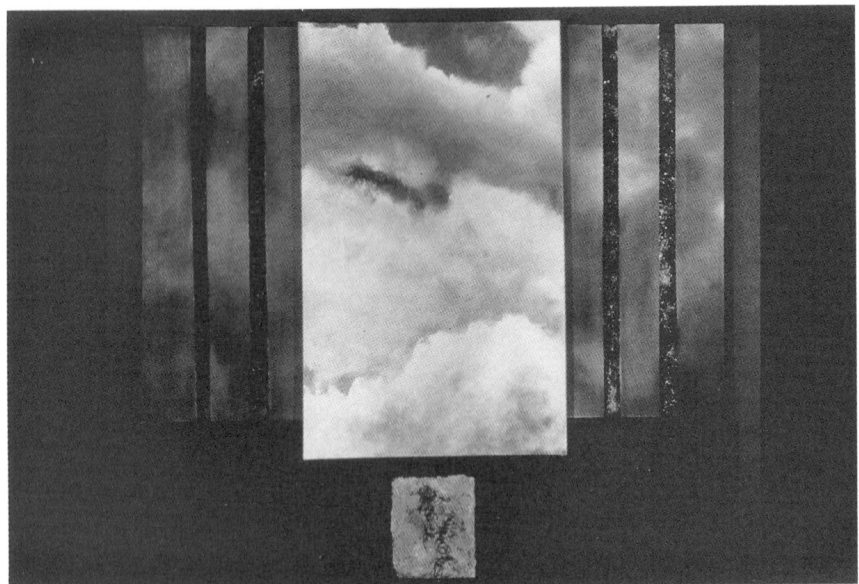

Dean Dresser, "Window" image created in collaboration with America Sosa, 1990, mixed media, from the series "Creation Myth For An Age of Despair."

To Light
Peace and Joy
for all of us
Dean 96

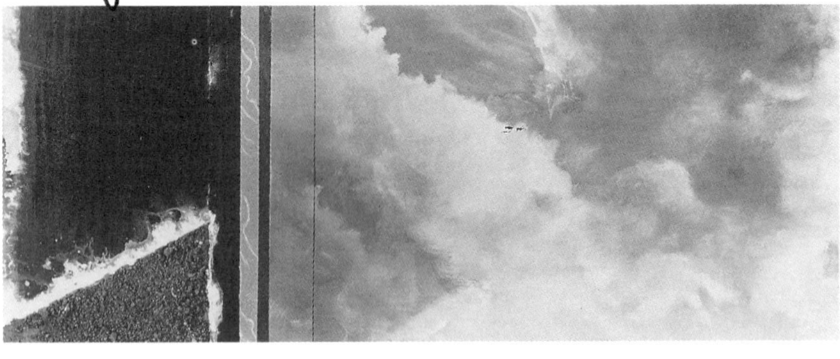

Dean Dresser, *Black Fire Into White Fire*, study, with Toby Levi, 1996, for the 1996-97 series "Marking Time In Eternity," a collaboration between three religious communities — Jewish, Christian, and Muslim — in contemporary Jerusalem.

Introduction

Here are four stories about women.

A woman leads a team of disadvantaged teens down into the cement-lined walls of the Tujunga River wash. The woman works with hundreds of these teens. They talk, argue, work together. Now they begin to paint. Years pass. A mural, over half a mile long, emerges. But something else emerges as well. Pride. Pride in themselves, pride in the histories of their people, histories that they had never learned before. Now their peoples' histories are painted on a wall, and their lives are forever changed.

A woman writes a world leader, someone whose name has been in the news. Then she writes a theologian, then a witch. Then she writes a Guardian Angel. She asks them all the same question, responds to their answers by doing paintings, asks them to respond to the paintings. Then she shares their responses with another leader, perhaps the founder of Amnesty International, perhaps an ex-President. Her paintings become a global network.

Two women live and work together. They are married, they are a family. Included in this family are many friends. For these women, as for many of us, friendship has by force or by choice replaced the bonds of blood. They create an artwork, an installation that challenges us to consider what the concept of family as community means today, and most particularly what it means for a lesbian family.

A woman performs a New Moon ritual. She is alone, in the wilderness. She returns to the city and to a group of eight other women. They pray, they bless, they heal. They explore their varied spiritual traditions, reach out to other women so they can touch other spiritual traditions. Then they invite us into their circle.

The "Communitas" Exhibition

These stories I wrote about women who use art as a community-building tool introduce this chapter, just as they introduced an exhibition catalogue for "Communitas: The Feminist Art of Community Building," an exhibition that I curated with Elizabeth Say at our shared workplace, California State University Northridge, in September of 1992.

These are the words of artist Dean Dresser that ended the catalogue: "My paintings communicate the way relationship can form. The work is accessible; it returns us to this world, which is sacred. The pinnacle of adulthood is not to transcend but to return to the community."

In Fall 1991, I had flown to San Francisco to see Dean Dresser's new paintings, since I wanted to do an article on her work. She picked me up at the airport and drove me to the industrial storefront that was her studio. I walked into a room lined with thick, heavy panels covered with some of the most radiantly beautiful, almost ethereal, paintings I had seen in a long time. So many artists in the 1980s had done what one critic called "Bad Painting": art that was intentionally ugly, awkward, unappealing. The unabashed loveliness of Dresser's work was quite a relief. But equal to the visual magnetism of the paintings was their conceptual basis. Dresser had identified several world leaders, people who she felt had or could make a real difference with their lives. She wrote to each of them, asking for a sign or symbol, something that might be etched on the metaphoric cave walls of the present to be seen by the generations of the future. hen she received each co-participant's mark, she did a painting incorporating the mark into a three-part composition, a triptych of earth, sky and cosmos, and then sent a reproduction of the painting back to the co-participant, asking for a written response. The marks — condensed ideological symbols — hovered over luminous painted surfaces, and were hung next to compelling texts in which the co-participants discussed global issues of capture and torture, personal issues of freedom and expression, or social issues of gender, race, and identity. Through her letters and images, Dresser was creating an unprecedented planetary community. I knew I had to write about the work, and was even further convinced the next day when I had lunch with Dresser and her life partner, Thandeka, an African-American scholar now teaching Religious Studies at Williams College. We discussed culture, politics, theory, and the need for artists to engage social issues in significant ways — the need for creative, aesthetic solutions to enter the discourses of national and international communities.

Linking global crises with the artistic imagination, we began to grapple with the issues bell hooks addresses when she writes, "How many of us in our daily life think about the connection between our capacity to imagine and resistance struggle? ... To imagine [is] a way to begin the process of transforming reality. All that we cannot imagine will not come into being."[1] Later, hooks writes, "[W]e rejoice in the power of community, because it renews our hope, intensifies awareness, and invites us to imagine together."[2] As often happens, hooks's writing helped me put it together. Alternative communities — communities that are resistance communities precisely because they are not patriarchal; creative communities like those conceived, facilitated, populated by women artists — these are the communities in which the power to imagine is nurtured, and it is the power to imagine that blossoms into transformation.

Returning to Los Angeles, I called Peter Frank, editor of Visions magazine, and told him I wanted to do an article on Dresser's work as a community building art form. He asked if I could make it a long piece, including other artists as well. I thought immediately of Lucy Lippard and Judy Chicago.

Lucy Lippard has been called "the first writer to attempt to devise a specifically feminist art criticism." As a critic myself, I have always found her subjective, poetic, and politically charged writing inspirational. I remembered her 1980 article [reprinted in Chapter I] in which she identified three models feminism was offering to art: "(1) group and/or public ritual; (2) public consciousness-raising and interaction through visual images, environments, and performances; and (3) cooperative/collaborative/ collective or anonymous artmaking."[3] While she didn't use the term "community" it was implied. Lippard had already mapped the terrain I would traverse in my article. One of the artists about whom she was writing, one who had pioneered all three of Lippard's models, was Judy Chicago.

Chicago's "Dinner Party" brought together porcelain-painting grandmothers from the midwest, radical women of color who felt disenfranchised by the dominant art practices, young lesbians who left their home towns to come work in an authentically women's environment, and many others. She integrated them all through shared meals, shared commitments, and consciousness-raising into a communal project. Chicago's work remains a brilliant model for community building, for the kind of feminist practices outlined by Lippard, but she had left California by the time I began the Visions article. What, I wondered, was the heritage she left? Which artists were building community here, in my own community?

I thought of Chicana muralist Judith F. Baca and her work to empower disadvantaged teens — Chicanos, African-Americans, Asian-Americans, and Native Americans from neighborhoods spread all over Southern California — and to help them image their peoples' histories in the "Great Wall of Los Angeles." I also thought of her more recent work on what she calls the "World Wall," a project that involves her traveling to various nations, working with communities to help them envision and generate positive images of global peace, and then assisting them to paint immense portable murals. As the number of "World Walls" increases, the resultant exhibition grows to become a circle of painted planes, surrounding the viewer in affirmative notions of the earth's future. Surely Baca's work could be paired with Dresser's.

I wondered if any male muralists considered their work community building as well. But when I telephoned one of the best-known Los Angeles muralists, a Euroamerican male, he assured me that, no, his work was his alone, no matter how many people assisted him. He, not they, developed and controlled the image as well as the execution. I got the same story from the other male muralists I called. It made me realize how important and unique Baca's work is.

Next I thought of Cheri Gaulke, the performance artist who had been there throughout the long and difficult history of the Los Angeles Woman's Building. Gaulke was working with high school kids in the El Sereno neighborhood of East Los Angeles. It became clear that she was also community building, that she was giving the kids the tools with which to articulate visually their community self-definition. Gaulke, with high school teacher Susan Boyle, helped the students create a three-dimensional self-portrait of their community, a houselike structure lined with video monitors. The students conceived of, built, and decorated the house; they also made the videos that portray both external (public/outsider) and internal (personal/intimate) views of their East Los Angeles homes and neighborhoods. This made Gaulke's work different from, for example, a well-known New York artist who also works with high school kids but stipulates historic, European models as central to his projects, rather than the diversified, self-generated ones facilitated by Gaulke.

Later, when public media artist Anne Bray showed me a video by African-American artist Portia Cobb and I heard one of the young black men say, "Real power is the ability to define yourself and have other people accept that definition," I realized that was an important distinguishing aspect. I now know that working within a community can be done through the dynamics of domination; artists can impose their own point of view. But to work on collaborative community building, artists work with the members of the community to help them come to terms with and articulate their own, internally-derived self-definition, a definition that validates, strengthens, and empowers the community that generates it. But I wasn't fully aware of that distinction when I wrote the Visions article.

The fourth artist was Suzanne Lacy. I thought especially of her "Crystal Quilt," the 1987 performance that brought together 430 women between the ages of 60 and 100 years. Lacy chose to work with these women because she realized that, although they represent the fastest growing population in the United States, our culture usually discounts them, assuming their value as human beings is diminished or even negated by their seventh decade. She worked with the elderly women of Minneapolis for two and a half years, asking about their stories, interviewing them, recording their answers. An edited tape of these conversations played throughout the performance, as the women sat down to an elegant array of tables, conversed about their lives, and moved colored squares over the tops of the tables to create a dynamic, many-hued quilt in the center of the Philip Johnson Crystal Quilt in Minneapolis. With Dresser, Baca, Gaulke, and Lacy, I figured I had something. I started to write.

I began by citing Elizabeth Say's book Evidence on Her Own Behalf: Women's Narrative as Theological Voice: "The vision of community is seductive. Women have been so long excluded that the invitation to 'belong' seems enticing. [But] we need to ask what is being conjured by the masculine image of community. It is a vision of cooperation toward a common good, but have they heard that patriarchy is not the common good? Until they hear this, there is no such thing."[4] I said that the women whose work was featured in the article shared common themes, precisely the themes Say says are representative of a feminist vision of community: a celebration of diversity, the inclusion of marginalized voices, and the grounding of social authority in concrete experience.

When I decided to do an art exhibit around the idea of women's community, it made sense to ask Say to co-curate. Dresser, Baca, and Gaulke were in the exhibition, as was Ruth Ann Anderson, whose installation explored feminist spirituality.[5] Say and

I talked at length about the ideas of the exhibit. Together, we interviewed all of the artists, worked out the installation plans, videotaped some of the teens who had worked with Judith F. Baca, physically worked on the exhibition lay-out, and gave interviews to the L.A. Times and Daily News. We split the work on the catalogue. Say wrote on Anderson and Gaulke. I wrote the introduction and essays on Baca and Dresser. I began to think that we — the curators, the artists, the artists' assistants, and the gallery staff — were forming our own community, however ephemerally, during the process.

In August 1992, with the camera-ready pages at the university printer, we nervously began to count the days until the exhibition opening. How would people respond to the concept of art as a community-building tool, as a tool for building feminist community — community that embraces diversity, celebrates the interconnectedness of all life, and values many different voices (rather than just those traditionally given authority)? In Fall 1992 there was much discussion of "family values." As a single mother, I felt excluded by the terms of that discussion, but I also had to acknowledge the compelling force of the conservative argument, which made me realize the controversial political resonance of the art exhibit. "Communitas" challenged the dominant culture's values of homogeneity, individualism, and hierarchy, the basis for almost all our social structures. How would people respond? Perhaps most people wanted, needed, for things in our personal and public communities to stay the same.

I didn't need to worry. We began the exhibition opening with a ritual organized by Nancy Ann Jones — an artist who had worked with Judy Chicago on the "Dinner Party" — and the women of her spiritual community. (This in itself seemed rather risky: it was, after all, a university gallery and academics are notoriously disdainful of anything that smacks of the spiritual.) We expected a few dozen participants. Instead, hundreds, many hundreds, of people came. And they stayed. And talked for hours, for days, about the ritual, the art, the ideas. They made "Communitas" a tremendous success. And they did something else. They — the artists, the ritual performers, the hundreds who attended and participated — became the midwives for this book. Many of them contributed to it. Through them, with them, the making of this book has become a community building project.

It has also become, as all books become, a learning project. It has forced me to conceptualize the history and issues of community building, to research and come to terms with the fact that this is a largely female, often feminist, and heavily West Coast art process.[6] And it has made me consider the continually expanding, complexly overlapping nature of the communities built by and through women's art.

Feminism: The Foundation

In Section I discussed the long history of women's communities and how they have often been centered around art work like quilts (although women's products have often been discounted as "craft" rather than "high art"). I also described how, in recent history, Judy Chicago and other artists began to establish women's art communities, and how that process required women to rethink both their identities as women and their identities as artists. It is important to keep in mind that this process developed out of feminism and, from this basis, to assess the nature[s] of feminist communities.

Chicago was aware that the new kind of community she was building in and through art was possible only because of the Women's Movement. "I realized that if the art community as it existed could not provide me with what I needed in order to realize myself, then I would have to commit myself to developing an alternative and that *the meaning of the women's movement was that there was, probably for the first time in history, a chance to do just that.*" [italics mine.][7]

Feminism is one of the basic movements for human liberty. Historian Gerda Lerner defines the nature of feminist consciousness.

> (1) the awareness of women that they belong to a subordinate group and that, as members of such a group, they have suffered wrongs; (2) the recognition that their condition of subordination is not natural, but societally determined; (3) the development of a sense of sisterhood; (4) the autonomous definition by women of their goals and strategies for changing their condition; and (5) the development of an alternate vision of the future. Because of the way women have been structured into patriarchal institutions, because of their long history of educational deprivation and of their economic dependence on males, women have had to overcome many obstacles before this process of coming-into-consciousness could be achieved. . . .[8]

Feminism has had two main epochs. What is sometimes called "old feminism" has its roots in the eighteenth century democratic revolutions of the propertied middle classes, such as the American Revolution that won independence from England and, soon thereafter, the French Revolution. The group of American women sculptors [the White, Marmorean Flock] who worked in Rome in the 1850s and 1860s benefited from old feminism. So did American Impressionist painter Mary Cassatt. Community and identity were important issues for all of these expatriate artists. The sculptors found support in their sisterhood of "emancipated females." Cassatt often returned to the United States to urge her monied friends to purchase the avant-garde art of her Parisian colleagues. She was a participant and supporter [along with Mary Fairchild MacMonnies] of the Women's Building at the World Columbian Exposition in Chicago, 1893, for which she created an immense mural (now lost) on the subject of "The Modern Woman."[9] Although old feminism identified and initially tried to grapple with several aspects of women's oppression, by the end of the nineteenth century it had narrowed its focus to women's suffrage. Soon after World War I, with the right to vote won in England and the United States, old feminism went into decline.[10]

New feminism, what is often called the Women's Movement, emerged in the 1960s. The women who had taken positions of professional importance during World War II had been, in the late 1940s and 1950s, ideologically — and sometimes forcibly — returned to their homes, to the narrow identity of decorative-but-mindless homemaker. Soon, they began to reevaluate their lives. They were spurred on by feminists like Betty Friedan, who gave voice to their angers and frustrations. Friedan's influential *The Feminine Mystique* documented the constricting nature of what was considered the "ideal" woman and sounded a clarion call for continued gender reform.[11]

In 1990, Vivian Gornick reminisced about the Movement.

> I wrote my first feminist polemic 20 years ago. . . . I'd been sent out by the [*Village*] *Voice* editors to investigate these 'women's libbers' who seemed to have sprung up out of the earth, and I came back converted. In one week I met Ti-Grace Atkinson, Kate Millett, Shulamith Firestone and Ann Snitow. The next week I met Gloria Steinem, Phyllis Chesler, Ellen Willis and Alix Kates Shulman. They were all talking at once, and I heard every word each one said.

> It was so simple, really: the idea that men by nature take their brains seriously, and women by nature do not, is a learned one; it serves the culture; from that central piece of information all else follows. . . . Not that the idea was unfamiliar — it wasn't. But now its time had come, and I felt it with the power of original discovery. It shed light and warmth. It healed and explained. It told me who I was in the world as I experienced the world.

> That is a moment of joy, when a sufficiently large number of people are galvanized by a social explanation of how their lives have taken shape, and are gathered together in the same place at the same time, speaking the same language. . . . It is the joy of revolutionary politics, and it was ours.[12]

I felt that same joy when I first experienced feminism, when I first realized I could be — was — part of the Women's Movement. But I didn't have those feelings, as Vivian Gornick did, through meeting feminist political activists in New York City in 1970. I first had those feelings five years later, and almost alone, as I began to read feminist literature in the isolation of my teaching job in the midwest. And I didn't feel the embrace of feminist community until I moved to Los Angeles in 1978. I had visited the city two years before, to attend College Art Association meetings and see the groundbreaking "Women Artists: 1550-1950" exhibition organized by Anne Sutherland Harris and Linda Nochlin. What an ironic contrast: the meetings were suffocatingly male-oriented, yet the exhibition demonstrated the limitations of such a perspective.

I have already told of how I came to feel "connected" as soon as I moved to Southern California. Feminist art historian Arlene Raven, who worked with Chicago to found the Los Angeles Woman's Building, was an inspiration for me. Raven has published several volumes on contemporary women's art. In *Crossing Over: Feminism and Art of Social Concern*, she gathered a group of her essays under the heading "The Women's Movement: Culture and Community." The second of these essays begins with a dialogue Raven had with artist Mary Beth Edelson about her design for an installation called "Unfinished Plans for Utopia."

(I am reminded that Daphne Patai once said, "Feminism today is the most utopian project around.")

Edelson says: On each side are paintings of women of all races looking at one another across the space, and ink drawings of womanforms interacting, to indicate a process women have undertaken together to prepare for Utopia.

Raven responds: Your metaphor for the women's movement . . . a decade of women looking at women — [shows] these six artists, myself, many others — passing through the gate of feminist process: gathering, bonding, building, expressing while moving together. . .

Gathering for consciousness-raising. . .

Bonding in the unity of our experience, finally spoken and shared. . .

Building community and a movement in kinship and common purpose. . .

Expressing our visions in work.[13]

Later in the same article, Raven writes, "Connection, community, kinship, network, are feminist word-concepts which have been actualized in the feminist art movement." She quotes artist Harmony Hammond: "For women, the meaning of sewing and knotting is 'connecting' — connecting the parts of one's life, and connecting to other women — creating a sense of community and wholeness."[14] I think once again of my great-grandmother, how she and many other women of the American frontier used sewing quilts as a way to connect. Then I think of how today, as I write, I am patching together the phrases and ideas of my friends and mentors to create a conceptual quilt, a community of words. I think of how much of this talking and thinking is the result of the Women's Movement.

Feminist Communities

Birthed by the Women's Movement, the creative communities discussed here are feminist in structure and intent. But just as feminism is not a monolithic ideological construct, the artistic communities created and populated largely by women are by no means uniform. However, they do tend to share several characteristics. As I have already written, they are not patriarchal or hierarchical. Instead, they honor diversity and often include traditionally marginalized peoples. Following the best-known feminist dictum that the personal is political, women's artistic communities ground social authority in concrete (lived) experience.

Elizabeth Say asserts that "the presumed centrality and normative quality of masculine existence is the foundation of patriarchy."[15] Women's communities are not patriarchal; they do not accept men or male experience as central. Many go further than this. They recognize, with Simone de Beauvoir[16] and, more recently, Helene Cixous,[17] that much of Western thought is dualistic, that is, based in systems of bipolar oppositions — male/female, culture/nature, self/

other, good/bad — in which one member of the pair is valued over the other. The valued member is considered central while the other is marginal, less than, deficient. The point is not to invert the oppositions; that would be reactionary and, as bell hooks asserts, "One has to build community on much deeper bases than 'in reaction to'."[18] The women/creators of these communities seek to establish situations where dualism does not dominate. Where oppositions are collapsed into variation. Where there is no hierarchy, no center/margin territoriality, no insider/outsider conflict.

[a] community of women is a rebuke to the conventional ideal of a solitary woman living for and through men, attaining citizenship in the community of adulthood through masculine approval alone . . . a community of women feeds dreams of a world beyond the normal.[19]

We're still working on dismantling all those old binary oppositions and the differences between the center and the edge. All those centers and all those margins are really parts of a very large framework of centers and margins together. We get community without unity, without understanding, accepting all the different parts without having to really understand everything, because there are some places where we truly can't.[20]

Since a community of women is a furtive, unofficial, often underground entity, it can be defined by the complex, shifting, often contradictory attitudes it evokes. Each community defines itself as a "distinct existence" flourishing outside familiar categories and calling for a plurality of perspectives and judgments. . . . The strongest community we can conceive is one with many voices.[21]

Embracing Difference

We no longer attempt to speak in one voice, but to appreciate and hear the many different voices. We no longer need to agree on one theory or one set of explanations and conflict, even among ourselves, no longer seems as threatening as it once did. Rather, it is a natural outgrowth of the breadth of our movement for cultural transformation.[22]

Difference as uniqueness or special identity is both limiting and deceiving. If identity refers to the whole pattern of sameness within a human life, the style of a continuing me that permeates all the changes undergone, then difference remains within the boundary of that which distinguishes one identity from another.[23]

In order to move out of patriarchy and away from dualistic thinking it is necessary to value diversity. But this is incredibly difficult to do in a culture that equates success with dominance[24]; a culture which has dealt with disagreement by exclusion or even death at various times in its history; a culture in which foreigners, Others, have been demeaned if not enslaved or disenfranchised. bell hooks tell us, "In this society it's easier to build our sense of 'community' around sameness. . . ."[25] But, as Audre Lorde writes in her profoundly important article about patriarchy entitled "The Master's Tools Will Never Dismantle The Master's House":

[D]ifference must be not merely tolerated, but seen as a fund of necessary polarities between which our creativity can spark like a dialectic. Only then does the necessity for interdependency become unthreatening. Only within that interdependency of different strengths, acknowledged and equal, can the power to seek new ways to actively "be" in the world generate, as well as the courage and sustenance to act where there are no charters.

Within the interdependence of mutual (non-dominant) differences lies that security which enables us to descend into the chaos of knowledge and return with true visions of our future, along with the concomitant power to effect those changes which can bring that future into being. Difference is that raw and powerful connection from which our personal power is forged.[26]

French philosopher Julia Kristeva also insists on our need to accept diversity, to embrace the Other.

As a still and perhaps ever utopic matter, the question is again before us today as we confront an economic and political integration on the scale of the planet: shall we be, intimately and subjectively, able to live with others, to live *as others*, without ostracism but also without leveling? The modification in the status of foreigners that is imperative today leads one to reflect on our ability to accept new modalities of otherness. No "Nationality Code" [certainly no feminist community] would be practicable without having that question slowly mature within each of us and for each of us.[27]

"There's an idea out there that things run better, smoother, if we're all alike, if we all conform," observes Rosalie Ortega. "But we're not all alike." Ortega's words make me think of Homi Bhaha, who wrote, "The postcolonial perspective forces us to rethink the profound limitations of a consensual and collusive liberal sense of community. The time for assimilating minorities to totalizing and organic notions of cultural value has passed. In this 'neurasthenic hour,' the very language of cultural community needs to be rethought, with an energy as powerful as that deployed by feminists, as well as gay activists, in re-examining the language of sexuality, self, and society. . . . Fiercely anti-assimilationist, women's movements not only generated conversations across political and cultural minorities but also, more significantly, sought to establish a sense of community that could tolerate difference and dissent."[28]

It is the issue of difference within community that Ortega deals with in her work. "I have always thought of myself as someone who was different," she says. "This is something that has formed my experience. And as I read, and speak to people, several things keep coming up. One of them has to do with confinement, what the experience of feeling different does to people, how it makes them feel confined, closed in. This happens within your body, almost physically. It's as if you've gone into a tunnel which gets tighter and tighter, as the level of judgement, both internal and external, constricts you further and further." Ortega's 1993 "Marginal Confessions" installation was a series of sculptures that resemble the confessional booths of her Catholic heritage. Tapes of her conversations with many disenfranchised people whispered through the sensuous architectonic structures. The confessionals got smaller and smaller, less and less able to accommodate a human participant, just as marginalized people have been given increasingly limited access to personal expression. Central to Ortega's work is the concept of giving voice to those traditionally marginalized and, through the process of marginalization, silenced.

Giving Voice

> [I]t matters to us what is said about us, who says it, and to whom it is said: having the opportunity to talk about one's life, to give an account of it, to interpret it, is integral to leading that life rather than being led through it; hence our distrust of the male monopoly over accounts of women's lives. To put the same point slightly differently, part of human life, human living, is talking about it, and we can be sure that being silenced in one's own account of one's life is a kind of amputation that signals oppression.[29]

> [W]oman speaks to her culture from the margins. While the margins have their limitations, they also have their advantages of vision. They are polyvocal. They are heretical . . . eccentric and alive . . . vital, unconventional. From them erupt, however suppressed they might be, rebellion, confusion, ambivalence, the uncertainties of desire.[30]

> [I]f white/Anglo women are to understand our voices, they must understand our communities and us in them.[31]

When Judith F. Baca taught her juvenile co-workers how to research the histories of their forebears and to paint them on the Great Wall mural, she was building community by celebrating diversity and giving voice to the marginalized. That is also what Cheri Gaulke did in her work with the high school students of East Los Angeles and what Ruth Ann Anderson did in the ritual space she erected for the "Communitas" exhibition. Anderson did it again in her recent collaboration with Suvan Geer entitled "In Living Memory." Aware that the dominant culture often treats both senior citizens and the environment as if they were invisible and of no account, the two artists asked Los Angeles seniors to talk about the city — particularly the air, water, and land of the city — that they recollect from their childhoods. They created a series of posters with photographs of the seniors paired with quotes from their interviews. "Remember," says Geer, "Los Angeles was a pueblo two hundred years ago. It was totally agrarian one hundred years ago. Our seniors recall what it was like sixty, seventy years ago, as the urban center came out of that agrarian era. They recall seeing cows on Wilshire Boulevard, getting water out of wells, putting their feet into the ocean and *seeing* them, because the bay water was so clear." In giving voice to the often ignored, Anderson and Geer's "In Living Memory" echoes many of Sheila Levrant de Bretteville's projects.

De Bretteville was running the women's design program at Cal Arts when Judy Chicago arrived there and became a co-founder of the Woman's Building. She is now at Yale University. In 1987, she covered the construction barricades surrounding the Los Angeles Grand Central Market renovation with phrases taken from multilingual interviews she and her Otis Art Institute student co-workers conducted with longtime residents of the market neighborhood. She used phrases like Bella Posey's: "Garlic reminds me of the hunger years when my mother rubbed it on a piece of bread and I would imagine the sausage sandwiches she gave me to take to school during the years of plenty." "The idea," says de Bretteville, "was to project into the public realm the feelings and memories of the actual people who'd be looking at those barricades every day. . . . I get pleasure from formats in which people who don't normally get to speak are heard from." And when graffiti appeared on the barricades, "That was interesting. Here we recognized the thoughts of some ordinary people — then a whole bunch of *other* people wanted their thoughts to be known as well."[32]

Two years later, de Bretteville collaborated with artist Betye Saar and historian Dolores Hayden to create a monumental wall honoring Biddy Mason, the African-American midwife and nurse who was born into slavery in 1818 and became the first black woman to own property in Los Angeles and the founder of its first black church. Embossed with photographs, artifacts, and quotations, the wall will "like fossils . . . carry the meaning of the life that previously existed there, a life not remembered in mainstream histories of the city. Discussing her work in general, de Bretteville states, "I continue to be exhilarated by a vision of graphic design functioning in much the same way Paolo Friere describes his class in Education for Critical Consciousness, as 'a meetingplace where knowledge is sought, not where it is transmitted.' This notion has led me to various kinds of graphic formats where there wasn't one answer but multiple voices. Information is given but it is not a closed declaration and a response is requested, directly or indirectly. The principle behind this exchange and encouragement of ideas is the initiation of dialogue, connection and community."[33] It's all part of her feminist process, de Bretteville believes.

Telling Stories to Honor Lived Experience

> Women will starve in silence until new stories are created which confer on them the power of naming themselves.[34]

> Women must turn to one another for stories; they must share the stories of their lives and their hopes and their unacceptable fantasies.[35]

> In their form, women's lives tend to be like the stories they tell: they show less a pattern of linear development towards some clear goal that one of repetitive, cumulative, cyclical structure.[36]

Another characteristic of much feminist community building is the grounding of social authority in concrete (lived) experience. Nancy Miller defines feminism as the wish "to articulate a self-consciousness about women's identity both as inherited cultural fact and as process of social construction" and "to protest against the available fiction of female becoming."[37] Parker and Pollock add, "Women are deprived of self-determination and self-knowledge at profound levels while they are barraged with others' definitions and imposed identities, roles and meanings."[38]

In other words, feminism analyzes the culturally determined definition of woman. As Simone de Beauvoir wrote in 1949, "One is not born but becomes a woman . . . it is civilization as a whole that produces this creature . . . described as feminine."[39] Carolyn Heilbrun adds, "What does it mean to be unambiguously a woman? It means to put a man at the center of one's life and to allow to occur only what honors this prime position. Occasionally women have put God or Christ in the place of a man; the results are the same: one's own desires and quests are always secondary."[40] Feminism exposes the limitations of the traditional definition of woman by expressing and valuing the diversity of women's lives. From the intimate, corporeal material of women's lives, feminism generates stories and images which in turn build community. "What matters is that lives do not serve as models; only stories do that. And it is a hard thing to make up stories to live by.[41]

Elizabeth Say has important insights on this matter:

> For men, the search for community must begin with a denial of the ego-centered self, as evidenced by the narrative critique of individualism. Community represents the ability of one man to transcend his self to embrace the good of others.

> Women's narratives are, on the other hand, a quest to find the self to which patriarchy has denied existence. Women know what it is to sacrifice their lives for others; what is difficult is accepting oneself as a legitimate claimant when there is a conflict of interests. Membership in a community, for women, must begin with recognition of the self, and women's stories are about discovering and validating this self.[42]

Again and again, women artists have built community by speaking, moving through all the vulnerabilities of self-revelation, and encouraging others to speak. This is revolutionary, as Arlene Raven makes clear: "When a woman artist positively identifies herself to us through her work, she commits a courageous and daring act of self-exposure, because she expresses herself outside of - and without the support of — a social, economic, and cultural base." Judy Chicago adds, "a woman's saying I am, I know myself, I understand on the basis of reality how I can act in the world, and I feel a fundamental optimism — a grasp upon my survival as a model for human survival — is saying something which challenges the existing and prevailing world view."[43]

But this speaking up, speaking out, is extraordinarily difficult alone. Women need to speak *with*. What is essential is "for women to see themselves collectively, not individually, not caught in some individual erotic and familial plot and, inevitably, found wanting."[44] It is when we find spaces of truth, spaces for speaking with, that change can happen. To create such a space is the impetus for the feminist art of community building.

Memories of a Community of Stories:
Suzanne Lacy's "Immigrants and Survivors"

> The point is not just to produce another thing for people to admire, but to create an opportunity — a situation — that enables viewers to look back at the world with renewed perspectives and clear angles of vision.[45]

In 1983, Suzanne Lacy invited me to join the group of women she was assembling to generate a new community building art work. Lacy brought together about a dozen women with whom she'd worked or wanted to work. We convened over a pot luck dinner at her studio in an old industrial warehouse in downtown Los Angeles to talk about what we shared with each other and with other women of Los Angeles. Writer Judith Stein notes that Lacy has "mined the informal collaborative tradition of the potluck dinner," citing Lucy Lippard's description of the potluck as "a classically feminist collage [that brings] together a highly disparate group of women and their culinary 'offerings'."[46] Those first dinners in Lacy's studio were the yeast that would allow the bread of our project to rise.

As our conversations over potluck dinners developed, we began to realize that as women, we are all immigrants to a foreign land — to man's land, the territory of patriarchy — and that we are all survivors of many forms of oppression — oppressions of fear, abuse, disregard, silence, threat. As we continued to deliberate, we chose not to focus on the perspectives of alienation or victimization in our project, but to celebrate our triumphs. We decided that we wanted to gather as many diverse women as we could, and bring them together for one night, for one immense potluck. We wanted to share food and stories. Stories of success and triumph. Stories of empowerment, of challenges met, obstacles overcome.

We began to spread the strands of our networks. At first, it seemed a daunting proposition. So many of us spend our private lives surrounded by people very much like ourselves. How could we reach others, Others? How could we convince them that to come together would create art, would establish community? That the experience would be valuable for them, not just serve our needs? It didn't happen overnight or without frustrations and dead ends, but eventually, after many discussions and many potlucks, the process began to "take."

We contacted women lawyers and teenage mothers. Nicaraguan refugees and battered Beverly Hills housewives. Black women from Skid Row, black women scholars. Lesbians. Prostitutes. Rabbis. Drug addicts. Artists. Then one night, hundreds of us sat around big tables in the dining room of the American Film Institute. We ate and talked. Then someone took the microphone dangling over her table and talked to all of us. Someone else spoke. Someone else. We shared our food and told our stories. It sounds simple. But it was incredible. We were so different, yet so connected. And there we were, together, in a single room, eating tamales and baklava, couscous and Irish onion pie, consuming signifiers of our diversity in a meal that unified us. I remember looking over the crowd and seeing women in braids and huipiles next to women in business suits. Women in black leather, women in polyester. Lots of make-up, no make-up. Lace. Men's clothes. Shawls. Veils. Beads. Silvery hair, shaved heads. Women in wheel chairs. The twelve of us had cast our nets as fishers of women and reeled in, however briefly, a dizzying catch of diversity. We spent the evening talking across the lines that usually divide us — lines of race, class, age, sexuality, physical ability — and as we did, the lines seemed to dissolve. The stories moved us to tears, to touching, to recognizing our oneness.

I still have the passport that Lacy printed and gave to each of us; my passport to the global community of women. I cherish it. I also cherish the resolute images of those women and the memories of their stories, the truths they told about their lives.

> What would happen if one woman told the truth about her life? The world would split open.
>
> — Muriel Rukeyser [47]

In creating spaces for the telling of truths, thereby honoring their truths and the truths of others, women artists begin the process of community building. In the essays of Section III, women tell their own stories and the stories of building community through art. This begins with my conversation with Suzanne Lacy and an article about Lacy's "Crystal Quilt" penned by Patricia Clark Koelsch. Suvan Geer describes two of her more successful community building projects. Cheryl Dullabaun discusses the work of New York artist Mierle Laderman Ukeles. Betsy Damon writes of her work building community around the issue of water pollution in China. Playwright Victoria Rue talks of the art and spirit of building community in feminist theater. Lorraine Serena joins several of her collaborators to discuss "WOMEN/ Beyond Borders," and art historian Frances Pohl interviews muralist Judith F. Baca.

> The longing to connect is not a breakfast food. You cannot have it instantly. I can't relate to the universality of all women. We make these bridges tentatively, we don't make assumptions, we build a relationship slowly — It's a long struggle, a long time building bridges.
>
> — Judith F. Baca[48]

Suzanne Lacy

in Conversation with Betty Ann Brown

Suzanne Lacy has pioneered community building art throughout the United States and in Europe. Recent projects include one in Chicago, where she put 100 boulders with women's names on the streets of the "Loop," followed by a dinner at Jane Addams' Hull House honoring several internationally known women. Lacy's work on violence continues with "Auto on the Edge of Time," a national series of exhibitions on domestic violence.

In Oakland, where she is Dean at the California College of Arts and Crafts, she has worked for five years with inner city teens, creating high school curricula, public policy, and large-scale media performances on youth identity.

> The interrogation of "public"— including art's interactive qualities, the artist's intentions, and the audience composition — defines this work. This action is a continuation of conceptual and process art, found in efforts to shift attention away from the object and toward the meaning of art and artmaking.
> — *Suzanne Lacy,* "Mapping the Terrain: The New Public Art"

I can't remember when or how I first met Suzanne Lacy. It seems like she has always been a formidable presence in my consciousness of feminism and feminist art. Seeing her "Making It Safe" performance (Ocean Park, California, 1979) was my first experience of women artists addressing rape. Involving dozens of women in visually and emotionally compelling situations, the performance heightened my awareness of the topic: I realized how many of us have been raped, how much we need to talk about it, how it is a cultural ill rather than an individual or personal problem. Lacy's performance also affected my view of the history of art: I can no longer look at, say, a Peter Paul Rubens painting of the abduction and rape of historical or mythological figures with indifference to the subject matter. I now realize that many celebrated canvases glorify violence against women.

I can't remember how or why I started working with Suzanne, either. But by 1982 I was attending meetings at her downtown Los Angeles studio, meeting more and more women over rich potluck dinners, talking through long nights about our experiences as immigrants to Los Angeles and the art world and about our triumphs of survival. Under Suzanne's guidance, we decided to extend and give structure to our dinners/conversations. We called the resulting performance piece, which I have described in the introduction to this chapter, "Immigrants and Survivors." I left the event feeling uplifted, transformed. I realized I had forged important and lasting friendships through the work leading up to and culminating in the performance event, and that the community of such friendships would not have been possible without the shared goal/shared labor of this artistically identified and crafted event.

Most of Suzanne Lacy's performances focus on the relationships between women; some include men as well; they all develop community. Some of her works are very complex and visually resonant, for example, "The Road of Poems and Borders," which Lacy organized in Joensuu, Finland, in 1990. Eighteen visual and performing artists collaborated with Lacy to orchestrate a four-day performance event. On the first day, 214 red-garbed Finnish youths raised crimson flags around a shallow lagoon, then leapt into the freezing water and swam to meet in the center as composer Jarmo Kakonen's sound piece echoed across the water. On the second day, senior women from the U.S., Russia, and Finland met on Finnish Public Radio to discuss the realities of their lives, of the spatial and cultural borders they had traversed. Day three was marked by meetings at Joensuu's central market. People, in pairs or groups, planned meetings and had their reclining bodies traced with chalk. By nightfall, when the market cleared, a portrait of the community was left on the asphalt. Throughout the performance there were continued readings of over 600 letters about border encounters that Lacy had solicited from all over the world. Every hour on the hour:

> Readers stopped whatever they were doing and read a border letter. They read at business meetings, over intimate dinners, on park benches, in stores and at home. Sometimes they read . . . in public places. . . . Most readings were in Finnish or English, and sometimes both together, but a few took place in Russian, German, Japanese, Spanish, French, Italian, and Portuguese. Each reading was introduced by an unobtrusive action: The reader, wearing a "Road of Poems and Borders" T-shirt, outlined his or her feet with yellow chalk. The reading was done simply, sometimes even whispered. . . . For days after the festival, 600 pairs of yellow footprints remained throughout the city like echoes of the stories that had visited there."[1]

In "The Road of Poems and Borders," Lacy worked to develop community in Joensuu with the youthful swimmers and the market-goers, using the splash of brilliant crimson against the icy blue water and the fine contour of chalk lines scattered, for brief moments, across the city. But the circles of community expanded globally, across national, political, and linguistic borders, through boundaries of age and gender, to establish, however ephemerally, the web of planetary community.

One of the participants wrote:

> My strongest memory is of working on a piece about borders in a world without borders. There was no border between day and night — it was light all the time. There was no border between work and play — we just worked all the time, but much of it had the quality of play. Between Joensuu and the larger world, I was so lost in what we were doing that Joensuu became the whole world. All activities, realms, relationships seemed to melt into each other. It was a wonderful way to live for a while, but it also made me aware of the value of the borders we construct in our lives.

Another wrote:

> The first thing that comes to mind about last summer's performances is the image of two old women who came to the market to be drawn. Giving support to each other, they lay down on the ground side by side. They talked about their lives for a long time and enjoyed the sun. Later on, looking at their figures on the ground, they hugged and laughingly said: "Hell, we're still beautiful." This, if anything, was aesthetic.

Yet another participant in Lacy's monumental performance wrote:

> Art cannot cause actual change, but it can give shape to changes already in the wind. It frames and expresses a reality, giving strength to that reality. Each artist's hopes and fears are reflective of the whole. Art lets you know changes are on the way. [2]

One of the artists with whom Lacy collaborated on this project was Allan Kaprow, the artist and theorist with whom she studied at California Institute of the Arts. During the 1960s Kaprow had begun to question many of the fundamental assumptions of the Western art tradition. Pointing out that historically, art had been made "in a rectangular studio, to be shown in a rectangular gallery, reproduced in a rectangular magazine, in rectangular photographs, all aligned according to rectangular axes, for rectangular reading movements and rectangular thought patterns,"[3] Kaprow had first done what he called "environments" (and what we today call "installations"), that is, room-sized space transformed by painting and sculpture. Realizing that the rooms were ultimately three-dimensional rectangles, Kaprow took his environments outdoors to create "Happenings." As Robert Pelfrey writes, "Happenings are difficult to describe. [They] stressed a minimum of direction and a maximum of participation. Kaprow, or whoever 'supervised' the happening, would provide the basic performance directives and materials, but people would be free to improvise as their mood dictated. Happenings merged drama, painting, music — and whatever else fit. In the happening, the boundary between life and art closed. The happening's problem, that of life itself, was its fragility. The experience stayed with the individual participant: the happening disappeared."[4]

Lacy combined Kaprow's art-as-life ethos and his Happenings format with her committed feminist politics and performance art structures — first developed while she was studying with Judy Chicago — to create a powerful community building strategy. Her work has profoundly affected thousands of women and men. Clearly, Suzanne Lacy is a figure whose work is central to the understanding of community building as an art form.

Our conversation began by speaking of her history because I wanted to know more about the genesis of her aesthetic process.

Betty Ann Brown: Tell me about the sources of your work.

Suzanne Lacy: The work that you're framing as community building art, which I frame as public art — that which explores the meaning of art within daily life — really began for me in the late 1960s and early 1970s when I studied with Allan

Kaprow and Judy Chicago. My work is influenced by the merger of Allan's theories and Judy's.

I met Judy in Fresno where I was getting a Masters degree in psychology. I was going to be a doctor but changed to art. I came to Cal Arts in 1969 and got a Masters of Fine Arts degree in design. I worked with Sheila de Bretteville to form the Women's Design program. Those years at Cal Arts were prolific ones for feminism: there were courses on Women Writers, Women in Sociology, Women's Art, etc. Feminists were a powerful, visible source of energy then. But after the first two or three years, the door slammed shut so hard that only in the last couple of years has Cal Arts begun to acknowledge that part of its history.

If you read publications on Cal Arts, it appears that everything that happened there from 1969 to 1972 had to do with [photographer/conceptual artist] John Baldessari. Allan Kaprow was there at the same time. The students chose between those two conceptual approaches, and feminists generally studied with Kaprow. Many of Baldessari's students went directly to New York. Kaprow's students became chiropractors, counselors . . . they did "art in life."

What was bigger than either of those two men was the presence of the Women's Movement. But today that part of Cal Arts' history is virtually ignored. By the mid-1970s, a European feminist who taught there told me she was ostracized for her political views.

BAB: Had you done any community performance pieces at Cal Arts?

SL: I don't think there was ever a time when community and performance were separated in my work. The aspect of Judy Chicago's work which influenced me in the beginning was performance. Judy did performance "skits" in Fresno, and although I didn't participate in any of them, I was quite interested. When I started working with Kaprow, I began to explore the incorporation of art into daily life. If you take Kaprow's ideas and you add to them a set of politics, you've got a perfect frame for including people in the art work. "If art is life," he would ask, "Is brushing your teeth an artwork or not an artwork?" Then we asked, How do you apply that to political and social issues?

BAB: Wasn't he doing things that involved non-artists then?

SL: Allan Kaprow had certainly done that in his Happenings. But he had shifted, by the time I met him, so that most of his venues were art galleries, and many of the people involved were at least familiar with the art world. Most of the acts he would ask people to do were so strange and esoteric that his community had to be the art community. He had become so philosophically reductive that he'd begun to work with smaller audiences. He felt that there was a quality of artificiality to spectacle, that he wanted to reduce things to their simplest manifestation, to the essence of experience.

BAB: What was the first step you took toward including a larger audience?

SL: I can't remember when I didn't. At Cal Arts, Nancy Youdelman, Dori Atlantis, Jan Lester and I did a piece called "I've Tried Everything" about breast enlargement. We were interested in American breast fetishism. We sent off to every breast development ad that we could find and then made Nancy Youdelman the guinea pig. For 28 days she tried everything and we took photos of her process. We displayed the photos plus the paraphernalia in the Cal Arts library.

Then we did "Ablutions" (a performance by myself, Judy Chicago, Aviva Rahmani, and Sandra Orgel in Venice, California, 1972), which was about rape. It was the first piece I know of that was about rape. We performed it for the Los Angeles art community, in the Venice studio of one of Judy's friends. For us, going public to the art world was a big step.

In 1974 I did "One Women Shows," which was my first major work explicitly about building community. I started by choosing three women, each from a different community — art historian Arlene Raven, performance artist Laurel Klick, and librarian Mary Holden. I designed a performance for them, and I worked with them each to pick two or three others for whom they would design performances. Those people in turn picked people, and so on, until there were about fifty people involved. That was phase one. Phase two was the opening night in the Grandview Gallery [a women's cooperative gallery in rented space at the Los Angeles Woman's Building, 1973-75]. I performed first, a statement about women who were raped, women who loved women, and women who were prostitutes. Then my three-woman audience — Arlene, Laurel and Mary — each went to different parts of the gallery, taking their personal "audiences" with them, and did their own performances. So it evolved from a single performance to dozens of simultaneous performances all over the gallery. The project continued in the gallery for a month. People would come into the gallery, bringing their own selected audiences, and do a performance. Their charge was to name themselves and then to leave evidence of the process on the wall. "One Woman Shows" was also a comment on my ambivalence about one-woman shows. [One-man shows have, of course, been the primary vehicles for promoting male artistic careers in the twentieth century.] One woman's show is another woman's show is another woman's show . . . and the idea was for each woman to teach another woman how to do a performance. When participants chose people, they had to teach them how to do a performance piece and support them in the development of their piece.

"One Woman Shows" was specifically about community, and a lot of the exercises I did with my students at the Woman's Building (I started teaching there in 1972) were also about community. There was an exercise that I used to assign for students to go out into the streets, locate and observe someone who represented a particular group, social situation, etc. Then they came back to the Building and did a project or performance about their experience of that person. That was part one. They could dress as the person, move as the person, or use whatever they could extract from the experience, but they would have to empathically unite with that situation through their piece. In the second phase, they had to go out and actually meet the person or someone like them and develop a work in collaboration with them. They had to grapple with the actual reality, as opposed to the empathic projection, of that person's experience. Many of the exercises I did were psychological and oriented toward relationship.

BAB: How did you come up with these exercises?

SL: My early postgraduate work was in psychology. And both Chicago's and Kaprow's work are about relationship. I began to consider that the artwork is the thing that takes place in the space between artist and audience — the space occupied by relationship.

In addition, conceptual artists from the Dadaists to Yoko Ono had been talking about art as the act. Merging the act with personal meaning, which was what Kaprow was doing, is straight out of feminist activist theory.

BAB: Do you think that it was "straight out of feminism" for Kaprow?

SL: Kaprow has stated often that he was very influenced by feminism. So the psychological/relational thing, coming through Kaprow, was one model for me.

The other model came from the notion of difference, and that's from Simone de Beauvoir. I saw that feminist art was or could be an attempt to move across some perceived difference, that the art act could be a bridging. Of course, Judy Chicago was most influential in developing the idea that art could *communicate* female difference.

> This transition from a model of individual authorship to one of collective relationship is not undertaken simply as an exercise in political correctness. There is a longing for 'the other' that runs as a deep stream through most of these works, a desire for connection that is part of the entire creative endeavor in all its forms.[5]

In the mid 1970s, I began working in Watts ["Evalina and I: Crime, Quilts and Art," Guy Miller Homes, Watts 1976]. I began by thinking: if as an artist, I'm going from Venice [the oceanside art community] to Watts [the African-American community in South Central Los Angeles] every day, the starting point for me should be to record my own experience, to become like an emotional Geiger counter. I relied on my experience to reflect the global reality [of, in this case, racism, and its relationship to crime and community]. I was convinced that good political art would deal with more than an issue, that it would deal with an experience of and empathic relationship to that issue.

BAB: Allan Kaprow said that "community change can't take place unless it's transformative within us . . . every prejudice, every misunderstanding that we perceive out in the real world is inside of us, and has to be challenged. . . ."[6] Sounds like "The personal is political" again, like the basis for feminism and feminist art, doesn't it?

SL: The art-as-life project which we developed in the 1970s, and which you are writing about as community building, seemed to split in the 1980s. One aspect of it came to be known as feminist art, and the other aspect of it came to be known as public art. Today, the multicultural/public art dialogue is taking place outside the context of 1970s feminism. Which is why you have people again interrogating issues that were raised during the 1970s — issues like violence, like racism — without any awareness of what went on then. In the transition from object-oriented public art, both feminist and community-based ethnic artists' theories have been lost. Of course process-oriented public art is pretty much what I was always interested in. Nobody knows what we did in the 1970s, so they're basically reinventing it, outside the context of feminism.

BAB: That's one of the problems with the history of feminism, isn't it? That we don't have a place in history and our accomplishments get erased even within one generation. People forget what women have done.

SL: My work, my strategies arose very specifically out of the political context of feminist activism. I was led to ask certain questions about audience because of the political needs within the work. For example, we developed mass media performances because issues of violence needed a public audience. Today it seems that audience has to do with the scope of your reach. The viability of a work has to do with the visibility of an artist — it sort of parades as the visibility of an issue.

We embarked upon the pursuit of visibility because the issues needed public exposure. Models of interfacing artists with non-artists, of constructing a community audience, and of involving the community within the actual work — these came from a feminist sensibility. Because people don't know the relationship between racial and feminist politics and the structure of the work, they don't know how to evaluate that work. They don't know what questions to ask.

BAB: There's ignorance. But it's not just ignorance, I think there's also an incredible arrogance on the part of people who are now getting involved with this kind of work. I just curated a show and this man did a project, this privileged white guy who worked with a bunch of disadvantaged black teenagers — which is in itself a problem since it recycled the dynamic of the dominant figure reaching down to the oppressed on his own terms, but that's another story. Anyway, he went about it like he was making it all up, like he was creating community-interaction-as-art and generating this whole strategy. I kept saying to him, "I think it's incredibly arrogant for you to go into this as if you're cutting new territory, to say nothing of the dominant white male thing that you're doing." But he was so ignorant about your work and Judy Baca's work! Judy's work is right here — tangible — you can see it in L.A. And yet he was totally ignorant of that. But I think there's also an arrogance.

SL: I think it's caused by the fact that the art world values innovation. In other words, you go into the history book if you do something *new*, not if you do something *better*. Even in the case of Judy Chicago, there's been a concerted effort not to know what she was doing. So that if you see yourself within a legacy of art, it's hard to claim you are original. When we're talking about social change, however, I don't think originality is the highest virtue.

A friend of mine just did a piece on domestic violence. I sat him down and said, "Let me send you some information, you need to know about the work that was done in the 1970s." But it was not to his advantage to acknowledge the earlier work women did on that topic. The piece that he ended up doing was structurally like what I'd done many years earlier. And very specifically like what Mary Beth Edelson did in the 1970s when she got people to come into a gallery and write things on a tablet and leave them on the wall. The piece of paper on the wall — the notion of response, of voice, of multiple voices that comes out within the art work — he duplicated that.

The guy you were talking about, the arrogant guy . . . well, there are as many artists who don't know the work who aren't arrogant. Then there are the ones who have the information and still don't align themselves with a legacy. I think that recognition of such an alignment is part of a political consciousness. If you have a political consciousness, you want to make connections and make coalitions; you want to make change, not make your mark.

The other problem is that nobody knows how to analyze this kind of work. And as a result, nobody can deconstruct the work and talk about the relationships between content and form. There are two tasks for us now, beside reconnecting with history. One is to delineate strategies. If you had a catalogue of how it has been done, you wouldn't have to reinvent all the time. We also need to see if there is, within the strategies, a specific construction of aesthetics in community work.

We also have to define certain kinds of terms that have become buzzwords, like community art and public art. One of the thing's I've suggested about public art is that it doesn't matter whether it's an object or comes out of a certain public tradition (like murals). What matters is that there's a notion of the public within the work. Public art is what happens between the artist and the audience, so public art can take place in the galleries as far as I'm concerned. I'm not so sure public art even has to have a diversity of audience, at least for any one work. Judy Chicago's work has not been called public art, yet it's profoundly public in the sense of involving an audience that's outside the art world. What happens is that it's classified as women's art. That means that even if appeals to a very large group — as in the case of the "Dinner Party," a very large group of middle class women — people rarely think it's important in terms of audience because that audience hasn't been portrayed in our thinking.

Another issue Suzanne Lacy has discussed and written about, in terms of analyzing community building artworks, is that of continuity.

The notion of sustaining or continuing a connection begun through the work is an expression of personal responsibility that has a pedagogical thrust, often expressed as educating engaged community members, students, or even the art world . . . the artist imparts a range of options for developing activist and aesthetic work, generally on the constituency's own terms. . . . If the artist does have stated political intentions — and the overtness of this varies from artist to artist — then continuity may become an important measure of the work's success. . . . For some, no less than concrete changes of social behaviors is demanded. For others, art is successful when it educates, or when it serves as a model for other artists. This raises the question as to whether this work is in fact an agent of change or whether it serves as a model for social change; whether the art is frankly and solely goal-oriented or, as I've suggested, is a more complex investigation of philosophical and personal meaning.[7]

Suzanne Lacy, "Whisper, the Waves, the Wind,"
La Jolla, California, 1984.

Building Community

Suzanne Lacy, "The Crystal Quilt," performance in the
IDS Crystal Court, Minneapolis, Minnesota, 1987.

Participants in "The Crystal Quilt."

The Crystal Quilt:
A Performance and Its Legacy

by Patrice Clark Koelsch

"I'm not aging — I'm ripening." This confident declaration by octogenarian poet and activist Meridel LeSueur concluded the narrative component of "The Crystal Quilt" — a Mothers' Day performance by 420 older women in the heart of downtown Minneapolis. Conceived and directed by Suzanne Lacy, "The Crystal Quilt" was the most visible component of the Whisper Minnesota Project, a multigenerational coalition of artists, policy makers, service providers, and community activists organized to challenge public perceptions about women and aging.

The role of older women in the public sphere is a theme that seems to have a special resonance for feminists who came of age politically in the late sixties and early seventies and are confronting the aging of themselves, their mothers, their movement. The initial euphoria of liberation has been replaced with the sobering recognition of how difficult it is to achieve change that is more than superficial.

Although the American mass media promotes idealized images of sexually active, career- and consumer-oriented women, an increasing number of women find themselves politically discounted and economically disenfranchised. Older women constitute the most rapidly growing segment of our society, yet they are relatively invisible and inaudible in the public sphere. When the disadvantaged situation of older women is publicly acknowledged, this stereotype camouflages the diverse and complex reality of older women's lives. And it was the scarcity of images which acknowledge both the strength and the struggle of older women that motivated Suzanne Lacy to develop the performance piece, "The Crystal Quilt."

Suzanne Lacy's performance work has always grown out of feminist issues of particular immediacy. While Lacy's pieces in the seventies addressed overt violence toward women (e.g., "Ablutions" 1972, "In Mourning and In Rage" 1977), her more recent performances have focused on the more subtle ways in which women's lives are constrained through racism, classism, and ageism. These concerns were at the heart of "Whisper, the Wind, the Waves" (1984) a stunning performance piece involving 150 older women who graphically represented the ethnic diversity of southern California. To symbolize continuity with the tradition of the suffragist pageants, all the performers wore white garments. They formed a procession to enter the gleaming La Jolla beach performance area and broke into quartets to sit at cloth-covered tables and discuss their lives while observers looked down from the boardwalk and listened to Susan Stone's audio collage. At the end of the performance the spectators were invited to go onto the beach and join in conversation with the performers.

In developing "The Crystal Quilt," Lacy adapted and expanded many of the aesthetic ideas and organizational principles of the California performance to fit the unusually hospitable artistic, political, and philanthropic climate of Minnesota. Lacy came to Minneapolis in 1985 with the notion of creating a piece on aging that would involve persons from the public policy sector in key organizational roles from the outset. Using stills and video from the La Jolla project as a presentation mobilized regional policy makers and philanthropists to help Lacy inaugurate the Whisper Minnesota Project. The Whisper Minnesota Project would work toward the realization of a major performance piece on the role of older women in the public arena, and collaborate with other service agencies and educational institutions to support significant auxiliary activities involving older women's leadership.

The fundamental premise of the Whisper Minnesota project has been that aesthetically complex visual images can challenge and eventually subvert the simple assumptions that dominate mass media culture. Lacy worked with the Minnesota Board on Aging (the state agency which plans and coordinates policies, programs, and services for the aging in Minnesota), the Reflective Leadership Program at the Hubert H. Humphrey Institute for Public Affairs at the University of Minnesota, and the Minneapolis College of Art and Design to conceptualize the project and to set up a state-wide network of women and men interested in presenting authentic images of older women as active participants in the public sphere. A core advisory group of artists, social service providers, arts administrators, clergy and community volunteers began to meet regularly to raise funds and coordinate activities. (One of the earliest project efforts to generate alternative images involved setting up a booth at the 1985 Minnesota State Fair to videotape interviews with older women about the experience of aging.)

In the spring and summer of 1986, in cooperation with the Whisper Minnesota project, the Humphrey Institute conducted a six-month leadership seminar for thirty-five women ranging in age from 60 to 87. These community leaders represented the diverse patterns of ethnic and geographic settlement in Minnesota. Although the seminar focused on the intermeshing of the personal and the political in women's assumption of leadership, the artistic mission of the project was not neglected. A documentation team of photographers and videographers were involved in producing authentic images of strong women struggling to make a difference in their respective communities. The products of the seminar — especially "The Time is Now," a videotape by Linda Brooks, and a slide tape presentation by Karen Bacing — provided additional images of aging which were quickly assimilated into the performance recruitment process.

An important goal was realized when the seminar participants became recruiters for "The Crystal Quilt" performance within their own communities. The involvement of these community leaders gave the project and the performance credibility in communities that were initially skeptical of performance art and wary of being exploited by a white, middle-class, feminist artist from California.

From its inception, the parent project and the ensuing performance were envisioned as collaborative efforts in which the process was part of the product. Both the administrative and the artistic components were committed to organizational models that valued inclusivity and cooperation more than efficiency and decisiveness. Lacy found Minnesota's socially progressive attitudes and its penchant for consensus-style politics especially suitable for the kind of organizational effort the project required. And she was willing to postpone the initial performance by nearly a year to accommodate the community-based fundraising and recruiting efforts.

In order to realize a performance with the scope and scale of "The Crystal Quilt," a substantial cast of collaborating artists was assembled. For many Minnesota activists, artists, and funders unfamiliar with Lacy's work, the inclusion — as peers — of well-respected feminists and artists from the Twin Cities was an important step in bolstering support from the local feminist and artistic communities. From Minneapolis, Phyllis Jane Rose, the artistic director of the oldest continuous women's theater in the United States, "At the Foot of the Mountain," became the associate director for the performance. (Coincidentally Rose was directing and touring "The Ladies Who Lunch," a play about older women and politics, as the Whisper Minnesota Project was taking shape.) Sage Cowles, a Twin Cities choreographer, became the movement specialist for the performance. Miriam Schapiro flew in from New York in December 1986 to see the performance site (the huge glass-enclosed Crystal Court of Philip Johnson's IDS Tower) and consult with Jeanne Spears of the Minnesota Quilters about the design of the stage. Susan Stone, the audio artist who developed the tape for the first Whisper project, also came to Minnesota to test the acoustics of the Crystal Court and discuss the form and content of the audio accompaniment for "The Crystal Quilt" performance. Although the artists focused on the aesthetic integrity of the performance and rarely identified themselves as "older" or "middle-aged," they implicitly represented several generations of women artists. (At the time of the performance Cowles and Schapiro were in their sixties, Spears in her fifties, Lacy and Rose in their forties, and Stone in her early thirties.)

Like the original "Whisper" performance in California, "The Crystal Quilt" was a rich mixture of artistic and political symbols. Once again, the performance was structured around the concept of an aesthetically compelling image of ethnically and racially diverse older women occupying a significant public space and discussing their concerns with each other. During the performance an audio collage of previously recorded conversations, songs, and ambient sounds provided content and context for the spectators and cued the performers to form kaleidoscopic patterns with their hands.

In contrast to the soothing natural environment of the La Jolla beach, the site of "The Crystal Quilt" was the glass-covered commercial center of downtown Minneapolis. The indoor image of a living quilt was particularly appropriate in a region where the inhabitants have had to act cooperatively to survive the rigors of the harsh northern climate. The aesthetics of the site and concept called for the transformation of a black stage into a colorful patchwork quilt. Lacy wanted the initial set to be somber, but not funereal. In order to avoid any visual or audial suggestion of mourning, the black-clad performers did not form a procession, but, accompanied by ambient sounds of "a typical Minnesota day," they entered gradually from the corners of the quilt and unfolded the black tablecloths to reveal the red or yellow color inside. This slow unfolding echoed the painstaking piecework of quilt-making. The audience listened to the participants talking [prerecorded] among themselves about their accomplishments and disappointments; reflecting on their hopes and their fears; self-image, sexuality, family, community, illness, invisibility, and activism. After a litany of the performers' names and ages, and Meridel LeSueur's ultimate characterization of aging as ripening, the performers applauded each other and the audience. The spectators were then encouraged to take hand-painted scarves from strategically situated volunteers and come on to the quilt to honor the performers by presenting them with these symbols of public investiture.

Judged by its goal to promulgate complex, artistically compelling images of older women, the Whisper Minnesota project succeeded in having local and regional mass-media venues distribute the striking and sensitive images produced by the two dozen photographers, videographers, filmmakers and writers on the documentation team. These visual, auditory, and literary images recognized the achievements of the performers while providing an opportunity for older women to speak out in the media on public policy issues. The Twin Cities public television station broadcast the live performance as a special Mothers' Day celebration. The live television coverage included brief interviews with Minnesota's Lieutenant Governor, Marlene Johnson, and her mother; critics Moira Roth and Lucy Lippard; and quilt designer Miriam Schapiro. Pre-recorded interviews with selected performers underscored the peculiar mix of limitation and liberation involved in aging.

The proliferation of images was designed to continue the project's goals: Larry Fink's photographs of the Whisper Minnesota project were the centerpiece of an exhibition at First Bank Saint Paul, while another exhibition of performance photographs by Tom Arndt, Linda Brooks, Gus Gustafson, Terry Gydeson, Edith Kodmur, Peter Latner, Wendy Olson, and Ann Marsden opened in the summer and then traveled to other sites in Minnesota, accompanied by older women from the project. These women hoped to use the exhibition as an organizing tool for conducting community hearings on public policy.

Led by Margaret Pederson, Avis Foley, Bea Swanson, and Muriel Vaughn (all alumnae of the leadership seminar), Quilt performers assumed initial responsibility for the continuation of the Whisper Minnesota project. They asked the original sponsors and advisors to renew their commitment to the project and planned to tap the resources of corporate funders in order to staff a very modest office, procure the use of a Winnebago, and travel the state to mobilize older women to occupy a more prominent place in the public arena. Suzanne Lacy returned from California to Minnesota occasionally to confer with project colleagues. The project continues to embody the message that older women are coming of age politically and artistically.[1]

The following quotes are taken from "The Crystal Quilt" soundtrack by Susan Stone, or "The Time is Now" a video tape by Linda Brooks]

> You get older in other people's eyes; you don't see yourself as old. You look out the window and not the mirror anymore.

> Why don't we just say "old"? What's wrong with the word "old"? You like old cheese, old wine, old furniture, what's wrong with the word "old"?

> I think it's true that we have a vocabulary that describes our beautiful young women, but we don't have as good a vocabulary to describe what is beautiful about older citizens.

> I don't think that being an old woman is ugly at all. It's different kind of beauty, like the difference between a rosebud and an old rose. Neither is more beautiful than the other.

> Personally I've never had it happen to me that I saw myself in a mirror and suddenly said "I'm old." I've been very aware of what's been happening gradually, so that it never came as a shock. I think I'm realistic about my age, but I just don't think of myself as "old."

> As a representative of my generation, I would like persons young or old to ask me what I thought my contribution to society is. I was raised by a family that believes strongly that you left this place better than you found it. That has been my whole impetus my entire life, and I would like people to be aware of that, to just ask the question.

> In many communities we are the ones who do the volunteer work now. Younger people are all employed. I deliver meals on wheels. Practically everybody who delivers meals on wheels is over 65. Since most of the people over 65 are women, most of the people delivering meals on wheels are women. More and more we are doing the volunteer work of the society.

> I don't want any particular recognition, I just want the sense of having done something well.

I would like to have a child say to me, "You lived during the Roosevelt administration, Grandma. What was so great about Roosevelt?" Rather than having them ask me what was transportation like then. I would really like children to be thinking about what we have to offer in terms of values.　　　　　　　　　　　　　　　　　— *Helen Wilbur*

I think a lot of senility comes from the fact that nobody asks you anything. Nobody includes you in the social ceremonials. Nobody asks you to speak. Pretty soon you lose your memory. I suffer a lot from people not listening to me. It's like not having a great aged tree to sit under, to protect you or to look at or to feel. I thinks it's a great cultural loss.　　　　　　　　　　　　　　　　　　　　　　　　　　— *Meridel Le Seuer*

As you approach your exits, you know, when you get to be 70 or 75, I think your response to stimuli is intensified. I feel as though I am living a richer life, because I am experiencing so much more. That sunset, you know, let's have it last a little longer!

I feel like I need to live about two years more, to bring in my crops before the frost, I call it. My unfinished work . . . I have three books to finish. But that is a patriarchal statement; women don't "finish' things."　　　　　　　　　　　　　　　　　　— *Meridel Le Seuer*

As I come to realize that death is going to be a part of my life in the next few years, I become more and more aware of what I have given and not given to my children. And I try to make my contribution to their lives more colorful, more exacting in standards, but also more enjoyable. So that if they have to go through that period of indignity with me, they will have the remembrance of a richer, better relationship.

The only terror of getting old for me is economic. I was put in the hospital a year ago and it wiped me out. Everything I had saved — I used to call it having enough to die on — all gone. Now I'm afraid. I'm not going to be dependent upon my children. What's going to happen to me? It's a terrible fear to have to be afraid to get ill.

I want to go directly from my home to the undertaker's. I wouldn't want to go into a nursing home.

I've done a lot to avoid being dependent upon my children. I've made a reservation in a retirement home, and right now one of the big decisions of my life is when do I go? Next week, or in ten years? But I have no intention of being dependent upon people who can hurt me as badly as my children can. Not that they would deliberately, but sometimes I feel so lonely here, sometimes I wish somebody gave a red hot damn about what I do. If I feel that way now, I would feel that way ten times more if I was near enough for my children to see me and they didn't.

Some Notes on "The Crystal Quilt": A Conversation Continued

by Suzanne Lacy

"The Crystal Quilt" was an extremely complex project, engaging the personal, political, and aesthetic experience of literally dozens of people. Patrice Koelsch wrote "The Crystal Quilt: A Performance and Its Legacy" shortly after the performance was over in 1987. In the intervening time some memories have emerged, while some have become less salient. These footnotes are offered in the spirit of a continuing conversation, not only between Patrice and myself, but with the many collaborators and points of view that made up the work itself. It is my hope that we will eventually piece these conversations together in a way that finally reveals the complexity of this collaboration.

1. Sometime during the 1970s it became quite apparent that not only were media images of younger women inaccurate, but those of older women were even more distorted. As I looked more closely at media, I remembered witch burnings, Shakespeare's three crones, and Walt Disney's old woman witches, and I began to understand how fears of aging were closely tied with the images of old women. It was as if our future was taken from us. We lived without aspirational images of wisdom and power that came with age and experience. We were women without a sense of where we were going.

It seemed that art was a place for our social reconstruction. Older women were everywhere, but invisible. Meeting articulate and active women well into their eighties convinced me that it was these portraits that were missing and needed.

2. During the 1970s, I was intrigued with ideas from Allan Kaprow's notions of art's close proximity with and resemblance to "real life," and from colleagues Judy Chicago, Shelia de Bretteville and Arlene Raven, who suggested that art could recreate women's reality from the point of view of women themselves. The line that divides the creations of the imagination from the daily life of common people was beginning to interest some art theoreticians. At California Institute for the Arts, where I was a graduate student, I worked with Kaprow and found his ideas had great political potential. If making art was not reserved exclusively for the white male artists currently in power, the "democratization" of art might include ideas from women, from ethnic minorities, from the working class. Even more important, if the subject matter for art might be found anywhere, particularly outside the confines of current art world subjects, then art might reasonable concern itself with the daily life and political reality of women. Working toward the notion of an "expanded performance" that took place in the public sector, including the mass media, I created performances, involving hundreds of people. They were to function on several levels at once: aesthetically, politically, and publicly. On the aesthetic level, the theoretical dialogues of art/life divisions, questions of how far you could go before it was no longer art, and an interest in shaping personal interaction into art-forms became a substructure. Politically, most of these works had a definite goal, or a series of them, and an activist thrust. Finally, inherent in the "expanded performance" was the idea of the mass public, and in each such artwork this public was carefully considered: how could the work alter both their political and aesthetic perceptions? In the case of Whisper Minnesota, for example, the entire project was seen as the work of art, from the beginning organization, through fundraising, administration, media work and promotion, and including follow-up after the performance. Thus "The Crystal

Quilt" performance, which took place on Mother's Day in 1987, was the central image in a three-year expanded performance, one which included the daily activities and framed interactions of scores of people.

3. The link between the San Diego Whisper and the Minnesota Whisper was important. In fact, the decision to do the project in Minnesota came as a result of an observation that repetition is an aspect of mass culture. I was curious to see how continuing with the theme of older women's visibility might contribute to a larger cultural awareness of these issues. Demonstrating the continuity between one performance and the other gave me a platform for organizing in Minnesota. Women who were leaders in the San Diego project visited Minnesota as our guests. They acted as witnesses to the Whisper planning, and experts who shared their wisdom with the group of Minnesota older women. Thus the continuity of the two projects linked older women from two cities in a network where they were positioned as leaders.

4. One of the major designer's of the Whisper Minnesota project was Sharon Roe Anderson, Associate Director of the Reflective Leadership Program at the Humphrey Institute for Public Affairs. Her creativity and vision gave pragmatic shape to my intuitive belief that such works could help to shape the public agenda. Usually artists' aspirations and desires toward change are limited by their access to the institutions that control such change. The Humphrey Institute is such an institution — a think tank in public policy for scholars and politicians.

Anderson insisted that we define clearly and in writing the rationale for this project, and together with analyst Karen Lehman we outlined the relationship between mass media imagery, social attitude, the creations of a public agenda related to the elderly, and the Whisper Minnesota project. We drew examples from the media's involvement with electoral politics to make our comparisons, and compared statistics of older women's visibility in the media with their social and economic situation. Anderson and her colleagues developed their contribution to Whisper Minnesota — a Reflective Leadership Program for older women.

As the project grew, other organizations, as well as individuals, continued to articulate the meaning of Whisper Minnesota, each from their own vantage point. The meaning of the project was thus consensual and evolving, including not only the vision of artists. From the beginning, Nancy Dennis served as Administrative Director, a position equivalent to mine as Artistic Director. She managed fundraising, personnel, board development, and participated in every aspect of planning and decision-making. Her belief in and dedication to this project was not only a great personal support, but was fundamental to its success.

5. Artists were central — not only with their images, but also politically generative in their own right. By introducing the subject matter of aging to artists, we encouraged an array of creative responses. Artists and social scientists were invited

as a team to participate in the Leadership Seminar, and others were invited to film, photograph, write about or otherwise speculate artistically on women and aging. In some cases, already existing artworks or exhibitions were conceptualized within the project. The play "Ladies Who Lunch" became a recruitment vehicle and advertisement for Whisper Minnesota while having an independent artistic life as a production of At the Foot of the Mountain Theater Company. In another example, an exhibition of art by elderly residents of a high-rise complex was advertised by Whisper Minnesota, and we hosted a reception for the artists.

6. Since we knew public awareness was a necessary precursor to change, we developed a mass media strategy, put together by various volunteers under the leadership of Phyllis Burns, a public relations professional. They decided to use public interest in the developing performance as a "hook" to get media coverage for older women — not just those in the project but others as well. They set out to raise the statewide awareness of older women's contributions by increasing their visibility. One tactic was to give women from the Reflective Leadership Program press kits and instructions on how to generate media coverage of themselves and other older women in their communities across the state. Another strategy was to use inquiries about the project as a way of generating strong media images of older women. They knew that the media has a penchant for "personal interest" stories, and like to focus on personalities. Rather than positioning me as "the artist" they worked to redirect the media attention; in some cases they were able to substitute interviews with older women for the requested interviews with me.

7. Although the majority of the people involved in the project were female, this seemed to stem more from women's higher interest in consensual and collaborative forms than from the subject matter of older women. Men figured significantly in all phases of the project. Particularly during production, men's skills were evident in all aspects of directing and producing the television documentary, soundtrack, and stage design. Yet there was no challenge to the creative centrality of women. It seemed that the subject of older women was a resonant one for men as well as women, and there was an acceptance of women's leadership in the project that is uncommon in other situations.

8. The whole discussion around the Quilt's colors was an intriguing connection between aesthetics and politics. When Mimi Schapiro visited Minnesota for the first time and we held a small dress rehearsal on the floor of the Crystal Court to decide on colors, we tried several ideas, including spring colors. But the two of us continued to return to black, sensing it was the only "color" that could "hold down" the complex and chaotic space, and bring it together into a unified stage. We were warned that it could be almost impossible to get older women in early spring, on Mother's Day no less, to wear black. We left that night to sleep on it, but the next day at breakfast Mimi and I agreed: black it had to be, to create the aesthetic power we were after. We believed strongly that the aesthetic vision

should not be compromised by the performers stereotypes of color. The performers, and ultimately older women, would be best served by the most powerful aesthetic statement we could make. Convincing the participants was only the first of our problems. Even after the project collaborators had accepted our choice of black as the ground color, and hence the costume color for the women, and even after it became apparent that the women performers understood and accepted our choice, there were still issues to be resolved. During one intense conversation with Elva Walker she pointed out the cultural associations linking black with age and death. Because of these, she said, we had to take particular care to transform this reference. Our public theme, after all, was older women as vital participants in the public arena, not harbingers of death. My original plan, to have performers enter the quilt as a processional through the crowd and down the escalators, would inscribe a funeral reference that could not be shaken, Elva stated with conviction. This discussion shaped both entrance and exit, which we staged in such a way that the performers would never be seen apart from the quilt background. They would enter four at a time from the corners of the quilt, assembling just under the eaves of the second balcony. Before the performance was over, each performer would be draped with a hand-painted scarf so that they carried away with them the red and yellow colors of the quilt.

9. Susan Stone's soundtrack was an amazing collage of information drawn from two full days of studio taping of seventy-five women. She chose the languages from the women's backgrounds and the songs they sang from their youth as two major themes in the work. Politically we stressed women's aspirations, accomplishments, fears and plans for the future — issues that pointed to their active and vital lives. The soundtrack, which played on multiple speakers placed around the second floor balcony, was our only method of cueing performers. At intervals the sound of a loon's cry, a church bell, a cuckoo clock, or a clap of thunder rang across the entire space, signaling the women that it was time to change their hand positions and their topic of conversation. Each group had four questions they addressed during these intervals.

10. When Patrice Koelsch wrote this article, shortly after the performance, the Whisper Minnesota project seemed destined to continue. They had moved into a smaller office in the Minnesota Women's Building and had secured enough funding to pay for a part-time staff person. For at least a year they continued, lecturing, attending conferences, and putting up small exhibitions of the photographs and presenting quilt by the Minnesota quilters. Then slowly the office closed down, and the women, who remained active and in touch with each other, stopped trying to maintain the "Whisper Minnesota" project as an entity.

In 1982 I wrote an article for the *New Art Examiner* in which I explored what was the real legacy of such performances. I compared my temporal works — art that took place in communities across the country rather than in my home town

— to those of my friend Judy Baca, who has lived and worked in Los Angeles for several years. Her presence there seemed to affect not only the scale of her work but its political longevity. Was the amount of time one was willing to stay in one place and commit to one work a measure of its continuing political viability?

Since that time I've watched Baca stretch to include different constituencies in different places. Continuing political activism in the shape of an ongoing organization seems related to the artist's ability to invest energy directly into the daily running of the operation. I suspect that it will not be that daily work for which the artist is remembered, and this leads me to consider whether the worth of political art is to be found in its ability to continue, after the artwork is no longer the focus, in an organizational form.

If so, how does one measure art's social values? As with all art, the aesthetics are at issue, and they must be evaluated. But what of its political nature? While we do not yet have the critical language to talk eloquently about these issues, perhaps what is called for is the inclusion of issues of meaning and value into the language of art. How do we change culture? By changing the images and words with which we describe ourselves, their rhythm and timing, the shapes and forms in which we recognize our experience? In what direction, and to what end, will our artworks serve the public imagination? What models for cooperation and consensual meaning are inherent in the art, and what is the vision of the future it evokes? There are critics at work developing this language, and more and more artists are tuning their creative insights toward public issues of profound consequence to all of us. It is not that we should leave the maintenance of organizing activities to others; artists are citizens who will naturally participate in the social order. But we have something additional to contribute to conceptualizing change and mobilizing the human spirit.

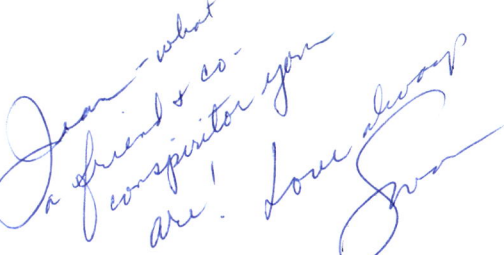

Confessions of a Community Artist

by Suvan Geer

In "Confessions of a Community Artist," Geer relates how her solo work led her to work with groups of women artists, which in turn led to the creation of her own group of artists committed to improving our specie's relationship to the earth (ACTS). She also discusses "In Living Memory" which brought together and honored elders and their recollections of growing up in a less polluted city.

Geer has written two sentences that summarize much of the content of this book: "to paraphrase a feminist credo, my personal has become not only political, but populated. Community for me has become an art of art, a natural method of engagement."

These are the words of a loner. Someone more comfortable apart. Someone always distracted and overwhelmed by conversations of more than two people. Someone who needs large doses of quiet and solitude just to keep sane and fully operational. Someone soul-mated to the emptiness of the California desert.

I make art — have always made art — from the depths of the aloneness that fills me like a grand stony cavern. Please understand, even though these pages are about a communal experience, I love and cherish my interior hollow space. My art resonates with the stinging sound I hear in that place. I find it to be a grand chamber in which any sound or word has a rolling echo of vibrating meaning. My installations whisper and drone, rumble and sigh with it. A kind of poetic, breathy, rustling poised just at the brink of language.

Six years ago I went into the White Mountains. I camped for nine days, letting the space of the high desert fill and match the vastness I felt inside of me. I went because I was drawn. I came out not-alone. The wind, the piñon, the beetles, lizards, rocks, sun and land all shared my campsite. Quite literally, I heard them speak. Once their voices echoed inside me, I guess you could say they took up residence.

A loner, but no longer alone, I slipped quietly back into the daily hustle of life as an artist and writer. My wild companions and I nested. I didn't know it at the time but I was beginning something of a personal paradigm shift, looking for a glimmer which reflected the loving, attended solitude I now felt.

The following summer I met a woman. An artist and a visionary named Betsy

Damon. Like me, Betsy had faith in the value of making art in a world gone nuts. But further, she was committed to the power of women artists working together. Betsy is a vibrant and charismatic woman with a seemingly infinite capacity to appreciate and nurture other people's best selves. Put quite simply, she wants to change the world, and is willing to do it one person at a time. To that end, she sets up support groups for women artists all around the country called "No Limits for Women Artists." These groups meet regularly to dream big visions for the participants/ art, while forging the underpinnings of strong communal caring and group faith to sustain and nurture them.

Where I have always been an artist mining an internal landscape somewhat privately in my studio and installations, Betsy is a woman of overt and public demonstration. In *Overlays*,[1] Lucy Lippard refers to Damon's "7000-Year-Old Woman" street performance in New York as a projection of "private rituals into the communal realm — the streets." Consistently, in art projects like her "Keepers of the Waters," which unites artists with environmental groups in a water-watch guardianship, Damon demonstrates art's ability to interrupt and interact in the daily reality of the world at large.

Betsy Damon's kind of communal art-life interaction resonated well with my own newly emerging sense of personal and natural interrelationship. Her support networks drew me into a fertile female community. For the first time, I understood the advantages of making art in collaboration, especially around important issues, and with the public at large. It struck me as ironic then, and occasionally still does, that artists — the long-idolized models of rebellious independence, painful isolation, and esoteric rumination — might ultimately serve as models for creative community dialogue and interaction. It seemed like an impossible contradiction. But I've found it works.

The River Calls You

On Earth Day 1990, artists joined residents from the neighborhoods lining the Los Angeles River to enact a cleansing ritual along the river's cement banks. Organized by artists Sandra Golvin and Leslie Diller-Zollo, "The River Calls You" performance was everything that one expects of good theater: uplifting purpose touched with the colors and textures of real life. At the finale of the piece, we participants — over 130 in number — stood along the narrow bridge arching across the river to pour small offerings of clean water into the river. We were exhilarated. Our "down and dirty" performance had recalled the beauty of the river running through our city, blessed its passage, and netted a small mountain of trash — bedsprings, shopping carts, and recyclables — from the quarter mile of the reed-covered river bottom. Art and action had come together for us and it felt wonderful.

"The River Calls You" was the inaugural gesture of our new artists group, Artists Contributing to the Solution (ACTS). It was a small collective aimed at drawing attention to artworks that dealt with ecological issues, which were, back in 1989 when we first started meeting, as thoroughly ignored by the art world as ecological warnings were by the popular press. The impact of Earth Day 1990 and the Exxon Valdez oil spill must be recognized as powerful honing devices that shaped the popular environmental movement. They made ecological awareness "politically correct" and open to individual activism. ACTS benefited from that energy and contributed to making local art a significant part of the public dialogue.

The core group of ACTS was a small cadre of wonderfully energetic women from the local chapter of the Women's Caucus for Art. We had discovered one another's work — and our shared activist aspirations — at an incredible charged weekend retreat of the local "No Limits For Women Artists" leaders' support group. In the security of that weekend, we shared our love for the planet and our fears for its future, without worries of being tagged "bleeding heart liberals" or "overly emotional women." The warmth of that communal reception and the fact that we were all artists just naturally seemed to lead to impassioned discussions of art's purpose and the practicalities of what art can do in the face of overwhelming disaster.

It was a discussion that deepened quickly into friendship. It is with real fondness that I recall the personal dedication and write the names of early ACTS artists like Lucy Blake-Elahi, Katya Williamson, Jean Towgood, Janice DeLoof, and the other artists who quickly joined us, Ruth Ann Anderson, Nancy Ann Jones, Sandra Golvin, Andreas Hesing, Elizabeth Jennings, Margaret Lazarri, and Leslie Diller-Zollo.

We started with a quarterly calendar. It was a constantly expanding listing of exhibitions, art events, and performances we either curated, created, or invited into our year of events. Every artist involved in the exhibitions or events was added to the growing list of participants. By the time that list reached fifty-two in number, it had become a "Who's Who" of artists who were exploring a "green" agenda. It included Helen and Newton Harrison, Rachel Rosenthal, Barbara Smith, Richard Misrach, Alan Sonfist, Lynne Hull, Beverly Naidus, Sheila Pinkel, Kim Abeles, Deborah Small, and Cheri Gaulke. As we continued to curate exhibitions (we organized six), we discovered many artists not known for making this kind of art. We also located several artists who had been longing for an opportunity to create work on the subject. So our list grew further to include Jerry Burchfield, Susan Gitlin-Emmer, Mark Niblock-Smith, John Outterbridge, and Jeffrey Valance.

ACTS did what it set out to do. It made ecologically-based art an acknowledged goad to discussion about the environment and individual action. It demanded an incredible amount of time and energy from all of us, but gave us back a sense of our own power, of what we could accomplish when we united. Drawing together, we found others who felt as we did and who had been working, sometimes for years, alone or in remote corners of the country.

The power of ACTS was the power of the people involved in it. What continues are certain events like the river clean-up which so pleased the local environmental group, Friends of the Los Angeles River (organized by poet Louis Adams), that the event is an annual Earth Day occurrence for them. Also continuing are the friendships. The expanded community that ACTS brought together now covers all of greater Los Angeles and reaches beyond to Minnesota, New York, and Wyoming. The experience of creating ACTS — all the panels, exhibitions, calendars, and discussions — taught me about our ability to care. It also showed me how effective a dedication to community involvement could be in keeping art active in political and social engagement. ACTS is no longer active, but I continue to believe that art is a good way to summon community.

In Living Memory

Art and its venues also offer ways to frame community dialogue. As Vito Acconci once said, "The [art] gallery . . . could be thought of as a community meeting place, a place where a community could be formed. . . ." I worked with the idea of community dialogue in a piece evoking ecological recollections of the city of Los Angeles. "In Living Memory" was done in collaboration with artist Ruth Ann Anderson and a group of ten elders who have lived in the Los Angeles area all their lives. To give the city back its invisible ecological history, we created posters using the elders' stories about what the land, water, air, and community were like up to sixty years ago. We hung the posters on bus shelters around Los Angeles.

There is something about the cement and asphalt sameness of Los Angeles that appears timeless. Like the weather that is repetitive and constant year to year, the city's environment seems unchanged decade to decade. Partly, it's because we change its detail so rapidly. Empty lots become buildings almost overnight. Vacant buildings get pulled down within months and mini-malls mushroom there before the dust settles. Add that rapid-change mentality to a population that routinely picks up and moves to another neighborhood every two years, and you have a formula for ecological blindness. How can one know the lay of the land when tractors keep flattening it or new buildings are forever cropping up between you and the hills? Transplants and new residents are like children; they have no lived history of place. Everything for them is present tense. There is no past for comparison. The future is always a whole new game to be made up on the spot without a sense of consequence or loss.

When we interviewed elders from around Los Angeles about what they remembered of the city of their childhoods, we were stunned. In one lifetime, the city had gone from being farmland with orange groves and cows along Wilshire Boulevard to the dense, faded industrial center we now know. In the space of one lifetime, the ocean had gone from a crystal-clear place to fish for dinner to brown-green muck often too hazardous to swim in. The air had gone from bright to blurry gray so thick the surrounding mountains are invisible most days.

For one month, during "In Living Memory," the city had a little bit of oral history at curbside. The stories reminded residents of the invisible, yet rampant change they are living through. It was a public gesture of anti-invisibility for the local environment and for the elders, but it was not enough. At the urging of our assisting collaborator, Sandra Golvin, we decided to use the added visibility of my participation in the "Utopian Dialogues" exhibition at the Los Angeles Municipal Art Gallery.

One afternoon, for a few hours, my installation — a hushed room lined with wax ears, melting words of longing, and native grasses — was transformed from a site of silent meditation to a public "town meeting" about the local ecology. We united the "In Living Memory" elders with local environmental groups and budding high school environmentalists, so they could network in small groups. The public was invited to eavesdrop on the groups and get a bit of past, present, and future all at once. The event was packed, noisy, and very moving. Friendships were started among some of the participants of all ages. The friendships continue.

All that being said, I wonder, do these projects make me a community artist? They seem such small gestures. The lives I'm touching are all over the place; it's hard to think of them as a community.

Or is it that I joined community during those nine days in the White Mountains? Last night an owl called in the backyard. It was a high, piping sound, so different from most owl calls that I didn't know what it was until the bird sailed from one tree to another. I have not heard the owl since and the silence bothers me. I hear ever fewer bird calls, ever fewer sounds I recognize from the desert. But more people are speaking and I value their words.

Still, I'm not sure what community means, or if I am a community artist in any typical sense. To me, community simply means connection. And on the most basic level, everything is connected.

Suvan Geer, Ruth Ann Anderson, et al, "In Living Memory," 1993. An oral history project of Los Angeles' environmental past written on bus shelters to draw attention to what senior citizens remember about local ecological changes project. Pictured: participants Ruth Ann Anderson, Sondra Golvin, and local children.

Touched by Ukeles

by Cheryl Marie Dullabaun

Mierle Laderman Ukeles is the unsalaried artist-in-residence for the New York City Department of Sanitation. She is also known for her Maintenance Art performances of the 1960s and early 1970s which involved washing, scrubbing and cleaning to bring these traditionally, ignored and devalued domestic activities to the public's attention. Ukeles went on to perform "Touch Sanitation," (1979-1984) which involved shaking the hands of all the sanitation workers in New York City and culminated in a parade of mirrored garbage trucks that reflected the image of those responsible for creating all of the solid waste. Her ongoing project "Flow City," asks viewers to consider the magnitude, responsibility, and effects of waste, waste management, and recycling on the members of the community. Ukeles is currently (1996) working on a project for the Los Angeles Museum of Contemporary Art.

I have never seen Mierle Laderman Ukeles's sanitation pieces in New York City. I've never been to one of her maintenance performances, nor have I witnessed her garbage barge ballet choreographed for the East River. The closest I've come to seeing her work in person was viewing the white rags tossed in the corner under the documentary images of "Washing, Tracks, Maintenance," (1973), installed in the "Division of Labor" exhibition at the Los Angeles Museum Of Contemporary Art in 1995. One might ask why I would write about an artist whose work I have only seen in photographs or slides.

But this is not an observational critique of objects, installations, and performances of Mierle Laderman Ukeles. It is about my relationship with an artist whom I met several years ago. Although I have not seen or spoken to her since, she stays in my thoughts and continues to influence my decisions about making art. Mierle Laderman Ukeles opened a door and I walked through to find a community of artists and a way of art-making that I had not known before.

I opened up my journal from 1990 and read these words next to the name of Mierle Laderman Ukeles.

beyond the vision

Ukeles was the "Atlantic Lecturer" at The Claremont Graduate School and I was a first-year student. Traditionally, visiting artists show slides of their work and lecture. Instead Ukeles asked us questions about ourselves, where we came from, where we thought we were going, and how we thought we were going to get there. Her questions probed a previously unexamined area. The emphasis was not on what we made — not on the pure materiality of the objects in our studios — but on how our work related to ourselves, to our audiences, and to the community in which we placed our "things"(our art works). She asked us to take a personal inventory and acknowledge who we touch, what issues we support with our art, and in return who touches and supports us.

transformational sites

The first meting of Ukeles's seminar continued outside under the cover of night. We students (only the curious and confused remained) formed a circle. Mierle persuaded us to act out — put into physical, visual terms — our interpretation of the support relationships we had identified.

support freedom dependency

carry drag pull lean lift

Two students did an impromptu ballet of each relationship. They moved in tandem. Their dance was an ephemeral documentation of their connection, their community. Their movements were sensual, loving, and interdependent. I envied their understanding and ability to perform so freely, so openly and so unselfconsciously.

We still had not seen Mierle's work.

Many of us were fresh out of undergraduate art programs and still clung to traditional views of art-making. We thought that art was a painting, a sculpture, maybe a photograph, perhaps an element found or constructed for an installation; an art work was definitely an object made by an individual for the purpose of being admired and eventually purchased by a museum, gallery, or collector.

That is why her ideas seemed so difficult to grasp. She was talking about art work that had no gallery price tags. Some of her ideas about art didn't involve materiality at all! She engaged us in a dialog that revolved around systems and ideologies — a dialogue that asked us to think about art beyond the object. It was a dialogue that included not only the community of students in our circle but our cosmos, our history, our relationships with past and future members of our blood-related families, and our extended world family.

As I searched through the files at the school looking for information for this article I found a copy of Mierle's original notes and outline for the seminar. These questions were written across the page in her handwriting:

Who do I make my art for?

Am I emotionally alive in my art making

or am merely a bill-paying-hanging-in-there person?

Building Community

What is my voice saying?

I remember as if it were yesterday. She inspired me to ask myself the same questions, and I was startled by the answers. It was clear I could never go home again. Not to my literal home with a husband who could never share my vision nor to the home of modernist ideas that I thought would house my "beautiful" objects.

Mierle's teaching propelled me into an examination of relatedness that started in the most personal of transformation sites: in my own consciousness. The motive, the voice of my art-making seemed unclear, out of focus, out of sync with who I was, what I was. Up to this point I had embraced without question the modernist premise that art-making was a highly individualistic endeavor, an enterprise conceived and completed in isolation. The products of art-making were to be placed in hierarchical institutions and have relevance only to a select few.

Before I met Mierle, I had been headed in a dangerous direction, ". . . running around in tighter and tighter circles, doing the same thing over and over again but trying to make it look and sound different."[1] Or as Mierle described it: "Show your work — show it again. Keep the contemporary art museum groovy."[2]

In our second seminar meeting Mierle asked us to make a list, a genealogy of self. We were to assemble not only a genetic kinship tree as well as a list of everything that contributed to the construction of our physical, emotional, and cultural selves. We incorporated our rituals, our relationships with the environment, with the land that we were tied to spiritually and geographically. It was while compiling this list that the door for me was unlocked. I saw beyond my current myopic vision, a vision that had been built by the patriarchal building blocks of traditional art history, traditional aesthetic philosophy, and traditional female roles.

I was actually surprised to find that I was not a white male creative genius! I realized that I was an artist and a woman, a mother, a daughter, a sister, a student, a sometimes wife, a sometimes sinner, a sometimes saint. I saw that I was physically tied to the flat plains of the Midwest and spiritually tied to the gilt, ritual, and smoke of Catholicism. I was a many-faceted being, an artist in a community of diverse points of view. From this moment of realization my art took on a new, specific direction. A gender specific direction. (In fact, the title of my first work after my seminar experience was precisely that: "A Gender Specific.")

On the last day of the seminar, Mierle Ukeles finally showed her work to us. Many of the students who had abandoned the seminar in the beginning rejoined the group for the final meeting. I remember Mierle's talk vividly. I recall the low gasps and muffled conversations as she progressed further into the slides of her work. Many of the male students had dismissed her circular, nonconventional, nonformalist, nonhierarchical ideas about art and teaching as "chick stuff," too touchy, too feely, too feminine (and too feminist!). They were stunned and I was thrilled as she explained "Flow City" and "Touch Sanitation." I was delighted and filled with a sense of pride as I saw images of mirrored garbage trucks and a tugboat ballet fill the screen. Her art was exciting, nonconventional, enormous in scope, organization, and execution.

More important I saw that it came from a place to which, as a woman, I could relate. I have lived in urban environments. I have experienced the sanitation strike in New York City that left mounds of uncollected refuse and created corridors of garbage on the city streets. I understand firsthand what happens if we don't take responsibility for our environment and waste recycling. I have cleaned up after others. I still do. At different times, I have washed, mended, cooked, sewed, worried about who I am and how I look and how I am perceived by others, only to devalue myself and allow others to undervalue my activities.

I read Mierle Laderman Ukeles's words written in 1969:

> Clean your desk, wash the dishes, clean the floor, wash your clothes, wash your toes, change the baby's diaper, finish the report, correct the typos, mend the fence, keep the customer happy, throw out the stinking garbage, watch out — don't put things in your nose, what shall I wear, I have no sox, pay your bills, don't litter, go to the store, I'm out of perfume, say it again — he doesn't understand, seal it again — it leaks, go to work, this art is dusty, clear the table, call him again, flush the toilet, stay young.[3]

These words contain the seeds, the core elements of much of her work. Whether about rinsing diapers, cleaning chicken feet, or building "Flow City," Mierle's work addresses maintenance and its ramifications on the community — from the nuclear family, to the largest and most industrialized of cities. The roles and functions of woman — wife, mother, citizen — defines who she is as an individual. They also inform and activate her art work.

July 1973/ Ukeles

"Washing, Tracks, Maintenance: Maintenance Art Activity III." Mierle washes several areas of the museum where visitors were sure to walk. She waits for the viewers to soil the floor. Then she rewashes the space, repeating the activity until the museum closes. The rags are collected in a corner and the area marked with the Maintenance Art Stamp as a further indication that an art activity has occurred and has transformed the space. From dirty, to clean, from dirty, to clean. . . .

> *You uncover secrets about yourself — but not to keep them hidden. . . .*

July 1991/ Dullabaun

"Becoming and Being," (The Claremont Graduate School.) I drag my bed into the gallery. I let others examine my biggest hang-up

while I observe how I am constricted by my roles, by my sexuality. I isolate the signals that motivate my behavior, influence my art work. Nipples, wedding ring, twisted sheets, discarded marital counseling tapes, lipstick, pictures of my cast-off lovers, all available for your viewing pleasure.

Fall 1974/ Ukeles

"The Trees Are Having Their Period: Time Slice." (Vassar College.) Mierle constructs a fifty-foot sanitary napkin under a 100-year-old tree and then she circles the "piece' with incantations to its "weeping womb," calling out the absurd woman/nature=ability/destiny correlation.

Summer 1992/ Dullabaun

"Sacrificial Daughters." (Lankersheim Center for the Arts, Los Angles.) I use images from found negatives and family photographs, anonymous couples depicting the portrayal and effect of romantic love, from fantasy to brutality. I hang out in front of the store windows and talk to people about what they see, their experiences with love betrayed and reciprocated. The viewers are incorporated into the art work through their reflection in mirrors that bear the words THIEF THREAT VIRGIN VICTRIX.

1978-1979/ Ukeles

"Touch Sanitation." Mierle wears the orange jumpsuit of the City of New York Sanitation Department workers. She meets them on their turf. She shakes each of their hands acknowledging, honoring their work and their importance to the community. The art work ends with a parade, complete with mirrored garbage truck that reflects the observers who are part of the community and affected by the production and disposal of waste.

November 1995/ Dullabaun

"Imprint Of The Interior: What Does She Require?" (Muses Exhibition, Armory Center for the Arts, Pasadena, California.) I scrutinize my relationships with my mother and my daughter, the emotional and physical separations and suffering. I work in collaboration with the anthropologist and writer Sondra Hale. During the opening, I present a performance with my daughter Jennifer Enders. We sit across from each other but are separated by yards of scarlet fabric. The blood-red drape is pulled through a narrow slit I cut into the pine table. We count pomegranate seeds one by one and place them in sets of three.

Mother/daughter/grandmother. Days/months/years. Row after bloody row. Hour after hour.

I see the impact of Mierle Laderman Ukeles's words and work in my own. I have tried to incorporate the spirit of her ideas. Her ideas about making art from the personal. Her belief in the importance of embracing the daily functions that constitute our humanity: nurturing, washing, questioning, loving, mothering, crying. In doing so, I endeavour to interrogate and reveal an alternative form of art-making, for an audience that exists outside of graduate schools, outside of collectors' homes and beyond the white gallery walls. Touched by Mierle Laderman Ukeles, I have become committed to art-making that is concerned with, "the applications, consequences and moral purpose of the activity."[4] Accessibility and relatedness are critical elements of art-making for the artist and the viewer alike. With Mierle, I recognize the significance of the actions and tasks that contribute to the construction of embracing these actions.

"Redemption through repetition," was the mantra my daughter and I whispered while "seed counting" during the Muses exhibition. I am reminded of the Zen teacher who answered the quest for enlightenment, "Prepare the rice. Eat the rice. Wash the bowl."

As Mierle intimated so many years ago, the transformation begins. Transubstantiation is found in the commonplace.

Mierle Laderman Ukeles, "Transfer Station
Trans Formation," performance.

Mierle Laderman Ukeles, "Sacrificial Daughters" (detail),
mixed media installation, 1992.

The Keepers of the Waters

by Betsy Damon

Conceptual artist Betsy Damon dedicates her art/her life to informing and awakening public consciousness to the need for and memory of clean water. Through community interaction and participation, Damon invites collaboration at all levels to structure projects creating a vision of living water gardens around the world. Damon has organized related projects from Castle Valley, Utah, to the shores of Lake Superior in Duluth, Minnesota, and to the Fu-Nan River in China, where the artist spent the summer of 1995. Damon plans to return there to work with the Chinese Government on an extended ecological awareness program that will involve traditional Chinese practices of holistic well-being. This project, when completed, will be the first of its kind to bring together water quality awareness with an artistic aesthetic, along with educational programs to generate community involvement at multiple levels for the sake of health and spiritual connections.

Damon notes that ecological and environmental programs have coincided with artistic awareness in the United States at least since nineteenth century Hudson River School painters Thomas Cole and Frederick Church. Recent interest in and support of environmental issues has abated as industrial giants push toward increasing financial gain at the expense of public health and well-being. The artist challenges such neglect in her work, making every effort to stimulate communities to respond to the cleansing of waters — the life-sustaining element and the source of everything that lives and breathes.

The following essay, which Damon wrote with the assistance of Jenny Starr and Roslye Ultan, describes "The Keepers of the Waters" project in China.

I am a conceptual humanist artist. There are few boundaries between my life and my art. They are interwoven, embracing each other as I change and grow. I have a strong personal aesthetic. I believe in art work that inspires, illuminates, and initiates a vision of possibilities. Life is the process of becoming conscious, coming to the recognition that everything a person does has ramifications in all parts of existence.

My work since 1980 has led me to the understanding of how a group of committed people can address any challenge and solve problems in ways that respect our dynamic universe and its every living part. I believe that working together and sharing information is exciting, creative, efficient and productive; everyone gets to be themselves. I facilitate the process as well as participate. I've found that displaced, isolated events have limited impact. When artists work together, our voice is loud, our voice is heard; we accomplish what we want to get done and we have fun As a person raised in the United States where materialism has created a separateness as the norm, my work insists on the reweaving of art with community

Although I have a distinct aesthetic, I acknowledge a space in which all collaborators initiate their own ideas, in which all collaborators are valued as necessary and equal. My artworks are individual and come from the situation, from a dynamic interaction between the people in a particular place. The aesthetic evolves through a process of building relationships around a human interaction, an activity, an issue or a place. Together, we create collaborations that are larger than any one of us and are the sum of the team.

I work under the premise that people are intelligent and creative. Human beings develop the communities in which we live. Each one of us has the power to be dynamically effective in taking charge of the world. We have the ability to create necessary changes and solutions.

Following closely the experimental studios founded by Judy Chicago in the early 1970s, I founded a Feminist Art Studio at Cornell University (1972-73). During this period, I initiated many experimental community events and created ways of sharing my ideas and artistic process. I placed my body in the streets in "The 7000- Year-Old Woman" (1976), and in "Blindbeggar Woman" (1978). I took the next step by creating performances in workshops. This form was a catalyst for acts of sharing, connecting, and inviting women to share their stories. It was the genesis for community as we developed rituals together and participatory performances as in "A Rape Memory" (1980) or the "Meditation on Knives" (1981). These works evolved into opportunities to share concerns about the environment with "Mediation with Stones for the Survival of the Planet" (1982-84). In this performance I became the container for the performance but not the event itself. In 1980 and 1985, I installed versions of "The Shrine for Every Woman" at the United Nations conferences in Copenhagen [as part of the International Festival of Women Artists] and in Nairobi. The shrines were sites for women to share stories and create events regardless of race, religion, or politics. Attenders of the conferences left their stories and prayers in bags and numerous groups met to create performance events within the Shrine.

The performance "Meditations with Stones" (1982-84) led to my search for a way to bring the natural environment back into the city. In 1985, I cast a dry river bed in hand-made paper, imagining this 200-foot piece meandering through a gallery space. During the casting process, I discovered the water in the pristine Utah valley was polluted with uranium tailings and agricultural chemicals. I could remember as a child drinking the water anywhere. The foundations of life were being challenged. I committed myself to working with water quality. Water became my archetype of the appropriate structure for projects that nurture community. Water is the planet's primary element. It forms and informs the nature of our world. It includes the shape and motion of our hearts.

I create projects that are accessible and comprehensible to everyone. They nurture community by inviting relationships. The underlying passion of my current work is rooted in the belief that water quality is effecting our cells, our DNA, the evolution of life. In 1989 I conceptualized a community project around water issues called "Keepers of the Waters." Part of this vision was to work with community to build spaces that would remind us of the interdependence of life and water quality.

I moved to Minnesota to begin a "Keepers" project. Minnesota has the largest supply of freshwater in the United States and is home to the headwaters of the Mississippi. I piloted the project in two communities, Anoka and Duluth, in 1990. The project built relationships among artists, scientists, community organizations, educational institutions and government agencies to form alliances that structured projects to create a language and a vision of living water in the world. It connected people, inspired initiative and hope, created new imagery and language about water quality, and facilitated change in the treatment of water.

Although there was great enthusiasm for my ideas, funding proposals that challenged the fragmentation of information and the material imperative of U.S. society were not initially successful. Then, at a time of great personal discouragement, I received a grant to research a site in China called the "God" water in 1993. The Chinese have a holistic view in which they do not equivocate about water quality issues, nor separate these issues from a profound understanding of the quality of life. Water is life and health. Traditionally, they neither question what water quality is nor wait for further proof that health is greatly affected by chemical pollution.

The Chinese have maintained a close connection to nature, and working cooperatively is integral to their society. Their art and medicine are based on thousands of years of observing nature and humans. I felt quite at home in Chinese culture. I was revitalized by the Chinese belief that uncompromised water quality is essential to human health. I was reminded that the most fundamental needs of human existence depend on relationships rather than material supports.

When I was invited to speak at the First International Conference for the Environment, Art and Qi Gong [a Chinese health practice, based on movement and breathing] in Chengdu, I proposed an international "Keepers" project on the Yangzi River. In 1995, funded by a grant from a private foundation and the contributions of numerous individuals, I initiated my first "Keepers of the Waters" project in Chengdu, China. I went with my heart on my sleeve, ready to learn as much as to teach.

At first, I felt overwhelmed by the task. There was garbage everywhere. The river was a sewer, and there was no apparent way to address it. I had gone to China with neither official permission nor sponsorship, and had no idea how to implement the project. One concept was dominant in my mind: relationships are everything. I was soon to learn the same was true in Chengdu. Jill Jacoby, an environmental educator; Ann Pilli, a water quality scientist; Jon Otto, my son (who is fluent in Chinese); and my assistant Kristen Caskey joined me on the journey to Chengdu. Upon arrival, we immediately began to meet with people. I was fortunate to encounter exceptional people whose lives were committed to China and the Chinese environment.

After numerous public presentations and discussions, artists began to come forward and many others came to assist with various parts of the project. The plans gradually developed through workshops with scientists, educators, and artists from China and the U.S. We hosted a variety of meetings and communal activities and people began to open up. For artists in China, speaking out in public is considered potentially dangerous. Joining the "Keepers" project was an unknown. To participate was seen as a very bold public step. For those who did, we were able to provide living expenses and airfare. We collectively figured out funding strategies, with each artist submitting a proposal and everyone publicly sharing their finances with each other. In the end, none of the pieces cost more than $400 U.S. dollars.

Initially I wanted to work in a remote area, but was gently encouraged to work on the river in the heart of Chengdu. "Here you will have the biggest impact," I was told. "It is where we need you the most." However, a major barrier still remained: I had no official permission to work and nobody thought it would be granted. After quietly doing research and planning for three weeks, we confronted the inevitable need for government permission. Miraculously we were granted permission to proceed by the Foreign Affairs Office. I became the liaison between the government and everyone else on the project — the artists, students, and others who had joined us. The government put the entire project under my direction. With all the responsibility on my shoulders, everyone else was free to come out and express their concerns about the river. This was a profound turning point. Artists had come from as far as Lhasa, Shanghai, and Beijing to join the many participants from Chengdu. The project suddenly become much larger than any of us had anticipated.

Jill Jacoby led the first event (July 27, 1995). She conducted the first teacher training workshop to implement programs with high school students on water quality monitoring. We started collaborations between artists and scientists in the schools. A few days later (July 29), we did our first performance on the river called "Washing Silk." The Fu-Nan river was once called the brocade river because when silk was washed in the river it became brighter. Dressed in white with red gloves, the artists rinsed long stretches of white silk in the river water. The silk turned brown and gray. The event was visually stunning and went right to the heart of the people of Chengdu.

In "Washing Ice" (August 7-9, 1995), we took large rectangles of ice frozen from river water and invited the public to come wash a pile of ice blocks with scrub brushes. In "Washing Face" (August 9), the public was invited to wash their faces in twenty Chinese wash basins full of river water. The Tibetan artists painted over seventy prayer flags and banners that animated the river front. One artist hung large earthenware food pots over the water from a bridge, while another placed over 100 tea cups on the floor of a tea house, as river water dripped down into the cups and onto a white cloth. We draped white pieces of cloth over every discharge pipe into the river. The cloth was immediately stained brown from the sewage. Another artist created a large propaganda board about water quality that became a public display about the project. A ritual storytelling session was held (August 12, 1995), where prayers were collected for the river. People blessed lotus flowers that were placed in bamboo baskets with candles and sent down the river, a radiant glow of candles floating on the water.

Every day we spoke with hundreds of people about water. Each event was televised on local TV, and there was a special program presented nationally. A closing ceremony was arranged. The river was alive with activity. Martial artists gathered to perform, pushing the vibrant energy to a new peak. Among the many officials who spoke, the head of the Chengdu Environmental Protection Agency expressed how our project had profoundly touched him to remember water as the spiritual basis of life. "Everyone says how the environment and economic development are in conflict. This is not true; the environment is a matter of consciousness" he explained. "I am rarely moved. But this project reminded me why I do my job; water is the basis of life." He described how papers often simply pass between governments but nothing gets done. "You actually did something. You are the first person to receive permission to do this kind of work with the public. We will continue to watch you very closely." His words moved me and I cried as we spoke.

I had brief moments of deep reflection during the project, quiet respites to recharge. Every morning I joined numerous others doing wushu (martial arts) and felt quite Chinese. I had a magical experience in a Tang Dynasty resort, and often sipped tea along the river in ancient teahouses, imagining the great history and the lives spent on the water. Images etched in my mind from this trip include: watching everyone open up; feeling the trust slowly develop between the participants from Tibet, China, and the U.S.; crying tears of joy when the ceiling opened after we received permission from the government; inviting everyone to hug one another; being hugged so tight that the chicken eggs in my hugger's pocket broke and covered us both in raw egg.

I learned from the Chinese, for whom cooperation is an integral component of society, what can happen when everyone pulls together. Relationships are truly everything; a group of people deciding to work together can make an enormous difference. I am now developing an international community of artists who can pull together and act in concert. I envision a new model that challenges the premise of radical autonomy in the arts and undermines the practice of funding one individual to be famous for a short period of time. However, creating trust and community across cultural lines is a challenge in the United States. I question the assumed dominance of my culture and country as I seek a place of real respect for everyone. My work brings people together to facilitate a dialogue between the arts and sciences. I cross borders that have traditionally been separated in order to create space for interdisciplinary collaborations and the exchange of images and information.

Betsy Damon with Cai Jian, Xu Hongbin, Yang Qi, Zhong Bo, Yin Xiaoten, and Yan Lijuu, "Washing Face," installation of twenty wash stands with water quality information on adjacent banners, 1995, at Fu Nan River, Chengdou, China.

The Keepers of the Waters

Judith F. Baca, "The Great Wall of Los Angeles"
(detail of strikers)

Judith F. Baca, "The Great Wall of Los Angeles," (detail depicting
"The Development of Suburbia").

Judith F. Baca: Community and Culture in the United States

by Frances K. Pohl

Judith F. Baca is known nationally and internationally as a muralist and a public educator, and she has taught in the University of California system since 1981. Her commitment to community-based art-making led her to found, along with filmmaker Donna Dietch and artist Christina Schlesinger, the Social and Public Art Resource Center (SPARC) in the mid-1970s in Venice, California. Through SPARC, Baca has not only facilitated the creation, preservation, and documentation of public art in the Los Angeles area, but has also provided a space for the images and voices of peoples of color. She has coordinated two major citywide mural projects in Los Angeles and has organized, along with the staff of SPARC, symposia and exhibitions that draw attention to the multiplicity of cultures that make up the greater Los Angeles area and the nation at large. Her most famous mural, *The Great Wall of Los Angeles* (1976-1983), extends for almost half a mile along a drainage canal in the San Fernando Valley and documents an alternative history of California, one that acknowledges the presence of Native Americans, Asian Americans, African Americans, Latinos, Chicanos, gays and lesbians, and working-class people. She has brought her coalition-building skills to other parts of California, including the farming community of Guadalupe, just north of Santa Barbara, and the city of Baldwin Park, just east of Los Angeles. She has also taken these skills and applied them to an international project, *The World Wall: A Vision of the Future Without Fear*, a series of 10- by 30-foot portable murals that has traveled around the world, joined by similar panels painted by artists from the host countries.

I first met Baca in 1988, when I invited her to speak to a women's studies class I was co-teaching at Pomona College. I was impressed by the nature of her work and her commitment to education, and I subsequently organized a retrospective exhibition, "Judith F. Baca: Sites and Insights, 1974-1992," for the Arizona State University, Tempe Art Museum in 1992 (it appeared the following year at the Pomona College Montgomery Gallery). I interviewed Baca in her studio in Venice, California on July 10, 1994.

Frances K. Pohl: In a December 1993 *Village Voice* review of an exhibition, Peter Schjeldahl wrote: "There is no art community, only more or less an art society. . . . Society is formal. Community is soulful. Many in the art world are so soul-starved they convince themselves of belonging to a community when they really don't. The art world is a fairly savage social and economic zone where values are always in doubt and often in conflict." What has been your experience of this "savage" society, and where do you see the "soulful" art community?

Judith F. Baca: My first thought is that the "savage" art world truly is a non-community. There's a certain brutality to it because it co-opts the truth of community and uses this language in such a way that people, particularly students, become extremely confused about professional group life. They talk about a professional group life as opposed to a community, which I would define more as a group of people who have shared values, mores, perhaps share a geographical space in which they have to live in some way in relatedness and connectedness. I think what the art community is really about is disconnection, in the sense that we really foster individuation. We foster competitiveness. We foster within our art schools and universities the sense of instantly disconnecting people from where they came to engage in the creation of what is called a "universal aesthetic," and that "universal aesthetic" is essentially a western-European aesthetic and it's very specific. It's geographically specific, ethnically specific. It's intellectually specific. And yet we call that "universal," and what happens is that people become very isolated. Right now we're recruiting the cream of the crop from our ethnic communities, for example the Chicano community. We're recruiting California students or people out of neighborhoods and we are putting them into the university and, as we recruit them and bring them in, we foster the disassociation from their origins. We say to them, "This is the highest form of achievement." It was put to me repeatedly - the highest form of achievement is to disassociate entirely, in totality, from where I came from. This means that, essentially, we're taking California taxpayer's money to recruit California students out of California neighborhoods so that they will never address the most salient issues, the most difficult and incredibly troublesome problems. We take the best of them and we take them away. Essentially we're doing a brain drain of those places, so that we can never solve the problems that plague those communities. We have a continuing cycle of feeding people off into this never-never land or non-space of professional group life. Basically what it means is we serve corporations with those people. Those kids never come back to where they came from. The biggest, biggest struggle in all of my life has been to stay connected in some way to where I came from. They've offered me every kind of imaginable goody if I would leave and even got as far as telling me I'm a failure because I haven't.

What I think is the future for us in terms of education is figuring out how to approach in a connected way what art-making is about - connected to the source of your own culture or ethnicity, connected to the geographic place that you came from. People would criticize that by saying, "You're localizing and therefore reducing the dialogue. You're keeping people from approaching global culture," and so forth. But in truth global culture is coming back to the same kind of solutions that we need at a local level. We have to work again in groups of collective consciousness. I would take our university systems and teach kids cooperation. I would teach them relatedness. I would honor where they came from. I would teach them to stay sourced in what they know and their own cultures, and use that as the basis for teaching. And by doing that you do a number of things. You teach them that achievement does not mean ignoring issues of homelessness or gang warfare or the failure to educate large masses of people. It doesn't require looking down on the work ethic of the working class.

FKP: This is assuming that these students are coming from backgrounds that allow them to think of those things as important.

JFB: Right. And I think I'm talking about the majority here. I'm not talking about the tiny, select number of people who go to university who are white and upper-class or upper-middle-class. I guess I'm jumping a step ahead here to parity and to equity. We're using a tax base for our educational systems that comes from the majority/minority and whether it's in the California State University system or the University of California system or the community college system we have to educate those people or our democracy will fail. You can't any longer in good conscience continue to recruit from the majority/minority group without addressing this issue.

FKP: When you say "majority/minority," are you saying that "minorities" are actually the majority?

JFB: That's right. Los Angeles, for example, is 70 percent people of color. We have to begin to address educating according to the tax base or we are stealing money from the people. And it is my opinion that we are stealing money in an incredible way from the Mexican population. We have recruited for the University of California system — all nine universities — 2,889 Chicano students. We have graduated over 2 million Chicano students from California high schools. These statistics are for 1993-94. They are alarming. I don't think we can sustain any longer these highly rugged individualist notions. We can't. We have to cooperate because we can't live here together anymore.

FKP: It seems rather than cooperating in the face of shrinking resources, people are digging in and becoming very resistant to sharing those diminishing resources. How do you think more of the people of color of California are going to make it into a university system that is state-run when the state itself is becoming increasingly reactionary in its attitude towards people of color? Are more people of color going to be allowed in or do you see that if they do come in, they're going to be turned into these individualistic kinds of people? Do you think that there's something much more radical that needs to happen, in terms of educational systems in general? Are they salvageable or do we really have to look at some other way of educating people for community-oriented ways of thinking?

JFB: I think all of the above. Every aspect has to be dealt with. I think university systems as a whole will come under greater and greater fire. This last year alone Cornell University, Stanford and the University of California at Santa Barbara had hunger strikes and walkouts just for the Chicano populations. These 20-year-olds now are getting in there and they're saying, "Wait a minute." They're becoming much more nationalistic. They're coming now with a very strong resistance to being assimilated and what I think is a very healthy rage. At the political level we are not making great strides, but we are getting people in key positions. What is going to happen is we're going to take the money away from them. The same way we had to do it with the arts councils and with the National Endowment. We had to attack the very premise of their funding to make them open it up. An African-American scholar and organizer years ago told me, "Judy, you keep expecting justice here because you think that if you are just logical enough and you convince people of what is just, they will simply open up the doors. They're never going to give it up easy. It has to be a struggle."

So I think there's a two-prong approach. One is to start attacking the funding base of the university system and the educational system in general, and the other is to start organizing at the student level. Now the counter-move of those opposed to change will be that they will abandon education, which is what is now happening within the local schools. The Save California Bill, signed by 600,000 people, basically says that any child of an immigrant who is now illegal cannot be educated. It also says they are not eligible for health care. People are running for political office on the basis of taking away those immigrant rights. Essentially that means that there will never be another Amalia Mesa-Bains [California educator and artist]. There'll never be another Judy Baca. We're now looking at an entire generation.

Okay, now take that logically to the next step. We have 80 percent Latino school children entering into the Los Angeles city school system. A healthy number of them are not documented. I don't know the percentage exactly. I guess we can't measure it. Okay, let's not educate them. Let's cut them loose. Let's put them all on the street, even people who have been here twenty years — my grandmother was here twenty-five years and was never documented. You've got Chiapas in about ten minutes. We're going to have a mass *mestizo* riot. We're going to have armed resistance. How long do you think it will take these heavily armed kids, who are now cut loose from the school system, to turn the guns away from shooting each other and begin to come after those who are responsible for the conditions in their lives? That's what's going to happen. It's not smart to do this. It's stupid. If they really wanted to do something about immigration problems, they simply would go after the employers who have a great addiction to this cheap labor source.

So we're talking about three areas of resistance: student protests, politicians saying, "Either do this or we take away your money," and people as a whole saying, "We don't want to pay for your schools anymore and we'll collapse the entire educational system." Reactionary people will say, "Tough. We don't want to educate anybody." There will be a different kind of opposition to educational institutions within the Latino communities. People are saying more and more, "We don't want to do this. You either have to open it up or lose it." They have to see that they have access to education and that it's part of what they can do with their lives. No one should ever underestimate the commitment of the Latino community to education. They believe that education is the ticket out, and they're going to be enraged as soon as they get that they can't have it. And it's becoming more and more clear as the numbers become more extreme.

I've been thinking about why this is happening and I can predict a few things. I think armed revolution is not out of the question if there is a decision to destroy the school system and not to have access for our people. Recent repressive immigrant legislation, which will eventually be thrown out as unconstitutional, may just push people over the edge. Fifteen years ago I went before the Los Angeles city council and told them they had a gang problem that they had to approach now, and they said, "It doesn't affect us, we don't have gangs in the [San Fernando] Valley." I said, "You will." These San Fernando Valley councilmen refused to look at a city-wide problem. Los Angeles is now the gang center of the entire United States and right now is putting satellite Crips in Arizona, for God's sake. We have satellites moving out to Albuquerque. I was in Albuquerque last week talking to people about the Crips and the 18th Street Gang. If you don't organize them and educate them, then they will educate and organize themselves, because they are resourceful. And if you don't give them an alternative, then they will create alternatives for themselves. Simple.

FKP: But giving alternatives to this many people means giving up some of the power, access, education, wealth, and all those things that a small number of people have been used to having all to themselves for all these years.

JFB: Yes. Sharing resources, not getting to come to dinner and eat it all. You have very, very intense resistance to this, and I think that's what you're seeing right now. Our major funders in America — the Rockefellers, the Fords — are all now talking about the civil society and saying, "Enough of this ethnic identification, enough of this nationalism because we're not talking about what will create a civil society any longer. We want to now fund people to talk about the spaces between us. We don't want you to talk about your own identity any more, because once you get too far into that, then there's no place for us."

FKP: I'd like to return to an issue you raised earlier. Many people argue that the key to artistic or aesthetic greatness lies in transcending the material world, which allows you to gain access to this notion of the "universal." How do you begin to take that apart on a day-to-day basis in teaching somebody art-making? How do you, instead, encourage connections with both one's immediate family and a larger community?

JFB: In a certain way I think it's easier to teach them connectedness than the opposite. When students come to the university they're in the process of building self-esteem. They're in the process of building an identity, and if you honor the identity they come with, if you tell them, "Value what you have in your own pocket," you actually build a healthier human being. For example, a young Korean woman came in with a photograph. It was a cloisonné medallion given to the bride and groom of two stork figures, one red and one blue, with a macramé cord. It's hung in the households of Korean families as a bridal gift to bring good luck to the bride and groom. For the student, it was just an object, one from which she was completely disassociated. She thought it was pretty but she didn't know the meaning of the object. She was going to use it in a still life that she was constructing for painting. I looked at the piece and I said, "You can't make anything until you know it, until you understand its meaning. Have you ever asked your mother?" "No. I don't really know what it is." That object had hung in her household every day and had been so devalued by the culture at large that she never thought to ask the question of its meaning. So sending her back home for an interview with her mother and a discussion of its meaning made a far more valuable connection for her to that image. It became actually a reinterpretation of the American experience through a Korean position, a one-and-a-half position (someone with Korean parents born in the U.S.). She could then use that image and actually begin to understand the power of its sources and why it resonates. Why does it move her? Why does that particular sound move you? Why are thousands of kids listening to *banda* music and dressing in western-like *vaquero* outfits with the great big buckles and the hats and the boots? Because it's a very nationalistic movement. Because they say, "This music makes me cry." Why does it make you cry? Why does it move your spirit?

So you need to do two things: you need to affirm their own experiences and you need to teach a respectful honoring of tradition. Now, this is absolutely counter to everything we are taught. Within the art world we believe that whatever is new is better. Innovation is prized above all other things, making art about art with a new twist. The standard way of teaching at the university is to ask people to source in some other artist. Who is your influence? The references are usually to white men, someone who's hot or current. Students are then taught that they must follow in that line. So what if you said, as I have tried to do with my classes, "Forget that. Make a tattoo. Study African scarification. Study the aboriginal marking of bodies as imprints on their soul. What would you imprint on your soul? Make a piece of work that has function within your daily life. Make it functional." That's another no-no. If it's functional, it's not art. Set up problems, ask kids to take the resources of their own culture and their own experience and bring them into the class and share them. Talk about the experience of others, which is, interestingly enough, a common experience, whether you're a dominant-culture person or an ethnic person. Talk about the commonality of immigration and what that means. Honor a traditional form that is thought of as folk art or not serious art. Look at tattoos and graffiti. Look at spray can art and see what these young people are making with those cans, which are incredible pieces of work. Study popular art that has to do with low-rider cars. By doing this you shift the emphasis from a world that is commodified and controlled, a marketplace. You take away the very basis of art-making as commodification, a practice to feed an elite, and think of it as a practice of healing. Make no object at all, but simply concentrate on the process. Devise a process that reminds you of the tradition of ritual sand painting or that is sourced in that, and then apply it to a contemporary time and make no object.

FKP: Do students sometimes respond, "But how can I support myself as an artist making this kind of art?"

JFB: Sure. I think there is a great push now within the state university system to give students practical skills, to make them employable. But my belief is that if you want to be employable, then don't become an artist. Become a graphic designer, become a dress designer, become a hundred other things. Focus on those things that are practical skills that can be used. Actually, if you exercise yourself and your intellect in these ways and also develop more theoretically or conceptually, in the end you are much more employable as a fine artist as well because you are interdisciplinary. You can address the most important issues of our time. You are problem-solvers based in reality. You are not carrying on an intellectual dialogue for fun and your friends. You can talk to your mother and father and are, in the end, a much better human being. You have more practical knowledge with which you can serve the community and make the arts relevant again. I think artists have made a terrible mistake over the years. It never served us to be "inspired by angels," to be mythological creatures who are somehow touched by the gods. A dealer said to me once, "I only want to show artists who are touched by the gods." I remember her telling me that I wasn't touched by the gods. So I thought, "How do you get this touch by the gods? Who are these gods?" Then I realized it was probably some white critic and if that white critic liked you, then you were touched by the gods. So I began to value, instead, what I understood and knew. I was terrified to death that I was going to be completely unemployable and completely a failure. There were no models for me to look at as a woman artist, as a Latina, as a person related to community, so therefore I figured maybe I wasn't an artist. That was actually incredibly liberating because then I could invent myself. These kids have got to invent themselves.

FKP: What about your own community, the one that has allowed you to survive as an artist?

JFB: On a spiritual and emotional level there has been a community of women, some within my own culture but many not. Donna Dietch was incredibly important in the process of me growing up to be an artist. She was doing the same thing but came from a completely different experience of a very wealthy family. And Christina Schlesinger. Both taught me something incredibly important. They taught me to perceive myself as entitled. I studied entitlement with those women, because I had never seen anybody who felt like they deserved to have things. They really knew about entertaining themselves, getting what they wanted, feeling that they deserved to have those things. And I learned that from them.

The women's community at critical points throughout my life has been really, really important — all of us struggling against male identities within the arts, there not really being places for us. And then parallel struggles. I've always been very connected to the African-American community because of being born in Watts. I grew up in African-American and Chicano communities and developed very close relationships with key African-American women who made present the parallel struggles of other ethnic groups so that I could see things relationally. It widened my world. And then most importantly has been an intergenerational connection with women and men older than I, like [actor] Gilbert Roland. He was absolutely an amazing model for me.

FKP: How did you meet him?

JFB: His wife called me. I had just done that Bill Moyers television piece and I was working on *The Great Wall of Los Angeles* and Gia Roland called me up and said, "I want to work for you. I want to take photographs. Can I follow you around? I'm interested in what you're doing." I didn't know who she was, and so she showed up and literally every day of my life for nearly ten years she was with me. She cooked, too. Not only could she take photographs, but she could make wonderful *menudo*. She fed me and fattened me up all of these years, making wonderful Mexican food. Then, of course, I met Gilbert. Gilbert was the *vaquero*, the ultimate *vaquero*. He had grace and was a man who refused to depict the Mexican people in a denigrated way. He was the "Cisco Kid." So many people later modeled what it was to be a Latino by virtue of actions he took in his early films. His favorite words were honor, dignity, courage. He was stalwart, patriotic. All those things.

So I had friends who were 80. And then I had friends who were 14, who gave me a sense of the range of the world I lived in. They really gave me a sense of perspective. I think that nurtured me. Jane Rule [Canadian writer] was the only lesbian I ever met in the early 1970s who was totally connected to community, not just an isolated women's community but a community filled with all ages and types of people. All these people had in common an incredible grace. Minnah [Agins] had the same grace. You know, this is really making me emotional because so many of them are dead, the 80-year-olds and the 14-year-olds. I feel such a sense of loss for Gilbert. He died the way he lived, too. Right to the end he wouldn't take his damn boots off! Minnah was important, too. She gave me a sense of a historical context. She told me about the hunger strikes and the bread strikes and the Detroit auto workers and I felt like I had met all these characters.

I could see first-hand what they went through to do the most basic things, like get us unemployment insurance.

FKP: Was this in the 1930s?

JFB: Yes, 1930s, the intellectual Left of the thirties. Minnah was the continuation of a long line of people who used art. When I put together her retrospective for her memorial I looked over the range of all these prints. It was an absolutely wonderful chronology of Left art-making and issues that ranged from the 1930s or late 1920s to the 1980s, when she died. You could see the preoccupations of the Left through all these different decades. I learned strategies for survival from the 14-year-olds and 80-year-olds, and also from staying connected to the humblest people, people who would not necessarily do good for your career, and with my family.

FKP: Have your experiences with these people affected the way you approach your own work as an artist?

JFB: Certainly. One thing they have taught me is to recognize the unrecognized seats of power, like the woman who looks out her window and watches the kids at the bus stop. That's a key role in the way that community moves. She keeps them from jumping out into the street. The gang that occupies the park, even if it's usually only a few little guys. Some of them are often much more harmless than they're perceived as being. Acknowledging these people. It's just the same as saying, "That tree is there." You don't pretend that the tree's not there.

FKP: And you don't try to cut it down.

JFB: No. You don't say, "Well, everything would be just great about this piece of land if the tree wasn't there." Instead, you come into a space and begin to figure out who's who. You look at the synagogue down the street, the passage of these people on a weekly basis past the site where the mural will be. The school, and the movement in and out of people who come from some distance. The local people across the street and their investment in being middle-class. Understanding what it is that they value, who they are. Recognizing those with the power and recognizing who's there. And then recognizing what is under the surface, almost like a spiritual half-life in the ground. Why do people get drawn, for example, to those exquisitely beautiful sites along Galiano's Coast where the Haida have been coming for potlatches for a few thousand years. People are drawn to those places, and they have a certain presence in the world by virtue of the spiritual investment of people for centuries. That's why you need to know what has happened there. You need to know who was there, who's there now and what is operating on them from another time. It's like digging up, revealing, digging away layers of information to the source of it.

FKP: Your words remind me of the series of murals you did for the farmworkers' community of Guadalupe, California.

JFB: Yes. The imagery in those four murals is an uncovering of the roots of the place. The ethnic contributors panel shows the Chinese as well as the Mexicans. A Swiss-Italian marble angel from the town's cemetery is the source of the central image in the *Future of Guadalupe*. Yet Guadalupe is also like every farming area. Farmworkers' issues are international issues. I respect both the local issues and their international ramifications. I want to build associations, relationships. I was taught to make family and to honor the family and that's what I do with the site, I make it family. I try to create order within that family, to develop some kind of community in order to approach the issue or the site and to become makers and problem-solvers together.

FKP: Do these families ever become dysfunctional?

JFB: Always is probably the case! Of course, that assumes that there is a perfect family out there somewhere.

FKP: Then there is that other "family" setting, the classroom or university, where conflict and dissension has increased as increasing numbers of people are coming in who want to see their identities reaffirmed and their cultures studied. How do you deal in a constructive way with this inevitable conflict?

JFB: Well, right now there isn't really any resolution except that if you're in charge, you win. People are not saying, "Okay, how do I make room for inclusion?" University professors often suffer from the same absence and poverty of thought that our students suffer from when we don't teach them relatedness. We don't teach them to connect. So who we have teaching and who we have as models are people trained in the old system, who really believe that individual achievement is to be valued above all things. We should begin as scholars to address in our writing, in our thinking, how we're going to move into this 21st century, into a really different time. I mean it's astounding how different it is. I have an incredibly difficult time keeping up within my own culture, with the changes, as it becomes "Latino" as opposed to "Chicano" and Chicanos come into positions of power and they have to reevaluate themselves because they can't speak for El Salvadorans. I don't know if one of us can ever begin to speak any longer for the whole.

FKP: Where do you see a commonality coming into play? Is it possible?

JFB: I guess what I'm advocating, for the most part, is working in smaller groups. We have to go down to smaller groups and then we have to make these little pods that have to make a relationship with another pod and then you start to create spaces between you. And I think the spaces in between have to do with our incorporation of each other. *The Great Wall* is a pretty good example of this process. It was important for me when I got the group together to represent each of the ethnic groups and then put them into a whole, and to move them between learning about each other's cultures so that Chicano kids were not encouraged to work only on Chicano history. In a similar way, our ethnic studies departments need to make relationships between each other. Every ethnic studies department should have within its core curriculum requirements that are relational studies. What is common about African-American and Chicano history? Where do those relationships really make sense? You can build that into curriculum. You can build it into committee structures. It allows people not to fear a kind of centrality within each culture. I used to really believe in integration in totality, and I don't think I believe in that anymore.

FKP: You want relationships but not integration?

JFB: Yes. Not integration in the total sense, all of us together, one planet, one people, all holding hands. I don't think we will. Not in my lifetime. I've worked really hard for twenty-five years to make things different and I've watched most of the gains rolled back.

FKP: What about these gains? You've done local work, but you're also out there on the national level, dealing with the National Endowment for the Arts (NEA) and with national commissions. There appears to have been, at least until recently, an increase in NEA funding for community organizations. Is this good or bad? Where do you see it going?

JFB: I think the NEA is not a good example because you probably would not see more money going to community groups from the NEA. But you do with organizations like the Lila Wallace Foundation, the e. e. cummings Foundation, the James Irvine Foundation, the Rockefeller Foundation, the Warhol Foundation. The James Irvine Foundation is on the cutting edge for its funding of community-initiated projects.

I'm working in a group now called the Tourism Industry Development Council, which comes out of Local 11 of the Restaurant and Hotel Workers union. This group formed to change the tourist industry vision of Los Angeles. It is the opposite of the Convention Bureau, which puts out videos that say you can come to Rodeo Drive and to Universal City and they don't show one person of color. Our program is very different. It takes tourists around the city to places like *The Great Wall.* People are enraged about it. We got calls all the way from the U.S. Department of Commerce. They fear that community-based people will destroy the tourism industry in Los Angeles, which means, basically, that we will share part of the wealth. You want to know what happened to Rodney King? Let's go out to Pacoima and the Foothills Division police station and hear the perspectives of community leaders. People are being given an alternative for the first time. And all of the tours are sold out during the World Cup soccer games. Yesterday I addressed a group of American Studies scholars from Syria, Israel, all over the world. There were forty chairs of American Studies Departments from various universities all over the world at *The Great Wall.* They want to know about race relations in America. They want to know if there is apartheid here. They want our perspective on what is happening. It's pretty exciting. There are spaces in between being made.

FKP: Do you see any down side to the increase in funding for community-based ventures by the foundations you just mentioned?

JFB: Absolutely. The Lila Wallace Foundation has been the most problematic. They've been giving major amounts of money — 5 million dollars — to the Mark Taper Forum to expand their audiences. Not to build a Chicano theater in Los Angeles, but to put Chicano theater under an all-white board of directors that comes from the very basis of power and authority in Los Angeles. . . .You're never going to get that board of directors to change. Five years from now there won't be a Chicano Theater Center. There won't be a parallel group to the music center that is ethnically run and governed and developed. There will be an incorporation within the music center of Chicano Theater. Maybe at the end of five years they'll have one Chicano on the board. They'll have all of our mailing lists. They'll have Latino theater without the control of the Latino population. There are many examples of this kind of funding, which is not about self-empowerment. Now, people would argue with me vehemently about this. But I honestly believe that the only thing to do in terms of cultural development in Los Angeles is to develop parallel institutions of equal size and stature for the ethnic populations.

FKP: But wouldn't you end up still having to accept money from these same institutions? I have another quote I wanted to read to you from Octavio Paz's collection *Essays on Mexican Art* (1993): "The idea of public art strikes me as a sentimental nostalgia and a dangerous anachronism. . . . Public art has invariably been the religious art of a state or of a church as powerful as a state. By definition, there is no such thing as public art made by isolated individuals or private groups. . . . The phrase 'revolutionary public art' not only contains a contradiction but is, in fact, meaningless . . . only through an abuse of language . . . is it possible to speak of a revolutionary art sponsored by the state."

JFB: Well, there's some validity to what he says. Yet if you look at *The Great Wall*, it received a certain amount of public dollars but it also received such a patchwork of funding from so many different sources that no one source could control the content of the piece. American philanthropic giving is not the same as Mexican philanthropic giving. They have no philanthropic giving in Mexico. They have patronage and they have government sponsorship, which is very direct. We have this other thing called non-profit giving. I think it's still possible, with multiple funding sources and with an artist who is uncompromising, to create work that does challenge the status quo. I think my Baldwin Park Metrorail Project is quite revolutionary. It really challenges the whole colonial mission system.

FKP: Did the people in charge know what you were doing?

JFB: Absolutely. Because I explained it to them. And because there were enough Latinos in that group. There were also people from Arkansas. There was an African-American woman who came from the oldest black family in Baldwin

Park. The head of the Department of Education for Baldwin Park was Latino. The mayor himself was a 24-year-old graduate of Harvard, a Latino. There was a Chicana, a working-class woman from the factory region, on the commission. I had four or five solid people behind me who said, "Yes, do it. It's about time somebody talked about the whole issue of the *mestijae* or mixing of races." The only problem I had was with one of the Catholics. The woman was working-class and very Catholic. She just wanted to make sure I wasn't going to offend the *padre* from the local mission. And then when I turned him upside-down on his head in one of the images, I said, "You know, Lupé, I'm turning him upside-down and, I'll tell you the truth, in native sign language it means 'not'." And she said. "They shouldn't have done what they did."

FKP: Who, the *padres?*

JFB: Yes, the *padres.* That's what she said, finally. Right on, Lupé! But I gave them a complete art historical and historical lesson. I brought the research in. They were with me through the whole process.

FKP: So they were not only engaged through the whole process, but had decision-making power, rather than simply being in an advisory position.

JFB: That's right. It was remarkable. Not to say they were all liberal and incredibly progressive thinkers. They said, "We want you to do something on the missions," and I think they thought "Taco Bell." They wanted my name recognition too. They wanted to say they had Judy Baca in Baldwin Park. It's interesting. They didn't really get what that meant. They just knew that I was a famous mural painter and I was a Chicana and had worked on projects with young kids. When they told me the subject was the missions, I said, "Okay, I'm going to do the missions but I have to tell you, I'm going to do the truth." "Well, we wouldn't expect any less," they said. So when I started developing the information, I started bringing it in because they met with me as I was progressing to the design. I started to tell them the numbers of people who were murdered, the numbers of native people lost, the loss of their names. It was really also about my passion for what I was doing and my belief system.

I brought in Vera Rocha, the chief of the Gabrieliños who lives in Baldwin Park, as an advisor for the project. And they know her. They've always known her because she had pow-wows in their parks. And she has twenty-two grandchildren who are all native people there. Her family grew up in a mission. Her great-grandmother made candles. She hates the mission. She wouldn't even step on the ground. She stood on the outside waiting for me when I went there to pick up materials. So convincing people was a combination of my passion and my ability to articulate it and Vera's ability to speak to what it meant to her. The mission fathers didn't participate except to impede the informational flow. But I had historians who helped me, and I just started bringing in material. I said, "First let me tell you what I'm going to do. Do you know what an archaeological dig looks like?" "No," they say. So I had to go through all these photographs of archaeological digs. That's how I began. I showed them photographs of archaeological sites. I really like the way they look. "I think this should be like an archaeological site," I said. "We're going to dig it up. We're going to dig it up and we're going to put it back in the ground. We're going to pull away the layers of the earth, literally, and see." Then the forms in the ground, the shapes of the mission, the native village, became the design in the concrete. And they really liked that. I was listening to Lupé talking to some kids on the day of the dedication. She said, "Well, just think of it this way. It's like she took a big steam roller and she smashed everything flat," which was a pretty close description of what I did! I used the language of the rednecks in the piece: "It was better before they came." And then there's Gloria Anzaldúa sandblasted into the big arch: "This land was Mexican once, was Indian always and will be again." And the words of this extraordinary young Asian woman, who said, "You know, it's not the adults leading only, it's the youth leading too." And so I used that too.

I had such a good time doing it. It was difficult working with the contractors. And the commission fought me on a couple of things, which I lost. I lost the benches in the plaza area. I wanted people to be able to sit in the plaza by the monument. And I wanted them to be able to cut *nopalitos*. I wanted edible food in the planters. I did get the oak tree, which represents the indigenous people, and I got the cactus, but not edible cactus, and I didn't get the benches because they didn't want people hanging out. So I didn't win everything. But I really felt like it was successful. And they seem very happy with it. The mayor told me, "I go to the Metro station and I sit on the bench and look down at my feet and it says 'memory' and 'will power' and I remember what my job is today." That's how you preserve a culture. It can still happen.

CancerBodies:
Building Community Through Feminist Theater and Spirituality

by Victoria Rue

Feminist theater creates community. During the creation of the play *CancerBodies*, my own process moved from isolated writer to collaboration and community. The content of the play mirrors this movement. In what follows I am describing a process of creation that spirals out from its genesis, building and bridging communities.

In January of l992, my mother called.

Hello, Victoria?

Hi, mom. I was just thinking of you. I was just about to call you about our coming down to LA for Easter. . . .

Victoria, your Aunt Marguerite has ovarian cancer.

It was my mother, you see. It was the sound in her voice. It was the catch of worry that runs deeper than life, smack into mortality. It was the helplessness I heard. "This is my sister. She's going to die." I saw my mother catch hold of her own mortality — and wring it until it twisted into grief, anger — and the fight to survive. She made her own doctor's appointment immediately. Later, she called to say it was negative.

This sequence of events changed the course of my academic work. My master of divinity thesis explored eros and lesbian spirituality. I was about to write a dissertation on medieval and contemporary women's spirituality. This experience turned me around. My celebration of eros and mysticism was enlarged to include illness, suffering, and aging. At the age of 46 my body was changing. My breasts had become troublesome with cysts. My health was fine, yet I felt the need to face my fears. As a friend said to me, "we do so much in this culture to deny our deaths." My great aunt and now my aunt had ovarian cancer. There is a good chance it would surface among me and my four sisters. I decided to face and explore my own mortality.

The Process of Creating *CancerBodies*:
Feminist Theater and Theology Make Community

I began to read. I found *Cancer in Two Voices* by Sandra Butler and Barbara Rosenblum. It is the story of two lesbians in a relationship: Barbara, who is diagnosed with breast cancer and Sandra, her partner and caregiver, who survives. Written in journal form and covering the five years Barbara struggled with cancer, this moving book raises the issues of women and health care, misdiagnosis, Jewish lesbian spirituality, lesbian community, body changes due to middle age and illness. As a lesbian in a committed relationship, the story of their commitment to each other was very important for me. It also helped me face fears that had arisen in me with my aunt's cancer. Years of work as both a playwright and theater director lead me instinctively to sense that Sandy and Barbara's story of relationship could form the core of a play about women and cancer. I was delighted when Sandy Butler agreed and encouraged me to adapt her book as part of our play.

My journey had begun. It was clear, my dissertation would have to be a play about women and cancer, and in it I would maintain that the struggle to create the play would be an enactment of feminist theology. The common ground shared between feminist theology and theater is in reclaiming women's histories, powersharing/mutuality, the necessity of multiplicity and process, recovering the celebration and unmasking the global suffering of women's bodies and the goal of building community. All these were part of the development of the play, and were represented in the play itself.

I began to find a plethora of books by women about cancer. In the last ten years, women have told their stories of diagnosis, treatments, and alternative treatments. We have been informing each other in the midst of our government's neglect of women's health care issues!

My reading introduced me to many communities of women and men who are involved with the cancer epidemic. I got to know the Women's Cancer Resource Center in Berkeley, In Our Own Image in Oakland (a cancer support group for African-American women), the Charlotte Maxwell Clinic in Oakland (for low-income women with cancer), Breast Cancer Action and The Cancer Support Community in San Francisco. From these activist organizations of women and men, I learned that, like my aunt, women's cancers are regarded as personal not socio-political tragedies. Cancer is the leading cause of death in women ages 35 to 54. It has become an acceptable private epidemic — and that is unacceptable.

Stories are the "stuff" of theater. Because I don't have cancer, I had to enter the experience of cancer through other women's stories. And so I found and recorded some thirty interviews with women cancer survivors: Bonnie, Cara, Nancy, Ann, Ruth, Sandy, Judy, Nancy, Terry, Evelyn, Chris, Donna, Rochelle, Teresa, Beth, Marie, Mary, Barbara, Susan, Leslie, Amay, Gaye, Francis, Susan. I was also privileged to attend weekly support group meetings of In Our Own Image. Twenty African-American women with breast cancer sat around a front room, sometimes laughing, sometimes praying, and always offering each other support. I listened, recorded, remembered.

Each week I was talking with my Aunt Marguerite by phone, attentive to new information I could find from my research and pass her way. I was also learning from her the daily struggle with this disease: appointments, conflicting opinions among physicians, other consultations, chemotherapy and its side effects, her body changing, her self-reflection.

June 27, 1992: (a telephone call with Aunt Marguerite)

The swelling in my abdomen has started all over again. I thought that was over in January with my hysterectomy. I poke out more than I did before. The oncologist put a needle into my abdomen and took some of the fluid. I guess I'll hear about it next Tuesday. I can't put on my old clothes. I used to wear a pair of pants and a tucked-in shirt. But now I have to wear all my shirts out. I may go back to the original diagnostician. But I don't like him. You know how he told me I had cancer? He walked into the room and announced, "all your blood works are good, except this one — you've got ovarian cancer." And then he went right on. He just sees too many people. You wait forever. He's too busy. He just cranks them out, like a machine.

Victoria's journal:

I feel so sad and angry . So the cancer is coming back. So why did they take out her womb? She goes on, waiting for test results, working with her volunteer organizations, and next Thursday she gets more of the chemo. Oh, Aunt Marguerite, I love you.

At the same time the interview tapes were stacking higher and higher and I felt more and more overwhelmed. I alone could not hold all these stories. It was clear, I couldn't sit in a room, at a desk, and write this play about all these women by myself.

I called my dear friend Martha Boesing, co-founder of At the Foot of the Mountain (a women's theater collective which survived for twenty years in Minneapolis before closing down a few years ago). She suggested I begin to work with a group of women to create the script. Of course! I needed to work in community! Isolation for this creation was not helpful. Another stage of the process began.

My work was already embodying some central themes of both feminist theater and theology. In each we begin with the premise of the importance of women's experiences. The process of listening and sharing with one another brings us into relationship. As we speak and listen, we understand the interdependence of our stories. Our stories point to the possibility of both survival and liberation. We begin to build the seeds of community based on our similarities and our differences. I looked forward to our process of making feminist theater as a relational web of healing — from the storytelling and improvisations to the writing and collaboration to rehearsals to performance.

In July I began working with five women who would form the cancer support group of the play: Jude Bell, Annie Hershey, Denise Jones, Tina Murray, and Diana Saenz. Some of these women were actresses, some acting students of mine, others were friends. There were many levels of acting experience, but all had a strong desire to follow the process wherever it would lead. All had known friends or relatives who had cancer, but none of them had "the big C." Later, Jude would say, "At first I thought, cancer, why do a play about that? And then I began to do my homework and gradually I understood the enormous need to do something about this disease!"

We began with character development. I gave each actress some of the interview tapes to listen to for story, voice timbre, for how things were phrased, left unsaid, implied — hearing a character into being. I gave Jude a tape of a woman older than herself. She took the medical information and life history and combined them with an older friend of hers who also had cancer to create the character of "Analese." Annie was given tapes of two ministers, one with breast cancer, the other with thyroid cancer. The character she created, "Mandy," a Unitarian minister, drew upon the stories of each. In deciding that her character had ovarian cancer, she was also able to include my Aunt Marguerite's struggle. During our weekly rehearsals, we began to build characters, relationships and situations that elaborated on the interviews. Our creativity was unleashed. Two would be best friends, two others shared religious beliefs, one was a cynic, another would be an activist, two would be married, one single, one in a lesbian relationship, and one a single mother. Each character would have a different form of cancer: melanoma, breast cancer, ovarian, and lung cancer.

A breast cancer survivor and an oncology nurse visited our rehearsals and shared more information. But the most important change occurred when we added another woman to the cast, Pat King. She was 72, and a lung cancer survivor. Pat's age was an opportunity for the play to span the ages of 27 to 72. This was most important for the content and immediacy of our work. Pat's process with us was different than others. She joined us not to create a "character," but to tell her own story. Thus, we bridged fictional and non-fictional work as Pat began to integrate her story in improvisations with the other actresses. In fact, we discovered that Pat was in reality a kind of "George Burns" with her dry wit. As she said, "I guess I cheered 'em up when I arrived! I just tried to talk about my life here, that's all." As the rest of the members of the cast got to know her, they formed a circle of protection around her. She didn't drive, so other members picked her up for rehearsals. Sometimes stage directions and movement were confusing to her, so a whisper from another cast member was never far away to guide her to the right spot on stage. Our community was taking new shape.

Because I wanted a poetic voice in the play, I asked Diana Saenz, a playwright and poet, to write a character who would add a third element/level to the play. When Diana began writing, a woman of ancient knowledge, a potion maker, a healer emerged. And all in poetry! The "Curandera" was born. This character intertwined the health of the body and the body's relationship to the healing of the earthbody. She contributed to the idea of connected living, living in community. The "Curandera" further created a kind of morality play that critiqued the hegemonic position of western medicine, offering instead the conspicuous reality of multiple alternatives — the efficacy of mixing medicines.

It is not a full picture of how this community of actors, designers, writers, musicians, and crew was forming without realizing that each person involved was affecting those around her. The stone in the lake has many reverberating circles. Conversations and so-called "chance meetings" were spiraling the issue of cancer out beyond our work. One of these chance meetings happened to a cast member, Tina, whose character in the play was an African-American activist, Nzinga.

October 28: Tina's journal*:*

I met Karen with some friends. She is an African-American woman who had just lost a breast and was recovering from her first six weeks of chemo. She was bitter, angry, and wanted to talk about it. It was a different energy than the women on the tapes who all seemed to have some kind of support. Karen was alone and had no support. She'd had mammograms for years and was continually told she was fine. Then she found a lump and had another mammogram and a biopsy and by this time the lump was quite noticeable. When she went for test results, her doctor had left on vacation and the nurse told her it was negative. She went for a second opinion luckily and her breast was removed by the end of the next week. She was really furious. With Karen's permission, we put some of her story into my character in the play.

By chance, the evening that Karen came to see the play, members of the cancer support group In Our Own Image were also there. Afterwards she met them and ended her isolation.

Tina's journal:

Karen not only got connected to a support group but she also was able to hear herself and her own experience re-enacted on stage in a play about women struggling with cancer only six weeks after she underwent diagnosis and treatment. Now that's empowering.

This was the fusion I had hoped for. Stories told are stories heard and stories heard are stories remembered, and remembered stories are stored fuel for the tough times. Stories bring us together. Shared stories can create community.

The Content of *CancerBodies*: Feminist Theology and Community

Ironically, cancer cells do not communicate with other cells, breeding subversive takeovers of other organs. Metaphorically, then, health would seem to be based on communication, relationship, and community-building. This movement away from isolation to communication and eventual community is a paradigmatic theological theme of *CancerBodies*.

Let's extend the discussion into the theological theme of community and how it is expressed in the play. I am working with Dorothee Soelle's three phases of suffering. The movement from isolation to community is mirrored in these phases: 1) isolation 2) expression/lamenting, 3) community/collaboration/change.[1]

Phase One: mute. Every woman in *CancerBodies* moves from an initial state of isolation, powerlessness, and suffering turned in on herself. Each is initially dominated by the situation of her private disease of cancer. In this mute phase. people experience their lives and suffering as being ruled by fate. Their "God" is mute as well. Any prayer is one of resignation. And if they have desires, this mute God seems to silence them or turns a deaf ear to the already deaf, isolated and powerless sufferer. Though Dorothee Soelle suggests there are sequential stages, the experience of the women in this play suggest that the phase of isolation, once left behind, can return with each new obstacle. Thus the three phases as represented in *CancerBodies* actually spiral, turning and returning.

Barbara's diagnosis of breast cancer pushes her into chaos and then anger. Since she is in relationship, her partner Sandy keeps her from immediate isolation. Yet even here, the experience of being the diseased one in a relationship can often work to isolate as well. Sandy and Barbara sit in silence in a doctor's office. Each strangers to one another — one well, one with cancer.[2]

Sandy, throughout the play, grapples with sustaining her own identity and being Barbara's primary caregiver. The fact of her own "guilt of survival" isolates her.

Deborah steels herself against the reality of cancer recurrence by obsessing about her weight, using denial to mute her fears.

Nzinga is diagnosed with breast cancer and says, "well, this is it" and rides home on the bus in tears, alone. For a time she isolates her feelings from everyone, most of all her children.

Mandy, in the face of recurrence, can't speak about it to her partner Melissa, though it is troubling her. Her denial includes denying that God is of any help, at least the God she has known up to now. She feels lost and alone.

Analese suggests she is "presented" with a rare form of cancer, as if driving on a highway and presented with a road block. Though not in the play, the interview that is the basis for the character, says that she called her daughter over, had a long talk, the daughter left and then Analese cried and cried. Muteness can also occur when only part of the story is able to be told. "I'll be fine, don't worry" suggests the rugged individual approach that tends to regard sharing feelings as inching toward emotional dependence. In general, Analese's approach is no-nonsense, and matter-of-fact. But perhaps it masks her aloneness.

Pat smoked knowing other people got cancer from smoking, but she wouldn't. This denial approach is a kind of powerlessness in the face of addiction.

Phase one, that of isolation, silence, and mute suffering, is mirrored in an "almighty" God who is above creation, above suffering, and silent. A church that expounds this theology teaches stability at the cost of language. Their liturgies do not participate in helping the individual to find words or expression.[3]

Phase Two: lamentation/expression. As the play begins, *CancerBodies* reveals most of the characters of the support group at this phase. Each has found or is finding her own language for her experience. Each woman has moved from isolation to a cry for help. As she expresses her needs, she comes into dialogue with herself. This dialogue/monologue is a way of discussing things. I agree with Soelle when she postulates this stage as a psalm, whether or not the dialogue partner (self or other) is spoken to theistically. This articulation concentrates will, rationality, and spiritual power.

The very act of writing journals for four years cataloging their struggle with cancer shows Sandy and Barbara to be sounding the alarm, a cry for help to the larger society about breast cancer. Along the way, as in the Psalms, we hear their fear, loneliness, desires, and lament. Barbara and Sandy gather a support group to assist them. This group receives their particular laments and offers help for everything from fixing meals to reassuring hugs.

At the support group meeting of Pat, Analese, Nzinga, and Mandy, Deborah is a new arrival. Each woman retells her story. As every new visitor is an opportunity to articulate the unfolding process of illness, each woman ventures to learn more about her cancer. Theirs is a continual attitude toward education as a hope for change. When Mandy's doctors tell her there's nothing else they can do for her, she is enraged, and sets out to find alternatives. This process of educating one's self, friends, and family, is an act that breaks the silence and isolation that surrounds cancer in our society. Rev. Annie Powell has said that the more one knows about cancer and treatment options, the greater control one has over one's own life. Otherwise, the cancer patient remains mute in the face of a medical profession that assumes ultimate authority but is not always as sensitive or as knowledgeable as they might be.[4]

In phase two, excavating for new knowledge, cries of help, and psalmic laments initiate the emergence from isolation into community. In this phase, God as sacred reality can become a dialog partner. Whispers, cries, even screams demand a God with "ears to hear." The play offers a liturgy for the grieving audience to name those they love with cancer; it collapses the space between audience and actor and invites those who have been weeping in the dark to enter the grieving community. At this moment, the play expands to incorporate the seen and unseen, and — for a moment — the audience becomes congregation, before returning to the final scene.

There must be other liturgies that reflect the painful expression of suffering. I recall at a recent Women in Buddhism conference, one of the participants suggested there be a room set aside only for lament. Yes. We need places to cry out loud or moan. The sounds release our hopes, needs, rage, and despair into a universe that resounds with others' sighs and cries. In this universe, God is not a silent watcher but a pained partner. When we feel we are not alone, that others and an Other participate with us in our suffering, we are moving away from the death of isolation into life.

Phase Three: community. The move of the suffering self to expression forges relationship. Yet often in this wailing, we learn that change is plodding, that in fact one has reached this place of conscious crying for help, only to realize that the suffering seems interminable. The waiting can push us back into despair and a continuous cycle of isolation and lament. Soelle suggests that the ground of one's being begins to fall away, and our trust of the world's and God's reliability is destroyed.[5] Again we return to our own loneliness and isolation. In this moment, some see God as the cause of their afflictions, as if God required suffering, as if suffering was a heavenly tool for submission rather than an earthly reality caused sometimes by random nature, sometimes by human oppression. The relationship to a God who is helper, true friend, and pained partner rather than avenger can be sustaining through relentless time. She who suffers can discover she is not alone. Suffering can expand reality. Not only is God a friend, but the sacred is experienced in other sisters and brothers who are suffering.

Women find their faith and resolve renewed with each other. Mandy confesses to Deborah her fears of recurrence; Sandy weeps in Barbara's arms at being left alone; Pat chides Analese to "wink at 'em (the wheel chair operators) flirt with 'em!" "Like I'm the Queen?" she retorts. "Like you're the Queen!" affirms Pat.[6] These women reach for a community that can assist with change in relationship with their own bodies to a relationship with another to the larger social body. Both Barbara and Mandy realize their suffering is not an isolated event but one experienced by many others in a community of women who are struggling, lamenting, living, and dying with cancer. Mandy describes her realization while ministering to a woman dying of cancer:

And then I heard you God. I heard you suffering with us. I saw your pain. I saw my pain, and the pain of the woman dying in front of me. Our suffering. Not my private little corner of fear. But concentric circles of humanity. I see now that our suffering must wake up everyone about the destruction of creation.[7]

Barbara contextualizes her own diagnosis of breast cancer as one in eight.

My friends gather in a circle around me, each of them laying hands upon my body. Rituals are strange to me. As I watch their faces, I come to understand that I am only the first among our friends to have cancer. There will be others as we grow older.[8]

With the awareness of something larger than themselves, each has moved into a circle of healing. This circle includes caregivers like Sandy. In this circle, the living and dying are achingly calling for change; rage and groans are demands. Activists are formed from the ranks of those who are ill and those who are not. Networks of activist groups collaborate in many localities. The suffering does not end, but its meaning is not lost. As women care for women in this epidemic, they create a cancer community. Churches and synagogues need to see God at work and share in the suffering that is birthing new resisting communities.

Conclusion

The ethos of individuality exudes isolation, separateness, self-reliance, self-identity. It is interesting to me that all of the women with whom I had conversations about their cancer at some point spoke of a realization of their own fragility. Their own permeability came to the foreground in the face of cancer, interconnected with a web of other survivors, western and non-western medical practitioners, caregivers, families, and friends. In a society in which everyone is a specialist and people are turned into bundles of functions, fragility does not seem to compliment survival. Yet as the Stanford study of women with breast cancer revealed, people live longer when they are engaged in and affected by each other's lives, something larger than themselves.[9]

The process of rehearsing *CancerBodies* deepened my understanding of the complexity of community. Occurring over four months, our rehearsals were a period of change where the actresses and myself learned patience with one another and acceptance of our human gifts and frailties. The trust that was given and the vulnerability that was demanded in creating a play about women and the disease of cancer formed and strengthened our ensemble. One of the gifts of working with a feminist approach to theatermaking is the joy of creating a web of interdependence. This web, however, is not created to make its members warm and comfortable. It is forged out of differences that sting and challenge. Its weave is lustrous and strong because there are differences. The web was formed as we elucidated multiple points of view about women and cancer which were located in the positions of race, class, and sexuality. In our rehearsal process we saw the changes wrought in each of us as we embraced our differences and similarities in the practice of community building.

Lorraine Serena

Elena Siff, "Global Vision," mixed media box, 1995.

Jean - So glad to re-connect through the conference. Hope to see your work soon [signature] Lorraine

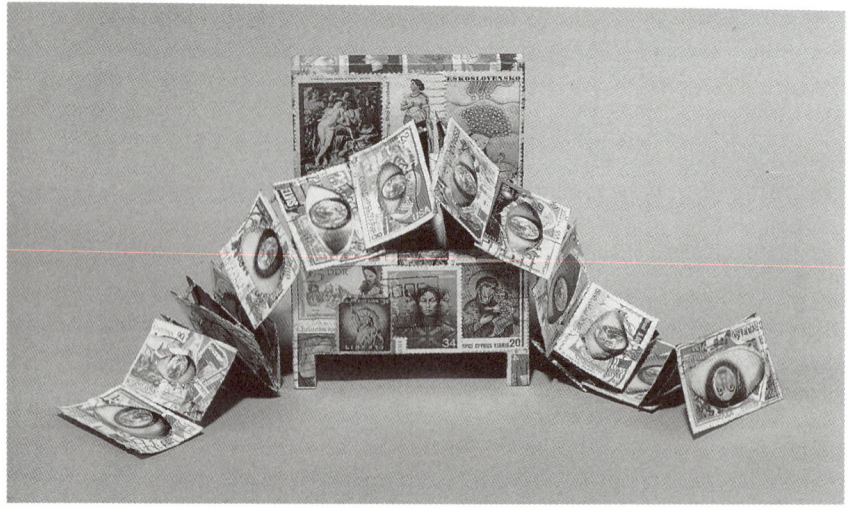

above:
Liliana Ribeiro, "Nostalgia Box."
left:
Lorraine Serena, "The Battlefield of Selfhood, A Box of Empty Shells to Ponder," mixed media, 1995.

WOMEN/*Beyond Borders*

by Lorraine Serena

Until a strong line of love, confirmation and example stretches from mother to daughter, from woman to woman, across the generations, women will still be wandering in the wilderness.

—Adrienne Rich

To honor and document women's visions

To build community through dialogue

To inspire all women to express their creativity

WOMEN/*Beyond Borders* is the possibility that women are honored for their untold visions and voices and that women support one another in this quest.

Modern technology facilitates this collaboration and in turn the building of a global community, opening the way for a new dimension of understanding as we move toward the 21st Century.

The Way of Women

Women in communication, sharing ideas, insights, dreams, joys, sorrows, and collective memories, connecting one to the other — it is an age-old activity. WOMEN/*Beyond Borders* is an extension of this continuum and represents women at their collective best. It is more than an exhibition, it is a worldwide conversation among women and about women. Over 200 artists and curators from diverse backgrounds and cultures collaborated for almost three years in order to create exhibitions traveling to fifteen countries and connecting the participants via modern technology. As we move toward the next century, we challenge ourselves to see beyond limiting categories of politics, geography, and belief in order to create images of who we are in a reality beyond definition. Through this experience we have been led to understanding, interaction, and trust. Together, we have envisioned this collaboration in a way far greater than we could have individually. The beauty and power of W/*BB* lies in the spirit of support witnessed across lines of class, race, ethnicity, nationality, and age, as women converse, exchange and send their visions further into the world.

My work with Suzi Gablik and Suzanne Lacy in the workshop, "Making Art as if the World Mattered," at Anderson Ranch, Colorado during the summer of 1991, was undoubtedly an underlying impetus for WOMEN/*Beyond Borders*. We acknowledge our human desire for community and our concern for our world through this project. As we cross borders and bring women into relation we have embarked on building a world community. This has become our art form.

A Grassroots Beginning

W/*BB* was born in a conversation at a gallery opening in Santa Barbara, California (September 1992) when Elena Siff and I contemplated the ease of shipping miniature works of art around the world. The idea spread by word of mouth and very soon we found ourselves collaborating with over a dozen area artists. At one of our studio meetings, we focused on a miniature wooden souvenir box from the 1950s which was on the table in front of us. "That's it!" someone said, and the "Box Project" began. Several hundred boxes, each 3 1/2 x 2 1/2 x 2 inches were constructed. Inspired, we swiftly began contacting artist and curator friends around the world who each invited up to twelve artists to participate.

In describing our inventive distribution process, artist Mary Heebner states, "Our selection of countries was made simply on the basis that someone in the group knew someone else abroad. Isabel enlisted the help of her 13-year-old son, Xavier, who carried plain boxes to artist Eliana Molinelli in Argentina. Elena's daughter Ravelle, a UCLA student studying at a Hebrew University, found Daphna Naor, a curator in Israel. A friend of Elisse Pogofsky-Harris, Carole Rosenberg, took boxes to Cubana women, and Elena traveled to Italy to find an exhibition site there. Mari Olguin, visiting from Oaxaca, left my home with an information packet in her suitcase, and a week later we had a fax from Tanya Coen, Director of Casa de Mujer in Oaxaca, Mexico: 'We seem to have hit a small gold mine of Oaxacan women artists — send boxes ASAP!'"[1]

There was no formal process at first. Evelyn Jacob Jaffe spontaneously walked into a gallery in Paris and left a half dozen boxes with a young woman who distributed them to friends. They returned as some of the most elegant, conceptual pieces. During a stay in Paris, Alice Hutchins discussed plans for a segment of the exhibition in France. My daughter, Stephania, contacted some of her artist friends in New York City. Beverly Decker enlisted her sister-in-law to locate Native American women in New Mexico.

At the inception of this project, Liz Brown, Curator of the University Art Museum at the University of California at Santa Barbara, said, "You have a conceptual elegance in your vision. Keep it flexible. Use a diversity of venues based on interpersonal connections. Allow the project to take on a life of its own." W/*BB* now moves forward and expands, as a living entity. We let it go and indeed, it now has a life of its own.

Artists included in Phase I are from the United States, Japan, Austria, Uganda, Kenya, Argentina, Spain, Mexico, Italy, Sweden, Finland, Australia, Vietnam, Israel, Cuba, and France. Arab women have joined artists in Israel. A Phase II of Women/ *Beyond Borders* includes Ecuador, Russia, England, Switzerland, Greece, and Germany. Another thirty countries await information. There are emerging artists, self-taught artists, nationally and internationally known women. Artists range in age from 18 to 88. Not only have geographical borders been crossed, but the borders of rejection and limitation as well. All boxes submitted to us were accepted.

After traveling to each of the participating countries, W/ *BB* returns to the United States in the year 2000 to become part of a permanent collection. A few of the exhibition sites include: The Santa Barbara Contemporary Arts Forum, California; Wifredo Lam Center, Havana, Cuba; The National Museum of Kenya, Contemporary Gallery, Nairobi; Kunstlerhaus, Graz, Austria; Tin Sheds Gallery, Sydney, Australia; ICC Contemporary Gallery, Jerusalem, Israel; Kulturhuset, Stockholm, Sweden; and the Extra Moenia, Arte Moderna, in Todi, Italy.

Beyond these exhibitions, participants have formed support groups, visited one another, raised funds, and organized panel discussions and workshops. A dialogue has been established among women, and doors have opened to new possibilities.

The Premier Opening

The Santa Barbara Contemporary Arts Forum was the site of the premier exhibition on November 4, 1995. The boxes struck a deep chord in those who attended. A record number of people came and responded to the quality and power of each work, as well as the collective pulse of the exhibition.

> WOMEN/ *Beyond Borders* exhibition surpasses all of our expectations, high as they were! I am quite sure that the exhibition will be received enthusiastically everywhere it goes. It is sure to be among one of our most popular shows. It was also one of our most meaningful exhibitions.

> W/BB is such a timely endeavor as it brings together women's visions at the end of a century marked by women's struggles to find their places and their voices. It is also particularly important in that it cuts across all borders — physical, political, religious, racial. W/BB has been transformed from a simple idea into a profound project that will engage and affect people as it makes its way around our world.
> *— Nancy Doll, Director, Santa Barbara Contemporary Arts Forum*

> Woman/ *Beyond Borders* is an inspiring, thought-provoking, and aesthetically thrilling project. The connections it has fostered between nations and among women are remarkable. It also becomes a testament to the unbounded possibilities of human creativity, tested here in the seemingly simple transformation of a small wooden box. Women representing various participating countries attended the opening. Meeting them was the highlight of the evening.
> *— Marla Berns, Director, University Art Museum, Santa Barbara*

Lizet Benrey-Fuller, artist and daughter of Mexico City artist-curator Shirley Chernitsky attended with her family. Ingeborg Pock and Eva Ursprung came from Graz, Austria. Annica Karlson-Rixon and Paulina Wallenberg Olsson represented Sweden. Darlene Nguyen-Ely, Suzie Vuong, and Be Ky Nguyen represented Vietnam.

Variations on the Theme of a Box

The box is a vessel with rich metaphoric significance. It refers to treasure, to shrines, to wombs and tombs, to gifts, to hope. As we began to receive completed works, it became clear that the humble container which we spontaneously selected was a powerful symbol — a resonating archetypal symbol of woman herself.

Completed works range from powerful, conceptual pieces to whimsical and nostalgic boxes. Some from Mexico are colorful, others sinister. Those from Israel are powerful and provocative; from Argentina, sculptural and earthy; from Paris, sophisticated and deliberate. Some works are fraught with the terror of oppression and others brim with hope and humor. There is a great variety, all compelling and unique. The images represent the spectrum of human experience: love, birth, relationship, power, courage, violence, death, and the sacred. These miniature boxes, which can be held in one hand, transmit a depth of vision which belies their size.

Writer Joan Crowder discusses individual boxes:

> The boxes are their own form of communication representing everything from universal women's issues to personal memoirs. A few artists took the boxes apart and reconstructed and transformed them. Carin Elberg of Sweden ground the box into sawdust and placed it in a Plexiglas box of the same dimensions.

> Kabura Simpiri of Kenya calls her box "My Culture, My Pride." It is a container for a miniature portrait painted on the bark of a tree sacred to her Maasai culture. "By revealing this beauty of the Maasai people, I hope my contribution in some way helps in the preservation of this priceless culture," she writes.

> The contradictions between the expectations of women and the realities of women concern a number of the artists. Rowena Galavitz of Oaxaca, Mexico, created an elaborate quilted satin box, fine and feminine. But inside, viewed through a blue scrim, is the photo of a nude woman and a sinister-looking knife.

> Akane Asoaka calls her box "Until Death Do Us Part." Inside is a tiny white cotton shirt that extends out from the box and becomes a wedding dress at the other end. In her statement, Asoaka says the piece comes from a collective memory of playing mother. "In Japanese, when we say 'to get married' we use the word 'to be tied up,'" she explains.

> The most poignant boxes are from Cuba. Jacquiline Brito Jorge's is a boat, set for escape. Another contains a lock of hair and a tattered bandage. Its title is "No Escape is Possible." Memory is the subject of Shuli Nachshon of Israel who filled

her box with slips of paper on which were words that she wished she had said to her mother.

Ciel Bergman's "Grief Repair" contains wax with blood behind it, threads and a needle. She calls it a metaphor for the efforts of women all over the world to heal, to keep communities whole, "despite a world which seems eternally based on war and conflict."

Lorraine Serena's box is filled with empty bullet shells, a statement about violence and anger and in a poem she asks, "Where is the greatest battlefield to conquer, on the terrain or in the heart?"

Judy Dater says she was shocked by the box she created, coated with lava and filled with green jelly buddies. She calls it "Virus Box." It feels appropriate at this time, she says, in view of "threats to the environment, threats to our health, to our civilization and our culture."

But there is an underlying tone of hope in the exhibition, with women recognizing their strengths and taking responsibility for their futures.

Japanese artist Chiori Ito's box refers to nature and natural history. She explains. "Each of us is connected by our umbilical cords through hundreds of generations of women into one continuous line . . . like the growing roots of a plant . . . we are simultaneously standing both in history and the frontier of the new world."

Lesley Tannahill, also from Japan, calls her entry "Pandora's Box," but the items in it are good, not evil. She offers the other version of the story: "The box which Pandora opened contained everything that was good and when (against her husband's advice) she raised the lid, all that was good escaped out into the world. I like this story and think it's a fine metaphor for the creative, open-minded nature of womankind."[2]

WOMEN/*Beyond Borders* "Gets Wired"

Audiences throughout the world are able to view the exhibition via the Internet. They can locate images of the boxes, exhibition sites and dates, essays, reviews, comments, etc. Artist Sky Bergman, Assistant Professor at Cal Poly San Luis Obispo, worked with her students to design a World Wide Web homepage for W/*BB*, in order to create accessibility and to promote communication between artist and audience. In commenting on this process, Sky stated, "The Word Wide Web is being used as a site to connect women who wish to participate in web chats and also to view the W/*BB* exhibition and individual artist portfolios." Hundreds of women and men from nations around the world have already logged on, including people from Chile, Brunei Darussalam, Bahrain, Lithuania, Thailand, United Arab Emirates, Malta, Russian Federation, Kuwait, Malaysia, Iceland, Indonesia, Slovenia, and Turkey.

Victoria Vesna, artist and professor at the University of California, Santa Barbara, created a component, "f-e-mail and beyond," to further elicit a dialogue among women which will assist in empowering them with the new technologies. The possibilities of this connection cannot be underestimated as women continue to discuss relevant issues as well as plan future events. Women are encouraged to gather around this electronic hearth to connect and create in a way more vast than we have ever imagined.

World Wide Web: http://cielo.libart.calpoly.edu/borders/index.html

f-e-mail & beyond: http://www.arts.ucsb.edu/f-e-mail

Stories Along the Way

In February 1995, Jony Waite from Nairobi, Kenya, arrived via a Greyhound bus just down the street from my studio to hand-deliver the first completed boxes from Africa. As she began to unwrap the boxes, I felt the initial impact of time, energy, and creativity invested by each individual artist. According to Jony, "African women have a strong desire to interact with women from other countries. WOMEN/ *Beyond Borders* is an enormous step in enriching and connecting us. In Kenya, women have been subjugated for years as chattel, but recently many have begun finding their voices and power. We are delighted to work with WOMEN/ *Beyond Borders* and look forward to networking with creative groups worldwide." Before Jony left to continue her journey, she expressed her gratitude for acknowledging women in Kenya and Uganda, and said that the Contemporary Gallery at the National Museum of Kenya had committed to honoring the African participants with their own exhibition.

When Eva Ursprung, artist/publisher from Graz, Austria joined W/ *BB*, she in turn invited women from the project to participate in a group she founded called Kunstverein W. A. S. "(Woman's Art Support)." As Eva states, "One of the main aims of W. A. S. is international networking of woman artists, so W/ BB fit perfectly and several participants have become members of the executive committee." When the completed boxes departed Graz, the townspeople pitched in to give the artists and their works a festive send-off. A copy shop printed the invitations gratis, a local bakery provided refreshments, and the neighborhood hardware store donated pedestals for the works of art — all generous extensions of the community support.

After a December 1995 poetry reading held in conjunction with the W/ *BB* Exhibition, Bunny Bernhardt was inspired by 16-year-old Jess Jaffe's compelling plea for support of young women afflicted with self abuse. She decided to form a group "Grandmothers to Protect Granddaughters." Wise women tossing a life raft to young women of the world: What a concept! If this were the only outcome of W/ *BB*, it would have been enough.

A father came to my studio with his daughter to view the boxes prior to the exhibition. They spend more than two hours discussing the issues expressed in the art: birth, death, conflict, the imagination. . . . It was a profound dialogue exemplifying the depth of human relationship.

An unexpected FAX arrived in May 1995 from Heide Hildebrand at the Museum Moderner Kunst Stiftung Ludwig und Sammlung Ludwig in Vienna: "I am a friend of [participant] Gina Ballinger and one of the twelve women in Austria who worked on a box. Last week we had a meeting in Tuscany and I want to report to you the following: Anne-Kathi Wildberger works at the Antikenmuseum in Basel/Switzerland and is assisting in the preparation of an exhibition entitled 'Pandora's Box: Women of Classical Greece." She had the idea of enlarging the exhibition in Basel with a Swiss segment of WOMEN/*Beyond Borders*. I find this a brilliant idea, as the exhibition will deal with antique boxes, vessels, etc. To actualize it by a present-day segment of female art work is just an ingenious idea." Dr. Margot Schmidt from the Antikenmuseum Basel also wrote of 'Pandora's Box,' I am looking forward to the realization of this project. If we can join W/*BB* with 'Pandora's Box' in Basel, it would mean that we would link not only women of our time, but we would also link with the ancient Greek women who, at their time, had a strong need for solidarity." With these two communiqués, we began Phase II. [The European exhibition is not to be confused with one similarly titled — "Pandora's Box: Women of Classical Greece" (November '95—January '96) — conceived, organized, and circulated by the Walters Art Gallery, Baltimore, MD.]

Reflections on WOMEN/*Beyond Borders*

From the participants:

> Most cultures have a tradition of working collectively, lending a hand. Native and pioneer Americans built kivas, raised barns, shared talk and talent in quilting, beading, or basket-making circles. It seems that the more self-sufficient we become, the lonelier the act of making things becomes as well. Today many women are seeking ways to meet informally or collaborate on group projects as a step toward undoing the isolation of solitary work.
>
> —*Mary Heebner*

> As contributing artist and team organizer of WOMEN/*Beyond Borders*, I learned to understand the world in a radically new way: one that is based in interaction and team work, versus the traditionally patriarchal view of individuality, competition and isolation. Woman is one and multiple at once; her strength resides in being so versatile to the extent that her individuality doesn't feel threatened by working in collaboration. This attitude is very valuable and very rare nowadays. Collaboration, exchange, dialogue are the elements that contribute to the impact of a show like this. Woman extends herself and becomes "female." Female exists beyond anatomical difference.
>
> — *Maria Velasco*

The feminine perspective needs to be seriously looked at and rediscovered. WOMEN/ *Beyond Borders* has been created in a female way. It has been very successful and powerful in this regard. What has been accomplished in this project is a real model to me of how the feminine process works. One doesn't have to bulldoze people over in process of moving forward. You can be nurturing, flexible, open, caring, non-judgmental — all of those wonderful female attributes which are very powerful in a every universal way. This would never have been done without give-and-take, without collaboration.

— *Beverly Decker*

A small box was given to me. I had to take a stand on what that box should mean. The more I worked on it, the more condensed the energy became. It came to mean a squared world of love and death in a 3 1/2 x 2 1/2 x 2" space. I felt it was like atomic energy, my life condensed. When my box took its place among all the other atomic reactions of love, despair, joy, fun and fear — all done by women, it was such a reaffirming commitment to living and being a woman that I felt the room explode with all the creative energy that was present.

—*Saritha Margon*

There is no hierarchy in this exhibition. We are all creating a piece from the same inexpensive pine box and there is a real sense of us supporting one another. We are women artists of all ages, from all economic backgrounds and with varying degrees of professional reputation in the "art world." As this project has grown and the dialogue with other international artists has increased, through the fax and Internet, it is apparent that there is a vital stream which is flowing among us as the exhibition begins it's epic voyage. Whatever happens on the way is the essence of WOMEN/ *Beyond Borders*!

— *Elena Mary Siff, co-founder*

Onward

W/*BB* honors the vitality, wisdom, sensitivity and collective power of women's expressions. As we move forward with a sense of solidarity and collective confirmation, there is no doubt that extending community has become the work. It is in this process that we find the greatest meaning of the word art as derived from the Latin root *ar* — to join together.

As artist/writer Suvan Geer states:

WOMEN/ *Beyond Borders* is a step in undoing the isolation and hopelessness of silence. It is not a panacea, a goal or a bandaid. It is simply a step. Next will be the visits between artists in various countries, the letters and the Internet communications. These are interpersonal communications which will be followed by more self exploration, expansion of presence, and confirmations of global and community importance. Although we are invited to witness these exchanges by viewing the various exhibitions, unless we actively join the discussions, most will be invisible to us. Documentation will never fully reveal what this dialogue will mean to the participants. That is to be expected, and in no way diminishes what this gathering together will signify to the world. Because every revolution is people. Not crowds, or movements or armies, but individuals coming to a common understanding that they have power. That they can change the world. And it always begins with knowing who we are.[3]

In the broadest sense, W/*BB* is not only about these women, it is about all women. Look and listen to these women. Hear their pleas for healing, justice, respect, and liberation. Observe their reverence for the home, the world and one another. These women express their deepest convictions. Look beyond these particular women — listen to and honor the voices and visions of all.

IV LIVING IN COMMUNITY

Sara Bates, "Honoring III" (detail), 1992,
natural materials, 7 foot diameter.

Introduction

No, no es la solucion
tirarse bajo un tren como la Ana de Tolstoy
ni apurar el arsenico de Madame Bovary
ni aguarar en los paramos de Avila la visita
del angel con venablo
antes de liarse el manto a la cabeza
y comenzar a actuar. . . .

Debe haber otro modo. . . .

Otro modo de ser humano y libre.

Otro modo de ser.

      No, the solution is not
      to jump beneath a train, like Tolstoy's Anna,
      nor to swallow Madame Bovary's arsenic,
      nor to wait on the barren plains of Avila
      for the visit of the angel with the javelin
      before tying the scarf around one's head and beginning to act. . . .

      There has to be some other way. . . .

      Another way to be human and free.

      Another way to be.[1]

It is 1985. I am in Madrid, looking for a convent reputed to have an excellent art collection. Finally, I find it: an austere, almost forbidding facade hidden in a tiny cul-de-sac behind an immense department store. I enter going from the blazing Spanish sun into the cavernous darkness of the entryway. The uniformed guards tell me that I can only see the convent on a tour, so I buy a ticket and go to the adjoining room to wait for the next guide. This room, too, is dark, and the gold-framed paintings that line it are shrouded by centuries of dust adhering to their glazed surfaces. As my eyes adjust, I see that what are depicted in the paintings are archangels, glorious androgynous creatures whose silvery armor and short brocade skirts glisten below cascading flowers. I smile to myself, pleased to recognize Spanish Baroque — the style of intentional visual redundancy that captured the imaginations of native peoples in the Americas and Philippines and which became the basis for so much Spanish Colonial art.

The guide enters, and in elegant lisping Castilian, introduces herself and the convent we are about to visit. The Monasterio de Nuestra Senora de la Asuncion y Nuestra Senora de la Consolacion, usually known as simply Descalzas Reales,[2] was founded in 1554 by Princess Dona Juana de Austria. Juana was the youngest sister of Carlos V (who was the most powerful European monarch of that time), wife of King Juan of Portugal, and sister of Felipe II (who was to formulate much of the colonial bureaucracy of the New World, perhaps outstrip his father in both military prowess and artistic patronage, then renounce his fame and retire to the severely self-abnegating life of a solitary monastery). I tell you all this about the founder so that you will understand Descalzas Reales was for women of high royal standing, women who had every opportunity in the outer world, but chose to retreat from it and join a cloistered community. Archduchess Dona Margarita entered Descalzas Reales as a very young woman, soon after refusing to become Felipe II's wife. Her bedroom is preserved, with one of the rough, harsh robes she wore and the knotted ropes she used for penitence.

Before we see Margarita's room, the guide takes us through the center of the convent structure, a courtyard that houses the nun's private chapels. Each chapel is a diminutive room, sometimes just a niche or closet-like space, with shuttered wooden doors that can secure it from outsiders. And each chapel contains the finest and most intimately personal art that the royal nuns could make, collect, and arrange to reflect their highest aspirations. Gilded archangels with lacy haloes point the way to salvation. Infant Jesuses, bedecked in jewels and sheer silk gowns, rest in thickly encrusted cradles. Female saints stand in regal affirmation, their magnificent robes adorned with pearls and inlaid stones. There is so much to look at that the chapels are almost dizzying; intentional visual redundancy is taken to unscaled heights by these wealthy women. I start to worry about the Stendahl syndrome (the illness brought on by looking at too much art), but am drawn on by the compelling individuality of each chapel. Here is one that celebrates the powerful women of the bible through delicate paintings on mirrors. Here's another with a creche sequestered in a coral cave. A Godiva-like saint reclines under mounds of golden tresses. A plaster skull peeks out from a bower of pink petals. It is so rich, so touching. So beautiful.

I am married and have a new baby when I first find Descalzas Reales. By my last visit, in 1990, I am divorced and my son is much older. But whatever my personal situation, the same questions come to me. Why did these women — who had every opportunity of wealth, power, position — join the convent? Why did they leave a world that promised them so much? And what was it like for them to build a community in which personal expression was articulated through making, collecting, and arranging such incredible art? How did these nuns live together? What did they share? I find the idea of living together in a community of creative women incredibly seductive. I begin to have fantasies of living in an art convent myself, maybe founding one in New Mexico where I'd gone to graduate school and where my mother now lives.

The vision of the convent haunts me. One night years later, back here in Los Angeles, I have a dream. I dream of establishing a salon, a meeting place for women to discuss their lives, their ideas, their art. I call a friend and tell her that I want to gather twelve women to meet once a month and discuss feminist art, theory and pedagogy. I tell her I think we can change the world. She shares my excitement. We start the salon. And soon, all too soon, it becomes a horrible experience for me. Some of the women don't take the salon seriously; they come late or not at all. Some of them want to gossip, especially about campus politics, rather than discuss the readings we've agreed on. Racism rears its ugly head. And homophobia. And, again and again, personality conflicts — some of the women just don't like each other much, even though they've agreed to the same agenda and share the same politics. I'm desolate. What's wrong with this community? What happened to my dream? How can people learn to live and work together, really? I remember my fantasies at Descalzas Reales convent. What does it take to build a creative community that works?

Convents and salons are the two most important precedents for the contemporary feminist communities. Historian Gerda Lerner points out that both institutions served to provide women with "sheltered spaces" where they could advance their intellectual development.[3] For over a millennium, Western European women were forced to choose between family life and a life of the mind (a choice few men have ever had to make). Opting for the latter, the women entered convents, where they found the support of like-minded women and the freedom to read, write, and create art (transcribe and illuminate manuscripts, embroider, weave tapestries, etc.). Nuns like the twelfth century Hildegard von Bingen were able to transcend traditional gender roles because they lived in female communities, "enjoying what Sara Evans has listed as a precondition for feminist consciousness, 'free space'."[4] Hildegard's work, which is honored in Judy Chicago's "Dinner Party," is elegantly described by Gerda Lerner:

> Hildegard's vision of cosmos, nature and humankind is powerful in its holistic integration of all aspects of Creation. The beautiful illustrations of the Rupertsberg Codex, which was created under her personal supervision by the nuns of her cloister, reflect the harmony and grandeur of her vision. Concentric figures hold sea, earth, sky, stars and the heavens in balance. Symbols are as frequently female as male and worshippers are evenly balanced among both sexes. Wherever the clergy is shown, it is represented by male and female religious. One senses in Hildegard a soul at ease with the physical as with the metaphysical, with life as with spirit.[5]

Beginning in the seventeenth century, women began to found and participate in salons, the meeting places for intellectual discourse that spawned so many of the publications of the Enlightenment, Romantic, and Modern eras.[6] Only noble and royal women possessed enough wealth to produce the dowry necessary for entry into most convents. Participation in salons was likewise limited to the elite. But classism was not the only form of inequity present in convents and salons — many other aspects of patriarchal oppression were active as well. Historically, then, convents and salons have not been the kind of alternative communities discussed in this book. So the question becomes, What does it take to create a genuinely alternative community?

I suppose that the first thing we need to know about creating alternative communities is that we have to change ourselves, reform our expectations and our behavior before we try to enter such communities, or we will inadvertently recycle the same old ideas and processes.

bell hooks: Sometimes I get really distressed by the extent to which we, in the United States, have moved away from the idea of *communities* — of people trying to have *different* world views and value systems. In the '60s there was a lot of focus on such communities, but that sort of died out and a refocus on the nuclear family emerged . . . we know that small alternative communities of people still exist, but they don't get a lot of attention. If I think about the communities that have gotten a lot of attention from the mass media (such as the Rajneesh town in Oregon), it was always *negative* . . . never attention on shared worship, shared eating of vegetables (and not being meat-eaters), or being peace-loving. . . . But whenever something goes wrong. . . .

Andrea Juno: . . The media are right there to report it. However, many "alternative" societies in the '60s brought their same dualistic oppressional thinking to their would-be "paradise" — they just inverted it a little, but it became just as oppressive.

bell hooks: Even then though, the question becomes, "Do you give up on making the beloved community . . . or do you realize that you must make it a different way?" Because I feel what happened was: a lot of people took the failures of the '60s as a sign that, "See — you cannot really make an alternative space." Whereas I'm convinced that you *can* — if, as you say, you have changed your consciousness and your actions *prior* to trying to create that space. I think that when we enter those new space with the same old negative baggage, then of course we don't produce something new and different in those spaces![7]

Rejecting Hierarchy and Domination

Tracing the historical development by which patriarchy emerged as the dominant form of societal order, I have shown how it gradually institutionalized the rights of men to control and appropriate sexual and reproductive services of women. Out of this form of dominance developed other forms of dominance, such as slavery. Once established as a functioning system of complex hierarchical relationships, patriarchy transformed sexual, social, and economic relations and dominated all systems of ideas.[8]

We must enter alternative communities already changed, but we must also structure them in alternative ways. The nuns of Descalzas Reales, like all members of cloistered Catholic communities, lived under the often oppressive standards of a set of rules established and approved by the Church fathers. These rules demanded absolute obedience and strict adherence to hierarchy. Reading through

Saint Benedict's Rule for Monasteries, I get some idea of what such rules must have meant on a daily experiential basis. A statement like: "An Abbot who is worthy to be *over* a monastery should always remember what he is called, and live up to the name of *Superior.* . . . [italics mine]"[9] tells me a lot about the hierarchy that is the basis for monastic structure. Later, when I read that members must "obey in all things the commands of the Abbott, even though he himself (which God forbid) should act otherwise, mindful of the Lord's precept, 'Do what they say, but not what they do',"[10] it begins to look like blind obedience is mandated. I read on. "The first degree of humility is obedience without delay. This is the virtue of those who . . . because of the holy service they have professed, and the fear of hell, and the glory of life everlasting, as soon as anything has been ordered by the Superior, receive it as a divine command and cannot suffer any delay in executing it . . . immediately leaving their own affairs and forsaking their own will, dropping the work they were engaged in and leaving it unfinished, with the ready step of obedience follow up with their deeds the voice of him who commands."[11] I realize that, historically, Catholic communities, like many other traditional communities, have been based on patterns of domination.

This begins to sound not only unappealing but dangerous. I turn to Sharon Welch's *A Feminist Ethic of Risk* to learn more about the relationship between cultural traditions and domination. Welch agrees that "a theology that valorizes absolute power through its concept of an omnipotent God is dangerous. . . ."[12] It is dangerous precisely because, in establishing a pattern of *power over* — the pattern reproduced in the hierarchy of Benedict's monasteries, for example — it legitimates the domination of others. "The claim of complete obedience to a higher power justifies control of others. . . . The results of the valorization of absolute power are indeed dangerous: either domination of others in the name of the common good or despair at not being able to readily attain the essential goals of peace, freedom, and justice. A theology that emphasizes the absolute power of God holds as an ideal a type of power not possible for those working for justice."[13]

Generating New Power Dynamics

A feminist community cannot embrace domination nor value absolute power. According to Celestine Ware, "Radical feminism, and this by no means includes all positions within the Women's Liberation Movement, postulates that the domination of one human being by another is the basic evil in society. Dominance in human relationships is the target of their opposition."[14] So, as Vietnamese-American filmmaker Trinh T. Minh-ha writes, "The challenge is thus: how can one re-create without recirculating domination?"[15] The answer that many women have come to, in creating alternative communities, is to redefine power as *power with* rather than *power over.*

The issues constituent of *power over* are fundamental to the arts. "Power of one group over another is sustained on many levels, economic, political, legal, or educational, but these relations of power are reproduced in language and in images which present the world from a certain point of view and represent different positions of and relations to power of both sexes and classes."[16] Not only those cultural products usually termed the "fine arts," but also advertisements, commercials, and billboards as well as film and television narratives present us with a deluge of images embodying the prescribed power dynamics of our society. There is no doubt that the daily flood of mass media images has potent impact, that it directly affects how we think about ourselves, our personal power, and our relationships with others. Over twenty years ago, Gaye Tuchman wrote that "Americans learn basic lessons about social life from the mass media, much as hundreds of years ago illiterate peasants studied the carvings around the apse or the stained glass windows of medieval cathedrals. . . . The societal need for continuity and transmission of dominant values may be particularly acute in times of rapid social change, such as our own. . . . Nowhere is that need as readily identifiable as in the area of sex roles — sex roles are social guidelines for sex-appropriate appearance, interests, skills, behaviors, and self-perceptions."[17] But few of us ask *who is speaking* when we turn on the television or enter a movie theater. Who is telling us how powerful or powerless we *should* feel?

Media artist Anne Bray has compiled unsettling statistics to answer this fundamental question. Of the thousands of people involved in creating images for mainstream mass media, only a tiny percentage is female. "Even 'Murder She Wrote' was not written by a woman!" quips Bray. In part to correct the inequities of access to broadcasting, Bray has organized an annual video festival in Southern California. Called "Los Angeles Freewaves," the festival connects hundreds of video-makers with dozens of venues, from university art galleries to cable television stations. Bray elects not to "choose" who can participate and who can't. That is, she doesn't select which videos are "artistically fine" enough or "politically correct" enough to be included. Instead, she endeavors to give voice to everyone interested. In doing so, she undermines the old high arts vs. entertainment hierarchy. She also acts as a facilitator of creative connection, and builds alternative communities across the airwaves.

Communications Professor Sut Jhally (University of Massachusetts, Amherst) addresses the relationship stories and attitudes, particularly as they pertain to gender roles, in his deeply disturbing educational video "Dreamworlds II: Desire, Sex, and Power in Music Video" (1995). Jhally suggests that a dominant story in commercial culture — not only music videos, but also ads, television programs, and films — is the adolescent male fantasy. There are many stories about sexuality in society. But when we ask who gets to tell the stories of sexuality in music videos, the answer is that over 90 percent are written and directed by men. The story of femininity, of what it means to be a woman in this culture, is told through the mythical women in the videos. Their primary role is to be decorative

— and always sexualized — objects of the (heterosexual) male gaze. Turned into objects, the women are stripped of subjectivity; their bodies become the ground on which action takes place. Jhally asserts that in the images of the videos, the invasion of the female body is welcomed and desired: "The women of the Dreamworld literally want to be carried away."

Jhally concludes that instead of censoring such stories, we need to hear more and different stories about sexuality, about subjectivity. He asks, "Whose stories are told? Whose visions of the world do we not see? Who is silenced in our culture?"

> The images and values of the culture that produces the television programs invade the subconscious cultural identity of its viewers. It's essential that the dialogue becomes two-way and interactive, respects and invites multiples points of view.[18]

Who can tell a story and how they can tell it has to do with power: "Power is the ability to take one's place in whatever discourse is essential to action and the right to have one's part matter."[19] I think again of the African-American boy in Portia Cobb's video. He talked about power being the ability to define yourself and have other people accept that definition, didn't he? But the power to speak and be heard does not mean the power to control your listeners. "Power understood as energy, strength, and effective interaction need not be the same as power that requires the domination of others."[20]

Writing about lesbian communities, Sarah Hoagland contends that "the norms we've absorbed from Anglo-European ethical theory promote dominance and subordination through social control . . . as a result they thwart rather than promote the successful weaving of lesbian community."[21] The same is true for any alternative women's community.

Forsaking Separation

> This relational model, whether expressed psychologically or politically, draws upon a spiritual tradition in art. Many new genre public artists express their connection, through memory, to traditions of ethnicity, gender, or family. They talk about their habitation of the earth as a relationship with it and all beings that live there. These essentially ethical and religious assertions are founded on a sense of service and a need to overcome the dualism of a separate self.[22]

In order to undermine the tradition of dominance and generate new power dynamics, we must restructure our relationships to eliminate arbitrary ranking and fixed hierarchy. We begin this process by accepting each other as equally valuable, if not equally experienced. Such acceptance is the basis for consciousness-raising, where everyone is given equal voice, where no one is ranked. Ranking, whatever the ranking is based on — whether it is gender, race, age, wealth, sexuality, ablebodiedness — is a way to distinguish and separate us one from the other. Creative feminist communities seek to *connect* rather than separate. Separation is antithetical to community building.

I love the way Eknath Easwaran expresses it: "With a higher image of the human being, we would cease to think of ourselves as separate fragments of life in a hostile universe. The more we think of ourselves as physical, the more we will see ourselves as isolated and alone, separate from each other and from the rest of life. Separate creatures are cut off from everything that gives life meaning: a sense of unity, a purpose for living that is larger than ourselves, and the lasting, loving relationships we must have to be human and whole."[23]

For many feminists, rejecting the dynamics of domination involves a spiritual act that extends beyond connection with the members of any discrete community to include connection with all people, all living things, and the planet on which we are living. Feminist theologian Carol Christ writes,

> With many spiritual feminists, ecofeminists, ecologists, antinuclear activists, and others, I share the conviction that the crisis that threatens the destruction of the earth is not only social, political, economic, and technological, but is at root spiritual. We have lost the sense that this earth is our true home, and we fail to recognize our profound connection with all beings in the web of life. Instead many people uncritically accept the view that "man" is superior to "nature" and has the right to "use" the natural world in any way "he" sees fit. Though often clothed in the garb of modern science, such views have their roots in theological conceptions that separate both God and humanity from nature and from finitude, change, and death.[24]

Artist Sara Bates believes we need to set up forms for "creating relationship, connection, integration with nature." A Cherokee from Muskogee, Oklahoma, Bates finds in her people's traditional worldview — a worldview which recognizes the mutual dependency between humans and the earth — the source for her artistic inspiration. Her installations are elegant geometric compositions that hover over museum floors. Rings of pine cones, crosses of stones, triangles of shells, leaves and feathers form lacy patterns radiating out from a central symbol of sacred fire. Viewers are invited to come, sit quietly, and experience their connection with nature, the planet, the sacred spirits — directly, without separation. Bates uses her art to weave the web of connection between herself and viewers, between the community of humans and the planet they inhabit.

Connecting Through Ritual

In creating environments for interaction, Bates creates art that is not only spiritual, but also related to ritual. The important relationship between art and ritual sheds further light on the nature of women's creative communities.

> The art world has been — both historically and cross-culturally — a world of ritual, an arena in which artists transform common materials into complex statements about the human condition. In an alchemy like the transubstantiation of communion wafers into the flesh of Christ, art-making has traditionally changed the raw materials of nature — light, color, line, volume, weight —into cultural artifacts . . . women artists find that their gender can be problematic, largely because of art's essential

basis in ritual — although . . . by 'ritual' I do not mean that all art-making is a shamanistic, visionary process, [but] transformative, by changing simple materials into complicated, culturally meaningful artifacts. As such, art is a medium for moving beyond the mundane. That which lies beyond the mundane is the sacred, and the corridor between the mundane and the sacred is ritual. . . . But . . . historically, creators of ritual tend overwhelmingly to be male."[25] Not allowed to lead the ceremonies of most global religions, women have employed art forms to craft rituals of community, of connection.

Ritual uses the body. Women's ritual uses women's body as divine.
Ritual is symbolic and spiritual.
Ritual moves in the circle.
Ritual is exchange, and makes a connection.
Ritual empowers. . . .
The ritual of speaking in turn, "speaking pain" [an expression for consciousness-raising] to heal pain.
To disclose our women's mysteries. To raise consciousness.
To raise power.
Feminism makes connection.[26]

In the "Communitas" exhibition I discussed earlier, artist Ruth Ann Anderson erected an elegant temple-like structure devoted to feminist spirituality. The external walls of the temple were adorned with poems on community, ritual, and womanspirit. Inside were four altars, dedicated to earth, air, fire, and water, sculpted by women who are on diverse spiritual paths.

The daughter of a fundamentalist minister and a religious educator, Anderson explains, "I have never really abandoned my childhood goal of missionary work. . . . Only my guidebook isn't the Bible any more." In the late 1970s, Anderson became involved in what she calls the Women's Spirituality Movement. The movement encompasses many different credos and practices, but the central belief is in the Goddess, a female divinity who is closely related to the earth and to life-giving forces. "When I first started, I saw the word 'goddess' as being a metaphor for nature," says Anderson. "I think now it's more an understanding of a feminine energy that I would qualify as nurturing and powerful and also terrifying in her destructive aspects — all the elements of the universe in a very powerful feminine entity who has a thousand ways of being manifested."[27]

Because Anderson's beliefs are not sustained by her family community (as are Bates's) nor by a church community, she has had to forge her own spiritual community. With seven other artists, she has founded a coven of women following the Wiccan traditions. In her essay in this chapter, she writes, with poet Starr Goode, about living in that community of creative women. They discuss the use of rituals as markers for life-changing events, as alternative art forms to give meaning and structure to the cycles of their daily lives.

Teaching Community

I am not a visual artist. I create neither images nor performances, nor do I build installations. I am not a member of an ongoing feminist community, like a coven or a commune. However, I do endeavor to incorporate the ideals and processes of feminist community building in my life, particularly in my professional practices of teaching, writing, and curating.

My teaching philosophy mandates the construction of the classroom as a learning community. I believe teaching should have more to do with empowerment than information dispersal. I see teaching as an opportunity to help people interact in ways they might not have previously, so I group my students into teams and assign collaborative projects which are self-evaluated. I also see teaching as a variant of consciousness-raising, and I constantly endeavor to make the classroom a safe space where all voices can be heard, and all voices are valued. Not all students are equally informed, but all of their stories, all of their opinions, are equally important. Many of my pedagogical values are shared by Judith F. Baca, Judy Chicago, Suzanne Lacy, and other women included in this volume who give significant time to teaching. Many of these same values echo those in bell hooks's writing.[28]

As I write this, I am about to start the Spring 1996 semester. I usually begin my classes by introducing myself to my students, telling them about my personal and professional history, my values, and my method of teaching. I let them know that I do this for pedagogical purposes. When I attended college the teaching paradigm was what I call the preacher-congregation model.[29] In most of my classes, the professors — almost always white men — stood in front of the room, separated from their students by a podium. They delivered lectures in as objective a manner as possible, as if channeling divine truth. Students were to memorize and repeat back what they heard. Studio art classes rarely involved lectures (although, when they did, the lecture format repeated that in other disciplines), but the pretense of singular truth objectively delivered was maintained.[30]

Most of my professors appeared to conceive of knowledge as a fixed body of data and insights about those data, which they were to reveal to their students over time. If they thought of themselves in relationship to "their" body of knowledge, it must have been as an impersonal revealer of truth. They seemed to think that allowing their personal lives to enter the classroom would be an embarrassing violation of academic propriety. I can not tell you which of my professors were married, which were heterosexual, what religions they practiced, even what they were working on outside the classroom. bell hooks comments that the "dualistic separation of public and private [encouraged] teachers and students to see no connection between life practices, habits of being, and the roles of professors."[31] She goes on to say, "While I wanted teaching to be my career, I believed that personal success was intimately linked with self-actualization. My passion for this quest led me to interrogate constantly the mind/body split that was so often taken to be a given."[32]

Like hooks, I approach teaching in a radically different way than my own professors did. I tell my students they might think of the classroom as more like a talk show than a traditional church service. The art historical images we analyze — whether slides of videos or films — are the "invited guests" and the students comprise the "audience." They all know that a talk show is only as interesting as the audience participation, which is often contentious. The students' job is to question and comment on the images. I tell them I will act as the talk show host. But the classroom is not a spectacle. I am not there to entertain.[33] I am there to engage them in expanding dialogue with the images that surround them.

Aware that whatever I say or do in the classroom is always informed by the sum of my personal experience, I feel it is incumbent upon me to alert my students to those aspects of myself I know to most influence my choices and interpretations of material. I tell them I am Euroamerican, a feminist, a pacifist, a heterosexual, a single parent. I tell them my age. I tell them I am on a spiritual path. I tell them I am communicating all of this because I know it all affects the dynamics of the classroom.

I seek not to practice the western cultural tradition of "separate learning," which promotes individual competition: Instead, I seek to develop what many feminist theorists have termed "connected learning," which brings the "personal is political" dictum into the classroom, as we realize students understand better and retain longer when the material they deal with is presented in relation to their personal histories and daily lives.[34] How can one interest students in the way images are composed? Show them an ad and help them "read" the way the designer leads the viewer's eye to various points of emphasis. How can one interest students in historic concepts of beauty? Survey movies and movie stars to examine what is considered attractive by the dominant culture, and how that changes. How can one interest students in the concept of dualism in western thought? Show them a series of children's commercials and allow them to see what characterizes those aimed at boys, what characterizes those aimed at girls. Or assign them a field trip to a toy store to analyze how the store is laid out according to gender divisions. That's connected learning.

I conceive of knowledge as something fluid to be created and interpreted, not as a fixed absolute to be discovered. I want to learn with my students, and I want them to be given the tools to learn together. At the beginning of each class, I have the students number off into teams. They spend several class periods in exercises aimed at helping them see that they all view and interpret visual information differently, and that each team member's opinions are valuable. For example, they start by introducing themselves to a partner, then reporting back to the class on what they learned about each other. Later, responding to various class material, each person makes a point, and the person to their right repeats what they heard. This forces the hearer to listen intently and to speak and listen with care.

Another exercise includes numbering each team member and asking one member to remain totally silent during a discussion. Being forcibly silenced allows team members to embody, however briefly, the alienation of exclusion and oppression. A second team role that is randomly rotated is that of note-taker. Having to serve by listening and recording can have a strong impact on those who are used to dominating conversations.

After several exercises on listening and honoring all members of the team, the students produce and enact two presentations. One is on a mass media narrative (a story told on television or film). The other is on a commercial production. The student presentations are always my favorite part of the semester. I am always impressed by their creativity, their willingness to risk, their developing insights. They deal with issues ranging from violence to the increasing objectification of men in the media to racial stereotypes. They dress up, make props, incorporate video and music, and use formats such as mock press conferences, political protests, or game shows.

Teaching is of course a performative practice. To establish the space for the students to co-create the teaching performance is to engage and empower them. It transforms students who are studying about art into artists themselves. At one point in her brilliant "Search for Signs of Intelligent Life in the Universe," Lily Tomlin talks about theater, saying that she doesn't know about what happens on the stage, but what goes on in the audience, that's art. A couple of years ago, a student used that analogy to comment on the student presentations, saying that he didn't know about the slides we'd viewed, but what went on in the classroom, that was art.

It's not easy to create community in the classroom. Students and colleagues expect old patterns to be followed; to violate them is to frustrate expectations. To change old patterns also requires a lot more energy. Whenever I'm exhausted as I face a day of teaching, I'm tempted to return to the well-paved path of lecturing. But I know that talking *at* people does not build community with or among them.

And it's not all positive. I remember with anguish when a student pointed out to me that although I acted like I wanted to hear from all the students, I didn't in fact seem to regard all their answers equally. I had to accept that I'd been dismissive and defensive at times. She really made me look again — as I must in an ongoing way — at how I negotiate the power of my position. Hopefully, I continue to grow in the process.

I remember the irony of another student comment. I was sitting on the floor speaking with a current student when a young man, a student of mine two years before, came up to us. "Betty Brown!" he exclaimed, using my first name rather than the (distancing) "Doctor" appellation he'd preferred in class. "You know, I thought you were a total bitch when I took your class. But now I think it really changed my life. I think about that class, about the things we talked about, more than any other class I've ever taken!" I keep his comment in the front of my mind, to armor me against the resistance and anger I so often meet as I work to break down barriers, rescind expectations, and teach to build community.

Curating Community

> Organizing and networking are crucial elements in activist art, despite the fact that they are not usually considered part of the creative process.[35]

As I composed an earlier draft of this book — this quilt — I was also organizing an exhibition called "Utopian Dialogues." When I tell you about the genesis of the exhibition, you will understand something of how museum work can also be community building. Then, when I tell you about the catalogue for that exhibition, you will understand more about weaving/writing and how this book itself represents community.

First, the idea behind the exhibition. April 29, 1992 was my son's eighth birthday. It was a school day, so we didn't have his party that day; instead, I took him and has best friend, our neighbor Matt, out to an early dinner. It wasn't until we returned home that I heard about the urban uprisings in response to the Simi Valley verdict on the police officers who beat Rodney King. Perhaps it was because they occurred on what for me began as a celebration that I didn't see the uprisings as totally negative. But for a long time it seemed my view was in the minority, particularly among Los Angeles artists. All over Southern California, art venues presented exhibitions in response to the uprisings and all of them seemed to me negative, if not apocalyptic. Was this all we were capable of, I asked myself. Could we only image a nightmarish future?

I decided to organize an exhibition about positive images of the future, about utopian dreams. When I discussed the idea with my boyfriend, a rock musician who was constantly challenging me about the elitism of the fine arts (just as I was ever criticizing the sexism in rock), he said something about artists commenting on the world from the safe (and privileged) distance of their hermetically sealed studios. He had a point. I decided to ask artists to develop work for the show from conversations they had with other individuals, groups, or institutions. Many of the artists with whom I initially spoke didn't feel comfortable with the concept. Doing work that truly acknowledged, indeed *sprang from*, another person's perspective was antithetical to their art practice. For these artists, creativity was firmly linked to their individuality. But other artists were intrigued. In the end, the exhibition was comprised of fourteen installations. Some were produced by single artists who worked with people outside the art environment, others by pairs of artists, others by artist collaborative groups. It should be no surprise to the reader of this book that most of the artists in "Utopian Dialogues" were women, and many were people of color. It is precisely women and people of color who, having had less historical access to the "benefits" accruing from the radical individualism aligned to traditional definitions of the artist, have less invested in maintaining those definitions.

The site for "Utopian Dialogues" was the Los Angeles Municipal Art Gallery. I chose such a public venue because I felt it was urgent for artists (and creative people in general) to enter the public discourse on the kinds of issues the "Utopian Dialogues" participants address. As with many public museums, more than half of the visitors to the Municipal Art Gallery are school children.

Nancy Ann Jones, who was born and educated in Pasadena, California, did her utopian dialogues with the students in Linda Slater's third and fourth grade class at Pasadena Alternative School. She began by brainstorming with the children. What problems did they see in the world around them? How would they like to change the world? I was amazed by the sophistication of the students' responses. They talked about environmental issues, pollution, whales, water supplies. They talked about the homeles. About race. Gangs. Graffiti. Jones's dialogues empowered the classroom. The thirty students from various races, classes, and home situations began to understand that their ideas were valid, their opinions mattered. Then Jones helped them develop images out of their conversations. The images were copied and bound in xeroxed books (one for each child) then hung on the walls of Jones's houselike installation. The house had barred windows, symbolizing the frequent inaccessibility of children's dreams. Graffiti scarred the exterior walls, representing the frustrated expressions of youths who are not allowed to articulate their dreams. The children's angelic faces formed a frieze around the interior, a space entered only through a door much too small for adults, a safe space for the community of children.

That is just one project of the "Utopian Dialogues." Anne Bray, the founder of the "L.A. Freewaves" video festival, was also in the exhibition. So was Suvan Geer, who built a room for listening, and invited numerous community groups to gather in the room and engage in public dialogues about identity, power, expression — many of the issues addressed in this book. Geer's room, and her interaction with community groups, was an outgrowth of years of collaborative art-making.

To ensure that the artists in the exhibition developed community, however ephemerally, in the art-making process, I scheduled a meeting at my home months before the exhibition was to open. The artists spoke about the topics of their dialogues and of their resultant installations, revealing the questions and challenges they'd encountered. As they interacted, we realized a lot about the collaborative process. It's difficult, sometimes painful. There are so few precedents that we constantly feel like we're "reinventing the wheel." But collaboration is also

Living in Community

incredibly rewarding. It allows for interpersonal connections far more profound than does working in isolation. And art does emerge. Identities shift, expand, overlap. Community grows.

> There is a need for new forms emphasizing our essential connectedness rather than our separateness, forms evoking the feeling of belonging to a larger whole rather than expressing the isolated, alienated self.[36]

Writing As Weaving

> The critic's role is to spread the word, propagate ideas, conceptualize, and network publicly with artists. We're mediums. And we need to help find complex and diverse ways to connect the private and public, the personal and the political.[37]

> The critical context is part of the concept of "community." Unlike standard definitions of community as individuals with common interests based on location alone (such as a state or commonwealth), the community that consists of artist and audience for artworks contains, as well, the commentative structure in which the audience and artist may view the process and product of art making. This "critical" component is present whether or not it is discerned or declared. Furthermore, community, like art itself, must be created from a practice that begins with the blank page or empty canvas.[38]

I think much art writing is inaccessible because the writer assumes a tone of mastery and a stance of objectivity that alienates most readers. I wonder why anyone would want to read something that puts them off, something in which they sense the writer is talking down to them. Because I am aware that the audience for most public art exhibitions is not primarily the art cognoscenti, I am determined to produce art writing and exhibition catalogues that are not elitist in form, cost, or content.

For "Utopian Dialogues," we printed a newspaper-like format that was distributed free of charge to all viewers of the exhibition. The text had three parts that ran side-by-side. The first was a series of quotes about utopia, starting with a simple definition of the word and excerpts from Sir Thomas More's famous volume, then working into theories and critiques of numerous utopian visions.

Readers could pick what they wanted from the quotes, what they felt comfortable with, as they scanned over to my essay, which reported on the utopian dialogue I had with my friend Cristina Guillen Cook, a dialogue in which we talked about her personal history, the influence of Cesar Chavez (who had recently died) and her renewed commitment to political activism. After our conversation, I thought and wrote a lot about difference, otherness, separation, and the cultured despair that discourages so many middle-aged, middle-class Euroamericans like myself from engaging in social reform. As I worked through the essay, I realized that it is through embracing difference, recognizing that we are all "other," and forging connections that we can defuse the despair that otherwise debilitates us. I realized these were things many of the exhibition artists had to go through in order to engage in utopian dialogues and incorporate those dialogues into their art.

The third segment of catalogue text described each of the fourteen installations. I developed the descriptions in collaboration with the artists, and in two cases, the artists generated their own texts (one a poem, the other a series of graphically presented fragments from American utopian texts). Arranged alphabetically, the descriptions ranged from Sara Bates's sacred circle inspired by dialogue with the spirits of nature; through Nancy Ann Jones's safe-space house developed in collaboration with grade school children; Rosalie Ortega's increasingly constricted confessional booths with taped conversations about identity and marginality; and Susan Silton's look at the balance/imbalance of lesbian/gay interaction; to Ruth Weisberg's presentation of the values and ideals passed from her Zionist-socialist grandfather through her mother to her. Readers could meander through the interwoven texts just as they could wander through the exhibition. They could read laterally, across quotes from Sir Thomas More and bell hooks through phrases from Cesar Chavez to the utopian writings that artist Sandra Rowe penned over a decade ago and came back to as source for her art work. Or they could read vertically. There was no single narrative, no fixed interpretation of the concept or the exhibition. I assembled the text but did not claim authorship in any traditional sense.[39] In "Utopian Dialogues," as in this book, the writer is not master. The fabric is not finished. I do not want to present closed or fixed meaning. Instead, I try to thread the filaments of my words with those of others to spin the gossamer strands of ideas. Readers must gather the threads and weave their own tapestry designs through interactive consideration.

Reading this book, you have seen that I often use writing to weave a tapestry of diverse voices, divergent stories. Perhaps a better analogy would be to say that I use writing to fabricate a "friendship quilt of words." I cut a scrap from one of my friend's articles, patch it together with a remnant from a role model or mentor's book, add an interview with an artist, then embroider them all with my own gloss. Writing this quilt, I acknowledge the women writers and artists who form my conceptual community — just as my great grandmother honored her friends, family, and forbears in the fabric quilts she sewed in "Indian Territory" Oklahoma a century ago.

Section IV, "Living in Community," begins with my essay on the CARA: Chicano Art Resistance and Affirmation exhibition as an example of curating community. This is followed by a conversation with Cheri Gaulke, Elizabeth Say's essay on Gaulke's "Lesbian Family" installation, then page art produced by Gaulke and her life partner Sue Maberry. Mindy Lorenz writes of the increasing conjunction of art, politics and community in her life. A conversation with Rachel Rosenthal focuses on her collaborative work with the new improvisational troupe "TohuBohu!" Ruth Ann Anderson and Starr Goode write of the art and poetry of their shared spiritual life in a Wiccan coven. The section ends with my memories of Jill D'Agnenica's "Angels" project.

To introduce her compelling volume *The Reenchantment of Art*, Suzi Gablik wrote, "I see it as a collective project, giving voice to what many people already believe and feel; ideas are expressed and woven together that are very much 'in the air,' seeking their proper articulation in the community."[40] That is precisely how I see this volume.

Gatekeepers, Silences, and Freedom: Moving Past Unexamined "Multiculturalism" to Teach and Curate Community

by Betty Ann Brown

I begin with a quote from African-American writer bell hooks:

> Now when I ponder the silences, the voices that are not heard, the voices of those wounded and/or oppressed individuals who do not speak or write, I contemplate the acts of persecution, torture — the terrorism that breaks spirits, that makes creativity impossible. . . . For us, true speaking is not solely an expression of creative power, it is an act of resistance, a political gesture that challenges the politics of domination that would render us nameless and voiceless. As such it is a courageous act; as such it represents a threat. To those who wield oppressive power, that which is threatening must necessarily be wiped out, annihilated, silenced.[1]

I begin with this for two reasons. The first is that as a privileged, middle-class, Euroamerican heterosexual woman, I feel it is imperative to use the words of a person of color to frame my comments on multiculturalism in teaching and curatorial practices. The second reason is that hooks's words establish the linkage of resistance to dominance, the threatening nature of speech, and the power of creativity. It was her words about this linkage that inspired my writing.

I want to challenge what I understand to be the consensus definition of "multiculturalism." Having been prodded by Shifra Goldman, Jewish Euroamerican art historian and critic of Latin American art, I have come to see multiculturalism as the outgrowth of imperialism, as the step in racist patriarchy to follow colonialism.[2] If we see imperialism as the European process of conquering people whom they (the Europeans) defined as of another race — and although I will not deconstruct the concept of race here, I do not accept it as a "natural" concept, but rather as a cultural construct that developed in the articulation of imperialist power hierarchies to position the conquered as "Other" — then colonialism is the process of maintaining dominion over and separation from the "Other" who are of a "different race" and, consequently, of a lower class. Multiculturalism is the process whereby the dominant culture, forced by the increasingly visible presence of the racial "Other" within its once homogeneous spheres of influence (that is, within the boundaries of its centers of power),[3] has elected to maintain dominance and control by acting as gatekeepers, by selecting exactly which "Others" are allowed access to which discourses, and under exactly what limited time spans.

To explain what I mean by this deconstruction of multiculturalism and how it is relevant to teaching and curating, I start by quoting from an article on the "Culturally Assaultive Classroom" by Clark, DeWolf, and Clark (Euroamerican scholars at Grossmont College in El Cajon, California), pairing this with statements from Euroamerican anthropologist Sondra Hale and from Vietnamese-American filmmaker Trinh T. Minh-ha, finally juxtaposing all of these with more from bell hooks.

Asserting that "stereotypes, rarely true 'facts,' and utter falsehoods are taught in most 'multicultural units'; [that] this type of curriculum hurts minorities feelings and makes them feel left out; [that] unwittingly, we [have been] teaching teachers to magnify differences, not to teach understanding and respect for diversity," Clark and her colleagues give a hypothetical example geared for the public school classroom:

> You are a "non-Indian." When you arrive in class, the "Indians" are all at the front of the room chatting with the teacher. She looks up. "Ah, the new student. Welcome! Have a seat. You're a non-Indian, aren't you? We were just talking about your people."
>
> The children turn to look at you. They giggle and whisper to each other. None of the people in the room looks or sounds like your family. You look around the room. No dolls in the beds or pictures on the book covers have eyes or hair or noses like those of your family members. Only one of the pictures of faces on the bulletin board looks similar to yours. The bulletin board says, "Thanksgiving: A Non-Indian Holiday" and has a grotesque picture of a non-Indian woman in Reeboks and a Pilgrim hat, holding a dead turkey in one hand and a machine gun in the other. Your classmates giggle when they look at the bulletin board. "Look at those funny shoes," they whisper. (You look down at your favorite pair of Reeboks and stuff your feet under your chair.)
>
> "Now class, it's very important to remember that our non-Indian friends are not responsible for what their forefathers did. They stole our land and ruined our forests, but that was a long time ago. We're not going to talk about that today."
>
> "Who knows what kind of houses non-Indians live in? Yes, that's right. They live in square houses with red tile roofs. Who lives in these houses? Mother and father and sister and brother. Yes, that's right. Grandmother? No; they don't live with their grandmothers, like we do. They send their grandmothers away to special places called retirement homes. Why? I don't know.
>
> "Next week, during Thanksgiving, we'll have a unit on non-Indians. We'll all make a non-Indian town out of clay. It's called a 'suburb.' Can you say 'suburb'? Non-Indians sleep in separate rooms, and they have little houses to keep their cars in.
>
> "Now this is a non-Indian hat." The teacher pulls out a Pilgrim's hat. "Non-Indians wore these when they first came to our land."[4]

When I first read that passage, I almost gagged. I could hear echoes of my teaching in almost every line. I realized that most of the students who have spoken with me before class are Euroamericans; it is Euroamerican students who have typically had the confidence to dialogue with me, with the parental/authority figure I become as soon as I walk into the classroom.

Next I thought about how I have taught segments on, for example, the Eskimo. I presented material on nineteenth and twentieth century Eskimo wooden masks as art forms that functioned in contradistinction to the Euroamerican traditions on which we were focusing in my "Art and Mass Media" classes. I shudder to think in what stereotypical fashion I presented Eskimo life. Certainly I emphasized traditional Eskimo culture, rather than the Eskimos of today, thereby inadvertently reinforcing my non-Eskimo students to continue to think of the Eskimo as "Other" — as exotic, romanticized "Other."

Then I thought about how much art historical curricula are written. At Cal State Northridge, for example, there are three art history classes in the core requirements. The first is a survey of western art from the caves to the Renaissance. The second is a survey of western art from the Renaissance to the present. (Actually, the second survey rarely comes into the present; it most often leaves the student with a gaping void after World War II — and even the term "World War" needs deconstruction, of course.) The third core class in art history is a survey of "non-western" art, that is, a survey of all of the world art outside the narrow confines of the Euroamerican tradition. In fact, the third core class — which has, in the last several years been taught by a part-timer — is rarely offered. Even when it is, enrollment never approaches that in the other two core classes. Faculty, advisors, and fellow students alike conspire, however unconsciously, to direct the vast majority of students into the western surveys. The rest of the curriculum reinforces this: the western surveys are prerequisite for most advanced art historical classes; the non-western survey is not required for admittance to any advanced class. In addition, the available art history survey texts underscore the emphasis on the western tradition.

Such problems in the teaching of the visual arts are no doubt paralleled in the other creative disciplines. The question becomes, What can we do? At a Huntington Museum conference on feminist pedagogy in 1990, Sondra Hale discussed one remedy: Instead of assuming the western tradition as central and positioning any other tradition as peripheral and therefore of secondary importance, why not invert the hierarchy? Why not begin with an African or African-American artist whose work is presented as a standard or ideal? This year, the first artist my students in "Art and Mass Media" studied was Chicana muralist Judith F. Baca, whose *Great Wall* of Los Angeles brought together youths from numerous diverse urban neighborhoods to portray the history of our city from the view of the underrepresented and disenfranchised. Their view was not from the role of victim, but was affirmative as well as resistant to the dominant culture's stereotyping definitions.

Speaking of stereotyping definitions, I am reminded of Trinh T. Minh-ha's words as she introduced her 1992 film on China at the Claremont Graduate School. She asserted that the only way war becomes possible is through arrested or restricted symbolic thought, that is, through thinking in stereotypical terms. (Although she was referring to the historically troubled relationship between China and Vietnam, I immediately thought of Desert Storm and how our government provoked our populace into support of the war by imaging Saddam Hussein as the incarnation of evil, as another Hitler — rather than trying to understand the cultural differences that made communication so difficult, rather than trying to understand the cultural context of Saddam Hussein's actions.) Trinh went on to assert that it is precisely art, in its ability to challenge and reinvent the symbolic order, that can lessen stereotypical thought.

If Trinh is correct, creative work becomes desperately important in this era of accelerated global change and conflict. And if my deconstruction of multiculturalism is correct, what we need to do both inside and outside the classroom is always share and sometimes relinquish the role of gatekeeper so that those who are not (like myself and like the vast majority of teachers of the arts) privileged Euroamerican, Judeo-Christian heterosexuals — so that those who are not like us can speak and create.

How can we do this in the classroom? Hale suggests that the "effective Euroamerican teacher may choose to engage in a process of self-subversion, a process much like de-centering the dominant culture. . . . This is the reverse of the usual self-centered or ethnocentered process whereby we try to understand the 'Other' through understanding the self."[5] This process requires first acknowledging the primacy of the "Other's' experience, which can come from the use of primary texts by people of color.

One thing I have done in discussing the art of Nigeria is to ask my students to compare a "Tribal Eye" television segment on the Beni, written and produced by British men, with a catalogue on Beni art by African-American scholar Paula Ben-Amos.[6] If the Ben-Amos text is accepted as central, the imperialist reading of history and cultural condescension of the British man become readily apparent. From that revelation come insights about both the subjective nature of all writers/ historians/presenters and the specific agendas of European colonialism.

Throughout most of my teaching career, even when I presented provocative material such as the contrast of Eurocentric and Afrocentric views of the Beni; even when I lay down the mantle of inappropriate power that most of us don when we step in front of the classroom, it was white males who dominated the discourse. Of course, much has been written about this domination. I think

Adrienne Rich, in her "Taking Female Students Seriously," has discussed it most eloquently.[7] But what can we do? How can we give voice to and thereby empower more of our students?

Curating Diversity: "Cara"

I will return to the concept of empowerment, but first I want to address the issue of multiculturalism in arts exhibitions. The people who hold positions as museum or gallery directors and exhibition curators also act as gatekeepers. Like the professors who set the supposedly multicultural agendas within the curriculum and the classroom, curators decide just which people of color are given access under what conditions and during what particular time spans.

In Los Angeles, all those who direct and curate in prominent (that is, large scale) museums and galleries [LACMA, MOCA, Getty, Huntington, Norton Simon, Lannan, UCLA, etc.] are privileged Judeo-Christian Euroamericans. Do they need to quit their jobs for the ostensive ideals of multiculturalism to become actualized? Well, some of them probably do for true diversity to be institutionalized. But in the meantime, I would suggest that they follow the excellent examples of Edith Tonelli, former director of UCLA's Wight Art Gallery and Karen Atkinson, founding director of Side Street Projects.

Tonelli oversaw the 1990 "CARA (Chicana Art: Resistance and Affirmation)" exhibition.[8] She realized that it is particularly inappropriate for Euroamericans to maintain exclusive control when they are curating the art work of people from other traditions. So she invited Chicano artists and curators from all over the country to form a curatorial board. The curators and artists set the agenda, named the exhibition, articulated its intentions, selected the specific artists and art works, and oversaw the related community educational events. It sounds like such a simple and logical manner in which to proceed, but CARA's community-based curatorial process was, to my knowledge, unique.

Tonelli is quite frank about how confrontational the initial organizational meetings for CARA were. "I knew that despite our openness and willingness to attempt new dialogues, I and the gallery staff generally thought of ourselves as the 'we' of 'those of us who are art museum professionals' and of any individuals outside of that museum culture as the 'they' of the 'community.' 'We' were inviting these people to our table of power and 'they' would hopefully 'assist' us in producing an important exhibition. I had no idea at the time how limiting that very common museum assumption was for *all* of us — but I learned very quickly."[9] Later Tonelli summarized, "Our concerns reflect[ed] a growing tendency on the part of many underrepresented groups and some museum people to question the traditional museological processes that separate the group's knowledge of its own culture from the institutional means of displaying that culture. Under particular attack is the conventional designation of a single curator for the ultimate determination of what is to be presented."[10] When Tonelli relinquished the traditional role of curator, that is, of cultural gatekeeper, the Chicano community was empowered to further creative expression and affirmation.

When I walked through the CARA exhibition, I recognized that it differed from other shows I had seen of Chicano art because it visualized a community's self-definition, rather than one imposed by the dominant culture. On my second viewing of CARA, I heard one Chicano father saying in Spanish to a young boy, "Come, I want to show you yourself, here in the exhibition."

Curated primarily by Chicanos who selected art works on the basis of content, CARA presented new parameters for judging art. Because of increased diversity in art production, selection, and exhibition, the canons of art — which have been historically constructed by dominant-culture gatekeepers — have been challenged and sometimes overturned. No longer limited to standards of technical virtuosity or a singular notion of beauty, art has been freed to play many roles. In exhibitions like CARA, for example, what is valued is the degree to which the art authentically reflects the artist's social/historical/political moment. But the linkage of art and politics threatens those who base their judgments on formalist criteria. Indeed, when the senior art critic of the *Los Angeles Times* wrote about the CARA show, he chose not to address the content of the art. Instead, he criticized it on the grounds of "quality."[11]

The discourse around quality has become fundamental to discussions of diversity and cultural relativity. Artist Howardena Pindell has written eloquently about how the concept of quality has been used to exclude people of color from presentation, acknowledgment, and validation in the arts: "The word quality is used as if it were synonymous with skin pigmentation and ancestry, but is stated publicly as signifying an unsullied and courageous color-blind standard."[12] David Bonetti adds, "The issue of quality . . . has been raised by those who favor the status quo as a smoke screen to disguise their own reactionary and exclusionary ideas about culture itself."[13]

Curating Community: "Fault Lines"

Many of the traditional definitions and roles of exhibition production have been challenged and overthrown by the mandates of cultural diversity. What, then, are the viable premises for ongoing commitment to curatorial practice? Artist Karen Atkinson has initiated an ongoing series of dialogues about this complex question. On February 24, 1996, she and co-organizer Lorne Falk invited a dozen curators, including artists who curate, to an all-day event they called "Gathering Voices: Curatorial Strategies for the Future." Atkinson and Falk acknowledged the necessity for curators "to give name to their practices and the potential for their reconfiguration. To do so is not to undermine existing institutions, but to articulate strategies and formations that can make institutions more responsive and relevant to contemporary culture." They added, "Society at the end of this century presents a remarkable confluence of issues that demand our attention, including: the changing nature of society (often described as multiculturalism, or what we prefer to think of as transculturalism), the ongoing integration of feminist ideologies into discourse, the problematic of the technological ethnos, and the renegotiation of our relationship with the environment (nature/culture). If the content of cultural programming does not include these and related social issues in a sustained manner, that programming may not be viable."[14]

The twelve of us sat at a large table as Falk introduced the "ground rules," which echoed those of consciousness-raising: we would go around the table and each speak our mind on the chosen topic. There would be no cross-talk. Any questions or comments had to be held until the conversation circle reached the questioner. There was also to be no whining. Instead, we looked for a spirit of generosity. In the morning, we addressed the ethics of curating. In the afternoon, we focused on strategies and methodologies.

We discussed our need to dismantle the traditional categories of curator/artist/ critic/educator (which are still maintained fairly rigidly by prominent arts institutions) and to acknowledge that many of us had already expanded our activities into all of these territories. As we spoke of categories, I realized that many of us are concerned with the false opposition or separation of categories such as artist/audience. We are all artists; we are all each others' audiences as well. One curator spoke of the perceived conflict between responsiveness to the needs of artists and the demands to maintain the edifice. Is this a remnant of continued dualistic thinking? Must we think of individuals and institutions as opposed? Can we not instead look to common ground? Individuals make up institutions.

Karen Atkinson insisted that all of us involved in creative practices have permission to redefine ourselves on our own terms rather than trying to fit into traditional ones. Later, we began to talk about exhibitions we had organized that redefined the very notion of curation. Mary Lou Knode of the new Huntington Beach Art Center spoke of experimenting with an "Open Call" exhibition, in which all art work submitted was displayed. Open Calls avoid the issues of selection and premises for selection altogether. Lorne Falk spoke of curator's needs to announce and clarify their intentions and their positions ahead of time. Noel Korten of the Los Angeles Municipal Art Gallery stated his preference for engagement as a strategy, rather than confrontation. Roberto Bedoya, formerly of the Getty Center and now president of NAOO, added that arts institutions can accommodate a number of agendas, as long as those agendas are declared. Bedoya also related what he had learned about getting people activated and interested in participating in cultural dialogues: he is certain that given a moment to speak, people will testify. So many have been silenced for so long that they welcome the opportunity to participate in creating the cultural record.

Atkinson ended the afternoon by recounting how she had conceived of the Side Street Projects arts organization. She stated that her personal conflation of being an artist and being an administrator/curator has always challenged many art world assumptions. She remembered that frequently, when an exhibition of her work was scheduled, she would invite other artists to collaborate by contributing a component to the art work. This was so often disconcerting to curators and gallery directors that Atkinson began to realize that existing institutions could rarely accommodate her practice. She decided to establish her own institution. She wanted a physical space to provide a "sense of place." She also wanted to rethink funding, access, functions of the space — as well as the curatorial process. I will describe one of the exhibitions Atkinson has overseen at Side Street Projects to clarify not only how she has developed her institution and the projects it presents, but more specifically, how she brings into collaboration and partnership — which is to say, into community — artists and organizations that don't necessarily tend to get connected.

"Fault Lines" was a project that culminated in October and November, 1995. Subtitled "Measurement, Distance and Place: A Montreal and Los Angeles Link," it was originally conceived by Chicago artist Ingrid Bacmann and Montreal artist Barbara Layne to be sited in Canada and California. The two artists linked the high technology of seismographs with the traditional technology of weaving on Jacquard looms. (Developed in eighteenth century France and based on a system of punch card programs to store and process information, the Jacquard loom was a precedent for the twentieth century computer.)

In the project description, the artists wrote: "'Fault Lines' involves the simultaneous production of two cloths in two distinct locations, Montreal, Quebec, and Santa Monica, California, that records, measures, and transforms information about these two sites into a woven record. A pattern is produced on information received through fax/modem lines during the month of October, 1995. The installation in both sites will include a computer-assisted loom and weaver within each gallery. Data consisting of seismographic waves will be exchanged through telephone lines to the computers attached to each loom. This information is translated by specially designed software into a woven structure. Weavers at both sites will operate the looms each day, producing a continuous length of cloth that records not only the shifts of the earth, but the passage of days and light waves, and the gestures of the weavers." A unique marriage of high and hand technologies, 'Fault Lines' employed both textile and computer language to explore issues of gender, information transmission and the scripting of technological practices in popular culture. Involving conceptual artists and weavers with computer programmers and geologists, 'Fault Lines' bridged the often perceived gap between art and science. It connected into aesthetic community people who initially considered their co-participants as "Others." Creating a situation for them to think and speak and work together, the exhibition empowered all participants through collaborative situations previously unimagined in their lives.

Does it all come down to power? Sondra Hale concludes her article on pedagogy and diversity with this sentence: "Although we may wonder if it's possible to intellectually empower everyone, such empowerment is an essential goal of the feminist movement."[15] I would add, thinking again of bell hooks's words, that creative empowerment needs to be a goal and that it needs to be a goal, not only of feminists but of everyone in teaching and curating. And I would caution against thinking of this empowerment in the terms usually intended. I do not mean the power of domination. I do not mean the power of control, or the power of exclusion through individualistically motivated and unexamined gatekeeping. I mean power that is, to use Nancy Harstock's words, "understood as energy, strength, and effective interaction."[16] I mean the power of freedom, the power to express creatively, the power to speak.

To quote bell hooks one more time:

> Moving from silence into speech is for the oppressed, the colonized, the exploited, and those who stand and struggle side by side, a gesture of defiance that heals, that makes new life, new growth possible. It is that act of speech, of "talking back" that is no mere gesture of empty words, that is the expression of moving from object to subject, that is the liberated voice."[17]

CHERI GAULKE

in Conversation with Betty Ann Brown

> [A] new [performance] aesthetic has emerged, informed by the collective experience of the feminist educational process. This aesthetic has moved beyond simple theatricality and incorporates elements of networking, working within real-life environment, and communicating with a mass audience.[1]

Cheri Gaulke is an internationally known performance artist. She has done work in venues from the Los Angeles Museum of Contemporary Art to the tiny Church in Ocean Park to the fields around Stonehenge in England. Her work often grapples with attempts to reconcile her Christian heritage and her lesbian identity. Her collaborative work, in groups like the rainbow-clad Sisters Of Survival, addresses social issues suck as the threat of nuclear destruction. Gaulke's work has been celebrated in numerous books and journals.

Gaulke and her life partner, Sue Maberry, have crafted a six-page portrait of their extended family, juxtaposing snap shots and stock Sears family portraits with their text and quotes from other family members on what it means to be part of this very committed alternative community. The art is preceded by feminist ethicist Elizabeth A. Say's essay on the exhibition installation from which the pages are derived, preceded, in turn, by my conversation with Gaulke about her work as a feminist community-building artist.

> When I was growing up I used to make my bed with precision movements, imagining that somehow the boy I wanted to marry was watching my performance and judging it. In the magazines and on television, we see women posing while mopping the kitchen floor, and we too learn to pose — as women. We played house only to grow up to get the starring role. Performance is not a difficult concept for us. We're on stage every moment of our lives. Acting like women. Performance is a declaration of self — who one is — a shamanistic dance by which we spin into other states of awareness, remembering new visions of ourselves. And in performance we found an art form that was young, without the tradition of painting or sculpture. Without the traditions governed by men. The shoe fit, and so, like Cinderella, we ran with it.[2]

I think Cheri Gaulke is one of the most important artists working today. In her work and her life, she fully embodies the feminist dictum of "the personal is political." (I visited her studio at the old Los Angeles Woman's Building site one afternoon and noticed she had a two-drawered filing cabinet. The top drawer was labeled "Life," the bottom drawer "Art."

She laughed when she saw my look. "It's getting harder and harder to figure out which drawer to put things in," she quipped.) The artist would concur with Suvan Geer who, in reference to one of Gaulke's performances, said that "the entire issue becomes less about intellectual generalizations and acquires personal implications that connect the audience to the performers."[3] Through such connections, community is built.

Los Angeles author Michael Ventura, writing about another of Gaulke's performances, points out how audience response and participation are fundamental to the artist's work.

> Gaulke sets up an environment that the audience is drawn to, without coercion or advertising, simply through curiosity — thus getting an audience that most performance art either can't reach or ignores. She strips the audience members of most of their defenses by making her "performance" a structure — an audio and tactile-visual structure — which they enter. The prime performer, Gaulke, sits in the center of the structure and does not move. Because she isn't moving, then, in the average audience's "vocabulary" of performances, she isn't asking them for anything. They don't feel directed toward a specific response, so their responses are extraordinarily open and free. The *spectators* do the moving, they are the active participants in the structure, and hence *their act of seeing becomes the performance.* This is as much a part of their delight (on levels which they're not aware of at the time) as what they see.[4]

Cheri Gaulke has participated in and organized numerous feminist groups, from the Community of Women Artists she founded as a student in Minneapolis, to the Feminist Studio Workshop, she studied, then taught in, at the Woman's Building, to the several performance collaboratives she started, such as the rainbow-clad Sisters Of Survival who traveled two continents to protest the nuclear threat. For many reasons, her work functions as an important educational tool. As Arlene Raven writes, "Her educative motive in individual artworks and collaborations . . . is, like the civic participatory pageants, directed to a general audience who have not 'read' contemporary events from a feminist/humanist perspective."[5] I discuss Gaulke's work in every class I give. I find that my students, whether they be working class kids from the inner city or San Fernando Valley housewives who have returned to school after their own children graduated, can relate to and learn from the sustained commitment and aesthetic growth evident in the artist's career.

As a solo performer, Gaulke weaves together art history, autobiography, and her ever-evolving agenda for social transformation, clearly establishing that art is, for her, the structuring of personal experience into new and significant form. I'm sure she would agree with Lucy Lippard that all art is political, that even art which appears "politically neutral" manifests the position of the artist in the culture in which she is working. "Performance art does represent inherent rebellion," the artist once said, "and I guess I've made a political choice."[6]

One of Cheri Gaulke's best known solo performances is "This Is My Body," a staging of eight tableaux in the Church in Ocean Park (Santa Monica, California, 1983). The artist combined slides of medieval and Renaissance religious paintings with text from Mary Daly's Gyn/Ecology (a feminist theological journey "beyond god the father") and personal narrative about growing up the daughter of a Midwestern Lutheran minister. As Gaulke merged with the Christian images, she poetically traced the connection between patriarchal beliefs, the domination of nature, and the threat of nuclear annihilation. I contemplated the performance in stunned silence. I had never before made all those connections. No one had, ever before, made me so powerfully aware of the relationship between my body, my religious heritage, and the rape of nature.

Three years later (1986), I saw Cheri Gaulke's "Virgin" in the same church. I had just returned from a year of falling in love with the churches and convents of Spain. My son was two years old. Cheri interlaced the concepts of female autonomy (did you know that the term "virgin" originally had nothing to do with sexual status, that it originally referred to autonomous women?), the Christian version of Immaculate Conception (did you know that the Church determined that Mary was impregnated through the ear?), and modern technology's processes of artificial insemination (do you have any idea how many scientific and pseudo-scientific ways have been developed to conceive extra-sexually?). I was swept into an almost hallucinogenic swirl of image and information. I thought of the nuns in Descalzas Reales Convent in Madrid. I thought of Artemis of Ephesus, the many-breasted goddess of coastal Turkey (where, they say, the Virgin Mary died). Then I thought about Cheri herself, who was trying to get pregnant, and about another girlfriend of mine who had spent thousands of dollars doing the same thing, in vain so far, and was at that time giving herself daily hormone shots. (My friend adopted a child the following year.) I thought about what it had been like to be pregnant, how women I didn't know constantly came up to me and talked to me, how I felt (as Erica Jong had felt) that, especially when pregnant, I was Everywoman. I thought about so much. About how intrusive Western medicine is. About how much of science is rape. And then I thought about how well, how beautifully, Cheri Gaulke was, again, telling Everywoman's story.

Fragments of the story of her life and art are taken out of their separate file drawers in the conversation that follows.

Betty Ann Brown: The first thing I want to talk about has to do with issues of identity. Did you, in your childhood or in your education, ever get the message that you couldn't be a woman *and* an artist?

Cheri Gaulke: I became a feminist at age 4. My first awareness that because I was a woman my life was going to be different came when I realized I wanted to be a minister like my dad but girls couldn't be ministers. I was pissed off about that. (In some ways, I did become what my dad is, though, because I became an educator and a person who expresses my spirituality in my work.)

At the same time, I learned that when girls grew up they had to change their names, because they'd get married and have to take their husbands' names. I was a Gaulke and I wanted to stay a Gaulke. So I guess I showed them — I became a lesbian and didn't have to change my name.

My mother introduced me to women artists in history. She didn't know about many of them, but she knew about Georgia O'Keeffe. What I got from learning about O'Keeffe was that I didn't have to be a traditional woman, that being an artist was somehow permission to be different. I loved the desert [where O'Keeffe chose to live and work]. I thought she was so beautiful, she wore black, she was married but she didn't let that stop her from living in the part of the world that she wanted to live in or from doing what she wanted to do. The other woman artist my mother introduced me to was Käthe Kollwitz. That was really powerful for me because I'm of German descent; when you're German it's hard to be proud of your heritage because of Nazism. Kollwitz was so gutsy! Her work was really passionate and was used as a vehicle to raise political issues, so she was an important positive role model for me.

I always had a good sense of myself as an artist and I really thank my parents. My dad worked for the church; so he was a model for doing what you believed in instead of doing something you hated just to make a lot of money. We were sort of middle-class. We didn't lead an extravagant life and I knew that that was a result of his working for the church, for what he believed in. I didn't have any pressures to make a lot of money; I felt I should do what is important for me.

I also got a lot of support from my mother, who was always encouraging me to do artwork. So I developed this sense of myself as a woman and as a feminist. It wasn't really articulated at that point, it was intuitive. When I got to art school it became more expressed, with the rise of the Women's Movement.

BAB: When did you go to college?

CG: I graduated from high school in 1971, went to junior college for two years in St. Louis and graduated in 1975 from Minneapolis College of Art and Design. When I was a senior in college, I decided to organize women students into what we called the Community of Women Artists (CWA). But I found an incredible amount of resistance to that; so many of the female students were afraid to identify as women. It was ludicrous. They kept saying things like, "I'm not a woman artist, I'm an artist." They thought it would endanger their careers to identify as women. It seemed like you almost had to be in the closet as a woman at that time in the art world. I think that attitude still exists some, but it has changed. And it's changed because of the Woman's Building and because of feminist art organizing.

BAB: Tell me about the Community of Women Artists. You organized that with some of the other women in school?

CG: Barbara Bouska was really important in all this. We had met in junior college where we had had a feminist photography teacher, a very "out-of-the-closet" feminist, who influenced us a lot.

Barbara and I moved to Minneapolis together and were roommates. When the two of us were introduced to video, we began collaborating. That was around 1973, so that was the beginning of my collaboration with artists. We began to have meetings, to invite other artists, and at one point we decided to organize a show of our work. But some of them felt that although they'd do just about anything to get into a show, this particular show — because it was female-identified — was too risky. It was so silly.

At the same time, we began to develop relationships with some professional women artists, who were starting to meet also. Their meetings were eventually organized into WARM (Women Artists Registry of Minnesota). Then in 1974, I heard about the Woman's Building from Arlene Raven and [feminist art historian] Ruth Iskin who were in town to lecture. Their talk was so powerful! They spoke for well over an hour about women artists from the beginning of history to contemporary times and I had not heard of any of the women — except maybe one or two — in any of my art history classes. I went up to Arlene afterwards and said I'm really frustrated, I'm trying to organize some of the artists here and nobody's cooperating. She said you should come to the Woman's Building. So I did.

Actually, Arlene said I should write to Suzanne Lacy. Suzanne wrote back: "I'm too busy to talk to you because I'm organizing a feminist performance art conference. Just come." I was so impressed that she was organizing a feminist performance art conference! I had been feeling all alone as a feminist performance artist. And they were having a whole conference on that kind of work! So I went. That was the fall of 1975.

BAB: Tell me how you became a feminist performance artist isolated as you were in the Midwest.

CG: In the summer of 1974 I went to Scotland and studied performance art with Sally Potter, the director of *Orlando* [the 1993 film version of Virginia Woolf's novel]. Potter is the one who taught me performance art. I returned to the Midwest, had one more semester at school and officially graduated in 1975. In Fall 1975 I started in the Feminist Studio Workshop (FSW) at the Los Angeles Woman's Building.

BAB: Tell me about your experience at the Feminist Studio Workshop.

CG: It was wonderful. We had a whole building dedicated to women's art, dedicated both to developing women's art in a personal way and to showing it to the public. I was absolutely committed to that concept. I remember the first day sitting in a room with fifty women in a circle, the teachers and students, all kinds of women from all over the country, some from foreign countries — it was so powerful!

BAB: You said you'd done some collaboration with the video, with Barbara. And you'd done some organizing, the Community of Women Artists. But you expressed some frustration with that. It sounds like it was not until you got to the Woman's Building that you felt your collaborative/community building impulses were actualized. What do you think the difference was? Was it simply that there was an organizational history of a couple of years by then?

CG: Maybe. There was strong leadership, there was really strong theory, and a sense of history behind it. In Minneapolis the organizing had come out of a few individuals' personal needs; there wasn't a sense that we had a legacy. I think that makes it very hard for women.

BAB: Have you read Gerda Lerner's *The Creation of Feminist Consciousness?* She says that until women have a sense of the legacy, a sense of history, then they have to recreate feminist consciousness every time. That is one of the most crippling things for women. Until we realize that there's a continuity, that we have a history, that we have a community, well then, everywhere we're reinventing the wheel, every generation.

So you got to the Woman's Building and because there was this sense of history and legacy *and* a theoretical context, you felt connected and actualized?

CG: I had teachers at the Building. In Minneapolis I had been trying to do something I simply didn't know how to do. It was frustrating. But when I moved to Los Angeles, I found my mentors. In fact, my initial reason for going to the Woman's Building was to go for a year, learn the skills needed to make a feminist art organization, and take those skills back to Minneapolis. But I never left. I was hooked.

BAB: Who were your teachers?

CG: Suzanne Lacy. From her, I got the theoretical framework for developing a performance as a conceptual structure. She had started calling her performances "performance structures" by then.

Arlene Raven was also very important to me. She did a "round table" class called Feminism 101. I remember at one point she said that capitalism was so big and so powerful that no matter what feminism created, capitalism would ultimately swallow it up, appropriate it. I remember thinking, "How will that ever happen?" Yet today, I feel like that's what I've seen transpire. Arlene is very wise.

There was one part of the FSW program where we got assigned to work with people we didn't pick — I got assigned to Ruth Iskin. Ruth was not somebody I had particularly good chemistry with, so I didn't much want to study with her. But she was really helpful. She helped me develop a whole series of shoe sculptures, all solo work. Up until that point I'd been collaborating. For most of the women, collaboration was the difficult thing, but for me it had been finding my own voice. I had become almost dependent on collaboration. I'm a very verbal person,

Living in Community

so collaboration works for me because I can get my ideas out by talking to someone else. But when I work by myself I have to get to that creative place alone, to find all the ways to get to it. Ruth was a sounding board for me, a critical sounding board.

Ruth Iskin also mentored me through curating the Grandma Prisbrey exhibition. [Grandma Prisbrey, an example of what is often called either an "eccentric artist" or an "urban folk artist," built a many-structured city out of bottles and other scraps around her home in the Simi Valley, northwest of Los Angeles.] We built a whole structure for the exhibition at the Woman's Building. We borrowed a lot of objects from Grandma Prisbrey [who was quite elderly at the time], she even came to the opening. It was really beautiful. Ruth helped me with writing, too. I wrote an essay, a feminist perspective on Grandma Prisbrey. Because she was an art historian and a writer, Ruth could help me with that. It's funny how that happens. The person who doesn't look like they're going to, ends up being your teacher. It happens to me all the time.

BAB: Why collaboration though? Why did you go to collaboration, first with Barbara? You said you got into video and then you immediately went into collaboration, why?

CG: I wasn't ever interested in video as an imitation of film; what interested me was (and is) the inherent nature of video — the immediate feedback aspect of it. Barbara and I started doing a series of interactive video installations. In 1973, we did a series called "Private Spaces" where one of us would point the camera at some abstract space and then watch the monitor while the other person would have to go find the camera and position themselves in that space. The process required the viewer to tell the performer what they looked like; it required dialogue.

I've always been interested in art as a vehicle for social change. That's why I make my art, that's always been my motivation. The "Private Spaces" videos had no overt politics but they were about connecting people, about having people play together and interact and feel the dependence on each other. In order for them to work, we had to cooperate.

BAB: I think creating new ways for people to interact is a very important part of art. At one point in Western culture, the aesthetic ideal was art as a separate thing with which the viewer had a closed, hermetic relationship. Today, so much feminist work is exploding that concept of art. Art isn't just a mute object you stare at any more, art can also be how you and I dialogue, or a situation set up for us to interact in.

So collaboration seemed to "naturally" develop out of your video work. And then you continued it at the Woman's Building.

CG: There was also the support structure at the Woman's Building. I realized I had moved away from the kind of artwork that was being made at school in Minneapolis — because my work was overtly feminist, because its form and content were not what anyone else was doing. When Barbara and I came back from Scotland in the fall of 1974, our teachers had never heard of performance art. They put us into a class called Intermedia because that's where they put all the students that didn't fit anywhere else.

We found a community of performance artists at the Feminist Studio Workshop. By December 1975 (which was the opening of the Woman's Building at the Spring Street site), I was doing a performance with five or six other women called "The Other Side Show." It was a big collaboration. Suzanne Lacy was our mentor on that piece and helped us develop it. It took the metaphor of the circus sideshow to explore how we women are cut in half, how we have two sides to our personalities. I was in a box that got sawed in half, which was about my public and my private self.

Then in 1976, in the summer art program, I taught a class called "1 + 1 = 3: Making Performances Collaboratively." I worked with my students on doing large-scale collaborative pieces. We did a piece that used all the windows of the Woman's Building; the audience watched it from across the street. We did another piece in a trashy vacant lot, then we used the train tracks next to the Building, then the whole environment. (In Scotland we had also done large-scale collaborative performances in public settings.)

After that teaching experience, in fall 1976 I co-founded Feminist Art Workers, which came out of wanting to combine performance art and feminist education and take it on the road. We felt like we could be ambassadors or missionaries for the Woman's Building. We wanted to share across the country what we were getting out of being in a feminist art community. We designed workshops, performances, lectures and we organized a tour that took us throughout the midwest. Feminist Art Workers was originally Laurel Klick, Nancy Angelo, Candace Compton, and me, and later Candace left the group and Vanalyne Green joined the group. We worked together from 1976 to 1980.

BAB: When did Sisters Of Survival come about?

CG: Sisters Of Survival started in 1981. It was comprised of members of the performance group The Waitresses and members of Feminist Art Workers. We'd started meeting and saying we've taken our work across the U.S., now it's time for us to go to Europe. What should we do? Should we do different performances? I remember seeing in the grocery store a cover of *Time* magazine with a skeleton face. It was a photograph taken from European demonstrations against the nuclear threat. I went back to the group and said that if we're going to go to Europe we have to address issues that are crucial for the Europeans. The issue of our country possibly having the next nuclear war with the Soviet Union on European soil is what they're concerned about and we need to address that issue. We didn't know much about the nuclear threat, so we decided to form a new group called Sisters Of Survival to deal with that issue. Nancy Angelo was the source of the nun imagery. She had been performing as a nun called Sister Angelica Furiosa. Nancy and I had done a performance called "The Passion" in which we had given birth to 13 nuns in different colored habits, a rainbow of nuns. We decided to adopt that visual image as a metaphor for a sisterhood ordered around hope, humor, and diversity.

BAB: Why is Sisters Of Survival no longer an active group?

CG: I think because the issues changed. The nuclear threat doesn't seem central anymore. Plus I think we really accomplished what we set out to do. Our mission had been to create a dialogue between artists in North America and Western Europe. We certainly contributed to that dialogue. We set out to do a three-part project [to develop events about the arms race for the media of this country, to collect American art on the subject and carry slides of that work to Europe, then to produce anti-nuclear performances on sites as diverse as Avebury standing Stone Circle and Covent Garden, England]. When the third part was culminated, there was no reason for us to continue working that way. Our last performance was in 1985. Occasionally people invite us to do a performance that we've done previously, and we did an artist's book in 1984 that the Museum of Modern Art toured in their "Committed to Print" show, but that's about it. Now I collaborate in different ways.

BAB: If you started collaboration in part because of the dialogue process with video, and in part because you needed a support structure since you were stepping out of what the university structure afforded you, why do you continue to collaborate?

CG: It's the "1 + 1 = 3" axiom. I truly believe that the result of the collaboration is more than the sum of its parts, that you really do create something beyond the capability of each of you to create individually. That really excites me. There's a chemistry in it that I love. I guess for me it's a way of creating community and creating family. The lasting relationships that I have forged have been relationships through work. Collaboration is a way of really getting to know people, working through something, working towards a goal.

I used to think that I could collaborate with anyone, that I was just such a good collaborator. Then I had a really bad collaboration experience. It was a situation where everyone involved acknowledged that it was a mistake. Our personalities did not go together and while I think two of the people really were effective collaborators, two of us were not. It just didn't work. Even so, we figured out a way to present the performance: we created a structure in which each of us could do our individual things and yet arrange them together. I thought we came out triumphant through that, that we overcame the limitations. We were even able to talk about it. It was really painful, though, I'd never go through that again. In the future I'll be very careful who I collaborate with and be clear about their personality.

BAB: Don't you think that's just one of the facts of life, that you can't work with everybody? Some people you work with really well. With other people, you assume that because they appear to share your values, they'll share your expectations and commitments. You only find out while working with them that they don't.

CG: Yes. That particular collaboration [the difficult one] was my conception, it grew out of my liking each of these people's work. So if I liked their work, I thought, I would like working with them, but that wasn't the case. It was a hard lesson for me to learn.

BAB: It seems to me that there's also a sense of creating a community, of developing female identity and feminist consciousness in your solo performances. I've certainly experienced that as a member of the audience. Both your individual works and your collaborative works have been about community, about community identity and building community. When did you become aware that you were doing that?

CG: I don't know if I know the answer to that. The word "community" was in my art vocabulary before I moved to L.A. Recently I've been sort of making peace with my past, making peace with my Christian upbringing. It's been very empowering, very healing. I'm starting to be able to embrace what positive things I've gotten from that heritage. I wonder if the idea of a Christian community — that certainly is something that you hear in the church, that the congregation is a community — if that's my earliest notion. Perhaps it comes from hearing about Jesus and his disciples being a community.

I also remember when I was a little girl, I used to say that I would never grow up just to marry and have kids. I wanted to live in a community where many adults and many children lived together and took responsibility for each other. I don't know whether it was grade school or high school, but I remember that used to be my vision of what I wanted my life to be like. To live in a community and raise children in a community.

BAB: Do you think that that was modeled after something you'd actually seen? Or was it an ideal you aspired to?

CG: I don't know. It didn't reflect anything in my life. My family didn't live near any relatives, we weren't part of an extended family, we were very much loners in relation to the relatives.

BAB: Maybe that's exactly why you wanted it, because you wanted more than what you were getting from your family. More connection.

When did you start using the word "community" in your art making?

CG: Probably in college. I don't remember using the word much before that. But recently, I've been using it in other ways. Like in the [East Los Angeles neighborhood] "El Sereno Serenade" project. My collaboration with Latino high school students was a case where, as a white artist with a lot of skills in collaboration and community building, I came into a community that already existed, already had values and culture and traditions I don't know a lot about. What I did was say to the kids, "Show me your community. Pretend I'm from Mars. Pretend I really don't know your community and I want to see it through your eyes." I would grab my video camera, hop in the car with different groups each day and let them show me what they were excited about. Then I facilitated their artistic expression of what their community is.

I am so turned on by cultural diversity. It's something that really excites me, interacting with people who are different than me, and gaining insights into what makes them tick and why they are the way that they are. I just love that. The students were really energized by the process, too. I started out working with a lot of kids, probably fifty in a classroom, working with every single one of them. But in the end it boiled down to just a few kids who followed the project through to completion. We edited the videotapes and installed them in a houselike structure (which they designed) in the El Sereno Senior Citizen Center. We had to work so hard through the summer, every single day, to get that project done. It was so ambitious. It was back-breaking. But when I have a vision of how something can work, I'm like a heat-seeking missile. I can go to that vision and I'm going to get there, damn it. It was harder for those teenagers. They weren't sure what they were going to get out of it. They hadn't had the life experience to foresee the end result, to know how their community would respect them more or how seeing their name or picture in the paper was going to make their self-esteem rise and make them feel like they could do the next thing. So I felt a little bit like I was dragging them along with the vision to get all the way through, but we did it. I think they felt really proud.

BAB: What are you working on now?

CG: I am working on a new video piece which is part of an installation called "Sea of Time." It's about my trying to get pregnant and my friend Mark dying of AIDS. It's about being a lesbian in a relationship, trying to create a family and at the same time dealing with losing a member of that family. Two years ago Sue and I and Mark Niblock-Smith [who subsequently died] and [his life partner] Roger Workman went to Bali together. The piece incorporates a lot of footage from our trip to Bali, but in a very metaphoric way. It's a metaphoric travelogue.

BAB: I want to get back to the issue of community, specifically the Woman's Building as community. We covered the Feminist Studio Workshop and your teaching there in the summer of 1976. Then you founded the Feminist Art Workers, but you remained involved with the Woman's Building.

Cheri Gaulke in Conversation

CG: Yes, and I'm still involved.

BAB: Why? And what does that mean to you?

CG: What it meant to me when I first moved to L.A. was that I could move to this big sprawling metropolis where people were alienated from each other and separated by great distances, yet I never felt like that was a problem for me. I would go to an opening in Santa Monica or Pasadena or Hollywood and I would run into members of my community. It touched on everything: when Barb Bouska and I were looking for housing, [feminist performance artist] Barbara Smith gave us space in her studio. Here was this older woman artist who became a mentor and introduced us to the art community, as we introduced her to our brand of feminism. I always felt this sense of community that had nothing to do with geography. In fact, it overcame the geography of L.A. You know a lot of people have a hard time with this city and I never did.

What does the Woman's Building mean to me now? I have said before that the thing that always turned me on about the Building was the two-pronged aspect of it. One prong was that it was a place where you had this "room of one's own" to individually and collectively explore what it means to be a woman and express that in your art, which doesn't mean that you're locked into a certain way of being a woman, it's not an essentialist thing at all. The other prong was public; the Building was a place that embraced and welcomed the public to come into that context and learn about women's issues. In that regard, the Building was about transforming society.

I am currently a Board member of the Woman's Building. It's an organization that exists on paper since it doesn't have any physical space. (Its archives have been moved into the Smithsonian.) Now I'm completely committed to the idea of legacy, back to that. Damn it, we're not going to be lost from history again! We have seen how that's happened time and again and how we've suffered from it. It's my chance, with the other women on the Board, to make sure that doesn't happen to us. So it doesn't happen to the next generation of women.

What we did at the Building will become a book. The Building's history is being recorded through oral history interviews — we're conducting about fifty — and we're going to commission different people to write essays, to do page art and poetry about their experiences there. It'll be a mixed media coffee table book. I feel really proud that we've managed our resources well and were responsible about closing the building when it was time to do so and not run it into the ground. And now we've insured this next step. I feel that's really good.

BAB: I didn't realize that you were thinking about doing a book. This issue of legacy, it's one of the things that Judy Chicago is talking about a lot, too. We do these things and then they're lost. How can we stop that process?

CG: Nancy Youdelman found, in a used bookstore, that book *Art and Handicraft* *in the Woman's Building of 1893.* That was so wonderful. Now we're going to make our own book and a hundred years from now somebody will find it in a used bookstore.

After we speak, I drive to Santa Barbara to see Cheri Gaulke's video installation "Sea of Time" at the Contemporary Arts Forum. The installation is placed in a corner of the gallery, with a barrier wall separating the viewing room from the rest of the exhibition space. On the outside face of the wall, framed by evocative stills from the video, Cheri has written: "Mark began dying of AIDS long before I began trying to conceive. . . . both of us racing against the inevitability of time. Although younger than me, he ran out of time first . . .his life blood poisoned and unable to regenerate itself. My womb blood is simply nearing the end of its fertility, making conception difficult." I enter the deep red viewing room as the video focuses on an image of Cheri floating in what appears to be a sea of blood. She talks about a previous pregnancy and miscarriage. A goblet tilts towards the screen and blood cascades over the rim. Then Cheri, in the video, talks about traveling to Bali with her life partner Sue and Mark and his life partner Roger. She talks about the sacred, ritualized nature of time there and about how she saw Mark's skill as a shopper. The narrative progresses, interspersed with a goblet of plastic babies, then one containing Mark's medicine ampules. Then Cheri talks about how, just before Mark's death, she and Sue curled up with him and asked him to shop for their child as he traveled through the realm of spirits.

He must have shopped well, I think. Cheri is having twins. I wipe a recalcitrant tear from my eye and think of what feminist theologian Carol Christ wrote about the web of life, about how it unites us all, about how Cheri and Sue have decided to name one of the girls "Marka" in memory of Mark's presence in our community. I think, again, about feminist art, about connection. Then I leave. [The twins, born May 21, 1994, are named Marka and Xochi].

Cheri Gaulke's and Sue Maberry's "Thicker Than Blood: Portraits of Our Lesbian Family"

by Elizabeth Say

As a first step to creating their installation, Cheri Gaulke and Sue Maberry went to their local Sears department store to have a family portrait done; they took a 7-year-old friend and neighbor with them. They felt some apprehension — how would the photographer react to photographing two lesbians and a child? Much to their surprise, the young woman taking the pictures appeared to have no negative response. She placed Sue behind Cheri, put Sue's arm around Cheri, and took the pictures. "I thought, this is great!" remembers Cheri. "She's not homophobic at all." Then they brought the child up to join them, and the young photographer called Sue "Mom." "I realized she thought I was Cheri's mother," says Sue, "and the little girl was Cheri's daughter — she thought she was photographing three generations." As Gaulke points out, "She clearly got that we were family, but she had to fit that into her notion of what a family is."

The idea for the installation came out of Gaulke's and Maberry's own experience of creating a family structure for themselves and the process of defining that over and against the dominant cultural model of the traditional nuclear family. "Every year, around the holidays, we get a family portrait from my brother and others. We have a stack of them. I said to Sue, one night, why don't our gay and lesbian friends do this? Why don't we have portraits taken?" "We have snapshots of our friends" said Maberry, "but not formal portraits. Going to have a portrait done is a cultural experience we don't participate in."

In American society, the family portrait functions as a kind of cultural icon. The Oxford Universal Dictionary defines an icon as "A representation of some sacred personage, itself regarded as sacred, and honored with a relative worship." The family portrait is a representation of a sacred cultural institution — the nuclear family. Go into almost any American home and you will find at least one such representation, proudly and prominently displayed. It serves to affirm the value that our society places on the traditional concept of the family as the foundation of the American way of life. There is no more sacred cultural image that a politician can conjure up than the American family, as evidenced by the rhetoric about family values we hear in Presidential campaigns.

Yet this is a model which represents fewer and fewer actual family units. The question of how to reconfigure our notions of family is a concern not only for lesbian and gay people, but for heterosexuals as well. Ironically, however, it may be lesbian and gay people — who have been excluded from the traditional family structure — who may provide all of society with models for how this reconfiguration can be accomplished.

"What happens when you come out to your family is that you often get rejected," according to Maberry. "You've grown up believing that 'blood is thicker than water.' Then your notion of family gets destroyed, and you have to be creative." The installation Maberry and Gaulke created is one expression of this creativity. As Gaulke points out, there is a lot of public dialogue around the question "Can gay people have a family?" "Psychologists, for example, often say one of the tragedies of being gay/lesbian is you can't have a family; you'll be alone." But these two women clearly identify themselves as a family, and fulfill all the functions we understand as familial obligations.

The difficulty is in making other people understand and accept them as a family. Gaulke recalls having to fill out insurance forms at her job. In the space where she was to designate a beneficiary she put Sue's name, and when the form asked for the relationship of this person she wrote "significant other." The woman who reviewed the form asked "What do you mean by significant other?" "Can you believe she didn't know what significant other meant? I had to explain, and I got all tense and nervous. I'm afraid of being completely 'out' at work, because I'm afraid I'll lose my job. This kind of thing happens all the time. You always have to answer these kinds of questions. It's difficult, and painful." Culturally dominant notions of family are narrow, and they do not make room for other, alternative models of family relationship.

Traditionally we have conceived of family as kinship networks based on blood connection — parents, brothers, sisters, children — and/or socially legitimated commitments — marriage and adoption. For lesbians and gays, such socially sanctioned commitments are not available, since lesbian and gay unions are not recognized under the law. Nevertheless, despite the lack of social legitimation, lesbians and gays (and others who fall outside of the traditional model) do create family structures. "In the lesbian and gay community," says Gaulke, "friendship becomes elevated to the level of family."

In the "Thicker than Blood" installation, Gaulke and Maberry utilize photographs and text to explore concepts of the family. The scale is large, intentionally bold. It is meant to capture the attention of the viewer; to shout "Look at us! Here we are! You can't ignore us any longer!" There are several layers of text employed, from the large exclamatory declaration of FAMILY, to smaller, more intimate texts which draw the viewer into a thought-provoking consideration of what does — and does not — count as family in American society. The following pages transform the public scale of the installation into the intimate scale of the book.

The involvement of community extended beyond the inclusion of photographs of friends/family in this portrait gallery. Gaulke explains that the entire project ought to be understood as a conceptual performance. "This is along the lines of what Suzanne Lacy was doing at The Woman's Building. Performance is not limited to a simply theatrical event; it can also be a conceptual structure." The various people who went to have their family portraits done at their local Sears store (at Gaulke's and Maberry's request) involved themselves in a live action they do not usually undertake. This experience varied from group to group; some explained the project in detail to the photographer while others were more reticent, leaving the photographers to draw their own conclusions. Thus, this performance also drew the photographers into the action and challenged narrow definitions of family construction.

"Thicker than Blood" also includes the element of humor, of parody. As Gaulke points out, "There is something about the banality of the photos. These are not, after all, glamour shots. These are more in the snapshot genre." Maberry goes on to say that "this is more of a working-class thing; going to Sears to have your picture taken. There is no idealizing going on here." These are not the portraits one expects to see in a portrait gallery; usually one sees images of the wealthy and powerful. So this installation turns expectations on end by elevating ordinary people to a place of artistic importance.

Maberry also points out the symbolic significance of putting a frame around alternative families; it is a way of moving them, in bell hooks's words, from margin to center.

The work which Gaulke and Maberry have created here celebrates the reality of this alternative understanding of family. They challenge each of us to rethink not only our understanding of family, but also of community.

The "page installation" artwork that follows this essay was derived from a large-scale installation of the same name, first exhibited in "Communitas" at the art gallery of California State University Northridge, Fall 1992.

Jean —
Best wishes on your work + thanks for your commitment to other women artists.

Cheri Gaulke

family

Much of the time, our lives do not intersect, however I count Sue and Cheri among the most important relationships in my life. I would do anything in my power to help them out if they needed it.

– Nancy Angelo

Thicker Than Blood:

In the summer of 1992 (the year of intensifying Republican "family value" rhetoric) we asked some of our closest friends and family to go to Sears and have their portraits taken. As lesbians, we accept the notion of family as a construction and have taken responsibility to create it in our lives. These are some of the people we cherish; this is a portrait of the family we choose.

– Cheri Gaulke and Sue Maberry

Kin are the people whose names and numbers are on my kid's school card to contact in case of emergency, the people in my will who want to care for my daughter should something happen to me.

– Lezli Davies

I was very nervous prior to the portrait-taking. I found my own internalized homophobia caming up, sitting there in the middle of Sears. The photographer seemed puzzled initially when Susan told her we wanted to pose looking at each other. Then, as if a light bulb came on over her head, she said, "Oh, like a couple?" "Yes," we agreed, "exactly like a couple."

– Terry Wolverton

As a coven we have shared birthdays, day-to-day life, and deep ritual experience. We handle deaths of family members, commitment ceremonies, weddings, coming-of-age and leaving home rituals, new homes and jobs, illness and healing together.

– Susan Gray

I want a word for queer family that's not about meschpuchah, which roughly translated from Yiddish means "the whole fucking extended family," and that's also about invention and vision... Because I can't envision a new way of being without the words to describe it.
– Sandra Golvin

Portrait of Our Lesbian Family

I wouldn't have known Sue and Cheri without the agency of making art, making culture, and most importantly, making an institution (the Woman's Building) in which other individuals could make and find and build. So, as "family" we are known to each other for what we have made.
– Eloise Klein-Healy

The chance gays and lesbians have for creating new family models, of blending family of origin with their community (read family) of choice, makes me hopeful. I am happy to include and be included in non-traditional family gatherings, particularly at holiday times.
– Rob Okun

With family, we feel content to lay around and read the paper in silence, to confide in them and trust them to give their most caring response, or we can be silly, sad, loud and brash, obnoxious, spontaneous or out of sorts.
-Elizabeth Canelake and Annette Hunt

Thicker Than Blood was first commissioned as an installation for *Communitas: The Feminist Art of Community Building*, an exhibition curated by Betty Ann Brown and Elizabeth Say, 1992.

Art, Politics and Community

by Mindy Lorenz

Mindy Lorenz was trained as an art historian and was a professor of art history for over twenty years. She has for some time been an art-maker, as well as an analyzer of the art-making process. In recent years, her art-making has entered the political arena. If I tell you that Lorenz ran for California State Assembly as a Democrat (1992) and was a Green Party candidate before that (1990), you may ask, what does that have to do with art? To answer, I need to go back to Germany in the 1960s when a highly respected artist and teacher named Joseph Beuys began to challenge himself, and his students, to break down the separation between art and life. Beuys, an early performance artist who is now considered one of the formative godfathers of Post-modern art, asserted that community work and political action could be aesthetically rendered if performed by artists. Lorenz was deeply influenced by Beuys, as well as by many feminist performance artists who cultivated the integration of their personal and professional lives. Like Lorenz, many were also teachers who viewed their teaching as part of their art-making. And, since "the personal is political," it should not be surprising that political activism was a natural extension of their work as artists. Beuys became one of the founders of the German Green Party in the early 1970s. A decade later, Lorenz was one of the founders of the Green Party in the United States.

I have always learned best from direct experience. After many years of theoretical study, I began using life experience as indelible lessons on art and politics and embarked on a journey of integrating the two. In retrospect, this process seems inevitable given my involvement in both arenas, but for a long time art and politics competed for my allegiance. This disturbed me enormously because I was so strongly attracted to both and could not dream of giving up one to pursue the other exclusively. It sounds like the classic dilemma of having two lovers who insist that you choose between them, and you cannot. The power of my involvement in art and politics forced me to search for their connections so I could better understand myself and try to resolve the conflicts of allegiances. What I discovered was how to apply the ecological model of interconnectedness to art and politics, thereby also discovering the spiritual basis of both.

At first, spirituality was far more discernible in art than in politics. From my first exposure to art in my freshman art history class, I could intuitively feel art's spiritual essence. As a young adult, art unlocked my spiritual and passionate center. Studying and making art gave me permission to delve into parts of myself and society that I would not have done otherwise. I cultivated the persona of an avant-garde artist, taking risks and throwing inhibitions to the wind. This process enabled me to tap into a deep wellspring of experiences, values, and principles that had been forming since childhood, but had been inaccessible. My fervent spirituality was being transformed from its doctrinaire Catholicism into a personal belief system.

Part of this self-discovery was recovering the memory of my life as a 4-year-old child. Day after day, I would spend hours alone in a sun porch, creating and acting out fantasies as a nun, a mother, and a teacher. I can still see the quality of the golden light, hear the soothing silence, feel the contentment. Although I was intensely alone, I felt connected to God and to the service of humanity. As in a dream, the inherent contradictions of my various identities were meaningless. My political awakening also occurred that year, as I discovered the cruel inequities of the world. Driving through New York's Bowery to visit my grandparents in Brooklyn, I was deeply shocked and incredulous at the sight of homeless men and women. My spiritual commitment of service to humanity suddenly gained the political focus of wanting to eradicate injustice.

During the 1960s, there were other powerful experiences that shaped my political perspective. When Reverend Martin Luther King, Jr. was assassinated, I was in graduate school at the University of Maryland and living near Washington, D.C. I watched in horror as the city burned. Bringing supplies into city churches, I maneuvered past gun-toting soldiers and tanks in the streets. At the same time, Vietnam War protests turned the campus into a chaotic melange of bomb threats and teach-ins. Filing past the White House with candles, I wondered if Richard Nixon cared at all about the suffering of war at home and abroad.

For the most part, my art history professors tried to deny the reality of the Vietnam War. Within their insulated classrooms, it was "business as usual." They made no attempt, and disallowed students from trying, to establish connections between art history and contemporary politics. While I wasn't clear how to do it, I knew it had to be done and deeply resented that it was not. Whether it seemed germane to the curriculum or not, we should be talking about what was happening in our society, and discovering the connections in the process. I promised myself that as a teacher, I would always stay open to that discourse.

In 1972, I moved to California where I had wanted to live since visiting my grandparents in Pasadena when I was seven. As a child, something told me one could get away with a lot of experimentation in California. I was right, and the 1970s were filled with it, My daughter was born in 1973 and within a year I had left her father, had no money, no job, applied for welfare, and applied for a doctoral program at the University of California Santa Barbara. I discovered the feminist movement and once again found that academia was not discussing major social issues, such as the politicization of women. Small wonder! The art historians were not even talking with the artists in the Art Department. I thought most of the artists were a lot more fun, much more curious and intellectually alive, and more engaged with life, than the historians. It was the artists who were more likely to make connections between art and life. Through them, I really began to understand the art-making process and began to see how it drew upon and integrated life experiences.

My first real opportunity to apply some of these lessons came with a teaching position at the University of Denver after receiving my Ph.D. I was eager to make the connections between my life values and my profession, between art history and studio art. Performance art seemed like the best vehicle, and I organized a summer performance art workshop in which I was both student and teacher. It was an intense experience for everyone as we created and critiqued each others' work. It was the first time I had incorporated highly personal material into art-making and it was exhilarating. The following year, I created a graduate seminar on the relationships between art and entropy. Art, politics, ecology, and autobiography became the ingredients for art-making and art history.

In the '80s I grew disillusioned and alienated from the art world as a curator and professor at the Claremont Colleges near Los Angeles. Too many of the artists I met in the Los Angeles art scene were on upwardly mobile career tracks, where the rules of the game were clear and unalterable. The graduate art students were eager to pursue this game to the exclusion of most alternatives. As a curator and teacher, I felt like I was servicing careers rather than providing opportunities for exploration and open-ended learning. At the same time, I was becoming repoliticized by my concern with American foreign policy in Central America and the nuclear buildup in Europe.

My renewed political work took the form of helping to organize a sanctuary network for Salvadoran political refugees in Southern California. I was deeply affected by meeting and hearing the horrifying experiences of people who had suffered at the hands of American-supported Death Squads. It changed my life. I dedicated myself to pursuing political activism at a much deeper level. The glitzy art scene seemed superficial and repugnant to me, as did many other symptoms of our materialistic consumer society.

In an attempt to bridge the gap, I created an outdoor installation in my backyard which integrated art and politics with my personal life. The piece evolved slowly over a period of three months. As I tried to come to terms with the specter of terrorism, torture, death, and dying, I spent time meditating under the large pine tree in the corner of my yard. As it became a personal sanctuary, the idea emerged to contrast the peacefulness of that place with the horror of the war in El Salvador. I divided the area into two sections after discovering the remains of a stone wall beneath the pine needles and grass. This became the dividing line between the "peace and war zones." In the "war zone," I made an earthwork cast of my daughter's body with a little red sock on her motionless foot. The carcass of a large seabird decomposed in a shallow grave. A large chunk of pig's flesh rotted in an army helmet suspended from a branch of the pine tree. In the "peace zone," I built a huge nest out of pine needles into which I placed two large, bandaged rocks huddled together for protection and healing. A circle of glass balls filled with blue liquid hung from branches and united the two zones. It was a tremendous joy to make the installation and to share it with a variety of people: my 10-year-old daughter, her friends, church people, students, political activists, neighbors.

As I struggled with how to make art relevant to my life, I left my job as a university curator and professor. I had discovered the Green Party in Europe, and I dedicated myself to the formation of the Greens in the U.S. in 1984. It was tremendously inspiring that Joseph Beuys, the German performance artist and sculptor, had been a founder of the German Green Party, since I had long admired his commitment to the integration of art, politics, and life. It hit me with the force of revelation that a political party based on ecology already existed and had elected people to a national parliament. For the Greens, ecology provided the model for understanding the fundamental interconnectedness of all life, where human systems took their place among other natural systems. People were held accountable to each other and to the rest of nature. The "Four Pillars" of the German Greens summed it up: Ecology, Social Justice, Grassroots Democracy, and Nonviolence. Since these were personal tenets I had formulated over the years, it was exciting to see them applied to political practice. Here was the integration of ecology, politics, and life I had been looking for!

It was more difficult for me to know how to apply these principles to art. I became rather critical and intolerant of making art objects for sale, as I became more intolerant of our consumer society. Art objects seemed like unnecessary consumer items with little socially redeemable value, often using environmentally destructive techniques and materials. In addition, art-making seemed elitist and quite divorced from most people's needs or interests. Avant-garde art, which I had venerated for so long, had become a commodity, subject to all the artificial trends of the marketplace, including planned obsolescence, fads, and the star system. Novelty had replaced real innovation.

So for a few years, I had a very uneasy relationship with art and politics, and it was not clear how to resolve my conflicts about them. Resolution eventually came in understanding the art process as an expression of interconnectedness. I came to think of art as signifying the integrative capabilities of humankind, that is, our ability to combine diverse, seemingly unrelated, or even conflicting parts into a unified whole: the art object. Art mirrors the fundamental reality of the interconnection of things. Experiencing a work of art can generate a deep sense of connection between our innermost selves and a new reality outside ourselves.

This experience of connection can lead to feeling less alienated and isolated from each other and our surroundings and, therefore, more aware of commonality rather than irreconcilable differences. Like art, politics, at its best, can involve a dialogue among diverse interests to reach some common ground: a law, regulation, treaty, or agreement. The spiritual underpinning of both art and politics, indeed of humanity, is our fundamental interconnection as a species and a planetary community.

This sense of deeply shared experience is an important characteristic of the concept of cultural transformation from a mechanistic to a holistic world view. Part of the crisis in the function of art in our society has to do with our loss of a sense of community. The struggle for liberation of individuals and minority groups, including many artists, within the dominant culture has created alienation and isolation. It is time to re-evaluate our concept of individualism and subjectivity to include solidarity and community. In *The Aesthetic Dimension*, Herbert Marcuse wrote, "Solidarity and community do not mean the absorption of the individual. They rather originate in autonomous individual decision; they unite freely associated individuals, not masses. . . . If art is for any collective consciousness at all, it is that of individuals united in their awareness of the universal need for liberation."[1]

Each of us is a complex web of identities functioning within many communities: our family, workplace, neighborhood, country and planet. As individuals, we must develop a variety of ways to move comfortably among these communities. Artists can examine the ways of best imaging the communities with which they identify. Political representatives must be clear about the communities with which they identify, in order to best represent them. If, as I suggest, the essence of art is to signify interconnectedness, and the purpose of politics is to create dialogue, then both art and politics are essential vehicles for individuals to discover and express their place in community.

These interconnections were being put into practice at an unexpected destination for me: the Instituto Armando Reveron in Caracas, Venezuela. In July 1992, I had the great pleasure of spending two weeks there as a visiting professor, giving a seminar on the relationship between art, politics and ecology. My former University of Denver student, Susanna Amundarain, arranged for my visit. She believed that my interdisciplinary interests would be very compatible with those of the new art institute. She was absolutely right. By that time, Susanna had become an internationally known artist and a faculty member at the Institute. The driving force behind this bold educational experiment was the Director, Manuel Espinoza, a renowned Venezuelan painter, and a political and ecological activist. I have never met anyone quite like Manuel, a man who loves his country, his people, and the earth as one loves close family members. Looking in his eyes as he spoke about Venezuela brought tears to my own eyes. Amidst rampant corruption, environmental devastation, and political instability, Manuel believes that Venezuela and Latin America are at a crossroads. Their future well-being depends on recognizing and acting upon the interrelationships of economy and ecology, social and economic justice. Individual and community decisions must be made from this holistic view. Manuel's contribution to establishing this connective process — indeed his legacy to his country — is the formation of the Institute.

The Institute curriculum was developed collaboratively with faculty, students, advisers, and the director exploring ways to study the integration of art and ecology. Among the art students, there was a great diversity in age, social and economic background, and approach to art making. What they seemed to have in common was the desire for experimentation and community. Life at the school became a model of community-building that could be brought into daily life and work.

Perhaps the most unique aspect of the program was the Taller El Territorio [The Workshop of the Territory], created by Manuel in his hometown Clarines, about three hours from Caracas. Through the workshop, Manuel developed a process whereby students and faculty directly experienced the land and people of that rural community. Theoretical discussions were combined with practical exercises that exposed the students to the realities of daily life. Students and community members worked on projects together each year. The effects are authentic and profound.

My visit to Clarines was a high point in my life. I still cannot fully explain the effect it had on me, but I know it was a catalyst for a new synthesis of my life experience. The "boundaries" between art, life, politics, and ecology disappeared for a fleeting period of time. I felt a sense of community that is rare; a belonging to, and belonging with people, as well as the natural environment.

My ongoing quest for an integration of art and politics reached a far deeper level as a result of my experiences in Venezuela, because learning from direct experience is the underlying premise of the Taller Territorio. Art-making did not feel elitist or irrelevant, because it took place and was experienced in the context of an integrative community. There, art is practiced as a deeply personal, spiritual reality and, at the same time, as an expression of social and environmental interaction. The process and product of art-making are equally valuable. The commercial viability of art is not the bottom line. Rather, the validity of art arises from the authenticity of the artist's process engaging in community, however that is defined. In many ways, this is a more traditional view of art, where the artist becomes a vehicle for community values, usually spiritual and sometimes political. The challenge for the contemporary artists is to rediscover the balance between expressing individual liberty and community values, between spiritual introspection and political action.

RACHEL ROSENTHAL

in Conversation with Betty Ann Brown

Rachel Rosenthal has been called "the cultish seer of human nature, a myth-puncturing spinner of parable . . . an outrageously giddy dowager who specializes in coquetry [and] a Shakespearean Kojak (with trademark bald pate and deep, richly resonant voice). . . ."[1] Her performance style has been termed "postmodern to the max."[2] Now the artist is the eyebrow-pierced materfamilias of a newly formed performance troupe that "provides a venue for several other talents who aspire to her level of sociopoetic commentary."[3]

Rosenthal was born in Paris to wealthy Russian Jews. After they fled the Nazi invasion, the young Rosenthal ended up in New York City, where she studied modern art with Hans Hoffman and dance with Merce Cunningham and worked with artists Jasper Johns and Robert Rauschenberg as well as composer John Cage. Coming to Los Angeles in the 1950s, she established and ran the avant-garde Instant Theatre. It was named as much for the pop-artiness of "instant coffee" as for the Zen awareness of "the instant, the now." "There was no such thing as performance art then, the word did not exist, and people's agents didn't want them to let the public see them doing the things we were doing . . . so I began working with non-actors. The rest of the company was a dancer, an artist, and an engineer."[4] In the 1960s, she gave up improvisational work because of the arthritic deterioration of her knees.

Rosenthal got involved with the Women's Art Movement in the 1970s and was inspired to merge her interest in art with her training in theater to become a performance artist. Her work from 1975 to 1981 was largely autobiographical. Since then, she has explored issues such as feminism, nuclear power, toxic waste, animal rights, the collision of spirituality and technology, and the relationship between humans and the planet.

The first time I saw Rachel Rosenthal perform, she did a piece called "Soldier of Fortune" (1981) in the parking lot behind a Los Angeles art gallery. She donned elegant attire and proceeded to eat a sumptuous gourmet meal, drinking French champagne with every course, as she spoke of financial vicissitudes, betrayal, bankruptcy. I had heard about her previous piece on female beauty and the fetishizing of hair in our culture — the piece in which she'd shaved her head. I knew she could be daringly autobiographical, but I was nonetheless stunned to see a performer become publicly intoxicated while discussing familial and financial loss — topics that had been shamed into silence throughout my middle-class upbringing. Her courage unnerved me; I can still remember how frighteningly personal it seemed when she ended the performance by throwing money at the audience.

I saw Rosenthal's "Gaia Mon Amour" performance two years later. Mixing moments of mystery and mythology, the artist traced our changing relationship to the planet. I still feel the majesty she instilled in her reenactment of the Celtic ritual of killing the old king to fertilize the fields. Her "Traps" (1982) had been equally impressive: I remember my awe at the fluttering moths she created with flashes of her snapping hands. "L.O.W. in Gaia" (1986) continued Rosenthal's exploration of environmental concerns. She spoke of a trip to the desert and her frustration over the lack of mystical unions with nature. She carried a huge trash sack, full of debris that increasingly burdened her. And she dripped hot wax onto her skin, to literally embody her anguish over environmental disasters. No one left that performance unmoved. Like "Soldier of Fortune" and "Gaia Mon Amour," it was informative, cathartic, and inspiring.

Rosenthal has attracted an immense following, which has led her to present her works internationally. When Robert Rauschenberg conceived of his "Tribute 21" — a project that honored, among many others, Mikhail Gorbachov for peace, Nelson Mandela for human rights, and Toni Morrison for literature — he chose Rosenthal to represent theater.

In Rosenthal's performances, she addresses vital social issues, constructs them around a framework of personal experience, and anchors them in rigorous research. She clothes the many rich layers of information in poetry and vision, thus providing viewers with both magical transcendence and profound intellectual satisfaction.

Rosenthal has recently re-engaged improvisational work in the collaborative ensemble "TohuBohu! This is a troupe of twelve actors, artists, and musicians whose performances can be characterized as surreal, collagist, Artaudian, thematic, content-oriented, compelling, and irresistible. Derived from Hebrew and often used in French, "tohubohu" means chaos, confusion, and disorder. I attended a "TohuBohu!" performance on Tuesday, December 19, 1995.

Rosenthal introduced the evening by stating that the troupe was finding its way into a totally protean art form. "It's a continuing challenge, an ongoing quest. We keep fighting the dragon. But we never get the boon!" The work would be non-linear as well as non-narrative, she explained, and it would incorporate all of the arts: music, dance, theater, and the visual arts. The process would be symbiotic: the performers would provide the ingredients from which the audience would construct their own images, their own dreams. In essence, the audience itself would actually create the art.

She was correct. I will never forget one particular moment from that evening with "TohuBohu!" One of the performers stood center stage, slowly threading a long circle of yellow police tape through his out-stretched hands. Behind him, two figures were locked in troubling repetitive gyrations, their costumes having transformed them into humanoid mechanical gears. To the far right, Rosenthal was seated as driving an automobile. She crooned hypnotically about collisions on the information highway. It was arresting, unnerving . . . and yet it made sense in an abstract, poetic way. Like dreams that linger long beyond waking, the images from "TohuBohu!" remain riveted in the viewer's consciousness.

The week before I saw the "TohuBohu!" performance, I interviewed Rachel Rosenthal about her collaborative work with the twelve young people who comprise her troupe. I wanted to know what it was like to work in improvisational community and what it was like to use performance art as the core for community building. As is often the case with Rosenthal, the conversation ranged from the personal to the political, from autobiographical to cosmic, from the joys and benefits of creative community to the anger and disappointment of people who have inappropriate expectations of a mentor. We began by talking about the Cambrian Explosion, then spoke of the space mission to Jupiter, soon to send back photographs of an ice moon that may have water (and perhaps life?) on it.

Rachel Rosenthal: That's the only annoyance about getting older. I would like to stick around to find out what happens next! I'll never be ready to go, because there will always be something new and exciting I want to understand and get to know. There are so many holes in my knowledge I would like to fill.

Betty Ann Brown: Tell me about your company.

RR: It's called The Rachel Rosenthal Company. It's really an outgrowth of my earlier Instant Theater.

BAB: Did you start Instant Theater at the Pasadena Playhouse?

RR: No, I was working at the Playhouse, but my theater was in Hollywood. [It was] a magical little company which ran for about ten years in all kinds of underground and secret places. It was totally improvised theater. It involved the most abstract, the most realistic, the most total theater. Not only the actors on stage, but the lights, the music — everything was improvised and everybody took turns doing these things. The kind of skills that it took to do that were developed in workshops. It was not just getting people together to do this collective creative process . . . we also changed people's lives.

In the 1970s, when I began looking around for a way to make an income, a friend said, why don't you do your Instant Theater as workshops? So I did. It was a time of many workshops, like EST. But those were workshops of 300-400 people. And they were all about authority and domination. That's not teaching, that's telling.

So I began the DBD ("Doing By Doing") Workshops. Many of the techniques and processes were adapted from Instant Theater. People who do the DBD classes are mesmerized by the kind of work that comes out of them. It's like nothing else, like no other theater you see. When people are in that slight trance that you need to be in, the kind of theater that they produce is so magical. It's amazing. You can't compare anything else to it.

I did the workshops for years. Then I did a performance called "Zone" with over sixty participants. [Performed at the Center for Performing Arts, University of California, Los Angeles in February 1994, "Zone" established the parallels between the Russian ruling class of the beginning of this century and the contemporary American situation. Rosenthal said of "Zone": "The ruling class didn't get it and neither do we. Here we are at the end of our century, putting machines before people, ruining the environment, the poor are starving. . . . It's a total downfall into materialism to the point where we've lost our perspective on our relationship to the whole: the planet, the cosmos, the soul."[5]]

Several of the people who worked on "Zone" remained. They formed a kernel of people who are beautiful, diverse, talented, and completely dedicated to what we're doing. We have been workshopping together. (I had to go back into the workshopping mode myself. I hadn't done improvisation myself in years and years, so I had to re-learn how to do it.) . . . We meet three times a week, five hours each session. It's a huge commitment but necessary to develop the requisite skills. And now we're coming out. We're developing an audience for this very, very different art experience. It's an art form that never culminates in total satisfaction, like coitus interruptus forever. It takes a certain kind of person to accept that. Most people want safety and security. They want finality and closure. If that's what you want, you won't be comfortable here. What we develop is a state of perpetual change, transmutation, metamorphosis, and growth.

BAB: Tell me about the people in your workshop.

RR: Most are trained as dancers, actors, performers. We also have two musicians, a light person and a woman who does live video that's projected at the same time we perform. The musicians have an electronic keyboard that works with a computer, sampling sounds in and out, and several instruments. I do a lot of vocal extensions, a lot of aural works.

The idea is to create a kind of environmental theater that deals with content, but is also very visual, very auditory, very movement-based. It has all the aspects of theater, but is not rehearsed. It is spontaneous, created in the moment.

BAB: How do you deal with content? Do you pick themes?

RR: Sometimes we do, sometimes we don't. Last week, I came to a meeting and I said, I want to do something about Bosnia and I want to do it as a duet, with Derrick [Jones]. I want to do it as a dissociation where it seems as though we're flirting, but what we're really talking about is the horrors of war. And so we did. We work so well, the two of us, me and a very young African American. We're the odd couple. . . . (laughter)

BAB: So you didn't script it at all, you just set the parameters and took off.

RR: Right. That was a short piece. Today, I'm going to give them a newspaper article on refugees to read, and then we'll do a rambler. A "rambler" is a longer piece. It involves the whole group and might have a set. It can be anywhere from ten to thirty minutes. When everybody reads the article, it gives the work a sort of collective consciousness about the subject. In a rambler, there can be two people working on the topic, or six, or more. We keep it fluid.

Sometimes, we go with absolutely nothing, like a high wire act without a net. And sometimes we have a specific point of departure, which may be as simple as saying, let's do two units of two.

We've developed this whole vocabulary. A "unit" involves more than one person. We can work together spatially very close or at a distance. If it's at a distance, we might do unison work, which can be movement-based or vocal or both. If it's not unison, it might be what we call "power at a distance," which is doing an exchange of power, working together so that it looks like one person is affecting the other person but there's a lot of distance between them. A unit can also be more than one person acting as the same thing, the same entity, for example a tree with branches. Or it could be many entities of the same kind, like a pack of wolves.

We have also worked on a technique we call "levels." A unit can be on one level and there can be a second unit on stage with them, working on a totally discrete level. The levels have to do with degrees of realism or abstraction, or degrees of conscious or subconscious activity, or degrees of being, as, this unit is a bunch of boulders and that unit is a bunch of crows.

BAB: You said that when people come together in such a community and work collaboratively for a time, that it really changes their lives. How? How does it change them?

RR: First of all, it centers you in the moment. This is one of the hardest things to do, since we live in a world that is so divisive and scattered and distracting, pulling us in every direction. I think one of the real problems for human beings right now is that we live in the past or the future — even if that past or future is just the moment before or the moment after — rather than in the now. This kind of work obliges you to surf the moment, to be in sync with the moment. And that, I think, is profoundly important for spiritual and psychological health.

The improvisational performance process heightens your sensibilities and your sensitivity to others. You have to know what their needs and wants are, and how to work with them, without losing yourself. If you are too sensitive to others, forgetting yourself, you become what I call "the social worker." You're always at their beck and call, always at the service of their wants. We need to become able to respond to others' needs without losing our own needs. We also need to initiate collaboration without invading another's space or coercing them to work with us.

The process teaches you respect. It teaches you a sense of space and time and grounds you in a kind of a cosmic world that is beyond the social world that you are usually rushing around in. This kind of work puts you in touch with your inner self, in ways which are sometimes very dramatic, but never destructive.

You learn, for instance, that there are no mistakes, there are just bad follow-ups. And you learn that within yourself, all the violence and all the monsters that you're so afraid of uncovering are simply segments, little aspects of a whole. You learn that they need to get a voice — to get expressed — so they don't remain repressed and start festering inside you. With this kind of work, you're able to create personae who embody all the aspects we usually call negative. They're not negative at all, they're just a different kind of energy. You start to become friends with them. You learn how to deal with them, how to bring them out of you and put them back at will. You recognize them and manage them in an art context.

It's a teaching process I've developed over decades. It's ironic that it's so much about community and collaboration because personally I am a loner. I am able to distance myself. And the more you can distance yourself, the more you can keep the love chakra open. I think that what enables me to do this [kind of work], is precisely the fact that I am a loner. My joy comes when everybody leaves and I'm alone with my animals.

BAB: I had a conversation related to the issue of love and distance just last night with a friend. We began talking about how we have this really ardent desire to see the divine in everybody, to love everybody, but that does not mean we want everybody close to us, in our lives. Love has to have boundaries and limits, for things like personal protection . . . and for the solitude necessary for creativity.

RR: When I teach in workshops, I truly love my students. But when we say good-by, I rarely remember their names. They're gone. For a long time, my students — particularly young female students — got upset with me because they wanted a friendship with me that would last beyond the workshop. But how could I do that? I've taught hundreds and hundreds of students.

BAB: The only model so many people have had of female authority is the "perfect mother," which means the mother who loves and forgives all, the mother who sacrifices herself constantly for the child. If you're a woman in authority and you step outside the perfect mother stereotype, you violate their expectations and incur their rage!

RR: But now it's different. People have evolved. Women have evolved. People now know that a powerful woman can be a good person without being the good mother . . . so they can enjoy her as a role model and then leave her alone.

BAB: Issues around female roles have definitely changed over the last several decades. Tell me about other issues you have dealt with.

RR: The issues I bring back into repertory from years ago — issues like animal rights, the environment, our relationship to technology and spirit — well, I can see that the language I used previously marks their age, but the issues are completely contemporary, because they are still around, not yet resolved.

BAB: In some of your pieces, you cite other thinkers who are coming to a kind of peak in cultural awareness, but they are often like tides: they come in and they go out.

RR: And very often, I bring them in when they haven't quite peaked. Then they do peak, and people say, "Oh, Rachel used such and such. . . ."

BAB: Tell me which issues you're grappling with most often now.

RR: I'm interested in population. We're under a Damocles sword of population. The explosion of overpopulation has been with us for forty, fifty years, but it hasn't crested yet. And when it does, I think it's going to be cataclysmic. Already, it's shown signs of great disturbance. Young people who are growing up now are becoming fertile earlier and mating earlier, mating without the understanding of rites of passage, of ritual. They are creating huge populations of children who cannot be cared for, by their parents or by the state. The ability to lodge and clothe and feed and educate and employ them is waning. The ability of the Earth to sustain them is disappearing with dwindling resources.

In maybe one decade, maybe two, maybe three, we will have a situation where people will be on the move, like army ants or locusts. . . . And what kind of horrendous clashes will that bring?

BAB: They *will* be just like locusts: they'll go into an area, wipe it out, and then have to move on.

RR: The kinds of clashes, the civil wars that are everywhere, are like the experiments done with rats. When rats are crowded into a small area, they start killing each other. Like rats, people need space; psychological and physical space. When their space is constricted, it becomes translated into issues of difference. They think, that person is different, so we can't live together.

The motion of masses takes two forms: invasion or refugees. The invasion aspect is much more aggressive, destructive, and demoralizing. The refugee issue is just as bad, but it's more passive. Both have the same common denominator: there are too many people.

The other issue that I think is extremely important is meat eating. Meat eating is similar to overpopulation. We raise and eat animals who are sucking resources far more extensively than a plant-based diet would. We are creating artificial animals. We are creating artificial situations which are uneconomic, unecological, and certainly unethical. Industrial farming and husbandry are like torture and concentration camps for these sentient creatures. Yet the industries that are involved are extremely powerful and are creating a demand for a totally unnatural situation.

BAB: Have you seen [New York artist] Sue Coe's work on pigs? She asserts that American farmers fatten pigs by injecting them with human genetic material. So if you eat pigs, you're a cannibal of sorts.

RR: The meat industry produces animals with such pain and suffering. When you ingest them, you're ingesting that violence and suffering and pain. One book that's really influenced my thoughts on this is Carol Adams's *The Sexual Politics of Meat.* You should read it. Also Jim Mason's *An Unnatural Order, Uncovering the Roots of our Domination of Nature and Each Other.*

BR: Domination. Yes, our relationship with animals, with all of nature, is premised on domination. (I guess you can trace that back to Genesis, when "man" is "given dominion" over the birds and beasts.) We're so species-centric. We think our intelligence is the only kind that matters. So we compare other species intelligence to ours and see them as less, as lacking. In fact, it's a difference of kind of intelligence not just amount of intelligence.

RR: Also their languages. We teach animals our language, but we never try to learn their languages. And they've got incredible communication skills. It always amazes me. Look at my dogs, look how they communicate. I take them everywhere, you know. The reactions of people are so strange. Some people act as if they've never seen an animal before.

BAB: Rachel, do your students share your values?

RR: They do. I couldn't work this way with anybody who didn't share them, at least on a broad level. Of course, we have differences of opinion on small political issues, but differences of basic values, no. I do a lot of propaganda in my workshops; I talk a lot about the issues that are important to me. I really don't think they would stay with me, with the kind of commitment and dedication they have, if we had completely different values.

Yet the people in the company are very diverse. There's an African American, an Asian American, a Filipino and some gay guys. There's a Latina and a woman who's half Native American. We come together three times a week for five hours, and have done so for months. We really have to click.

BAB: An issue that comes up with collective creativity, especially among such diverse groups, is the issue of credit. You are called The Rachel Rosenthal Company. Do they have any trouble with that?

RR: No, I don't think so. I have the name that's going to ring the bell . . . which is precisely why I named the company that way. If I'd called it the La-Di-Da Company, we'd have to do all the promotion, PR, etc., to create awareness of the new name. But people already recognize my name, so they come to see the work.

BAB: And the others? Are they comfortable?

RR: These people are my students, primarily, and they are where they are because of that relationship. I've said to them, I'll put you on the map. Perhaps individually, they could make it. But as a company, we all have to rely on my name to promote our efforts.

I don't think the issue of name or of credit is a problem. The only thing that bothers me is that whenever there's a problem, they don't come to me.

BAB: You're so powerful. . . .

RR: I know that. I've always been powerful. But I don't throw my weight around. I make myself very accessible. I teach them, I direct them. And I never put people down, I never humiliate them. I never put myself on a pedestal or demand certain attitudes. But they still treat me with kid gloves and don't come to me with their problems. I don't mean their personal problems, I mean their professional ones, group ones.

> *As I left, I thought about the experience of community centered around such a powerful personality as Rachel Rosenthal. Then I thought of the comment a mutual friend had made to me years ago. She'd said how much she admired Rachel Rosenthal, how she knew anyone so charismatic could easily encourage a cultlike following. But Rachel Rosenthal hasn't. Instead, she has held steadfast to her own art and, in the last few years, made remarkable commitment to collaboration, community, and "creating mutual understandings for the benefit of all."*

The Rachel Rosenthal Company: Imesol Moreno (foreground),
C. Derrick Jones, and Rachel Rosenthal; live video: Rula
Kaliroi.

Source: The Spirits of the Air, Fire, Water and Earth

Text by Ruth Ann Anderson

Poetry by Starr Goode

Ruth Ann Anderson is an artist and long-time veteran of the Los Angeles Woman's Building. She grew up in a devoutly religious household. "I never really abandoned my childhood goal of missionary work," she explains. "Only, my guidebook isn't the Bible any more." Shortly after beginning her advanced studies in art, Anderson read *The Mists of Avalon* and took a Spring Equinox workshop. "I felt like I had come home. It was where I belonged, what I'd been looking for . . . I felt ecstatic." She became involved in feminist spirituality and turned her attention to the Goddess. "When I first started," she remembers, "I saw the word 'goddess' as being a metaphor for nature. I think now it's more an understanding of feminine energy that I would qualify as nurturing and powerful and also terrifying in her destructive aspects — all the elements of the universe in a very powerful feminine entity who has a thousand ways of being manifested. For me, emotionally, she is personified in the moon." As part of her personal search for the Goddess, Anderson has created an ongoing series of "Full Moon Rituals." She has also sought the company of other women similarly committed to feminist spirituality.

Starr Goode is a poet and spokesperson for feminist spirituality. She is a founding member of Goddess Project LA, originally a month-long arts festival dedicated to the creative spirit of the Goddess. For the last six years, she has produced the cable television series "The Goddess in Art." As moderator of this program, she has interviewed numerous notable scholars and artists in the field of feminist spirituality. Her series has been used in university courses throughout the country. Goode's poetry has appeared in *We'Moon*, *Squaw Valley Anthology*, *Return of the Goddess 1993*, *High Performance*, and other publications.

Together, Anderson and Goode write of how they use art, poetry and ritual to build community and structure the spiritual underpinnings of their lives.

A Gaia Hypothesis

In Paleolithic Europe
an ancestor carved the figure
of a woman in limestone and
the art of sculpture began.
What is the need of our time?
To be in a sacred fabric,
to have a place,
like the shakti woman in the tree
or like Laksmi floating on a lotus?
The elephants bathe her life giving waters.

Has the drama passed from us,
are the lights in the sky sacred
but not the earth?
Is there a god out there
who created the world once
then despised it?
Or is the earth alive and creating herself,
an ocean clad,
mountain breast goddess
from whose smoky caves
comes the life force!

I am tired of science
as a religion
and starved for a new story
from the cleansing North wind.
I long for the call of the white she bear
dancing on an ice floe.
Her green eyes know the way
of the blue water rimmed with star moss.

In a village in Czechoslovakia,
an old woman died. After her burial
the village was abandoned.
Years later,
her remains were discovered;
she had a broken jaw
and a fox bone in her hand.
Also found was
a face carved from stone,
a serene, crooked face.
You can hold her in your hand,
you can call her Crooked Fox,
she is thirty thousand years old.

When the moon begins waxing full, my energy takes on a new excitement. I know that soon I will be sleeping on the earth, out of the concrete of the city, under the healing, cleansing rays of the full moon. When I am at my chosen spot for the month, I wait anxiously as I watch the eastern sky begin to lighten. Time stands still as the stars take over the sky's magic. What is this strange intensity I feel towards this heavenly body at this particular time in her cycle? I have no rational explanation. What I do know is that this is my time—my link to the universe—my solitude; my connection to the spiritual forces. This is my time—with my whole being—to understand the ancient ways, the ways of honoring the earth as life holder, the ways of honoring and finding joy in each expression of life, the ways of honoring women and children, the ways of knowing the interweaving and spiral connection of all life. Under the moon a sense of oneness with nature permeates my body I call upon the spirits of the air, the fire, the water and the earth to be with me. I call upon Selene, Moon Goddess of wisdom to be with me. This is my time of introspection, of seeking and knowing my innermost self. It is a time of tears, joy, anger, love and reconciliation, a time when I come away with a sense of wholeness.

In WICCA, as in many earth centered religions, sacred–safe space is cast–created by invoking–honoring the four elements - earth, fire, air and water. Once a circle– sacred space is cast, spiritual work can begin. The elements become a focal point for transformation and spiritual process. I am invited to participate in an exhibit about women and community. My art is to be about women, community and the sacred. I decide to create a room–circle which will hold sacred space – a space in which the viewer can feel safe, become active participant, and experience the individual elements as transformative powers. To initiate the spectator for this experience, I decide upon poetry for the outside walls of the installation which will invoke a meditative/ thoughtful/playful/open state of mind as one enters. The women I ask to join me to present this space are as different as the elements themselves. We come from different spiritual paths, different cultural backgrounds, different ethnic make up and different artistic processes. What we have in common is a deep commitment to this earth, to all that exists upon it and to the empowerment of women. Together we create ritual, explore our private beliefs and make art. The room, angular and linear on the outside with poetry painstakingly hand stenciled on the outer walls, undulates on the inside with low flickering lights, seeping water, mysterious female body shapes and the circular. A pillow for meditation, a sound track of women chanting, this room senses of the magical. In the center of this room, the busyness of our lives disappears and time stands still. Alone with the air, the fire, the water and the earth, there is a sense of the interweaving. One woman's response: "I am in an abusive marriage. I am trying to finish my B.A. in order to support myself and my children. This morning was a really awful morning and I felt like the abuse would never end. I walked into that room and remembered that women can be powerful."

The winter holiday draws near. I approach the circle of my sisters with anticipation. I know that we will be doing healing, cleansing work We will honor this season of the

Source: The Spirits of the Air, Fire, Water and Earth   299

dark's triumph even as we welcome the return of the sun. We will journey inward. We will chant together, seek the ancient ways together, call upon the spirits of the air, fire, water and earth together. We will call upon the Goddesses of the Winter Sun. It is a time of introspection, of seeking and knowing our innermost selves. We will exchange delightful gifts of the winter solstice. From one member, a trophy for each of us with a witch flying on a broom in full glittering painted plastic. From another, a sculpture of Medusa and yet another, fanny packs decorated with spirals, stars and moons. More gifts of handmade books, candles and cups all about our particular identity as a circle. It is a time of tears, joy, anger, love and reconciliation. We come away with a sense of wholeness.

A member's father has died. We come together to guide her through this transition. She has gathered several dozen stones from her father's garden. We begin by casting sacred–safe space in that same garden. We call upon the spirits of the air, fire, water and earth. We call upon Hecate, a Greek Goddess of the crossroads. We assist our sister on a guided meditation to seek within herself her deepest knowing of her father's well-being on the other side, knowing that we all came to this beautiful earth to live; we all came to this beautiful earth to die. We guide her to the center of the river that separates the living from those who have passed over. We invite her father from the other side to meet with her. She truly understands that he is content. She returns to our time and space. She takes the stones and one by one lays them in a spiral on the earth, each stone representing an attribute or way of being of her father of which she would let go, such as his critical judgements of her, his inability to take her goals seriously. She picks up the stones, one by one, washes them and places them in a pot. This time each stone represents an attribute or way of being of her father which she wants to honor and remember about him, such as his love of gardening, his sense of humor and pursuit of the intellectual. A year later, she will take the stones to his graveside and do a solitary ritual.

Water Movements

I. A Creation Myth

Before all beginnings
was a black bird hovering over
darkness,
its cold eyes, a mouth
like a circle
out of which poured
the first creation:
water in all directions.
Next there were four quarters,
four points in which to create

a cycle,
a way of becoming,
a way of creating
the beauty of the physical world.

II. Where Are Our Lives Now?

Tonight my nerves are bad.
My dreams are filled
with the darkest of images:
a dark day in the middle
of the afternoon,
murky shapes floating
on the surface of the sea.
They are coming ashore.

III. Where Have We Been?

Lepenski Vir,
on the banks of the Danube,
we carve our fish stones
to the wet Lady.
This stone is for the altar
that stands at the end
of the blood red floor.

IV. Myths To Live By

The history of religion
is the history of symbols.
Some examples:
A curtain of Fate arches over us,
exalting us,
condemning us.
Will it give us
another chance?

The Gaia conspiracy–
it's the little bacteria
that are running the show;
they are the earth goddess.
All life regulates
for their survival.
Our bodies are but a shell
for their pleasure.

V. Myth of Departure

Over the rolling seas
across the water to the west
our funeral ship
sails in a fading light.
We leave our bodies for the birds,
then our white bones for the hypogeum.
We go as our ancestor went
on the final journey
of our souls as they are now.

VI. Myth of Return

White Lady of death,
lover carved of bone,
take me inside your stiff embrace.
Or will you appear as a bird or a snake,
perhaps a beautiful woman.

Lady with no eyes,
take this death
into your chrysalis belly.
The magic womb makes life
come again, in the wet
spring morning.

Her first encounter with the runes was accidental. She was doing some research on ancient Sun Goddesses, reading the material available from Scandinavia on the runic alphabet. She discovered that the 16th rune, Sowilo, stood for the Sun Goddess Herself. She was hooked. What was the Sun Goddess doing in the middle of an alphabet supposedly sacred to a warrior people worshiping a sky god? How had the Goddess come to remain a part of the sacred alphabet? As she looked at the accepted meanings for the oldest form of the runes, she felt a kind of vertigo. Here were all the same symbols she had learned to associate with the Goddess and Her diverse aspects and Epiphanies. Was it possible that the mysteries of the Great Goddess, originally transmitted in rock carvings, and oral tradition, had led to the development of a "Goddess language" that had simply become associated at a much later date with the new runic alphabet? By re-examining the runic alphabet could an ancient Scandinavian view of the Goddess and Her world be recovered? Certain themes began to grow clearer. Each rune represented a cluster of related ideas, together weaving a picture she could begin to identify. She came to this work both as an artist working intuitively with symbols and as a modern priestess of the Goddess, a member of the circle, familiar with the changing cycles of nature. Soon she was compelled to write a book; she calls it *Lady of the Northern Light: A Feminist Guide to the Runes.*

A member teaches the old ways, the traditional ways of the earth. She reaches out to help women learn to create safe–sacred space. She travels with them on their personal journeys of heroism, seeing how the ancient ways bring the sacred of the feminine to their current everyday lives. Together they call upon the spirits of the air, the fire, the water and the earth. They do healing, cleansing work, learn to trust their bodies, learn their deepest knowing. They learn the wheel of the year, the agricultural holidays, the high holidays based upon the seasons. Together they chant, learn new songs, laugh and experience ritual. They share tears, joy, anger, love and reconciliation. They come away with a sense of wholeness.

> Equinox
> Sit at Donegal Bay,
> the white dunes and healing
> sea air.
> forget the pain in your head
> and that you are all alone
> and lonely.
> Forget the machine guns at
> the border,
> the soldiers that made you
> wait
> while they took apart your
> car's spare tire.
> Just know that you are alive.
> It is a glorious autumn day,
> the sky stately with clouds,
> the ocean gently rocking,
> the mountains calm and
> peaceful.
> Forget your despair.
> Thank nature for your life.
> Thank the spirit in the grass
> for its beauty and resilience.
> forget all your hopelessness,
> the tears that stain your blue
> blouse.

Thank the shadows on the
mountains;
there are some who cannot
live in light.
Thank the shoes that are on
your feet
for having carried you this far.
Thank whatever mystery is to
be
when this day is gone
and so are you.

She is many breasted. She is the great nurturer in a modern waitress uniform. She stands silent and stoic at the center of the restaurant. Around her, dozens of customers demand attention and food from the single mortal waitress who runs from table to table while drawing strength and patience from Her. She is a contemporary Goddess in the video, Our Lady of L.A., a collaboration by three members. The lights during the filming are constant. She must stand perfectly still for over an hour. She faints. She is revived. She takes a short break. True to the Goddess whose role she is enacting she returns to her pose to finish the taping. Our Lady of L.A.: modern day Goddesses in the images of Kuan Yin, Diana of Ephesus, Coatlicue, the Venus of Willendorf and the birth of Venus all set in the Los Angeles landscape interspersing with artists interviews. Our Lady of L.A. is a search for the Goddess in the contemporary urban environment–of how the Goddess is found and worshipped in Los Angeles.

A member is nervous under the hot bright lights, time is suspended, altered as she watches the cameraman's fingers count off 5-4-3-2-1 and then the finger points to her: it has begun, her twentieth show of The Goddess in Art. She has interviewed many of the great ones and feels privileged to talk to the artists and scholars who have influenced this international movement of consciousness about the Goddess. Tonight before her is Starhawk, author of The Spiral Dance, a seminal book on earth based pagan ritual and the quintessential image in Goddess cosmology of the ebb and flow of the sacred life energy. Moderator and guest have met for the first time, just minutes before the taping. Once begun, the show is live, there is no editing, no going back, the race is on to fill 28 minutes with all it can hold. She has no notes, only all that has sunk into her mind from the last few weeks of reading all of her guest's books and distilled in her imagination. She decides to go for the controversy. "Starhawk, the Pope tried to fire you from the Catholic college you were teaching at; how does it feel to be censured by the Pope?" "Well, I felt like little Frodo Baggins in the Lord Of The Rings when he says, 'How did the name of Baggins come before the great Dark Lord?'" The show ends as Starhawk sums up the future, "The next ten years are crucial in deciding the fate of our planet and what the quality of life will be for the centuries, even millennium. We still have a chance if we act now."

A member of the circle is facing a hysterectomy. We gather together. Her life partner and extended family members join us. We call upon the spirits of the air, fire, water and earth. We call upon Glispa, the Great Navajo heroine who brought healing, beauty and chant to her people. We call upon Hsi Wang Ma, the highest Goddess of ancient China who cured disease. We call upon Hera, ancient Greek Goddess of women, their sexuality and aging. We lay her in the center of the circle. We guide her on a visualization that she might open to a sense of love and trust. We focus our energies upon the healing process. For nearly an hour, we chant to her, drumming a cleansing beat. We sing to her, songs of community and love. We touch her, a laying on of the hands. We resolve together to alter reality by filling her soul with our love and healing intentions. We center our thoughts upon a successful operation. we end by celebrating and affirming the wisdom and honor of age. We crown her crone: wise woman.

The little girl is made of flatware, springs, keys, hardware and kitchen utensils. She clatters as she is led across the stage, throwing the broken egg into the sky. A cackle is heard. The witch–body parts made from sheep shears, barbecue forks and head from a raccoon skull–flies by. The audience, all adults, laughs. The member, invisible behind the stage backdrop, pulls the strings to manipulate the puppets. The magic is working; the puppets are alive; the strings are staying disentangled. For the production Icons and Other Strangers, she has recreated the folktale of the little girl and the witch. In the story, the townsfolk tell the little girl not to give the egg shells to the witches but she does anyway. Later, when she is trapped on an island during a flood, the witch flies by in a boat made from the egg shell and rescues the little girl. Together they fly through the sky in the boat.

Walking into the room, one immediately notices the wonderful smell of leaves and wood. The room is painted a deep green. Shavings and sawdust cover the floor. A soundtrack has forest sounds and interviews with people talking about their relationship with the forest and sounds of clearcutting. We are in an indoor forest. We are in Spirit of Place: Clear Cut Memories, part of The Forest Project. The member who created this interactive installation is present to chat with the viewer. Here we are reminded that Earth's first temples were the forests where we knew the kinship of owl, fox and deer, where we could know ourselves as a part of that great interdependent cycle of life, death and rebirth that spanned the generations. We are asked to re-member our own experience of the forest, of a tree — reawaken the points of contact. We are asked to participate by imprinting our hand on a paper leaf and writing a memory of a tree on it and then hang the paper leaf on the wall for others to read. We are further asked to participate by filling a bag with sawdust left over from clearcutting and attach it to a postcard we are to sign. The postcard will be hand delivered to the Chair of the House Interior Committee, Morris Udall with the help of The Wilderness Society to emphasize the need to permanently protect the remaining Ancient Forests. As we leave we are charged with the knowledge that each time we share our memories of our own relationships with trees, something sacred inside ourselves is reawakened and revalued.

The Mystery of Coming to Earth

Under a sky layered in blue,
I feel a power, until the wind
comes and dries me out,
makes my shoulder ache.
My body is living and dying.
Standing barefoot in the low tide algae,
I don't want to be a part of nature.
Decay is for others.
I am condensed light
broken into colors.
Let nature be — orchids in a vase,
not the black beetles lumbering
like old Buicks across the dirt,
not the sparrows that cry the end
of this day then suddenly,
are silent.
Serve me up
on an altar of mysteries,
and don't let me crack.
The birds turn their backs to me
and fly into the west.
Out of nowhere, more appear
in the sky above my head.

A member plans for six months an event that will take place in one evening. She has dreamed of producing this event for five years. It is a lecture about and a book signing for Dr. Marija Gimbutas' magnum opus, *The Civilization of the Goddess*. It is the culmination of her life's work, the capstone of an impressive body of scholarship that documents the peaceful artful society of Old Europe ruled over by the Goddess or the soul of nature. The member wants to give something back to a woman who is over 70 years old and has spent a lifetime in struggle and recently poor health to write the truth that has become the sturdy foundation from which feminist spirituality rises. It is an immeasurable debt. Finally the evening arrives. No one has seen the book yet. There is a sense of history in the air. The member wonders, will all her decisions prove to be right? Will people come? Will they buy the book? Will Marija see how she is loved? Will she see how she has earned the gratitude of women and men interested in the fate of the earth? The hall is filled with flowers and art; people begin to arrive. The tickets are sold out. The book sells out. People sit in the aisles — lean against walls. Dr. Gimbutas arrives on the stage and receives a standing ovation from the audience of over 700. She gives the speech of a lifetime, "I spent thirty years reading thousands of books, visiting hundreds of museums, years supervising the dig at Achilleion, a decade of writing . . . my book is not a novel." All are ecstatic. Is it so strange that the many generations represented at this event, all of whom have grown up under the weight of two world wars, the cold war and the threat of nuclear annihilation would seek a new way of being and find an ancient model in Old Europe — a civilization that did not make weapons of war, but turned its energy to life.

Two members collaborate to produce a video installation exploring the fragile balance of our earth's ecosystem. They look at creation myths from around the world and how they effect the people who live by each story's specific ethics. They explore how these stories teach a different way of being upon the earth; a different way of interacting with the earth, its creatures and its peoples. One story they choose is of Mawu, the creatrix from the Dohemy tribes of West Africa. Because of Mawu there exists the Sekpoli — soul — which is a broader understanding of soul than western theology offers. In the Dohemy tribes, it is because of the existence of the Sekpoli, as a part of Mawu in every person, that aggression and fighting are wrong. Thus those who are wise, treasure the Sekpoli in each and know that it is from Mawu, only Mawu, that we receive the gift of the breath of life.

A member creates a performance about her mother who has Alzheimer's Disease. She weaves the stories of her mother's past and present as she walks a narrow path while invoking the spirits of the air, the fire, the water and the earth. She tells of her mother's inability to recognize family members. She tells stories such as her mother's confusion of the daughter, thinking that she is a secretary to the father and accusing them of having an affair. She agonizes over the loss of her mother to such a bizarre state of mind. She honors the life of her mother. She tells stories such as her mother's commitment in prayer to restore her daughter's hearing. She tells the story of her mother's one time relationship with a woman as she begins to understand her own lesbian identity. Slides, bigger than life, follow her mother's youth and flowering while the member simultaneously creates an installation on the floor and asks "Why hast thou forsaken me?" She recognizes the beauty and the pain of her mother. She ends the performance by lighting a candle to her.

Source: The Spirits of the Air, Fire, Water and Earth

Reunion in L.A.

At your funeral, where were you?
Strange to think
that you were in that expensive coffin,
that your body which walked upon this earth
forty seven years and bore one child
was in that cramped space.
Still, you don't need to breathe now.
is your spirit everywhere?
I am thinking of my own wasted life.
Last night in a dream you visited me,
said you had been
in a library, learning things.
We were as close as in the beginning.

Right now,
there are no diversions from death.
Two days after the funeral, our city is in flames.
The calendar marks the midway point of spring
and the May fires are lit.
I see how much I have left to fate. I know
my death is near;
it causes such intense anxiety,
I may die right now from fear.
Against this terror, I roll on the floor and cry out
as if to a lover, for my life to come and take me.

The curfew settles on the grimy city.
At the ocean's edge, there is much physical beauty:
a soft light of fairy gold and green,
the wind, the trees,
a hillside full of flowers.
With people banned from the beach, the dolphins return to
Santa Monica Bay.
I know myself to be in the presence of a vast turning.
Irreplaceable things are passing;
each of us plays our part.
I have reconciled with those from whom I was estranged
and count myself blessed for such a chance,
that I am still alive.

A member climbs the ladder to take her place. Minutes ago she was ravenous, gulping down a plateful of food; shoveling in mouthfuls of endurance. Now she wonders why she has created yet another performance which requires that she tackle her fear of heights, not to mention that she has to schlepp this ladder all over the country while taking the performance on tour. She takes her pose, the lights find her: she is Eve in the garden; she is the dead Christ on the dead tree; she is a hanging corpse of a woman accused of witchcraft; she is in the midst of a burning bush, a woman accused of having made a pact with the devil; she is the dead Christ on the lap of Mary; she is the snake airing its way up the tree of life. She wonders, will people understand how badly the Church has damaged the tree of life? How badly it has damaged the bodies of women? Will they understand that she is taking in these images, trying them on and throwing them off? This is My Body is above all a declarative sentence, stating the very fact of having a female body.

Two members of the circle are life partners. In a ceremony they sit in the center of the circle. They are about to become mothers. In May the twins will be born – two girls to enter the circle. Each priestess, in turn, offers a blessing to the unborn babies: a promise to teach the ways of the moon, a prayer for the new sisters to be close to each other all their lives, in the mysterious intimacies of twins. All the wishes are placed tenderly in a black egg and a blue egg, one for each. Later, at the birth, the circle will attend the mothers, chanting in the hospital halls, anointing the doctors with holy water from the cave of Elitheia, ancient Goddess of childbirth. Finally, after two days of labor – the miraculous cries. The twins are weighed, measured, held by all of the circle. From the first day of their lives on this earth, the babies are imprinted by loving hands that they are part of a community.

Two Cards On My Desk

The first is a card -
blank inside if one were to open it -
whose cover is a detail of a kimono sleeve
in muted fall colors -
gold yellow and brown chrysanthemums.
It will be sent to a woman
whose husband died suddenly
in a car accident.
I remember her brown eyes - burning and moist -
just last week thanking me at the death ritual
of a mutual friend.
I do not know with what words to fill
that inside blank space.

Source: The Spirits of the Air, Fire, Water and Earth

The other card is a white bootie
with a pink bow,
inside is an invitation to a baby shower.
Two little girls are about to be born
into this world of transitory shapes.
They will enter by way of pain
and compression,
squeezed down a dark hole
into a totally alien world
- a universe beyond
the soft waters where
the heartbeat of their creatrix
is always present.
But after the suffering and the blood,
they will be placed in their mother's arms.
She will enfold them back
to the familiar beating of her heart.
Peace, for now, will be restored.

What awaits the tragic victim
of the other card,
I do not know.
After the dark transformation,
the loss once again of all that is familiar,
is there another mother waiting
to protect and guide us,
to initiate us into that final mystery?
And will there be another heartbeat
that we have heard all along
but did not know its source?
So sure,
so steady,
so pervasive,
that we were unconscious
of its presence and only
when all the trappings and distractions
of the vanished world have departed,
only then,
do we know completely

the guidestar that has been with us
from the beginning -
the heartbeat of the Mother
calling all into creation and passing,
calling us back
to her unfathomable waiting arms.

The members of the circle talk about their identity. Who are they in the community of women? How do they want to serve it? They have been given a rare opportunity but it has risks. What should they do? What do they want to do? A journalist wants to put them on the cover of the largest alternative paper in the country, the *LA Weekly*, she wants to do an extensive profile of the circle which would include lengthy interviews with each member and a group photo on the cover with the word "witches" underneath it. It is out of the broom closet for sure if they agree. Some are afraid of what their families will think. Some are afraid they will lose their jobs. Some are afraid of the violence of hate. Perhaps that is the final reason they all decide, each one, to do the article and take the risk of exposure: to replace ignorance with education. They want to say in a large public forum, "We are not devil worshippers. We love the earth, the creative spirit of the life force. We follow the ways of the earth, the changing seasons through time. We celebrate the wheel of the year in her many moods; Solstice to Equinox, Beltane to Samhain." The new year begins with the publication of their story.

Together we create art, family, ritual. Together we follow the threads of each other's lives. We make up ritual to help a member weave together those threads when they become entangled. Separately we create art, family, ritual. Separately we follow the threads of each other's lives. Separately we weave our own threads. We reach out to others, we create art and ritual with others. Coming back together, we are family. We honor one another and the ancient ways. We honor the earth. Together we are Nemesis. Together we are a coven.

Jill D'Agnenica — Look for Angels

by Betty Ann Brown

The act of looking for angels is an exalting gesture.

April 29, 1993 — the first anniversary of the Los Angeles riots. Jill D'Agnenica and her husband Michael drove into South Central, along the burned scars of the uprising. Initially, Jill had thought she'd place Angel #1 at the corner of First and Normandy, where the riots supposedly began, but she realized that to focus on where the chaos surfaced would validate the media infatuation with violence. Then she remembered the First AME Church, which she knew was a center of healing for the city, They headed for the church.

Jill had originally intended to place the angels alone, anonymously, in the middle of the night. But that night, she'd been exhausted and slept through the first alarm. It wasn't until just before dawn that she and her husband filled the back of the truck with magenta putti and started driving. They arrived at the church just as the sun was coming up, just as it illuminated the banner over the sanctuary door: "Brothers, Come Help Us, Stop the Madness." Jill knew the bold words were a sign that what she was doing was right. Michael selected the site for the four angels. She placed and photographed them, aware that the art work was already a collaboration.

A year after the Los Angeles uprisings, conceptual artist Jill D'Agnenica began depositing bright magenta plaster angels around the city of Los Angeles. Although she initiated the project alone, the artist soon realized she needed a community of co-creators to help accomplish her goal of ten angels per square mile of city territory. Throughout 1993 and 1994, she and a growing army of volunteers distributed angels on street corners, at bus stops, in front of buildings, beside freeway offramps, and at numerous other locations within the city limits. D'Agnenica's intention was to leave these angels throughout the entire city, to be happened upon by motorists and passersby and adopted by interested parties. But as the project progressed, people sought after the angels more and more. Awareness grew that the candy-colored putti were random messengers of blessing, to be highly cherished by those who saw or received them.

Each time D'Agnenica or a volunteer placed an angel, it was photographed and its location was recorded. In addition, any special encounter with site or recipient was noted. The resulting documentation was a diverse, alternative and affirmative portrait of the city so often characterized by the disasters it suffers rather than by the spirit with which it survives them.

What follows is my personal account of one of the days I drove with D'Agnenica to distribute and document angels.

Jill D'Agnenica's Angels Project

July 10, 1994. When I got there, people were already working, loading the angels into the backs of several pick-up trucks. For you to understand what that sentence really means, I need to describe the angels. They're gaudy. They're candy-colored putti with crossed legs and coy smiles. They're bright, hot pink. Screaming magenta. A color that, out of context, looks so kitschy, artificial, and, well, *tacky*, that when I first saw an angel, months ago, I just groaned to myself. But my friend Nancy Jones had told me she'd gone out with D'Agnenica to place angels and that the color, surprisingly, looked great against foliage, surrounded by cement, bracketed by brick. I wasn't convinced, but I decided to withhold judgement until I went out with Jill myself.

So there I was, driving up on the scene of a half dozen people loading hot pink angels into the group of pick-up trucks clustered around Jill's Brewery Building studio. I'd made the mistake of wearing a white shirt and immediately wondered if the hot pink pigment would stain my fabric. But Jill told me not to worry — she had hot pink tee shirts for us all to wear. I climbed the rickety stairs to her studio bathroom and exchanged the hot pink shirt for my white one, then commenced loading angels. Not only were they candy-colored, they were also candy-feeling. The acrylic paint in which Jill had dipped them was glossy and sticky, as if the putti were sugar-coated. Their chubby seated bodies formed irregular S-curves when laid on their sides, so they looked like they were snuggling together on the foam rubber pad in the back of the truck. Jill and I loaded in about fifty for our day's work; that meant we were going to put out the last of the third thousand angels.

Jill D'Agnenica is an artist who lives in the artists' community based in an old brewery in downtown Los Angeles. One day she was driving west on the 10 freeway, staring straight at the city. "It popped into my head that I should put these little angels around. I had painted one already, one I'd bought at a party supply store, and placed it in various places in my studio. It looked great everywhere. . . . So that day I realized I wanted to put them all around. I started on . . . the first anniversary of the Los Angeles riots . . . at dawn. . . . We photographed them with the sun coming up behind them. It was sublime!"

The concept for the project came in a flash. Jill would create ten angels per square mile of the city territory, a total of 4687 angels in all. That's a pretty formidable number, so formidable in fact that Jill immediately realized that she would need to use the most basic sculptural technology possible to create the angels — casting them in plaster — and she also realized she would need help, lots of it. So she applied for and won a couple of grants and began recruiting volunteers to help her place the angels throughout the city.

As she did with me and the other people who worked that Sunday, Jill invited all of her volunteers to her studio home, fed us breakfast, clothed us in tee shirts (the uniform of the 1990s), and sat us down to brief us on the process. She started out by explaining that what we were about to do was technically illegal. That is, legally, you weren't supposed to place objects on public or private property. But nobody seemed to mind. In fact, as I was to find that very day, lots of people were thrilled to receive the candy putti. Some even helped, like the police officers who escorted her through the ruins of the Northridge Meadows apartment buildings a few days after the earthquake. Even those who seemed fairly neutral were often curious, she said, which was why she had printed up pink post cards which explained the project, which we were welcome to distribute, along with the pink bumper stickers that said "look for angels."

Our mission was to find places for the angels, put them there, photograph them, and record, in the carefully organized ring binder she provided us with, the address of their new site. The addresses would in turn be recorded on a map of Los Angeles through a new computer program a friend of hers was working.[1] Sounded easy enough. We grabbed notebooks, maps of the parts of the city we were to cover, cameras, film, and food and water for the drive, then headed out. I felt like I was departing on some kind of an art round-up. Mostly I wanted to spend the day with Jill. I had admired her work since first seeing it at Claremont Graduate School and wanted to understand better what she had been doing all these months. And I liked Jill, wanted to get to know her better.

We drove down from Jill's studio, exited the Harbor Freeway, turned east, then north onto Avalon. There was a filling station at that first intersection and we pulled in. As we placed the cross-legged angel on top of the Pepsi machine, a man in a van came up to Jill. "Are you the angel woman?" he asked. "I saw you on TV." So we gave him an angel. We documented our actions with photographs, made note of the address, then drove on. And it suddenly seemed as if every street, every corner, every store front beckoned us, sirenlike, to approach and leave an angel. Every place I looked it seemed as if a hot pink angel would "go" and "go" well. A deep green facade, a chartreuse corner, a brick doorway. Emerald leaves promised to frame the angels. Polished windows vowed to reflect them. Bright, animated murals swore they would oversee and protect any angels we left in their keeping. So we did. Then we photographed the angels in front of forests of walls and swamps of doors, recorded their new dwellings, and drove on.

But even more than the mute bidding of the architecture, we and the angels responded to the articulate asking of the buildings' inhabitants. Let me tell you about three instances. The first was a tangerine apartment building crowding a corner and covered with graffiti. I wanted to place a single angel below the arc of sprayed letters. But as I arranged it below the defiant alphabetic tag, the building's tenants noticed and came down to ask what I was doing. As it happened, they were all recently arrived from Mexico and spoke little English. As it happens, I speak a lot of Spanish. So we spoke.

I told them, those first spirited children, that Jill was an artist who had made these angels as little gifts (*regalitos*) to the city of Los Angeles. I told them that we had placed the angel on the sidewalk near their building as a gift to them. "For us?" they enquired dubiously. "For us? Can we have it?" And Jill and I decided to gift them, individually, with angels. So we gave each of those first three an angel, and photographed them with their angels, and recorded their names and the address on Avalon Boulevard. And as we did that, three other children came out, more timid than the first, to ask for their angels. Then two more. Then five from down the street. Then two men who'd been working on their car and watching the activities approached us and asked for angels. Then they brought a third friend whose wife was in the hospital. "She's really spiritual," he smiled. "She'll love this. I'll take it right to her." With rolls of film exposed and our truck carrying a much lighter load, we left that corner twenty minutes later. I was excited because speaking Spanish in this country always animates me and also because I kept thinking that it might very well have been the first time a Euroamerican gave, freely gave, anything to those children. How lucky I was, I thought, to have been able to share in that giving. Those tacky little figures, their fat legs crossed under their pudgy fingers, weren't just *regalitos*, I realized. They were blessings.

A few blocks north of the apartment building, we drove up to an intense kelly-colored structure circled by shrubs. As we passed the front, we saw that it was a church, so we stopped, certain that angels should adorn it. When we got out of the car, we heard the service echoing through the open windows. The congregants were shouting their responses to the preacher, who expressed his truths more and more intensely. As we lingered, debating where to place the angels, how many, how to photograph them, the dialogue reached a feverish pitch. I wanted to stay. I wanted to share the feelings. But Jill reminded me that we had dozens more angels to distribute. So, after sheltering a pair of angels beneath the bushes, we continued our journey.

We took a detour. A woman in the area had seen Jill featured on CBS "Good Morning" and called the artist to ask for an angel. The woman wasn't going to be there that afternoon, but had instructed Jill to leave an angel with her neighbor, Rose. We turned west off Avalon onto Rose's street and started checking the house numbers. Rose's was a small white house with a trim garden. We walked up to the barred door and knocked, then hollered through the dark screen that we had been sent by her neighbor to deliver some angels. She opened the screen, apologizing that she was conditioning her hair with beer, which was why it was damp and swept against her skull. We reassured her that we conditioned our hair as well, then accepted her invitation to enter. Her house was lined with photographs. They blanketed the walls and cluttered every horizontal surface, even the wooden expanses of the dining room table. When we complimented her on some of them, she told us that she'd been horribly depressed, feeling so alone, so lonely. Then her preacher asked her if she still had photographs of her family, especially of those who'd passed on. He instructed her to bring them all out of their boxed hideaways and surround herself with them. Now there is not one spare foot of space not inhabited by images of her family. Dead and alive, they all live with Rose, and her depression is gone.

Now an angel lives with her, too.

As we left Rose's house and drove back toward Avalon, we passed a yard that virtually screamed for angels. The yard was faced with a picket fence and the fence was covered with crocheted doilies and baskets and dolls and hats made by the woman who lived there. When I say covered, I mean it literally: This was truly an example of intentional visual redundancy. Layer upon layer of brilliant colorful objects fluttered over the fence, like immense petals. They were for sale; this craft work was being displayed as a kind of porch-front market. We knew that an angel would feel quite comfortable there. When we drove up and parked, we found a Salvadoran family so shy and withdrawn in English that it was a relief to be able to reach out to touch them in Spanish.

Back on Avalon, down a few blocks, we found a fence displaying the same aesthetic of abundance and overlap: but this time it was dozens of baseball hats. (Which reminds me that I haven't mentioned when we drove by the baseball field and put the putti in the forest green bleachers to the roars of the other fans.)

As we ended our trek, we drove by a truck full of watermelons. Their deep green skins screamed for companionship. for a pink angel to snuggle happily in their midst. Across the street was an office with "City of Los Angeles" in an arc of golden letters over the reflective surface of a dormer window. We sat an angel there, and I thought about how the photograph, capturing the angel below an official announcement of the presence of the city, caught so much of the essence of the work Jill is doing.

The angels are gifts the artist and her many diverse volunteers are lucky enough to be able to give to their urban environment, which includes both the people and the places which receive their magenta blessings. Creating a network, however open and ephemeral, across this immense city, they serve to unify it in symbols of generosity — in marked contrast to the usual symbols of our urban angst.

But the angels are also the currency of exchange between the artist and her volunteers. They unite us, even as they unite us with the city. We become, for a moment, members of an alternative community, a community based not on profit or gain or judgment, but of shared effort, shared generosity. We come together to share the process, share the traveling, share the giving, and then as the day ends, we come together to share our stories about our day of angels.

In both respects, as the material of a network of generosity strewn momentarily across the face of this troubled city and as the stuff of an ephemeral community of workers, collaborators, co-creators of new and different stories of exchange, the angels stand as art that creates dialogue and builds community. These new ways of relating, these new ways of working and talking and being together, through generosity of the angels exchange, these are the art of Jill D'Agnenica's work. These, not the singular experience of an isolated angel in its candy-colored physicality, these are what make the angels effective art.

Jill D'Agnenica's Angels project, South Central Los Angeles, 1994.

Jill D'Agnenica

Jean ~
To a future of
intersections.
Much love
~ Jill

Coda: Continuing

In January 1985, I left a stable job in academic administration to move my unemployed husband and 8-month old son to Madrid, Spain, where I ran a university "study abroad" program. It was a wondrous year. We traveled, made friends, ate incredible food, saw blindingly good art. It was also a terrible year. My son was ill several times, and we never found medical care we felt comfortable with. My husband went into severe culture shock and became virtually nonfunctional. The students, almost all from homes of privilege, were often spoiled and intolerant. I remember one phone call in the middle of the night. "Betty, we're in jail. We met some guys at a disco and came out here to their country villa and, can you believe it, they tried to get sexy with us. So we told them to drive us back to Madrid and we got in a car wreck. Now we're in jail. What should we do?" About that time, my son woke and cried out in fear. We were scheduled to take the entire group of students on a long field trip early the next day.

When we returned to Los Angeles in January of the next year, we had no place to live, no jobs, no money. My marriage was ending. My husband was to face almost another whole year of unemployment. I got a job, then a second job, then a third while supporting the family and doing all of the child care. Disoriented, overworked, frightened, far from the broken home of my childhood, I was in desperate need of the kind of support only a community can provide.

My friend Joan Hugo, the editor who had given me my first art criticism assignment, called to ask if I might consider joining the board of directors of the Los Angeles Woman's Building. It might be a great way for you to reconnect, she said, not realizing how very right she was.

I went to a board recruitment party one night in Hollywood and was surprised to see so many old friends there, artists whose work I'd admired, scholars I'd shared podiums with, writers I'd published with. I joined the board, joined a group of about a dozen women whose accomplishments and commitments to feminism were inspiring. There was an anthropologist who had spent years doing field work in Africa, adopted two young African girls, and now spends much of her time (when not in the classroom) in zealous political action. There was a musician/song writer who was, while on the board, to produce a music video that raises women's self-esteem by honoring a diverse range of female role models. There was a scholar of Spanish Renaissance history, an executive from a major corporation, a therapist, a caterer. There were artists. (You may be thinking that the presence of artists on the board of arts organizations is a given, but in fact very few of the major museums in this country have artists on their boards.)

We worked together, ate together, did consciousness-raising together, traveled together. We sponsored a dozen art exhibits, dozens of classes and lectures, a symposium on feminist criticism that opened to a standing-room-only crowd. We flew to New Mexico to study women's art, then to Chicago. We organized honors ceremonies that moved hundreds of women to tears of fierce pride. After only a few months, I began to feel the embrace of feminist community in a way I'd never experienced before. I remember walking into Woman's Building openings and potlucks and classes and feeling buoyed up by the sense of shared effort. I looked into the faces of the Building staff and board members, gazed around the funky walls of the old brick structure, and felt profound personal pleasure. Validated by our mutual commitment to work, by our ideals and our mission to change the world, I was supported and sustained by the Woman's Building community in a way I have not know before or since.

Our duty as members of the board was to oversee the activities of the Building. I thought this would mean organizing exhibitions and symposia, and it did involve work on such programs, but I soon learned that keeping a non-profit organization going required much more than programming. What it mostly required was financial oversight: paying salaries, paying bills, paying taxes, balancing the books, fundraising. On the heels of that awareness came the realization that previous boards had been, for years, remiss in their duties. Bills hadn't been paid. Taxes hadn't been paid. For years.

I didn't find out about this until my second year on the board, after I had been elected board president. I didn't find it out until I had, through work and play and love and trust, bonded so strongly with the other women on the board that the financial crisis we found ourselves in the middle of became, immediately, a personal crisis. Depressed, we hired an accountant and a lawyer. We attempted extraordinary fundraising projects, tried to sell components of the building, cried. Many of us left when our terms ended; others stayed on. We stopped programming exhibitions and classes. And then the institution ended. Unable to face financial problems in the declining economy of the Reagan/Ford years, the Woman's Building disintegrated. Many of us are still friends, and these friends remain the central core of my writing, teaching, and curating work. But the institution did not endure. When the next generation of women artists recognizes the need for the special support a feminist arts organization can provide them, they will have to build another building, another community, from the ground up.

As I peruse this weaving of words, I realize there is one point I may not have made strongly enough: in order to sustain alternative feminist communities, we need to work consciously, deliberately, and in a committed, ongoing fashion to *continue* the consciousness we have created.[1]

We need to continue to eliminate bias and prejudice. We need to celebrate difference. History has shown us that if we listen to only one (dominant) group, we hear only one kind of solution. But the levels of crisis we face today — the ecological, medical, political and social problems — require as many alternative *and that means creative* solutions as we can produce.[2] If we give voice to only a few, we hear only a few solutions. But if we give voice to, and really listen to all speakers, we hear many suggestions, many solutions. I think again of what Judy Chicago said about redefining leadership. Our leaders must refuse the mantle of authority, if that mantle is woven of mastery and lined with the seductive satin of domination. Leaders must act as facilitators, empowering rather than controlling. Creativity, whether it is casting a sculpture or calculating mathematical formulae or proposing the solution to a social problem, is based on discovery. But discovery is impossible if the outcome is predetermined, and expression of creativity is impossible if people are silenced. As we embrace new identities, build new affinity clusters, live in newly conceived communities, we must continue to work against bias.

We must also continue to tell our stories. Identity-forging and community-building are ongoing processes. There is no fixed, centralized self[3] and there should be no rigid boundaries of inclusion or exclusion defining community. Our identities must be flexible and our borders permeable, to allow the flow of change, which is constant. One of the problems with traditional communities is that they tend to be configured around rigid regulations (I think again of the monastic rules) which do not acknowledge the ever changing nature of human experience. A similar problem has plagued most utopian speculation: idealists have often imagined a static state populated by fixed personae.[4]

As we continue to value the truths of lived experience, and give public authority to the revelations of the private, we must also work to eliminate hierarchy. Like the women who gather for consciousness-raising, we must value all members of our communities equally. In doing so, we will continue to carve out safe spaces for them/us to speak. We will continue to hear the truths of their lives and to know ourselves and our communities through that hearing.

> Without support to help me through my changes, I'm not sure I'd have had the courage to make some of the choices I've made. The community as a whole, and individual members, have always been there to back me up. Outside, I think it's harder to hook into a group that you can count on consistently being there for you. People in mainstream culture tend to be more mobile; relationships peak and fall; there are always distractions. Of course, there's turnover in community, too, but the community endures, and so does the support.[5]

Another thing history has taught us is how easy it is for women's accomplishments to be disregarded, erased, written out of the dominant culture's stories. Judy Chicago said it clearly in our conversation. We can create, and we can create the context for our creations, but until women develop a new relationship to history, all of our work may very well be erased. Always, as we create, we must work to *preserve* our creations.

Gerda Lerner, in her brilliant *The Creation of Feminist Consciousness, From the Middle Ages to Eighteen-seventy*, convincingly argues for the need for ongoing feminist consciousness:

> Creativity became the instrument by which women emancipated themselves intellectually to a level from which they could think their way out of patriarchy . . . women of talent existed, they struggled valiantly, they achieved — and they were forgotten. The women coming after them had to start all over again, repeating the process. . . . It helped individual women to authorize themselves and in some cases to create important works of lasting impact. But what we need to note is the discontinuity of the story of women's intellectual effort. Endlessly, generation after generation of Penelopes rewove the unraveled fabric only to unravel it again.
>
> In order for women to verify the adequacy, even the power, of their own thinking, they needed cultural confirmation, exactly as men did. The mystics and women religious could find such an affirmation in their actual or spiritual communities. Secular women attempted to and sometimes did find it in women's clusters or networks. . . . Out of these clusters of women active in reforms for women, arose the first woman's rights organizations, the National Society for Women's Suffrage in 1867.[6]

Out of the Women's Movement arose creative communities like those discussed in this book. As Lerner insists, we need communities to sustain our feminist vision. We need the safety and support of communities to correct the inequities of patriarchy, to model a world without dominance, to give place to the marginalized and voice to the silenced. If we do not weave the fabric of sisterhood from the many-plied threads of artistic, intellectual, and spiritual connection, then our daughters will face the daunting task of reweaving the world again.[7]

Michelle T. Clinton

Joana Frueh

1975 members of HERA, a women's cooperative gallery:
Top row, L.to R.: Donna Croteau, Alexandra Broches, Pamela Brown, Marlene Malik, Roberta Richman;
Second row: Althea Smith, Constance Greene Alexander, Jacqui Kanis, Frances Hamilton, Merle Barnett, Frances Powers;
Third row: Linnea Toneg Leeming, Martha Cooper, Toby Bornstein, Mary Jane Christofferson, Bernadette Hackett, Elena Jahn (Clough).

1984 members of Front Range: Women in the Visual Arts, photographed for the announcement of the exhibition "A Decade of Women's Art," Boulder Center for the Visual Arts (Colorado).
Standing: Helen Redman, Linda Herritt, Barbara Baer, Fran Metzger, Cath Murphy, Virginia Maitland, Barbara Takenaga, Marilyn Duke, Margaretta Gilboy;
Seated: Meridel Rubenstein, Alice McClelland, Sally Elliott, Sandra Kaplan, Barbara Ball Shark, Virginia Johnson, Geraldine Brussel, Megan Perry; Models: Jerry West, Baby Kevin Baer.

Notes

INTRODUCTION

[1] Harmony Hammond, "Creating Feminist Works," cited in Arlene Raven, "harmonies: Harmony Hammond," reprinted in Raven's *Crossing Over: Feminism and Art of Social Concern* (Ann Arbor/London: UMI Press, 1988).

[2] It is in these dictums that art is first referred to as propaganda. See, for example, Robert Pelfrey with Mary-Hall Pelfrey, *Art and Mass Media* (NY: Harper & Row, 1985) p. 363. "[Propaganda was] originally, part of the name of the Roman Catholic office charged with the propagation (or spread) of the faith."

[3] Robert Rauschenberg, "Tribute 21" pamphlet. (See further reference to this project in the "Conversation with Rachel Rosenthal" in Chapter IV.)

[4] William Raspberry, syndicated columnist for the *Washington Post*, writes eloquently about what he terms the "Crisis of Community" in *Sewanee*, January 1996, pp. 16-21. Although it may be said to have a different resonance in the 1990s, the desire for community is of course nothing new. bell hooks, for example, remembers Martin Luther King's impassioned "Community or Chaos" in her *Teaching to Transgress, Education as the Practice of Freedom* (NY and London, Routledge, 1994).

[5] Russell Fergusson, William Olander, Marcia Tucker, and Karen Fiss, eds., *Discourse: Conversations in Postmodern Art and Culture* (NY: The New Museum of Contemporary Art, 1990).

[6] Suzanne Lacy, "Affinities: Thoughts on an Incomplete History." In, Norma Broude and Mary D. Garrard, eds., *The Power of Feminist Art, The American Movement of the 1970s, History and Impact* (NY: Harry N. Abrams, 1994) p. 268.

[7] Suzanne Lacy, ed. *Mapping the Terrain: New Genre Public Art* (Seattle: Bay Press, 1995).

[8] For example, a collaboration between Faith Wilding and local high school students, scheduled as part of the "House Project" events at the Los Angeles Museum of Contemporary Art in late 1995, too late for our deadline.

[9] I refer you to the Compendium at the end of Suzanne Lacy's anthology (op. cit.), which lists many of the artists here, as well as dozens of others.

[10] Ralph Waldo Emerson, *Emerson's Essays* (NY: Harper & Row, 1951) p. 214.

I   WOMEN'S ART COMMUNITIES IN CONTEMPORARY HISTORY

[1] Much of the criticism leveled at Judy Chicago seems to be due to her gender, which is to say she has been maligned for what is often commended in men. For example, while successful men with aggressive personalities are often praised as "having balls," women with active, assertive characters have often been called "uppity" or "bitches." Male artists who employ numerous assistants to help or even execute their art are called "masters," while women who

work with others yet leave their own names prominent (instead of retiring into the anonymity to which women were traditionally consigned) are called inconsiderate, exploitative, and domineering. Judy Chicago probably has been subject to this kind of double standard more than any other woman artist.

[2] All of the collaborators on the "Dinner Party" were listed and credited in the documentation that preceded entry into the installation itself.

[3] The classic article on what is termed the "male gaze," that is, the presumption of the male viewer in Western culture, is Laura Mulvey's "Visual Pleasure and Narrative Cinema." *Screen* 16, no. 3, Autumn 1975, pp. 6-18.

[4] In Suzanne Lacy, ed, *Mapping the Terrain, New Genre Public Art* (Seattle: Bay Press, 1995) p. 32.

[5] See especially, Norma Broude and Mary D. Garrard, *The Power of Feminist Art, The American Movement of the 1970s, History and Impact.*

[6] Linda S. Klinger, "Where's the Artist? Feminist Practice and Poststructural Theories of Authorship," *Art Journal*, Summer 1991.

[7] In 1972, in a paper delivered to the American Sociological Association, Jacqueline Skiles asserted that the writings of Shulamith Firestone, Robin Morgan, and Judith Hole and Ellen Levine gave "ample documentation of the indignities suffered by women in the New Left on occasion, so it is not hard to understand the marginality of most women artists vis-à-vis the New Left." Skiles argued that instead of trying, with the New Left, to agitate for revolution that would transform the entire culture, the Women Artists Movement began with a goal of equitable inclusion.

[8] A brief but excellent summary of this chronology is found in the "Backtalk" exhibition catalogue published by the Santa Barbara Contemporary Arts Forum in 1993.

[9] Mary D. Garrard, "Feminist Politics: Networks and Organizations." In Broude and Garrard, op. cit. p. 91.

[10] The first all-woman co-op, Gallery 15, opened in NYC in 1958 with 15 members; it lasted only through the following year. Cited in Cynthia Navaretta, *Guide to Women's Art Organizations* (NY: Midmarch Arts Press, 1982) p. 17.

[11] Faith Wilding's *By Our Own Hands, The Women Artist's Movement in Southern California, 1970-1976* (Santa Monica: Double X, 1977) is an excellent summary of the early developments in that area.

[12] See The Guerrilla Girls, *The Confession of the Guerrilla Girls* (NY: Harper Collins, 1995).

[13] Teresa de Laurentis, "Alice Doesn't: Feminism, Semiotics, Cinema," p. 186. Cited in Carolyn Heilbrun, *Writing a Woman's Life* (NY: Ballantine Books, 1988) p. 45.

[14] Broude and Garrard, op. cit., p. 21.

[15] Suzanne Lacy, "Affinities: Thoughts on an Incomplete History." In Broude and Garrard, op. cit., p. 264. Because identity remains central to community-building arts, it is discussed further in Chapter II of this volume.

[16] See Broude and Garrard, op. cit., p. 22, on identity and art making in the 1970s.

[17] According to Coco Fusco, "Even the limited ability one might acquire to alter aspects of one's identity cannot completely obfuscate the impact of outside social, political and economic facts in the constitution of the self." Coco Fusco, *English is Broken Here, Notes on Cultural Fusion in the Americas* (NY: The New Press, 1995) p. 32.

[18] Judy Chicago, *Through the Flower: My Struggle as a Woman Artist* (NY: Doubleday, 1975; NY: Penguin, 1983) p. 80.

[19] Ibid., p. 86.

[20] Ibid., p. 178. Also cited in Judith E. Stein, "Collaborations." In Broude and Garrard, op. cit., p. 228.

[21] Stein, op. cit., pp. 227 passim.

[22] Chicago, op. cit., p. 66.

[23] Lacy, op. cit., p. 264.

[24] Thomas Albright, "Guess who's coming to Judy Chicago's dinner," *ARTnews*, January 1979, pp. 60-64.

[25] Suzi Gablik, *The Reenchantment of Art* (London and NY: Thames and Hudson, 1991) pp. 2-7.

Conversation with Judy Chicago

[1] Sandra Gilbert and Susan Gubar (*The Madwoman in the Attic* (New Haven: Yale University Press, 1979) p. 241, assert that a woman's pseudonym functions "as a name of power, the mark of a private christening into a second self, a rebirth into linguistic primacy." Gerda Lerner (*The Creation of Feminist Consciousness, From the Middle Ages to Eighteen-seventy*, Oxford and NY: Oxford University Press, p. 185) points out that Emily Dickinson had "given up her baptismal name (role definition) which had not been her choice." Since the "Second Wave" of feminism, scores of women have changed their names as a symbol of their independence.

[2] Central to Comini's scholarship has been an exploration of the difference between female and male artistic interpretations. See Alessandra Comini, "Gender or Genius: The Women Artists of German Expressionism," in Norma Broude and Mary D. Garrard, eds. *Feminism and Art History: Questioning the Litany* (NY: Harper & Row, 1982).

[3] Judy Chicago, *Through the Flower, My Struggle as a Woman Artist* (NY: Doubleday, 1975) p. 67.

[4] Carolyn Heilbrun (*Writing a Woman's Life* (NY: Ballantine Books, 1988, p. 15) writes extensively about how important it is for women to express their anger. "If one is not permitted to express anger or even to recognize it within oneself, one is, by simple extension, refused both power and control. . . . Forbidden anger, women could find no voice in which publicly to complain; they took refuge in depression of madness." Chicago's Womanhouse was of crucial importance because it gave physical form to the expression of women's anger.

[5] Heilbrun (op. cit., p. 98) agrees. She notes that there was "the supporting group of friends behind many outstanding women in the past whose public lives could hardly have endured without such support."

[6] Judy Chicago, *The Dinner Party, A Symbol of Our Heritage* (NY: Anchor Books, 1979, pp. 12-13.

[7] Chicago, *Through the Flower*, pp. 107-108.

Lucy Lippard, "Sweeping Exchanges:

"Sweeping Exchanges: The Contribution of Feminism to the Arts of the 1970s" is reprinted from *Art Journal* (Fall-Winter 1980), pp. 362-365.

[1] Lucy R. Lippard, "Introduction: Moving Targets/Concentric Circles: Notes from the Radical Whirlwind" In *The Pink Glass Swan, Selected Essays on Feminist Art* (NY: The New Press, 1995) pp. 5 and 28.

[2] Ibid. p. 28.

[3] Even Hilton Kramer, though he fears it is "lowering the artistic standards."

[4] Judy Chicago, *Artforum*, Sept. 1974.

[5] Surrealism was also self-described along these broad lines, and with Dada has proved that it, too, was never a movement or a style, since it has continued to pervade all movements and styles ever since.

[6] Ruth Iskin, quoting Arlene Raven at the panel on feminist art and social change accompanying the opening of *The Dinner Party*, March 1979.

[7] Harmony Hammond, "Horse-blinders," *Heresies*, no. 9, 1980.

[8] May Stevens, "Taking Art to the Revolution," *Heresies*, no. 9, 1980. Many of the ideas in my article emerged in discussions with the collective that edited this issue and with Hammond and Stevens in particular.

[9] Suzanne Lacy at the panel accompanying *The Dinner Party*.

[10] Jack Burnham in the *New Art Examiner*, Summer 1977.

[11] The distinction between ambition (doing one's best and taking one's art and ideas as far as possible without abandoning the feminist support system) and competition (walking all over everybody to accomplish this) is a much discussed topic in the women's movement.

[12] Jemake Highwater, quoting Joseph Epes Brown, in an unpublished manuscript.

Conversation with Arlene Raven

[1] Raven, "The Circle: Ritual and the Occult in Women's Performance Art." Reprinted in her *Crossing Over: Feminism and Art of Social Concern* (Ann Arbor/London: UMI Research Press, 1988) p. 24.

[2] Impressionist painter Mary Cassatt and Mary Fairchild MacMonnies (American artists living in Paris) were commissioned to paint murals for the Chicago Woman's Building. For additional discussion of the founding of the Los Angeles Woman's Building, see Faith Wilding, op. cit., especially pp. 61 passim, and Raven's "At Home" catalogue, reprinted in her *Crossing Over*. For a history of the 1893 World's Columbian Exposition Woman's Building, see Jeanne Madeline Weimann, *The Fair Women* (Chicago: Academy Chicago, 1981).

[3] In the 1960s, several artists working in and around Washington, D.C. moved beyond the gestural excesses of New York-based Abstract Expressionism to working with areas of lyrical color that evoked poetic responses in the viewer.

[4] Art critic Clement Greenberg championed the Abstract Expressionist work of artists like Jackson Pollock and also "discovered" Washington Color School painters Morris Louis and Kenneth Noland.

[5] Raven, "Women Look at Women," p. 18.

[6] Raven, in the preface to *Crossing Over*, p. xvii.

[7] Raven, "At Home" (exhibition catalogue), in *Crossing Over*, p. 93.

[8] Donald Kuspit, in the Editor's Preface to *Crossing Over*, p. xiii.

[9] Raven, "The New Culture," in *Crossing Over*, p. 8.

[10] Raven, "The Circle," in *Crossing Over*, pp. 26-27.

[11] Mary Daly, *Beyond God the Father* (Boston: Beacon Press, 1973) p. 8. Cited in Raven, "At Home," p. 108.

[12] Raven, "At Home," p. 110.

[13] Raven, "Women Look at Women," p. 18.

[14] Kuspit, op. cit., p. xiv.

[15] Raven, "The Art of the Altar," in *Crossing Over*, p. 79.

[16] Raven, "A Hunger Artist," in *Crossing Over*, p. 62.

[17] Raven, Preface to *Crossing Over*, p. xviii.

[18] Raven, "The New Culture," in *Crossing Over*, p. 5.

Terry Wolverton — "Requiem"

[1] Excerpted lyric from "A House Is Not A Home," lyrics by Hal David, music by Burt Bacharach

Collection of Collectives

[1] Miriam Schapiro, quoted in Thalia Gouma-Peterson and Patricia Mathews, "The Feminist Critique of Art History," *Art Bulletin*, September 1987, Vol. LXIX, no. 3, p. 332.

[2] Jeanette Winterson, *Art [Objects], Essays on Ecstasy and Effrontery* (NY: Alfred A. Knopf, 1996) p. 12.

[3] Indeed, the U.S. feminist movement of the last three decades has given rise to numerous women's organizations. In 1966, the National Organization for Women (NOW) was founded to fight sexual discrimination. The New York-based Women's Action Alliance was established in 1971 as a national organization dedicated to realizing the vision of self-determination for all women. The list is extensive and diverse.

[4] Prominent among these are Cynthia Navaretta's *Guide to Women's Art Organizations and Directory for the Arts* (1978, rev. ed. 1982) and her *Whole Arts Directory* (1987), both from Midmarch Arts Press. Gouma-Peterson and Mathews summarize the early development of women's art organizations in their comprehensive "The Feminist Critique of Art History," pp. 329-332. These data are amplified in Broude and Garrard's *The Power of Feminist Art*, especially Part II, "Building a Network: Feminist Activism in the Arts."

[5] As with any selection process, I am here forced to "select out" as well as "select in." In doing so, I have been forced to eliminate organizations such as the New York Feminist Art Institute (NYFAI) in New York City and W.E.B. (West-East Bag). Launched in 1979, the NYFAI began as a full-time program. Its enrollment began to decline during the conservative political climate of the 1980s and in 1989 it changed its name to the Women's Center for Learning. It was forced to close its doors in 1990. W.E.B. began as network system — initially conceived by Judy Chicago, Grace Glueck, Lucy Lippard, and Miriam Schapiro and started in 1971 by Ellen Lanyon — for linking women artists from coast to coast by means of a slide registry and newsletter.

[6] FAX from A.I.R. Director Alissa Schoenfeld on March 21, 1996.

[7] Ibid.

[8] Telephone interview with Irene LaPapa on March 22, 1996.

Notes

[9] A.R.C. press release, March, 1996.

[10] Artemisia Gallery brochure, March 1996.

[11] Confirming the statistics in the Artemisia Newsletter, was the 1996-97 exhibition schedule I received for the Los Angeles County Museum of Art issued by their Office of Media and Public Affairs. For the period of the schedule — March 1996 through March 1997 — six one-person exhibitions were given to male artists. Even more distressing, this is a public museum, mandated to serve the populace of the Los Angeles County area. Four of the six male artists are local residents, but it has been decades since a local woman artist was given a one-person show!

[12] From the Athena Art Society membership pamphlet, n.p.

[13] Sally Valongo, "Drawn Together, Women artists find support, recognition in local peer group." Toledo, Ohio *Blade*, Saturday, March 23, 1991, p. 27.

[14] Telephone interview with Leslie Adams, April 4, 1996.

[15] From telephone interview with Sarah Lejeune on March 20, 1996.

[16] Shifra Goldman, "Bridging Troubled Waters" (catalogue essay) (El Paso, Texas, Bridge Center for Contemporary Art, October 1990) n.p.

[17] Ibid.

[18] Shifra Goldman, *Dimensions of the Americas, Art and Social Change in Latin America and the United States* (Chicago, The University of Chicago Press, 1994) p. 235.

[19] Shifra Goldman, "MAS==More + Artists + Women == MAS," *Revista Xhisme Arte*, Vol. I, no. 7, January 1981, pp. 21-22.

[20] Ibid.

[21] From telephone interview with Sylvia Orozco on March 22, 1996.

[22] From telephone interview with Ruth Humpton on March 22, 1996.

[23] Ellen Lubell, "SoHo 20," *Womenart*.

[24] From telephone interview with Lucy Hodgson on March 28, 1996.

[25] From the Soho 20 membership pamphlet of 1995, n.p.

[26] Mary D. Garrard, "Feminist Politics: Networks and Organizations," Broude and Garrard, op. cit., p. 91.

[27] Kay Brown's article "Where We At Black Women Artists," *Feminist Art Journal,* April 1972.

[28] From telephone interview with Alexandra Broches on April 27, 1996.

[29] From "A Brief History of CWAO" prepared by Sylvia Moore, editor of CWAO's original quarterly newsletter.

[30] Christina Baldwin, "Welcome to the Circle," (excerpted from her *Calling the Circle: The First and Future Culture*, 1994) in *Science of Mind*, Vol. 69, no. 4, April 1996, p.

II   IDENTITY IN COMMUNITY

[1] Marge Piercy, "Looking at Quilts," quoted in Arlene Raven, *Crossing Over: Feminism and Art of Social Concern* (Ann Arbor & London: UMI Research Press, 1988) p. 13.

2 For more on friendship quilts, see Linda Otto Lipsett's *Remember Me, Women & Their Friendship Quilts* (SF: The Quilt Digest Press, 1985).

3 Louis Daguerre took out the first patent for a photographic process in Paris in 1839, but photographs were not readily available to frontier families until this century.

4 Rozsika Parker and Griselda Pollock, *Old Mistresses, Women, Art and Ideology* (London: Routledge & Kegan Paul, 1981) pp. 75-76.

5 Lucy Lippard, "Up, Down, and Across: A New Frame for Quilts" in *The Artist and the Quilt* (exhibition catalogue), New York, 1983.

6 My *Webster's New World Dictionary* defines community as "any group living in the same area of having interests, work, etc. in common . . . a sharing in common." (1979 edition, p. 126.)

7 Sharon O'Brien writing about Willa Cather. Cited in Heilbrun, op. cit., page 96.

8 Betty Ann Brown & Arlene Raven, *Exposures, Women & Their Art* (Pasadena, CA: New Sage Press, 1989) p. 112.

9 Judy Chicago, *Through the Flower, My Struggle as a Woman Artist* (New York: Anchor Books, 1977) pp. 37-39.

10 Lucy Lippard, *Eva Hesse* (NY: New York University Press, 1976) p. 24. Cited in Parker and Pollock, p. 155.

11 Ibid., p. 106.

12 Much Post-Structuralist discourse argues against the possibility and/or valorization of originality in any form of late twentieth century cultural production. See especially, Rosalind Krauss, "The Originality of the Avant-Garde: A Postmodernist Repetition," *October*, no. 18 (Fall 1981). Reprinted in *Art After Modernism: Rethinking Representation*, ed. Brian Wallis (NY: The New Museum of Contemporary Art, 1984).

13 Ibid., p. 112.

14 First published in 1962 by Prentice-Hall, Englewood Cliffs, N.J., and Harry N. Abrams, New York.

15 In spite of the title, which implies it has global scope, Janson's text — like almost all those used in art history surveys— is focused almost entirely on the EuroAmerican tradition.

16 Parker and Pollock, pp. 69 and 49.

17 Thalia Gouma-Peterson and Patricia Mathews, "The Feminist Critique of Art History," *Art Bulletin*, September 1987, Vol. LXIX, no. 3, p. 329.

18 Tillie Olsen, "One Out of Twelve: Writers Who Are Women in Our Century," in *Silences* (NY: Delacorte Press/Seymour Lawrence, 1978) p. 25. Cited in Mara R. Witzling, ed. *Voicing Our Visions, Writings by Women Artists* (NY: Universe, 1991) p. 3.

19 Witzling, op. cit., p. 9.

20 Griselda Pollock, *Vision and Difference: Femininity, Feminism and the Histories of Art* (London and NY: Routledge, 1988), pp. 41-42. Cited in Witzling, p. 8.

21 Dinah M. Craik, *Olive* (1850). Cited in Parker and Pollock, p. 83.

22 Linda Nochlin, "Why Are There No Great Women Artists?" In Vivian Gornick & Barbara K. Moran, *Woman in Sexist Society, Studies in Power and Powerlessness* (NY: New American Library, A Mentor Book, 1971) pp. 480-510.

[23] Simone de Beauvoir, *The Second Sex* (NY: Vintage Books, 1952) p. 149.

[24] Suzi Gablik, *The Reenchantment of Art* (London and New York: Thames and Hudson, 1991) p. 5.

[25] Parker and Pollock, p. 82.

[26] From an interview with Christo in *Flash Art* magazine. Cited by Suzi Galik in her "Connective Aesthetics: Art after Individualism." In, Suzanne Lacy, op. cit., p. 78.

[27] Michael Ventura, "Notes on a Blind Spot" in *L.A. Weekly*, August 23-29, 1991.

[28] Steve Hohenboken, "Comfort Cut on the (Gender) Bias: Out of the (Linen) Closet" in, *New Art Examiner*, September 1993, p. 12.

[29] Parker and Pollock, pp. 50-51.

[30] This is but one example of an ongoing historical process, as Gerda Lerner notes: "In general, education becomes institutionalized when elites — military, religious or political — need to assure their position in power by means of training a group to serve and perpetuate their interests." (op. cit., p. 23.)

[31] Ibid., p. 70.

[32] Parker and Pollock, op. cit., p. 35.

[33] Karen Peterson & J.J. Wilson, in their *Women Artists, Recognition and Reappraisal, From the Early Middle Ages to the Twentieth Century* (NY: Harper & Row, 1976), discuss the restrictive nature of guilds. "For example, in the making of tapestry, the fourteenth century guild rules, like taboos from some early tribe, forbade pregnant or menstruating women (which included just about every woman in those days, after all) from working on the big tapestry looms."

[34] For example, at California State University Northridge (CSUN), of the 25 full time studio professors, only 4 are female. Racial and ethnic exclusions continue to operate as well. In an area as diversified as Southern California, only one of the CSUN studio faculty is African American, only one is Hispanic, only one is Asian American. At Cal State San Bernardino, there is only one full time studio faculty member who is female. There are no people of color on the full time studio faculty there. [Statistics given are for 1995.]

[35] Hilary Robinson, *Visibly Female, Feminism and Art Today, An Anthology* (London, Camden Press, 1987) p. 4.

[36] Ibid.

[37] Olsen, op. cit.

[38] Susan Rubin Suleiman, *Subversive Intent, Gender, Politics, and the Avant-Garde.* (Cambridge: Harvard University Press, 1990) pp. 28 & 33.

[39] Chicago, op. cit., p. 82.

[40] Simone de Beauvoir, op. cit., p. 794.

[41] Otto G. Ocvirk, et al, eds. *Art Fundamentals, Theory & Practice*, 7th edition (Madison, WI: Brown & Benchmark, 1994) p. 149.

[42] Coco Fusco, *English is Broken Here, Notes on Cultural Fusion in the Americas* (NY: The New Press, 1995) p. 26.

[43] Cited in bell hooks, *Feminist Theory from margin to center* (Boston: South End Press, 1984) p. 90.

[44] Lerner, op. cit., page 47.

⁴⁵ Witzling, p. 7.

⁴⁶ Lerner, op. cit., p. 238.

Adrian Piper: You and Me

¹ "Adrian Piper and the Indexical," *Reimaging America* (Philadelphia, Pennsylvania, and Santa Cruz, California: New Society Publishers, 1990) p. 290.

² Ibid.

³ The Mythic Being I/You (Her) #7, 1974.

⁴ I Embody, 1975, photo and oil crayon (poster image original) 8" x 10".

⁵ Adrian Piper, "Flying," in *Adrian Piper: Reflections 1967-1987* (NY: Alternative Museum 1987), p. 24.

Conversation with Rosalie Ortega

¹ Coco Fusco, *English Is Broken Here, Notes on Cultural Fusion in the Americas* (NY: The New Press, 1995) p. 36.

² Fusco, pp. 32-33.

³ Ibid., pp. 34-35.

⁴ See especially Carol Christ, "Rethinking Theology and Nature" in Irene Diamond and Gloria Feman Orenstein, eds. *Reweaving the World, The Emergence of Ecofeminism* (SF: Sierra Club Books, 1990).

⁵ Betty Ann Brown, *Utopian Dialogues* (exhibit catalogue) LA: Municipal Art Gallery, 1993) pp. 12-13.

⁶ Fusco, op. cit., p. 29.

⁷ Fusco, p. 9.

⁸ Ibid., p. 33.

⁹ bell hooks also addresses poignantly the issue of home in her *Teaching to Transgress, Education as the Practice of Freedom* (NY: Routledge, 1995) p. 60.

¹⁰ Maria Lugones, "Playfulness, 'World'-Traveling, and Loving Perception" in Garry and Pearsall, *Women, Knowledge and Reality* (London: Unwin Hyman, 1989) pp. 275-290.

¹¹ Fusco, op. cit., p. 26.

¹² Ibid., pp. 32-33.

¹³ Fusco, op. cit., p. x.

Katherine Ng "My Name is Not My Own"

Trinh T. Minh-ha in her "Difference, A Special Third World Women Issue"

Ruth Weisberg Jewish Identity

¹ Rachel Alder, "Talking our Way in," *Sh'ma: A Journal of Jewish Responsibility*, 23/441, November 13, 1992, p.6.

² Jewish illustrated scrolls or *megillahs* are usually restricted to the story of Esther where there is no mention of God and Passover Haggadot. There is a proscription against illustrating the *Torah* itself.

[3] "Entering the Scroll," Performance by Ruth Weisberg and Meredith Stone, Hebrew Union College, New York, Oct. 21 and Nov. 9, 1987; Los Angeles, May 10 and 11, 1989.

[4] Rabbi Laura Geller, "Women's Spirituality and Our Tradition," *Sh'ma: A Journal of Jewish Responsibility* 17/325, January 1987.

[5] Doris Sosin, "The Wimple, A Jewish Folk Art Expression" (Hebrew Union College, Skirball Museum, Los Angeles, undated).

[6] 18th Century German Torah Wimple, Skirball Museum, Hebrew Union College, Los Angeles.

[7] Thalia Gouma-Peterson, "Passages in Cyclical Time: Ruth Weisberg's Scroll," *Arts Magazine*, February 1988, 59.

[8] Nancy Berman, "Tradition and Self," *Ruth Weisberg - The Scroll* (Hebrew Union College, Jewish Institute of Religion, NY, 1987), p. 9.

[9] Helen Racine, *Vision of the Temple: The Image of the Temple of Jerusalem and Christianity* (London: Oresko Books, 1979) p. 186.

[10] *The Scroll* has been exhibited at Skirball Museum, Hebrew Union College, Los Angeles, (which owns the work); and at Hebrew Union College, Jewish Institute of Religion, New York; and has been written about in several periodicals including *Arts Magazine* (Thalia Gouma-Peterson) and *New Art Examiner*, (Arlene Raven).

[11] The author [Ruth Weisberg] would like to thank Rabbi Laura Geller, Alicia Weisberg-Roberts, and Kelyn Roberts. Some of this material was first published in *Arts: The Arts in Religious and Theological Studies*, United Theological Seminary, New Brighton, Minn., Vol. 3 no. 3, Summer 1991, "Creating the Scroll: A Jewish Artist Reflects on Her Work," pp. 4-9.

Michelle T. Clinton — "Warrior Council"

"Warrior Council" originally appeared in Clinton's book of poetry, *Good Sense and the Faithless* (Albuquerque: West End Press, 1994).

Joanna Frueh — Building the Body of Love

[1] Joan Nestle's "My Mother Liked to Fuck," in Nestle, *A Restricted Country* (Ithaca: Firebrand Books, 1987) is, to my knowledge, the only account given by a feminist about her mother's love of sex. Sara Ruddick, *Maternal Thinking: Toward a Politics of Peace* (Boston: Beacon Press, 1989) discusses the characteristics and value of maternal attentiveness. Many feminists have written about the Great Goddess, or Triple Goddess, one of whose phases is the Mother. Interestingly, in "My Mother Liked to Fuck," Nestle removes her mother from "sacred" status. She writes, "My mother . . . was not a matriarchal goddess," and "My mother was not a goddess, not a matriarchal figure who looms over my life bigbellied with womyn rituals."

[2] Julia Kristeva, *Powers of Horror: An Essay on Abjection*, trans. Leon S. Roudiez (NY: Columbia University Press, 1982) pp. 54-55, 59.

[3] See Mary Caputi, *Voluptuous Yearnings: A Feminist Theory of the Obscene* (London: Rowman and Littlefield, 1994).

[4] Laura Mulvey, "Visual Pleasure and Narrative Cinema," *Screen* 16: 3 (Autumn 1975) pp. 6-18.

[5] *Webster's New World Dictionary of American English*, Third College Edition, p. 540.

[6] Alphonso Lingis, *Libido: The French Existential Theories* (Bloomington: Indiana University Press, 1985) p. 90.

[7] Laurie is Laurie Fierstein. I use only her first name in the body of this piece in order to be consistent with my use of women friends' first names in both autobiographical and fiction sections. While I call "Evolution F" a fascinating spectacle, it was also a disorganized and sloppy production, some of whose characters and metaphors should have been more subtly conceived and richly developed.

III   BUILDING COMMUNITY

[1] bell hooks, "Narratives of Struggle" in *Critical Fictions, The Politics of Imaginative Writing,* Philomena Mariana, ed. (Seattle: Bay Press, 1991) p. 55.

[2] Ibid., p. 61.

[3] Lucy Lippard, "Sweeping Changes: The Contribution of Feminism to the Art of the 1970s," *Art Journal* XL, 1980. Critic Lawrence Alloway concurred. In his "Women's Art in the '70s" (*Art in America*, May/June 1976), he suggested that collaboration was the most important criterion for a working definition of a feminist: "a woman who is willing to work with other women to reduce inequity in the long run or to achieve a specific short-term reform." Cited in Gouma-Peterson and Mathews, p. 345.

[4] Elizabeth A. Say, *Evidence on her Own Behalf, Women's Narrative as Theological Voice* (Savage, MD: Rowman & Littlefield, 1990).

[5] Ruth Ann Anderson created a templelike structure oriented to the four cardinal directions. Women artists created altars for each of the four walls. Three of the women whose work is discussed further in this volume were involved: Jill D'Angenica's altar focused on fire, Rosalie Ortega's on earth, and Anderson's on water. All around the outside of the temple were poems by women writers, including Starr Goode who co-authored with Anderson an essay in Section IV on their shared spiritual community.

[6] Of course community building through art is neither exclusively female nor attributable only to the West Coast. A decade ago, Lucy Lippard wrote an article entitled "Trojan Horses: Activist Art and Power" (reprinted in *Art After Modernism: Rethinking Representation,* Brian Wallis, ed. (NY: The New Museum, 1984) in which she described many of the community-building processes discussed here as activist art processes used by cultural democrats, both male and female, all over the world. Of the eight examples of activist artists she lists at the beginning of the article, the first is Suzanne Lacy and all but one of the others is female. Lippard asserts, "Much activist work is collaborative or participatory and its meaning is directly derived from its use-value to a particular community. A true cultural democracy would encourage artists to speak for themselves and for their communities . . . in order to make heard and seen those voices and faces hitherto invisible and powerless . . ." which sounds a lot like the art described here. While working on this book (August 1993), I traveled to Chicago and saw an exhibition in the Museum of Contemporary Art called "Cul De Sac," which was clearly a community building art supervised by two men, Inigo Manglano-Ovalle and Paul Teruel, with Street-Level Video, a crew of young adults from Chicago's West Town neighborhood. The exhibition reminded me a lot of Cheri Gaulke's work in El Sereno.

[7] Chicago, *Through the Flower*, p. 66.

[8] Lerner, op. cit., p. 274.

[9] Anne Sutherland Harris and Linda Nochlin, *Women Artists: 1550-1950* (exhibition cata-

logue) (NY: Alfred A. Knopf, 1976) p. 239.

[10] Miriam Schneir, *Feminism: The Essential Historical Writings* (NY: Random House, 1972) pp. xi-xxi.

[11] Betty Friedan, *The Feminine Mystique* (NY: Dell Books, 1963).

[12] Vivian Gornick, "Who Says We Haven't Made A Revolution? A Feminist Takes Stock" *New York Times Magazine*, April 15, 1990, pp. 24-25.

[13] Arlene Raven, *Crossing Over: Feminism and Art of Social Concern* (Ann Arbor and London: UMI Research Press, 1988) pp. 13-14.

[14] Ibid., p. 18.

[15] Say, op. cit., p. 130.

[16] Simone de Beauvoir, *The Second Sex* (NY: Vintage Books, 1974) p. 54 passim.

[17] Helene Cixous, "The Laugh of the Medusa" in *New French Feminisms, An Anthology*, ed. Elaine Marks and Isabelle de Courtivron (NY: Schocken Books, 1981).

[18] bell hooks, in *Angry Women*, Andrea Juno and V. Vale, eds. (SF: Re/search Publications, 1991) p. 85.

[19] Nina Auerbach, *Communities of Women, An Idea in Fiction* (Cambridge: Harvard University Press, 1978) p. 5.

[20] Sheila de Bretteville, quoted in Lacy, *Mapping the Terrain*, p. 38.

[21] Auerbach, op. cit., pp. 11-12.

[22] Lerner (op. cit., p. x) is speaking here about the community of women historians, but her comments seem applicable to the Women's Movement in general.

[23] Trinh T. Minh-ha, "Difference: A Special Third World Women Issue" in her *Woman, Native, Other* (Bloomington: Indiana University Press, 1989) p. 79.

[24] This is discussed more fully in Section IV of this volume.

[25] hooks, op. cit., p. 85.

[26] Audre Lorde, "The Master's Tools Will Never Dismantle the Master's House" in *This Bridge Called My Back, Writings By Radical Women of Color* (NY: Kitchen Table: Women of Color Press, 1983) p. 99.

[27] Julia Kristeva, *Strangers to Ourselves* (NY: Columbia University Press, 1991) pp. 1-2.

[28] Homi K. Bhaha, in *Critical Fictions, The Politics of Narrative Writing* (Seattle: Bay Press, 1991) p. 63.

[29] Maria C. Lugones and Elizabeth V. Spellman, "Have We Got A Theory for You! Feminist Theory, Cultural Imperialism and the Demand for "The Woman's Voice'" in *Women's Studies International Forum*, Vol. 6, no. 6, 1983, p. 573.

[30] Sidonie Smith, *A Poetics of Women's Autobiography: Marginality and the Fictions of Self-Representation* (Indianapolis, Indiana University Press, 1987) p. 176.

[31] Maria C. Lugones in Lugones and Spellman, op. cit. p. 581.

[32] These quotes are from a telephone interview with the artist in Fall, 1993.

[33] See *The New York Times*, "The Living Arts," Thursday, December 7, 1989, for further discussion of the Biddy Mason Place.

[34] Cited in Carolyn G. Heilbrun, *Writing a Woman's Life* (NY: Ballantine Books, 1988) p. 33.

[35] Cited in Heilbrun, op. cit., p. 44.

[36] Suzanne Juhasz, "Towards a Theory of Form in Feminist Autobiography: Kate Millett's *Flying* and *Sita*; Maxine Hong Kingston's *The Woman Warrior*" in Estelle C. Jelink, ed. *Women's Autobiography: Essays in Criticism* (Bloomington, Indiana University Press, 1980) p. 224.

[37] Cited in Heilbrun, op. cit., p. 18.

[38] Parker and Pollock, p. 155.

[39] Simone de Beauvoir, op. cit.

[40] Heilbrun, op. cit., p. 21.

[41] Ibid., p. 37.

[42] Say, op. cit., p. 131.

[43] Ibid., p. 145.

[44] Heilbrun, op. cit., p. 46.

[45] Patricia C. Phillips, "Public Constructions" in Lacy, op. cit., p. 70.

[46] Judith E. Stein, "Collaboration" in Broude and Garrard, op. cit., p. 235.

[47] Muriel Rukeyser, "Käthe Kollwitz" in *The Collected Poems of Muriel Rukeyser* (NY: McGraw-Hill, 1982) p. 482.

[48] In Lacy, op. cit., p. 274.

Conversation with Suzanne Lacy

[1] "The Road of Poems and Borders" (the performance publication), p. 43.

[2] Ibid., p. 57.

[3] Allan Kaprow, "The Shape of the Art Environment," *Artforum* (Summer, 1968), p. 33.

[4] Robert Pelfrey with Mary Hall-Pelfrey, *Art and Mass Media* (NY: Harper & Row, 1985, p. 320.

[5] Suzanne Lacy, "Mapping the Terrain: The New Public Art (part 2)," *Public Art Review*, Vol. 4, no. 3, Fall 1993, p. 30.

[6] Ibid., p. 28.

[7] Ibid.

The Crystal Quilt

[1] Patrice Clark Koelsch is a Minneapolis critic and writer. She previously directed the Center for Arts Criticism in St. Paul. Koelsch coordinated the documentation team for "The Crystal Quilt."

Confessions of a Community Artist — Suvan Geer

[1] Lucy Lippard, *Overlay*

Touched by Ukeles

[1] Jack Burnham, "The Problems of Criticism IX," *Art Forum*, January 1971.

²Ibid.

³Ibid.

⁴Suzanne Lacy, ed. *Mapping the Terrain, New Genre Public Art* (Seattle: Bay Press, 1995) p. 77.

Judith F. Baca: Community and Culture in the United States

Frances K. Pohl's essay, "Judith F. Baca: Community and Culture in the United States," is reprinted from *Women's Studies: An Interdisciplinary Journal*, Vol. 25, no. 3, 1996, pp. 215-238.

Victoria Rue *CANCERBODIES*

¹Dorothee Soelle, *Suffering*. trans. Everett R. Kalin (Philadelphia: Fortress Press, 1975), p.70.

²Victoria Rue, *CancerBodies: Women Speaking the Unspeakable* (Ann Arbor, Mich.: University Microfilms) l994).

³Soelle, *Suffering*, op. cit., p. 74.

⁴Rev. Annie Powell, "Response to *CancerBodies*. Remarks at the American Academy of Religion, November 18, l992," in *CancerBodies*, Appendix 6, p. 267.

⁵Soelle, *Suffering*, p. 86.

⁶*CancerBodies*, Act 2, Scene 10.

⁷Ibid., Act 2, Scene 12.

⁸Ibid., Act 1, Scene 5.

⁹David Spiegel, J.R. Bloom, H.C. Kramer, and E. Gottheili, "The Effects of Psychological Treatment on Survival of Patients with Metastatic Cancer," *The Lancet 2*, October 1989, pp. 888-901.

Lorraine Serena WOMEN/*Beyond Borders*

¹Mary Heebner, "Box Network," *Santa Barbara Magazine*, Fall 1995.

²Joan Crowder, "Box Populi, 'Women Beyond Borders' crates a worldwide web," *Santa Barbara News Press*, Monday, February 6, 1995, p. B5.

³Suvan Geer, "Pieces of Dialogue," *Women Beyond Borders* (exhibition catalogue), Santa Barbara, 1995.

Coordinators/Curators:

USA, Lorraine Serena, Founder; Elena Siff, Co-founder; Santa Barbara, CA coordinators: Mary Heebner, Victoria Vesna (e-mail & Beyond), Alice Hutchins, Sky Bergman (World Wide Web), Elisse Pogofsky-Harris, Rose Bilot, Isabel Barbuzza, Beverly Decker, Ciel Bergman, Evelyn Jacob-Jaffe, Saritha Margon, Maria Velasco and Joan Tanner; Israel, Daphna Naor; Austria, Gina Ballinger, Ingeborg Pock, Eva Urspring; Spain, Rosa Martinez, Esther Regueira; Kenya, Jony Waite, Wendy Karmali; Italy, Guilian D'Orazio; France, Dominique Grangeon; Sweden/Finland, Elizabeth Haitto-Connah; Cuba, Llillian Llanes; Mexico, Shirley Chernitsky, Conchita Benevides, Tanya Coen, Mari Olguin; Argentina, Eliana Molineli; Japan, Shoko Tomo, Toshi Ohi; Vietnam, Lan Huong Nguyen, Darlene Nguyen-Ely; Australia, Therese Kenyon, Jan Fieldsend; Native American, Dr. Leona Zastrow

Phase II

Ecuador, Pilar Flores; Russia, Katya Galitzine; England, Penny Paine; Germany, Vera Giesel, Annerose Bekuhrs; Switzerland, Dr. Margot Schmidt, Heiderose Bilderbrand, Anne-Kathi Wildberger

IV LIVING IN COMMUNITY

[1] Rosario Castellanos, "Meditacion en el Umbral/Meditation at the Threshold" in Angel Flores and Kate Flores, eds. *The Defiant Muse, Hispanic Feminist Poems from the Middle Ages to the Present, A Bilingual Anthology* (NY: The Feminist Press, 1986) pp. 98-101.

[2] Descalzas Reales means "barefoot royal women" and indicates that the aristocratic inhabitants of the convent had taken vows of poverty.

[3] Gerda Lerner, op. cit., pp. 26-29, passim,

[4] Lerner, op. cit. p. 58.

[5] Lerner, op. cit. p. 59.

[6] Lerner notes that convents remained a refuge throughout these eras, however, and cites the remarkable example of Sor Juana de la Cruz of Mexico (1651-95), pp. 33-36.

[7] bell hooks, in Andrea Juno and V. Vale, eds. *Angry Women* (SF: Re/search Publications, 1991) p. 85.

[8] Gerda Lerner, op. cit., p. 3.

[9] Leonard J. Doyle, trans. *St. Benedict's Rule for Monasteries* (Collegeville, MN, The Liturgical press, 1948) p. 7.

[10] Ibid., p. 17.

[11] Ibid., p. 18.

[12] Sharon D. Welch, *A Feminist Ethic of Risk*, (Minneapolis, Fortress Press, 1990) p. 111.

[13] Ibid., p. 113.

[14] Celestine Ware, in her book *woman power*, quoted in bell hooks, *Feminist Theory*, p. 83.

[15] Trinh T. Minh-ha, "Cotton and Iron" in Russell Ferguson, Martha Gever, Trinh T. Minh-ha and Cornel West, eds. *Out There: Marginalization and Contemporary Cultures* (NY: The New Museum, 1993) pp. 327-336.

[16] Parker and Pollock, op. cit., p. 115.

[17] Gaye Tuchman, Arlene Kaplan Daniels and James Benet, eds. *Hearth & Home, Images of Women in the Mass Media* (NY: Oxford University Press, 1978) p. 3.

[18] Lynn Hershman, quoted in Lacy, *Mapping the Terrain*, p. 26.

[19] Heilbrun, op. cit., p. 19.

[20] Nancy Harstock in bell hooks, *Feminist Theory*, p. 89.

[21] Sarah Lucia Hoagland, *Lesbian Ethics: Toward New Value* (Palo Alto: Institute of Lesbian Studies, 1988) p. 2.

[22] Lacy, op. cit., p. 36.

[23] Eknath Easwaran, "Three Harmonies" in *Parabola Magazine*.

[24] Carol P. Christ, "Rethinking Theology and Nature" in Irene Diamond and Gloria Feman Orenstein, eds. *Reweaving the World, The Emergence of Ecofeminism* (SF: Sierra Club Books,

1990) p. 314.

[25] Devorah Knaff, "The Sacred and the Mundane, Gender and Southern California art world politics," *Artweek*, July 22, 1993.

[26] Arlene Raven, "The Circle: Ritual and Occult in Women's Performance Art," in her *Crossing Over: Feminism and the Art of Social Concern* (Ann Arbor: University of Michigan Press, 1988) pp. 23-24.

[27] From Brown and Raven, *Exposures*, p. 92.

[28] bell hooks, *Teaching to Transgress, Education as the Practice of Freedom* (NY and London: Routledge, 1994).

[29] hooks, p. 51, writes about the "banking" system of education, "an education that in no way expressed my social reality."

[30] The concept of objective truth extended to the belief in a unitary "right" art style. During the late 1960s, as Minimalism swept west from New York City, I told my professor I wanted to paint images of people. He shuddered and insisted I go back to laying smooth, Frank Stella-like stripes of colorful acrylic across the canvas. When I told him I wanted to take photographs and translate them into paintings (in anticipation of what I now know as photorealism), he shuddered again, urged me to go back to the stripes, and disdainfully suggested I think about teaching art to children rather than pursuing graduate studies in painting.

[31] hooks, op. cit., p. 16.

[32] Ibid., p. 18.

[33] hooks discusses the dangers of the classroom becoming a spectacle, a place of entertainment, especially when it is overcrowded, on p. 161.

[34] hooks addresses connected learning when she cites the writings of Paolo Friere and Thich Nhat Hanh, who both endeavor to link awareness with practice, p. 14.

[35] Lippard, "Trojan Horses: Activist Art and Power," p. 356 in Brian Wallis, ed. *Art After Modernism: Rethinking Representation.* (NY: The New Museum, 1984).

[36] Gablik, op. cit., p. 6.

[37] Lucy Lippard, quoted in Lacy, op. cit., p. 42.

[38] Arlene Raven, "Word of Honor," in Lacy, op. cit., p. 161.

[39] Certainly the most poetic discussion of the post-structuralist theory of the "death of the author," is in Jorge Luis Borges's *Labyrinth, Selected Stories and Other Writings*, trans. Donald A. Yates and James E. Irby (NY: New Directions, 1964) pp. 36-44. Reprinted in Wallis, op. cit., pp. 3-11.

[40] Gablik, op. cit., p. 2.

Gatekeepers, Silences, and Freedom

[1] bell hooks, "Talking Back," in Russell Ferguson, Martha Gever, Trinh T. Minh-ha and Cornel West, eds. *Out There: Marginalization and Contemporary Cultures* (NY: The New Museum, 1993) p. 339.

[2] See especially Shifra Goldman, "Latin American Art's U.S. Explosion," *New Art Examiner*, Vol. 17, no. 4, Dec. 1989, p. 27.

[3] Julia Kristeva discusses the presence of the "other" in the centers of power at length in her *Strangers to Ourselves* (NY: Columbia University Press, 1991).

[4] Leilani Clark, Sheridan DeWolf, and Carl Clark, "Teaching Teachers To Avoid Having Culturally Assaultive Classrooms" in *Young Children*, July 1992, pp. 4-5.

[5] Sondra Hale, "Pedagogy and Diversity" in *UCLA Center for the Study of Women Newsletter*, Spring 1991, p. 15.

[6] Paula Ben-Amos, *The Art of Benin* (London: Thames & Hudson, 1980).

[7] Adrienne Rich, "Taking Women Students Seriously (1978)" in her *Lies, Secrets and Silences, Selected Prose 1966-1978*. (NY: Norton, 1979) pp. 237-246.

[8] "Cara" means face in Spanish; the exhibition title acronym underscored, for Spanish speakers, the fact that the Chicano community was showing itself — its face — through this art. Tonelli was forced out of UCLA soon after the CARA exhibition and has left the museum world altogether.

[9] I have written further about the CARA exhibition in "A Community's Self-Portrait," *New Art Examiner*, December 1990, pp. 22-24.

[10] Ibid., p. 21.

[11] William Wilson critiqued CARA for what he perceived as an absence of quality, and defensively argued for maintaining quality as the standard in his *Times* article of September 12, 1990. All of the full-time art editors and critics on staff at the *Los Angeles Times*, the *Daily News*, and the West Coast trade *Artweek* are Judeo-Christian Euroamericans. People of color are only "allowed" (and I put that in quotes to reiterate the power differential implied) to write on an occasional, part-time basis.

[12] Howardena Pindell, "Breaking the Silence," in *New Art Examiner*, October 1990, pp. 18-21.

[13] David Bonetti, "The Battle Cry Over Quality," *Image (San Francisco Examiner* weekly magazine), September 23, 1990, p. 6.

[14] These words are taken from a hand-out Atkinson and Falk distributed at the beginning of the day-long dialogue.

[15] Hale, op. cit., p. 16.

[16] Nancy Harstock, quoted in bell hooks, *Feminist Theory*, p. 88.

[17] hooks, "Talking Back," p. 340.

Conversation with Cheri Gaulke

[1] Cheri Gaulke, "Performance Art of the Woman's Building" in *High Performance*, Fall/Winter 1980. p. 156.

[2] Ibid.

[3] Suvan Geer, "Stamping on Fertile Ground" in *Artweek*, September 26, 1987, vol. 18, no. 31, p.8.

[4] Michael Ventura, "Nature in Ourselves" in *High Performance*, issue 26 (1984). The performance he refers to, "Leap of Faith," was done on UCLA campus with the Sisters of Survival.

[5] Arlene Raven, "Passion/Passage," in *Crossing Over*, (Ann Arbor: UMI Press, 1988) p. 48.

[6] Darcy Diamond, "Art in the Combat Zone, Woman Warriors Create New Arenas Through

Performance Art" in *L.A. Theatre*, Vol. I, no. 4, June/July 1983, p. 13.

Mindy Lorenz

[1] Herbert Marcuse, *The Aesthetic Dimension* (Boston: Beacon Press, 1978).

Rachel Rosenthal

[1] Donna Perlmutter, "The New Rachel Rosenthal Company," *Dance Magazine*, April 1995, Vol. LXIX, no. 4, p. 87.

[2] Anne Marie Welsh, "Rosenthal refines message to planet Earth," "The Arts," *The San Diego Union Tribune*, November 11, 1995, p. D-5.

[3] Perlmutter, op. cit.

[4] Pleasant Gehman, "Rachel's World," *The Los Angeles Reader*, February 4, 1994, Vol. 16, no. 17, pp. 10-11.

[5] Quoted in Gehman, op. cit., p. 11.

Look for Angels

Lead-in quotation is from *Time* Magazine, December 27, 1993

[1] The computer program, "GeoFinder II," was donated to the Angels project by Thomas Brothers Maps of California.

Coda

[1] Mary D. Garrard, in discussing "Feminist Politics: Networks and Organizations," notes that many feminist communities, as they became institutionalized, went through the "four entropic stages of regression: self-satisfaction, complacency, internal Balkanization, amnesia" in Broude and Garrard, op. cit., p. 88.

[2] As Suzi Gablik notes, "Exalted individualism . . . is hardly a creative response to the needs of the planet at this time, which demand complex and sensitive forms of interaction and linking" in *The Reenchantment of Art* (London and NY: Thames and Hudson, 1991) p. 6.

[3] Jacques Derrida, father of deconstructive thought, writes about the "abandonment of all reference to a center, to a subject, to a privileged reference, to an origin, or to an absolute *archaria* [beginning]" particularly in his "Structure, sign and play in the discourse of the human sciences" in his *Writing and Difference*, trans. Alan Bass (Chicago: University of Chicago Press/Routledge & Kegan Paul, 1978). David Tripp and Elizabeth Say continue critique of the concept of the unitary, centralized self in their "Positioning the Self: From Post-Structuralism to Ethical Agency" (unpublished manuscript).

[4] See especially George Kateb, ed., *Utopia* (NY: Atherton Press, 1971) p. 9 passim.

[5] Julie Mazo, "Women in Community," *Intentional Communities*, (Rutledge, MO, Fellowship for Intentional Community and Communities Publications Cooperative, 1992).

[6] Gerda Lerner, *The Creation of Feminist Consciousness, From the Middle Ages to Eighteen-seventy* (NY and Oxford, Oxford University Press, 1993) pp. 274-276.

[7] It is with pleasure that I end this essay with the words which my friend Gloria Orenstein used to name her book, *Reweaving the World, The Emergence of Ecofeminism*, edited and with essays by Irene Diamond and Gloria Feman Orenstein. SF: Sierra Club Books, 1990).

PHOTO CREDITS

Wayne McCall, 2
Tina Freeman, 33
Rena Hansen, 64 (left—top & center)
Pam Pierson, 107
Erl-Hwa Hsiao, 133 (top)
Maja Kihlstedt, 144 (bottom)
Peter Latner, 169 (top)
Terry Gydesen 169 (bottom)
Li Pan, 199
Betty Ann Brown, 200 (top)
Martin Cohen, 296
Jill D'Agnenica & Betty Ann Brown, 317
Dana L. Walker, 318
Suzanne States, 323 (top)
Russell Dudley, 323 (bottom)

Contributors

Betty Ann Brown is an art historian, critic, and curator, trained in Latin American art history, B.F.A., M.A., Ph.D.(art history, University of New Mexico, 1977). After moving to Los Angeles in the late 1970s, her interest began to shift from Latin American art in Mexico to chicano art in the United States and, ultimately, to all contemporary art. She has written extensively on Latin American art in journals world-wide, and has been writing contemporary criticism since 1982. Brown has worked as a contributing editor for *Arts, Artweek* and the *Los Angeles Reader*, was founding editor of *Visions;* and co-authored, *Exposures, Women & Their Art.* She has curated several exhibitions focusing (as in her writing) on feminism, identity, and the use of art as a community building tool.

Brown is a professor at California State University, Northridge, and has been active in art world politics. She is a longtime member of the Women's Caucus for Art, (organized national meeting program, 1985), is currently President of the Southern California Chapter, and also served as president of the Los Angeles Woman's Building Board (1985-86). Brown recently curated the exhibition "Muses," which paired women artists with women writers, for the Pasadena Armory for the Arts. Betty Ann Brown lives in Pasadena, California, with her son Wiley.

Betsy Damon has been creating and performing community-based and issue-oriented art works since 1977, when her "The 7000-Year-Old Woman" appeared as a street event in New York City. Other works have dealt with rape, violence, gender, spirituality, and the survival of the planet. Damon has been committed to teaching and empowering other artists since the mid 1960s. She continues to offer workshops, particularly her "No Limits for Women Artists" which she developed in 1984 to teach women to lead and build community while establishing networks of support around themselves. Since 1978, she has done "Reevaluation Counseling" workshops intended to assist people in reclaiming what she terms their "complete intelligence. . . . A large part of this work is the elimination of internalized oppression that results from living in a classist, racist, sexist society." Damon also organizes exhibitions and writes about her art and the values it embodies.

Joanna Frueh is the author of *Erotic Faculties* (1996), a collection of her critical and performance writings, and *Hannah Wilke: A Retrospective* (1989). She is co-editor and contributor to *New Feminist Criticism: Art, Identity, Action* (1994) and *Feminist Art Criticism: An Anthology* (1988; 1991). She has written extensively on contemporary art and women artists and is recognized as a powerful, provocative, and articulate performer. She teaches at the University of Nevada, Reno.

Margot Fortunato Galt, who contributed the history of WARM gallery, writes and publishes poetry, essays and memoir stories about traveling with her daughter, growing up Yankee in the South, ecology and the visual arts. Her work has appeared in a variety of publications, such as *The Iowa Review* and *Milkweed Chronicle*, the recent anthology *Looking for Home*, as well as *Minnesota Monthly, Mpls/St. Paul Magazine, Twin Cities* and *Artpaper*. Her book, *The Story in History: Writing Your Way Into The American Experience* was published in the fall of 1992. She hold a Ph.D. from the University of Minnesota in American Studies and has taught at several Minneapolis institutions.

Cheri Gaulke's work has been celebrated in numerous books and journals. She has received national and international recognition in the form of grants (including several from the National Endowment for the Arts), awards (including The Woman's Building VESTA Award), and diverse artist-in-residence programs.

Suvan Geer is an installation artist, art critic, and political activist. She has had a dozen one-person and over three dozen group shows since starting to exhibit her work in 1981. She has written extensively for the *Los Angeles Times* and for art publications such as *Artweek, Artscene* and *Visions*. She has taught both studio arts and critical theory classes at the Claremont Colleges. In addition, she has been active in the Women's Caucus for Art on both local and national levels, organizing symposia, sitting on the boards of directors, and curating exhibitions. In 1990, Geer began working as coordinator for Artists Contributing to the Solution (ACTS), an artists' ecology activist group. In 1992, she founded Health + Education + Art + Law (HEAL), a mentor/mentoree program for artists working in battered women's shelters, hospices, homes for abused children and hospitals. Geer's art work engages the planetary environment both metaphorically and physically.

Patrice Clark Koelsch is a fiction writer, freelance critic, and cultural worker living in Minneapolis. A native of the Bronx, Koelsch came of age during the resistance to the Vietnam War and the flowering of the feminist movement. After completing graduate school in Ohio, she taught philosophy at Augustana College, then worked for the Minnesota Humanities Commission, and finally directed the Center for Arts Criticism for its first eight years. Currently a member of the National Book Critics' Circle and an advisor to *Public Art Review*, Koelsch also serves on the Board of Directors for the Minneapolis Center for Neighborhoods. She has been awarded writing residencies at Ragdale Foundation and Norcroft: A Writing Retreat for Women. Koelsch was a co-editor of *Looking Out: Perspectives on Dance in a Multicultural World* (Schirmer Books, 1995). Her recent essays and reviews have appeared in *The Women's Review of Books, Art Papers, The Hungry Mind Review On-line*, and *Tractor*. "Satisfaction," Koelsch's first published story, appears in *The Slate* (Winter 1996).

Suzanne Lacy studied with Judy Chicago first in Fresno then at California Institute of the Arts in Valencia, where she received her graduate degree. She went on to teach and present art at the Los Angeles Woman's Building but her work soon spread far beyond the walls of that institution. Lacy is internationally know for her monumental community-building art projects. In California, she has worked to "Take Back the Night" (1978); "Immigrants and Survivors" (1983); "Black Madonna" (1986);."Whisper, the Waves, the Wind" (1984); and in Minneapolis, "Crystal Quilt" (1987).

Lucy Lippard is one of America's most provocative and influential art writers, activists,. and curators. She has published sixteen books, including most notably *From the Center: Feminist Essays on Art, Overlay: Contemporary Art and the Art of Prehistory, Get the Message?: A Decade of Art for Social Change*, and *Mixed Blessings: New Art in a Multicultural America*. She has produced monographs on artists Eva Hesse, Tony Smith, and Ad Reinhardt, as well as dozens of exhibition catalogues and essays. Her recent *The Pink Glass Swan* is an anthology of some of the scores of articles and reviews she has written for periodicals such as the *Village Voice, In*

These Times and the *Nation*, and includes "Sweeping Exchanges," reprinted in *Expanding Circles: Women, Art & Community.*

Adrian Piper is a professor of philosophy at Wellesley College, Mass. and a leading conceptual and performance artist who devotes her art activity to attacking racism, sexism, and xenophobia. She has had solo exhibitions at major museums and galleries in the U.S. and Europe, and has been the recipient of many grants and awards. Additional biographical material is included in the introduction to "You and Me."

Frances K. Pohl received her doctorate in art history from the University of California, Los Angeles, and currently teaches in the Department of Art and Art History at Pomona College. She is the author of *Ben Shahn: New Deal Artist in a Cold War Climate, 1947-1954* (University of Texas Press, 1989); *Ben Shahn* (Pomegranate Press, 1993); two chapters on American art in Stephen F. Eisenman's *Nineteenth Century Art, A Critical History* (Thames and Hudson, 1994); and *In the Eye of the Storm: An Art Conscience, 1930-1970* (Pomegranate Press, 1995). She has also written numerous articles for women's studies and art history journals on feminist art and American art, and is working on a project on working-class culture and the visual arts and writing a survey text on American art.

Feminist art historian and critic **Arlene Raven**, M.F.A., M.A., Ph.D., is one of the most important conceivers and recorders of the history of women's art and women's art institutions in this country. She has written dozens of significant articles for journals and newspapers such as *Arts*, the *Women's Review of Books*, the *Village Voice*, the *New Art Examiner*, and *High Performance. Crossing Over: Feminism and Art of Social Concern*, an anthology of her writing was published in 1988 by UMI Research Press. She co-edited, with Cassandra Langer and Joanna Frueh, an anthology on feminist art criticism, also published by UMI in 1988. In 1989, Raven and Betty Ann Brown co-authored *Exposures, Women & Their Art* (NewSage Press), which featured photographs of and essays about fifty contemporary American women artists. The essay on Adrian Piper, reprinted in this book is part of a larger study Raven undertook on Piper's work in the early 1990s.

Aleida Rodríguez is a poet and prose writer. She has been publishing her poetry in Spanish and English since 1973 in newspapers (*L.A. Weekly*), journals (*Ploughshares, Prairie Schooner, The Kenyon Review, Phoebe*), and anthologies (*In Short*, W.W. Norton; *Indivisible*, New American Library/Plume Books; *Blood Whispers: LA. Writers on AIDS*, Silverton Books; *Grand Passion*, Red Wind Books; *Cuentos: Stories by Latinas*, Kitchen Table Press). Rodríguez has taught writing workshops at the Woman's Building, the California Institution for Women at Frontera, and various public schools. She has received grants and awards for her work from the California Arts Council, the National Endowment for the Arts, the Woman's Building, George Mason University, and Barnard College.

Sandra Rowe has taught and lectured at California colleges since 1979 (currently professor at Cal-Polytechnic University, Pomona) and is a multi media artist who addresses issues of race, gender and perception in her exploration of art, identity and community. She uses words as well as images to convey her "intention" to the viewer. She was the first Artist-in-Residence at the Afro-American Museum, Los Angeles, and has exhibited her work in museums and galleries including a retrospective exhibition at the Riverside Art Museum, 1993.

Victoria Rue is a feminist theologian, playwright, director, and teacher. As Director of the Institute for Religion and the Arts in Oakland, California, Rue creates plays that include

CancerBodies and *Ecstasy in the Everyday*, which she co-wrote with Letitia Bartlett. These plays have toured to conferences and houses of worship throughout the country. Rue's theatre directing has been seen at the New York Shakespeare Festival, the Women's Project (NYC), Manhattan Theatre Club, the Mark Taper Forum (Los Angeles) and BRAVA! For Women in the Arts (San Francisco). Other plays she has written include *The Terry Project: An Exploration of Schizophrenia* and *The Landscape of My Body*, which connects lesbian sexuality and spirituality. She is a Visiting Professor at the California Institute of Integral Studies in San Francisco and is also on the teaching faculty of the American Conservatory Theatre.

Elizabeth A. Say is an Associate Professor of Religious Studies at California State University, Northridge. She received a doctorate in religious social ethics from the University of Southern California in 1988. Her first book, *Evidence On Her Own Behalf, Women's Narrative as Theological Voice* (Rowman & Littlefield, 1990) explored the way women used narrative as a forum for entering the moral debates of their day at a time when the more formal means and institutions of such debates were closed to them. She is currently completing *I Want a Word: Lesbian, Gay and the Family Mystique*. Co-authored with Mark R. Kowalewski, *I Want a Word* enters the debates about family values and challenges the claims of the Religious Right to ownership of a singular valid definition of family. She is the Executive Secretary of the Western Commission on the Study of Religion. Say co-curated the "Communitas" exhibition.

Ruth Weisberg's art work has been included in over 60 one-person and over 150-group exhibitions, both nationally and internationally, from the Los Angeles Municipal Art Gallery to the Municipal Art Gallery of Oslo, Norway. Her work is included in collections such as the Metropolitan Museum of Art and the Whitney Museum of American Art, New York; the National Gallery of Art, Washington, D.C.; Chicago Art Institute; and the Los Angeles County Museum of Art. Weisberg's oeuvre has been discussed and reproduced in several books. *A Mid-Life Catalogue Raisonné of Ruth Weisberg's Prints* was published by the Fresno Art Museum in 1992 in conjunction with an exhibition. She has published art criticism in many journals, including *Artweek*, the *New Art Examiner*, and *The Tamarind Papers*. She is the past president of the College Art Association (the national professional organization of artists, art historians, and museum personnel) and was a founder of the Southern California chapter of Women's Caucus for Art in 1976.

Terry Wolverton is the author of *Black Slip* (Clothespin Fever Press, 1992) and of *Bailey's Beads* (Faber and Faber, 1996). She was one of hundreds of women who left their home-towns (in her case, Detroit) to be part of the Woman's Building in Los Angeles. Beginning as a student in the Feminist Studio Workshop in 1976, Wolverton spent thirteen years working in the context of the Woman's Building. Her activities there included co-directing the Lesbian Art Project with art historian Arlene Raven; self-publishing her first book on the antique letterpress; producing numerous works of performance art; participating in the Incest Awareness Project; founding an anti-racism consciousness-raising group for white women; serving as newsletter editor, membership coordinator, typesetter, administrative assistant, member of the Board, development director, and eventually, executive director; and making life-long friends with other women artists, writers, and performers. "Requiem" mourns the closing of this vital institution.

Index